# JOHN OF SALISBURY AND THE MEDIEVAL ROMAN RENAISSANCE

Manchester University Press

# Manchester Medieval Studies

SERIES EDITOR   Professor S. H. Rigby

The study of medieval Europe is being transformed as old orthodoxies are challenged, new methods embraced and fresh fields of enquiry opened up. The adoption of interdisciplinary perspectives and the challenge of economic, social and cultural theory are forcing medievalists to ask new questions and to see familiar topics in a fresh light.

The aim of this series is to combine the scholarship traditionally associated with medieval studies with an awareness of more recent issues and approaches in a form accessible to the non-specialist reader.

ALREADY PUBLISHED IN THE SERIES

*Peacemaking in the middle ages: principles and practice*
Jenny Benham

*Money in the medieval English economy: 973–1489*
James Bolton

*The commercialisation of English Society 1000–1500 (second edition)*
Richard H. Britnell

*Reform and the papacy in the eleventh century*
Kathleen G. Cushing

*Picturing women in late medieval and Renaissance art*
Christa Grössinger

*The Vikings in England*
D. M. Hadley

*A sacred city: consecrating churches and reforming society in eleventh-century Italy*
Louis I. Hamilton

*The politics of carnival*
Christopher Humphrey

*Holy motherhood*
Elizabeth L'Estrange

*Music, scholasticism and reform: Salian Germany 1024–1125*
T. J. H. McCarthy

*Medieval law in context*
Anthony Musson

*Constructing kingship: the Capetian monarchs of France and the early Crusades*
James Naus

*The expansion of Europe, 1250–1500*
Michael North

*Medieval maidens*
Kim M. Phillips

*Approaching the Bible in medieval England*
Eyal Poleg

*Gentry culture in late medieval England*
Raluca Radulescu and Alison Truelove (eds)

*Chaucer in context*
S. H. Rigby

*Peasants and historians: debating the medieval English peasantry*
Phillipp R. Schofield

*Lordship in four realms: the Lacy family, 1166–1241*
Colin Veach

*The life cycle in Western Europe, c.1300–c.1500*
Deborah Youngs

# CONTENTS

| | | |
|---|---|---|
| *Acknowledgements* | | *page* vi |
| *Editions and translations used* | | viii |
| *Abbreviations* | | x |
| Introduction | | 1 |
| 1 | The Roman inheritance | 25 |
| 2 | Nature and reason | 67 |
| 3 | Defining duties: the cooperative model of the polity | 92 |
| 4 | Political relationships in context: the body politic | 117 |
| 5 | Moderation and the virtuous life | 145 |
| 6 | The princely head | 181 |
| Conclusion | | 221 |
| *Select bibliography* | | 226 |
| *Index* | | 239 |

# ACKNOWLEDGEMENTS

Many of the ideas in this book originated in my PhD, awarded by the University of Cambridge in 2010. First thanks must go to Anna Abulafia, my MPhil and PhD supervisor, for her diligent attention to my studies and well-being during my time in Cambridge and beyond. Further valuable feedback on my work was provided by Peter Stacey, Magnus Ryan and Joe Canning. I am grateful for opportunities to have presented parts of this work to colleagues, notably at the John of Salisbury Colloquium held in Durham (2012) and at 'Jean de Salisbury: Nouvelles lectures, nouvelles enjeux' at the Université de Lorraine, Metz (2015). My studies at Cambridge were funded by the Arts and Humanities Research Council (UK), a Robert Gardiner Memorial Scholarship, the Cambridge European Trust, an Isaac Newton Research Studentship, the Elizabeth Kolb Memorial Trust and Gonville and Caius College; my thanks to all of these for their financial support. Meanwhile, I owe a huge debt of a different kind to Alex Bamji, Lucy Rhymer, Graham St John and Alex Sapoznik, with whom I shared my PhD years and many years of friendship since.

I'm particularly grateful to Eddie Hyland and Ian S. Robinson of Trinity College Dublin, my alma mater, for their introductions to political thought and medieval history, respectively. Although they are now scattered far and wide, thanks are also due to my circle of Dublin friends – Alison MacIntyre, Mánus de Barra, Kevin Byrne, Karola McGetrick, Helen Airton, Susannah Gibson and Audrey Harwood. The book was written between three countries. Kate Pruce has experienced all three with me, providing kindness and tea throughout. Sarah Courtauld has been a continuous source of friendship, hospitality, and sound advice. Nicola Cossburn, Krista Kajberg, Tereza Pavlickova and Eva Streglova have inspired and supported me every summer during our annual holidays.

The writing of this book occurred alongside a number of other projects and posts. From 2011 to 2014, I worked at Leiden University on the Nederlandse Organisatie voor Wetenschappelijk Onderzoek-funded project 'Turning Over a New Leaf: Manuscript Innovation in the Twelfth Century'. My colleagues Erik Kwakkel, Jenneka Janzen, Julie Somers and

Jenny Weston became great friends and made those three years incredibly enjoyable, as well as intellectually stimulating. Peter Liebregts has been an essential source of steady support, inspiration, and patient kindness since my time in Leiden – *bedankt*. From 2014 to 2017, I worked at the John Rylands Research Institute at the University of Manchester, which proved a fruitful environment to complete the draft manuscript of this book; Katharina Keim, Stefania Silvestri and Julianne Simpson were particularly encouraging cheerleaders throughout this process. Mariken Teeuwen at Huygens ING generously gave me the time required to complete the final manuscript. Thanks are due, too, to the editorial staff at Manchester University Press for their practical aid and advice, and to Stephen Rigby, who, along with the anonymous reviewers of the manuscript, offered valuable suggestions of how to improve its text.

While this book is a product of time spent in different places, an important constant has been my family, who have provided practical and emotional support throughout. The last thanks go, therefore, to those who were there from the first – to my parents and brothers for the wonderful opportunities for education I had, both in and out of the classroom. This book is dedicated to the memory of Dorothy C. Connor (1913–2004) and Paddy 'Panda' O'Daly (1911–2006), who supported this project (and me) at its start, and, I know, would have been proud of its completion. *Requiescant in pace.*

# EDITIONS AND TRANSLATIONS USED

The edition of the *Policraticus* used is *Ioannis Saresberiensis Episcopi Carnotensis Policratici sive De Nugis Curialium et Vestigiis Philosophorum Libri VIII*, ed. C. C. J. Webb (2 vols; Oxford: Clarendon Press, 1909). To date, this is the only complete modern edition of the *Policraticus*. Books I–IV of the *Policraticus* were edited as part of the CCCM (118) by Katharine Keats-Rohan, but Webb's version – which used Cambridge, Corpus Christi College, MS 46 as its base manuscript – is preferred throughout, although I am aware of its editorial shortcomings. The edition of the *Metalogicon* used is *Ioannis Saresberiensis Metalogicon*, ed. J. B. Hall, *auxiliata* K. S. B. Keats-Rohan (CCCM 98; Turnhout: Brepols, 1991).

All translations from the *Policraticus* and *Metalogicon* are my own, although I have been informed in my readings by existing translations, notably *The Statesman's Book of John of Salisbury: Being the Fourth, Fifth and Sixth Books and Selections from the Seventh and Eighth Books of the Policraticus*, trans. J. Dickinson (New York: Knopf, 1927); *Frivolities of Courtiers and Footprints of Philosophers: Being a Translation of the First, Second, and Third Books of the Policraticus of John of Salisbury*, trans. J. B. Pike (Minneapolis: University of Minnesota Press, 1938); *Policraticus: Of the Frivolities of Courtiers and the Footprints of Philosophers*, trans. C. J. Nederman (Cambridge: Cambridge University Press, 1990); and John of Salisbury, *The Metalogicon: A Twelfth-Century Defense of the Verbal and Logical Arts of the Trivium*, trans. D. McGarry (Berkeley: University of California Press, 1955).

I have used *John of Salisbury's Entheticus Maior et Minor*, ed. and trans. J. van Laarhoven (3 vols; Leiden: Brill, 1987), as it offers a highly readable translation of these poems that captures their dynamic literary form. Translations of John's letters are taken from *The Letters of John of Salisbury*, vol. 1: *The Early Letters (1153–61)*, ed. and trans. W. J. Millor, H. E. Butler, and C. N. L. Brooke (rev. edn, Oxford: Oxford University Press, 1986); and *The Letters of John of Salisbury*, vol. 2: *The Later Letters (1163–80)*, ed. and trans. W. J. Millor and C. N. L. Brooke (Oxford: Oxford University Press, 1979), by permission of Oxford University

Press. I have also used *The Historia Pontificalis of John of Salisbury*, ed. and trans. M. Chibnall (Oxford: Oxford University Press, 1986). I have indicated any variance from these translations when necessary, and have preserved editorial presentations of spelling (particularly with respect to the use of u/v) and punctuation throughout. Bible quotations in Latin and English are taken from *Biblia Sacra Vulgata* (Stuttgart: Deutsche Bibelgesellschaft, 1994) and *The New Oxford Annotated Bible: New Revised Standard Version with the Apocrypha* (Oxford: Oxford University Press, 2001) respectively. Other editions and translations used are noted throughout; if no translation is cited it can be assumed that the translation is my own.

# ABBREVIATIONS

CCCM     Corpus Christianorum Continuatio Mediævalis
CCSL     Corpus Christianorum Series Latina
LC     Loeb Classical Library
*Letters* I     *The Letters of John of Salisbury*, vol. 1: *The Early Letters (1153–61)*, ed. and trans. W. J. Millor, H. E. Butler and C. N. L. Brooke (rev. edn, Oxford: Oxford University Press, 1986)
*Letters* II     *The Letters of John of Salisbury*, vol. 2: *The Later Letters (1163–80)*, ed. and trans. W. J. Millor and C. N. L. Brooke (Oxford: Oxford University Press, 1979)
*Met.*     *Ioannis Saresberiensis Metalogicon*, ed. J. B. Hall, aux. K. S. B. Keats-Rohan (CCCM 98; Turnhout: Brepols, 1991)
*MHTB*     *Materials for the History of Thomas Becket: Archbishop of Canterbury*, ed. J. C. Robertson and J. B. Sheppard (7 vols; London: Rolls Series, 1875–85)
PL     Patrologia Latina cursus completus, ed. J.-P. Migne (221 vols; Paris, 1844–64)
*Pol.*     *Ioannis Saresberiensis Episcopi Carnotensis Policratici sive De Nugis Curialium et Vestigiis Philosophorum Libri VIII*, ed. C. C. J. Webb (2 vols; Oxford: Clarendon Press, 1909).

# Introduction

## Biography

The Chapelle Saint-Piat, attached by dramatic flying buttresses to the rear of the Cathédrale de Notre-Dame in Chartres, is the final resting place of John of Salisbury (late 1110s–1180). He was interred here in 1911 after archaeological investigations in the abbey of St Marie de Josaphat at Leves uncovered his remains in their original ornate Romanesque sarcophagus.[1] John now rests under a medieval fresco of the miracles of another famous scholar who made his home at Chartres, Fulbert (d. 1028), in a conjunction that links the eleventh- and twelfth-century intellectual life of the cathedral city. A plaque outside the chapel commemorates John's career as Bishop of Chartres from 1176 to 1180, the twilight of his life and a period from which little evidence remains.[2] John's early years are similarly shadowy. We know he was born in Old Sarum some time between 1115 and 1120 during the bishopric of Roger (d. 1139); he may have been the son of a married canon.[3] Letters from John to his brother Richard and half-brother Robert survive.[4] References to John as canon of Salisbury, and to revenues held by him within the diocese, demonstrate his continued connection to that area.[5]

It was in Salisbury that John's early education occurred, as memorably recorded in the *Policraticus*. John describes being entrusted to a priest to be taught the psalms – that is, how to read – but the unscrupulous priest attempted instead to teach John and another student the art of crystal gazing.[6] It is to John's *Metalogicon* (II. 10), where he describes his studies in France from 1136 to 1147, that we must turn to receive a detailed account of his later, and more intellectually challenging, education.[7] John names his teachers on the Mont Sainte-Geneviève, in the heart of Paris: Peter Abelard (1079–1142/43) for dialectic, Alberic, 'the best of the

1

other dialecticians', and Robert of Melun (c.1100–1167) also for dialectic.[8] John then became a pupil of William of Conches (c.1090–after 1154) for grammar from 1138 to 1141, while simultaneously studying rhetoric with Thierry of Chartres (c.1100–c.1155) and the German Hardewin, who taught John the *quadrivium*. In 1141, John began to study theology with Gilbert of Poitiers, and from 1142 to 1144 he studied with Robert Pullen (d. c.1146).[9] His final years of education were spent under the tutelage of Simon of Poissy, a theologian, whom John describes as 'a faithful but dull teacher'.[10] Other figures mentioned by John in connection with this period of learning include Peter Helias (c.1100–after 1166), Richard l'Évêque (d. 1181) and Adam du Petit Pont (1100×02?–1157×69?).[11]

The location of John's education has provoked substantial debate. In the 1890s, Alexander Clerval, at one point superior of the choir school at Chartres, reinforced the narrative that John's studies with William of Conches and Thierry took place at the cathedral school at Chartres.[12] This view was refuted by Richard W. Southern in a paper delivered in 1965, in which he argued that the association of these scholars with Chartres had contributed to an inflated sense of the importance of the school in the development of medieval education, questioning not only whether John ever actually studied at Chartres, but also the existence of a specific genre of teaching unique to that cathedral school.[13] Southern pointed out that John could equally have heard William's teachings in Paris, though Peter Dronke has pointed out that there is insubstantial evidence to link Thierry, often called '*Carnotensis*' but never '*Parisiensis*', with that city.[14] The definitive resolution of whether or not John ever studied at Chartres seems intractable on the basis of the current state of evidence.[15] Bearing that in mind, more recent studies that seek to look beyond the chronological and locative issues raised by the account in *Metalogicon*, Book II. 10, and to reconstruct, instead, what John actually learned during his period in France seem to be pursuing a more productive line of enquiry.[16] Katharine Keats-Rohan, noting that John's account of his education in the *Metalogicon* is at times highly critical, has pointed out that this passage can be read not simply as a biography, but also as a polemical 'cautionary tale' demonstrating the dangers of over-absorption in dialectic, which instead must be balanced with studies of all parts of the *trivium* (grammar, logic and dialectic, rhetoric) and *quadrivium* (arithmetic, astronomy, geometry, music).[17] John's account also emphasises the diversity of the teaching available in the schools of northern France, and highlights the fluid nature of education in this period; he spent time not only as a pupil, but also as a teacher.[18] There is little doubt from John's narrative that he was exposed to the foremost educative trends in the twelfth century, from the neo-Platonic theories forwarded by Thierry of Chartres to the nominalism of Peter Abelard.

Under the recommendation of Bernard of Clairvaux (1090–1153), who described him as 'a friend and a friend of my friends', John joined the episcopal court of Theobald of Canterbury (d. 1161) in late 1147.[19] Between 1148 and 1162 he had a broad range of administrative duties in the episcopal court of Canterbury, which permitted him to travel repeatedly to Italy and France, as well as throughout England, as attested to in the prologue to Book III of the *Metalogicon*.[20] Notable among these trips are his journey to Rheims in the spring of 1148 to attend the papal council, and a period at the papal court of Pope Adrian IV (1100–1159) in 1155–56 to obtain the grant of Ireland as a hereditary fee for Henry II (1133–89). During his time in Canterbury, John composed some 135 letters, which he wrote either under his own auspices or for his master, Archbishop Theobald.[21] It was in this milieu that John's major works – the *Metalogicon* and the *Policraticus* – were completed by the late 1150s.

On 3 June 1162, Thomas Becket (1118–1170) succeeded Theobald as Archbishop of Canterbury. Tension with Henry II heightened throughout the early years of Thomas's episcopate, and in November 1164 Thomas fled into exile.[22] John was already in exile, having left in either late 1163 or early 1164.[23] John first went to Paris, and then to Rheims, where he lodged with his friend Peter, abbot of Celle (1115–1183).[24] Although John did not join the Becket contingent he remained in constant contact with its members, and wrote many letters on their behalf.[25] John's period of exile seems to have been one of soul-searching, as evidence of increased reference to biblical and patristic texts in his letters suggests.[26] During this period, under the encouragement of Peter of Celle, John wrote a continuation of the *Chronica* of Sigebert of Gembloux (*c*.1030–1112), the *Historia pontificalis*.[27] Unfortunately incomplete, covering only the period from the Council of Rheims in 1148 to around 1152, it provides not only valuable material about this period, but also an insight into John's methods as a historian.[28] In November 1170, John returned to Canterbury in advance of Becket's arrival. He was present at the moment of Becket's murder, although it seems that he fled from the scene, as evinced by the derivative account of it preserved in his *Vita Thomae*.[29] After the murder John probably remained in Canterbury, where he assembled the collection of his letters and promoted the cult of Becket. In 1176, John was elevated to the see of Chartres, where, as noted, little evidence of his episcopal career has been preserved. He died on 25 October 1180, bequeathing his books and belongings to the Cathédrale de Notre-Dame.[30]

## The scholarly tradition

John of Salisbury has been extensively studied. The subject of three biographies, he has also come under consideration in analyses of political theory of the Middle Ages, in histories of educational development and for his role as a witness to many events in the 1150s and 1160s.[31] Often, these studies have sought to situate John's work within larger narratives, such as the history of twelfth-century scholasticism, the development of medieval Aristotelianism and the rise of medieval humanism. The present study seeks to establish an alternative context within which to view John's intellectual contributions, namely what I will term the 'Roman Renaissance' of the twelfth century. It offers a thorough contextualisation of John's political thought, while, by extension, demonstrating the way in which Roman classical philosophy, particularly the works of Cicero and Seneca, shaped philosophical theorising in the Middle Ages. In so doing, it aims to demonstrate how John's work epitomised many of the trends now seen as characteristic of the transformation of the twelfth-century educational environment. As an Englishman who travelled abroad to the schools of Paris, he was part of a cosmopolitan educational elite that participated in cutting-edge theoretical debates led by some of the foremost teachers of the day. John was described by Charles Homer Haskins in his study *The Renaissance of the Twelfth Century* as 'the best classical scholar of the age'.[32] Of course, such a presentation is somewhat circular; we regard John as characteristic in part because so much of our received narrative about education in the twelfth century depends on what can be learned from his extensive surviving works. This has led, in the past, to an over-emphasis on John's significance (and on the twelfth century more generally) in the context of the medieval classical revival. This study aims, instead, to show how John accessed, read and used his sources, with the goal of demonstrating ways in which he was exceptional, as well as ways in which he incorporated ideas familiar to his contemporaries. Even if John was – to paraphrase the words he ascribed to the teacher Bernard of Chartres – a dwarf standing on the shoulder of giants, the interesting question is how he reached that position.[33]

This approach aims to redress the dismissal by Charles Howard McIlwain in the 1930s of John as a 'systematiser rather than an innovator', given to 'rapid skimming' of classical works without real engagement, a historiographical position that has remained persistent in studies of John's use of sources.[34] In many respects, Hans Liebeschütz's *Mediaeval Humanism in the Life and Writings of John of Salisbury*, an authoritative work published in 1950, exemplifies this stance.[35] While Liebeschütz correctly identified the Roman origins of many of John's theories, he based his conclusions on an image of John as a vapid scholar given to excerption and devious invention, while overestimating the range of texts at John's disposal. Janet Martin, on the other hand, presented a more conservative impression of the breadth of John's knowledge. Her unpublished thesis, 'John of Salisbury and the Classics' (1968), assessed John's access to classical sources, concluding that much of his material was obtained through compilations and extracts.[36] One, no doubt unforeseen, contribution of her findings, however, was a lasting impression of John's views as derivative or unoriginal in some fashion. In thinking about what is 'original' about John's works, it is necessary to tread a middle ground between the implication that only 'radical originality' counts as a marker of value for a text and the relativist position that values 'synthetic originality', but in doing so, risks making all texts 'original'.[37] Nevertheless, it is undeniable that synthesis and borrowing can be regarded as cornerstones of John's compositional methodology, and are at the root of how he treated classical and Christian sources. Hans Berman noted how John achieved such synthesis in his writings 'through the use of concepts which combined contradictory norms by abstracting their common qualities'.[38] By this reading paradox, not plagiarism, characterises John's work, while such methods of synthesis and extraction can still be seen as innovative, if not 'radically original', in the context of the historical moment of production of his texts.

Scholarship on John since the early twentieth century has been marked by several phases of analysis. As noted, John's career was first examined extensively as an exemplar of twelfth-century scholasticism. The great contribution of Clement C. J. Webb, editor of the *Policraticus* and the *Metalogicon*, was an impetus to this tradition, which is exemplified in the later work of Reginald L. Poole.[39] Arguably, Liebeschütz's study established John at the forefront of medieval humanism, while in the second half of the twentieth century, studies of John received a new catalyst with the publication of the first volume of his letters (1955) and of the *Historia pontificalis* (1956), both of which prompted revisions of the chronology of John's career. Martin's contributions revised impressions of John's sources, while the structure of the *Policraticus* was analysed in 1977 by Max Kerner.[40] In 1979, the second volume of letters by John was published, heralding the culmination of a new phase of Johnian scholarship.

Coinciding with the 800th anniversary of the death of John, a colloquium was held in 1980, which resulted in a volume (1984) containing a provocative and wide-ranging series of articles covering the scope of his learning and career.[41] The outline of John's later years was established in more detail through the work of Anne Duggan on the Becket correspondence.[42] Meanwhile new editions of John's works were prepared: the *Entheticus* was edited by Jan van Laarhoven in 1987; the *Metalogicon* by J. Barrie Hall and Katharine Keats-Rohan in 1991; and the first half of the *Policraticus* by Keats-Rohan in 1993.

Throughout the 1980s and 1990s these studies have provided the basis for further analyses of John's life and works. A significant figure in this 'new wave' of research on John is Cary Nederman, who has produced substantial work on John's Aristotelian debt, although his appraisal of John's political contributions is, on occasion, at the expense of acknowledging their strong ecclesiastical dimensions.[43] In contrast to this are the unpublished PhD thesis and articles of John McLoughlin, which focus on John's role in ecclesiastical circles, and a number of articles by Julie Barrau which illustrate the extent of John's dependence on biblical and patristic sources.[44] These studies can now be supplemented with the account given by Christophe Grellard of John's scepticism, which focuses largely on theological aspects of his writings.[45] The range of essays in *A Companion to John of Salisbury* (2015) shows the breadth of themes John's works offer for scholarly analysis.[46] However, it remains the case that accounts of his political thought have tended, by and large, to concentrate on the supposed highlights of John's works: the theory of tyrannicide and the metaphor of the polity as a human body.[47] A tradition of overemphasising Books IV–VI of the *Policraticus* would seem to stem from John Dickinson's selection of these 'political chapters' of the *Policraticus* for his translated part-edition (1927), a limitation in scope also suffered by the latest part-translation of the *Policraticus* by Nederman (1990).[48] John Hosler's recent study of John's military knowledge has, by contrast, brought the less-studied books of the *Policraticus* to the fore, while David Bloch has given renewed attention to the *Metalogicon*.[49] Following this momentum, this study seeks not only to examine the *Policraticus* as a whole, but also to look at it in the context of John's other works, notably the *Metalogicon* and *Entheticus*, texts alongside which it circulated in the earliest manuscripts. Such an approach will lead to a more nuanced account of John's political theory and use of classical sources.

## The case for a 'Roman Renaissance'

The application of the term 'Renaissance' to the twelfth century is a contested one. However, like other so-called renaissances of the medieval and early modern period, it has as one of its dominant features a resurgence of interest in classical texts. Much attention has focused on the influence of Plato and Aristotle, despite the limited availability of their texts at this juncture. Plato's *Timaeus*, which circulated in partial form with the commentary by Calcidius (*fl.* 321), was a very popular text in the twelfth century, with thirty-three extant manuscripts dating from the second half of the 1100s.[50] In all, there are over 150 extant medieval manuscripts of *Timaeus*, either in the Calcidian translation or in the translation by Cicero.[51] Twelfth-century interest in the text is also clear from the number of commentaries on it, notably those of Bernard of Chartres and William of Conches.[52] While the continuity of the Platonic tradition is assured through its absorption into other classical and patristic sources, particularly through its neo-Platonic manifestations, the paucity of texts available rendered Plato's views opaque, at times, to the medieval scholar. Meanwhile, the logical works of Aristotle were slowly becoming part of the medieval curriculum in the twelfth century, with John one of the principal witnesses to their reception. At the start of the twelfth century only *Categoriae* and *De interpretatione* were known in Latin, through the translations of Boethius (forming, along with Porphyry's *Isagoge*, the so-called *logica vetus*). From about 1120 onwards, the rest of Aristotle's logical works became known, although full translations of his ethical and political works (most notably of the *Eudemian Ethics*, *Nichomachean Ethics* and *Politics*) would not be made until the thirteenth century. John's access to the *logica vetus* and to the *logica nova* – the *Analytica Priora*, *Topica* and *Sophistici Elenchi* in rediscovered translations by Boethius, and the translation from Greek of the *Analytica posteriora* by James of Venice – has been much studied.[53] The *Metalogicon* can be read, thus, as an exposé of Aristotelian logic, with the second book introducing the value of Aristotle's logic, the third book summarising the *Topics* and the fourth containing a summary of the *Prior* and *Posterior Analytics*.[54] John refers to Aristotle as 'the philosopher', although Bloch has recently questioned the degree of John's familiarity with the available Aristotelian corpus.[55] While John was indisputably an 'early adopter' of Aristotelian ideas, their influence on John's work has frequently been overstated, and this has led to the under-appreciation of other, more accessible, streams of influence.[56]

To turn to the Roman inheritance, one of the philosophical streams most easily accessed in the twelfth century was Stoicism, an inherently varied political discourse frequently mingled with other philosophies. Roman philosophers of the late Empire and early Republic reworked Greek sources and ideas, as demonstrated by Cicero's *De officiis*, a revision of the treatise *On Duty* by the Greek Stoic Panaetius.[57] Cicero, an eclectic thinker, identified himself as a sceptic – denying the plausibility of absolute knowledge in favour of what was most probable – but despite this difference of opinion, he remained an important conduit for Stoic ideas for later readers. A purer Stoicism was found in the writings of Seneca, also popular in the medieval period.[58] While John's use of Roman sources has long been recognised as one of the dominant features of his works, the specifics of how they served to shape his philosophical and political position has not yet been determined. No complete synthesis of his utilisation of Roman Stoic texts has yet been undertaken, and many of the studies have thus far focused mainly on John's use of Cicero.[59] The specifics of John's access to the writings of Cicero and Seneca, and other classical works, will be discussed in Chapter 1. In part, one purpose of this investigation is to probe the answer given by Sten Ebbesen to the question: 'Where were the Stoics in the Middle Ages?' – to which Ebbesen answered, 'everywhere and nowhere'.[60]

This theme was elaborated in Alisdair MacIntyre's *After Virtue: A Study in Moral Theory*, where Stoicism is regarded as 'one of the permanent moral possibilities within the cultures of the West'. In that text, MacIntyre characterised the confrontation between Becket and Henry II as a conflict of authoritative roles, secular and divine, but he also recognised that the protagonists shared a common 'narrative structure', a 'shared framework of detailed agreement on human and divine justice', that is, an understanding of what constitutes the common good.[61] Thus, an intellectual consensus existed between these political actors on the need for common interests to take precedence over those of the individual; by this reading, society is an arena for maximising the good of the community, not for achieving individual ambitions. This agreement on the common good was partially shaped by a set of shared Christian values, which emphasised one's obligations towards others within the community of the Church. It was also, however, shaped by an antique tradition of discourse on the appropriate content of the law for social groupings, found in the writings of Plato, Aristotle and other classical thinkers, as well as in the biblical book of Deuteronomy. In this present study, it is argued that a normative ideal of community similarly underpins John of Salisbury's writings. In this respect, the *Policraticus* marks an important milestone in the development of medieval communitarian thought. Cary Nederman has also identified communitarian traits in John's writings, deriving his argument from the mutuality of relationships within the organic model of the body politic, memorably presented by John in Book V of the *Policraticus*.[62]

This study, however, will show how the organic model went above and beyond Nederman's claims on its part, with particular reference to how John developed a sophisticated theory of political duties, emphasising solidarity and moral obligation within the community. Chapter 2 discusses two philosophical aspects of John's political theory: his understanding of nature and of reason. It will demonstrate how 'following nature' was linked with correct exercise of reason and regarded as the foundation of political sociability. Chapter 3 illustrates how following nature necessarily involves exercising political duties that are limited and extended by a rational understanding of personal and social bonds, a view that is intellectually shaped by both the Christian and Roman traditions, notably by the simultaneous presence of Christian ideas of *caritas* and the Stoic theory of *oikeiôsis* (the extension of a sense of duty from the self to those who are akin to the self) in John's writings. Chapter 4 takes a deeper look at the application of this perspective to the organic model of the body politic, demonstrating how the body model does not simply serve to show how the parts of the organic whole work together, but also provides an entirely original way of representing political responsibilities, distinct from the works of John's contemporaries and with important implications for his understanding of rulership.

In the final two chapters, the focus turns to the implications that John's ethical perspective had for political behaviour. Chapter 5 examines what moderation consists of according to John, and how it influences virtuous behaviour. John adopts a Ciceronian interpretation of what constitutes the 'mean', and his insistence on an internal mental orientation towards virtuous behaviour is influenced by Stoic ethics. John applies his recommendations to the ruler, but also to other members of the polity, as demonstrated through a series of case studies on the practice of the individual virtues. Chapter 6 turns to the head of the body politic, the prince. A number of case studies (King Stephen, Frederick Barbarossa and Thomas Becket) show how John's perspective on contemporary society was influenced by his theoretical position regarding right rulership. A good ruler cannot rule without the support of a well-ordered polity, but a well-ordered polity can come about only through the actions of a good ruler.

## Methodology

At the heart of this study is an interpretation of what is 'political' about John's works. As Quentin Skinner memorably noted, the historian must avoid construing the 'political' as the projection of whatever we now regard as to be the proper level of rational discourse on politics.[63] John Pocock, in turn, recognised that the historian faces a challenge in identifying the presence of political language; anachronism endangers the capacity of the reader to determine reliably the political content of a text.[64] One solution is to adopt a contextualist approach, as advised by Skinner, who advocates examining what the subject 'was doing' when the text was composed. By this reading, political language, in addition to being circumscribed terminologically through its reference to unambiguously political entities (such as the *res publica*, *senatus*, *princeps* and *rex*), also defines itself in terms of context: political language discusses 'the political', whatever that is determined to be at the point of composition.[65] Furthermore, if we consider the text to be an 'authoritative artefact', whose authority determines the manner in which it is read, then the language in which it is written carries certain implications that determine the modes of its usage.[66] This approach to the history of political thought, which requires the investigation of political ideas as situated in the historical context that produced them, has come to be known as the 'Cambridge School' method, and has dominated the field since the 1960s. It marks a departure from the idealist approach that looked at political ideas abstracted from their context – thus neutralised of their historical content – and the normative approach that sought to find in the history of political thought lessons which could usefully be applied to a contemporary present. Adopting the 'Cambridge School' method requires, instead, that three categories of information are to be investigated when searching for the political content of a text. First, we need to isolate the normative propositions it delineates for political conduct. Secondly, we must examine the description it gives of the political world contemporary to its composition. Finally, we must look at the immediate context in which the text was written, including the sources used.

Informed by this method, the present study seeks, in part, to determine what constitutes 'the political' in the twelfth century, using the oeuvre of John of Salisbury as a case study. As an extension, it seeks to demonstrate the way in which works of Roman philosophy had a profound effect on shaping the way in which social and political life was viewed in this period. However, such a task also provokes a variety of theoretical questions concerning how transmission and influence are valued and determined. Explicit approval of sources alone cannot suffice; this denies the influence of explicit disapproval, as well as the significance of allusion, quotation and veiled reference.[67] Skinner suggests three conditions which serve to confirm direct influence of one thinker on another: that genuine similarity between the doctrines of A and B can be determined, that B could not have found the relevant doctrine in any other writer apart from A and that the probability of the similarity being random is low.[68] These criteria may also be used as a standard against which indirect transmission can be judged. However, it can also be suggested that much transmission of classical ideas in the medieval period occurred through unconscious channels. Stoic thought, for example, was gradually absorbed and assimilated into early Christian texts. By this process the 'authoritative' influence of classical texts is compromised and counter-balanced by the 'authority' of the patristic corpus in the Middle Ages. The question of what constitutes 'influence' in this period will be investigated in more depth in Chapter 1.

### Finding 'the political' in John's work

From the mid-1150s on, John wrote a series of works with significant applications for the understanding of medieval society.[69] Emanating from the context of the episcopal court at Canterbury, they deal with the full spectrum of political life, clerical and secular. First among these is a long poem, *Entheticus de dogmate philosophorum*.[70] Finished during Thomas Becket's chancellorship (1154–62), it may date in earlier drafts from John's time as a student.[71] A shorter version of this poem, *Entheticus in Policraticum*, was appended to John's principal works, the *Policraticus* and the *Metalogicon*, which were completed in 1159. The former, dedicated to Thomas Becket, is subtitled '*De nugis curialium et vestigiis philosophorum libri*' – 'On the Trifles of Courtiers and the Footsteps of Philosophers' – and is a polemical work on the nature of rulership and society. The latter, primarily an educational treatise, is a descriptive work exploring the arts of the *trivium* in the light of the Aristotelian logical revival. It was originally intended to be read alongside the *Policraticus*, as is clear from the earliest manuscripts where the two texts (and *Entheticus in Policraticum*) appear together. This suggests that John regarded the two texts as companions, each informing the reader on a different aspect of life.[72] Meanwhile, John's extensive letter collection covers a period from his time at the episcopal court in Canterbury, stretching into his exile in France during the Becket conflict and concluding with a brief series of letters pertaining to his later life. These letters offer a valuable counterpart to the formal works, demonstrating John's views on significant political and social events.[73]

The *Policraticus* has often been situated within the 'mirror for princes' genre, although, as Julie Barrau noted, this intention was secondary in John's mind; the book is formally addressed to Thomas Becket, and a theory of monarchy was not at its core. Barrau referred to a set of marginal annotations in Cambridge, Corpus Christi College, MS 46 (hereafter CCC 46), the manuscript traditionally regarded (on the basis of its *ex libris*) as Thomas Becket's own copy of the *Policraticus*, to illustrate her point. These annotations, which Barrau terms '*un guide de lecture*', seem to have been added at the time of the redaction of the text but do not, by and large, provide a commentary on the main sections where rulership was discussed in the *Policraticus*. Instead, as Barrau notes, they are scattered throughout the manuscript, dealing with public affairs, the nature of making just decisions and the practice of moderation, and highlighting various classical and biblical *exempla*.[74] While the thrust of Barrau's assertion – that Becket, not Henry, is the intended principal (and first) audience of the *Policraticus* – is persuasive, these marginal additions to the text deserve re-examination, as they illustrate how the *Policraticus* was intended to be read by its earliest audiences, and, by extension, what the vocabulary of the 'political' was in this period.

CCC 46, the base-text of Webb's 1909 edition, has held traditional primacy among manuscripts of the *Policraticus*, by reason of its association with Becket and its Canterbury provenance. This primacy was questioned by Keats-Rohan, who rejected CCC 46 as the base-text of her part-edition, on the grounds that, when compared with other key manuscripts, it never presented a unique reading of the text in any instance. However, as Guglielmetti has demonstrated, CCC 46 is the source of two other early copies of the text: London, British Library (hereafter BL), Royal MS 13 D IV and Oxford, Bodleian Library (Bodl.), MS Lat. misc. c. 16, thereby explaining such textual similitude.[75] Guglielmetti has further determined that corrections in BL Royal MS 13 D IV indicate likely collation with what she terms the 'French family' of manuscripts, notably Soissons, Bibliothèque municipale, MS 24. The latter manuscript has recently been re-dated by Patricia Stirnemann to England, *c.*1160.[76] On palaeographical and decorative grounds, Stirnemann's analysis seems sound.[77] Furthermore, Stirnemann has proposed that this manuscript may be identified with John's own copy of the *Policraticus*, left upon his death to Chartres Cathedral, even suggesting that John's hand can be identified with that of the *ex libris* on fo. 1r, a hand that provides some careful corrections throughout the manuscript.

Regardless of the weight of evidence attributing ownership to Becket in the case of CCC 46, or to John in the case of Soissons MS 24, these manuscripts, along with BL Royal MS 13 D IV and Oxford, Bodl. Library, MS Lat. misc. c. 16, represent the earliest surviving exemplars of the English copying tradition of the *Policraticus*. The production context of BL Royal MS 13 D IV can also be closely linked to John's circle. Copied at St Albans, it is, according to Rodney Thomson, one of the earliest surviving books made during the abbacy of Simon (1167-83).[78] Thomson suggests that Simon and John were actually acquainted, noting that at a point between 1171 and 1173 Abbot Simon is listed as a witness to a settlement between Oseney and Eynsham along with 'Master John of Salisbury' and Nicholas, prior of Wallingford. Furthermore, in 1174, John would act as a papal judge-delegate in a dispute between the abbey of St Albans and the monks of Durham over the status of Tynemouth priory. Thomson goes so far as to suggest that the addition of *Entheticus maior* to BL Royal MS 13 D IV (the earliest witness to that text) and some textual revisions throughout the manuscript may demonstrate continued contact between John and Simon, and perhaps personal intervention by John in the make-up of the manuscript. Thomson observes that the aforementioned Nicholas, prior of Wallingford, who was prior of Malmesbury (1183-87) and a monk of St Albans, was an acquaintance of Peter of Celle.[79] Although Thomson points out that this relationship is indicative of contact between St Albans and 'the world of continental reformed monasticism', he does not make explicit the fact that Peter may have been a potential conduit between Nicholas and John. Malmesbury's own copy of the *Policraticus*, now Oxford, Bodleian Library, MS Barlow 6, was copied during the abbacy of Robert (1187-1205) and was the source for a further copy made at Cirencester in the 1180s, now Oxford, Bodleian Library, MS Barlow 48. Bodl. MS Lat. misc. c. 16 also comes from a monastic context, and is recorded as having been donated to Battle Abbey by Abbot Richard (1215-35). As it dates from the last quarter of the twelfth century, however, Guglielmetti posits that this was actually the copy given to Odo, a monk of Canterbury, who was prior of Battle from 1175 to 1200, a speculation given strength by the fact that Odo is named in *Entheticus in Policraticum* as one of the recipients of the 'best wishes' of his 'little book', that is, the *Policraticus*.[80]

While Barrau's analysis was confined to CCC 46, the copy associated with Thomas Becket, it is intriguing to note that the other early manuscripts mentioned here also contain a comparable set of marginal annotations. In Book 1, for example, the annotations which refer to classical figures and authors, like Ulysses, Virgil, Horace and Ovid, among others, are found alongside identical passages of text in the four manuscripts. Barrau drew specific attention to a series of annotations in the margins of CCC 46, fo. 92r–v (alongside the account of the successive kings of England, Book VI. 18), suggesting that these may have been added to the manuscript to draw Henry II's attention to this part of the text, pleasing him by highlighting his rightful dynastic succession.[81] An alternative interpretation of this set of annotations can now be posited following comparison of the four manuscripts in question, where this section is one of the most consistently glossed. The annotations, in fact, follow a broader narrative arc, commencing in Book VI. 14, following John's detailed discussion of the responsibilities and duties of soldiers. A notation symbol in the form of a *chi-rho* marks the textual bridge, where John points out that a ruler is useless if he does not maintain discipline and train his soldiers, with the chapter concerned with how Roman leaders led their armies.[82] The annotations then draw attention to the reference to Nero in this chapter, adding in the margin '*De nerone*', to stress how he corrupted Rome through his indulgence, while Julius Caesar is similarly emphasised in Book VI. 15 ('*De Iulio cesare*') as a contrasting example of powerful leadership.[83] The annotations then proceed to refer to leadership in the contemporary period and to Britain, through the addition of a marginal note alongside Book VI. 16 reading '*De coaetaneis nostris*', before the addition of '*De Brenno*' (in two manuscripts) alongside the account of Brennus, leader of the Senones, who John believed to have originated from England (Book VI. 17).[84] Book VI. 18 is a comparative study of discipline and rulership in England; the annotations to Book VI. 18 refer in succession to Cnut, William Rufus, Henry I, Henry II, Stephen and Stephen's son Eustace.[85] Reading the annotations in Book VI. 18 in conjunction with those that precede them broadens the scope of their applicability beyond seeking favour with the king. Instead, the annotations bring together a number of examples of good and bad rulership, setting the contemporary history of England within a wider frame of reference stretching back to ancient Rome, while reinforcing a general message regarding discipline in leadership.

Furthermore, the presence of these annotations in multiple manuscripts elevates their status beyond a *guide de lecture*, confined to one manuscript and intended for one reader, to that of a paratextual apparatus that circulated alongside the text, was copied from manuscript to manuscript and was seemingly regarded as integral to its understanding. Analysis of the precise relationships of the annotations in the manuscripts, and what they can tell us about the transmission and collation of copies of the *Policraticus*, lies beyond the scope of this book.[86] However, it is clear that they were conscientiously replicated in manuscripts of the text, as most clearly demonstrated by one of the later manuscripts, Bodl., MS Barlow 48, which rubricates the annotations and encloses them in penwork borders, according them a visual status akin to that of its chapter headings.[87] As noted earlier, to understand what is 'political' about a text we must look at the context within which it was written and read. Annotations of this type provide an insight into the contemporary reception of the text. For example, the annotations alongside Book VI. 14–18, which highlight the necessity of discipline in leadership, point to a subject that was of interest to Becket and Henry II alike, but was also relevant to all. Georges Duby suggested that the *Policraticus* can be read as a '*speculum curiae*' intended for study by the whole court.[88] This approaches the truth; the *Policraticus* was not intended as simply a 'mirror for princes', but rather is a mirror for the whole polity. The following chapters will investigate the political lessons which John hoped to impart.

## Notes

1 R. Joly, 'Josaphat: Lieu de sépulture de Jean de Salisbury', *Notre-Dame de Chartres*, 11 (1980), 10–14; J. Villette, 'Le tombeau sculpté de Jean de Salisbury, un chef d'oeuvre trop peu connu', *Notre-Dame de Chartres*, 11 (1980), 15–17.
2 For contrasting opinions of John's legacy as a bishop in Chartres see E. Türk, *Nugae Curialium: Le règne d'Henri II Plantegenêt (1145–1189) et l'éthique politique* (Geneva: Droz, 1977), pp. 92–4; J. van Laarhoven, '*Non iam decreta, sed Evangelium!* Jean de Salisbury au Latran III', in M. Fois, V. Monachino and F. Litva (eds), *Dalla Chiesa antica alla Chiesa moderna: Miscellanea per il Cinquantesimo della Facoltà di Storia Ecclesiastica della Pontifica Università Gregoriana* (Rome: Università Gregoriana, 1983), pp. 107–19; K. Bollermann and C. J. Nederman, 'The "Sunset Years": John of Salisbury as Bishop of Chartres and the Emergent Cult of St. Thomas Becket in France', *Viator*, 45 (2014), 55–76; J. Barrau, 'John of Salisbury as Ecclesiastical Administrator', in C. Grellard and F. Lachaud (eds), *A Companion to John of Salisbury* (Leiden: Brill, 2015), pp. 105–44 (pp. 118–43). See list of episcopal *acta* from John's period in Chartres in *Letters* II, pp. 809–10. See also A. Piper, 'New Evidence for the Becket Correspondence and John of Salisbury's Letters', in M. Wilks (ed.), *The World of John of Salisbury* (Oxford: Blackwell, 1984), pp. 439–44, which points to evidence of some untraced correspondence of John, possibly dating from his episcopate.

3 C. N. L. Brooke, 'John of Salisbury and his World', in Wilks (ed.), *World*, pp. 1–20 (p. 3); D. Luscombe, 'Salisbury, John of (late 1110s–1180)', *Oxford Dictionary of National Biography* (Oxford: Oxford University Press, 2004; online edn, May 2011), www.oxforddnb.com/view/article/14849 (accessed 24 January 2017).

4 To Richard: Letters 164, 169, 172 in *Letters* II; to Robert: Letters 145–8 in *Letters* II. John's visit to his mother, Egidia, upon his return from exile in December 1170 is detailed in Letter 304 to Peter of Celle, *Letters* II, pp. 716–17. F. Barlow, 'John of Salisbury and his Brothers', *Journal of Ecclesiastical History*, 46 (1995), 95–109.

5 See Letter 152 to Thomas Becket (late summer 1165), *Letters* II, pp. 52–3. John is referred to as a canon of Salisbury in William Fitzstephen's *Life of Thomas Becket*, *MHTB* III, p. 46.

6 *Pol.* II. 28; 1, p. 164. For analysis of the practice see N. Orme, *Medieval Children* (New Haven: Yale University Press, 2001), pp. 102–3.

7 *Met.* II. 10, pp. 70–3. C. Giraud and C. Mews, 'John of Salisbury and the Schools of the 12th Century', in Grellard and Lachaud (eds), *Companion*, pp. 31–62 (pp. 32–47, 60–1). The account given in *Met.* II. 10 should be read alongside the additional details on these teachers provided in *Met.* I. 5, pp. 20–2.

8 On the tradition of teaching on the Mont-Saint-Geneviève see W. Courtney, 'Schools and Schools of Thought in the Twelfth Century', in C. J. Nederman, N. Van Deusen and E. A. Matter (eds), *Mind Matters: Studies of Medieval and Early Modern Intellectual History in Honour of Marcia Colish* (Turnhout: Brepols, 2009), pp. 13–45 (p. 20). Courtney notes (p. 25) that the scholars who taught here were probably granted some sort of teaching licence by the abbey of Saint-Geneviève, although they were not directly associated with teaching at the abbey, living, instead, in rented quarters, a situation that would have allowed several masters to teach within the same area at the same time.

9 John provides further information on Gilbert in *Historia pontificalis*, recounting his summons before the Council of Rheims in 1148: *The Historia Pontificalis of John of Salisbury*, ed. and trans. M. Chibnall (Oxford: Oxford University Press, 1986), pp. 15–41; see C. Monagle, 'John of Salisbury and the Writing of History', in Grellard and Lachaud (eds), *Companion*, pp. 215–32 (pp. 221–8).

10 *Met.* II. 10, p. 72: '*fidus lector, sed obtusior disputator*'.

11 See Letter 201 to Richard l'Évêque, which John composed during exile, *Letters* II, pp. 292–5.

12 J. A. Clerval, *Les Écoles de Chartres au Moyen-Âge (du $V^e$ au $XVI^e$ siècle)* (Chartres: Selleret, 1895). The suggestion was originally made in C. Schaarschmidt, *Johannes Saresberiensis nach Leben und Studien, Schriften und Philosophie* (Leipzig: Teubner, 1862), pp. 21–5. A notable supporter of this perspective was R. L. Poole, *Illustrations of the History of Medieval Thought and Learning* (London: SPCK, 1932), pp. 177–89. The literature on the school of Chartres is extensive; a summary can be found in E. Jeauneau, *L'Âge d'or des écoles de Chartres* (Chartres: Éditions Houvet, 2000), pp. 19–24.

13 R. W. Southern, 'Humanism and the School of Chartres', in his *Medieval Humanism and Other Studies* (Oxford: Blackwell, 1970), pp. 61–85. Southern's

later responses to the developing debate can be found in his 'The Schools of Paris and the School of Chartres', in R. L. Benson, G. Constable and C. D. Lanham (eds), *Renaissance and Renewal in the Twelfth Century* (Cambridge, MA: Harvard University Press, 1982), pp. 113–37, and his *Scholastic Humanism and the Unification of Europe*, vol. 1: *Foundations* (Oxford: Blackwell, 1995), pp. 61–101. See also I. O'Daly, 'Revisiting the Evidence for the Study of Rhetoric and Dialectic at the School of Chartres in the Time of Fulbert (d. 1028)', *Viator*, 47 (2016), 23–43, which reassesses the state of teaching in the eleventh-century school.

14 P. Dronke, 'Thierry of Chartres', in P. Dronke (ed.), *A History of Twelfth-Century Western Philosophy* (Cambridge: Cambridge University Press, 1992), pp. 358–85 (p. 358).

15 It is likely that John had some links with the diocese, as his later elevation to the episcopate suggests, as well as the informed references he made to Gilbert of Poitiers's chancellorship (see *Met.* I. 5, p. 20).

16 For example, K. M. Fredborg in 'The Grammar and Rhetoric Offered to John of Salisbury', in J. Feros Ruys, J. O. Ward and M. Heyworth (eds), *The Classics in the Medieval and Renaissance Classroom: The Role of Ancient Texts in the Arts Curriculum as Revealed by Surviving Manuscripts and Early Printed Books* (Turnhout: Brepols, 2013), pp. 103–30.

17 K. S. B. Keats-Rohan, 'John of Salisbury and Education in Twelfth-Century Paris from the Account of his *Metalogicon*', *History of Universities*, 6 (1987), 1–45 (6). See also K. S. B. Keats-Rohan, 'The Chronology of John of Salisbury's Studies in Paris: A Reading of *Metalogicon* II. 10', *Studi medievali*, 3rd series, 28 (1987), 193–203.

18 This fluidity is captured by S. Ferruolo's analysis in *The Origins of the University: The Schools of Paris and their Critics, 1100–1215* (Stanford: Stanford University Press, 1985), pp. 22–3. John refers to a period as a teacher, provoked by penury, in *Met.* II. 10. See D. Bloch, *John of Salisbury on Aristotelian Science* (Turnhout: Brepols, 2012), pp. 12–19.

19 Bernard of Clairvaux, Letter 361, in *Sancti Bernardi Opera Omnia*, vol. 8: *Epistolae*, ed. J. LeClercq and H. Rochais (Rome: Editiones Cistercienses, 1977), pp. 307–8. Bernard describes John as '*amicum meum et amicum amicorum meorum*'.

20 A. Saltman, *Theobald, Archbishop of Canterbury* (London: Athlone Press, 1956) gives details of the early charters to which John was a signatory (p. 170). Barrau, 'John of Salisbury as Ecclesiastical Administrator' (p. 110) notes that he held no specific title, but suggests (p. 114) that he effectively held the position of *secretarius* by Theobald's later years.

21 A notable example of John's administrative writing is Letter 131, *Letters* I, pp. 227–37, written in 1160 on behalf of Archbishop Theobald to Pope Alexander III, regarding the dispute between Richard of Anstey and Mabel de Francheville.

22 C. Duggan, 'The Becket Dispute and the Crimonious Clerks', *Bulletin of the Institute of Historical Research*, 35 (1962), 1–28.

23 L. Robertson, 'Exile in the Life and Correspondence of John of Salisbury', in

L. Napran and E. Van Houts (eds), *Exile in the Middle Ages: Selected Proceedings from the International Medieval Congress, University of Leeds 8–11 July 2002* (Turnhout: Brepols, 2004), pp. 181–97.
24 J. McLoughlin, 'Amicitia in Practice: John of Salisbury (c.1120–1180) and his Circle', in D. Williams (ed.), *England in the Twelfth Century: Proceedings of the 1988 Harlaxton Symposium* (Woodbridge: Boydell Press, 1990), pp. 165–81. On this friendship see also J. Haseldine, 'Introduction', in John of Salisbury, *Metalogicon*, trans. J. B. Hall (Turnhout: Brepols, 2013), pp. 23–4.
25 A. Duggan, 'John of Salisbury and Thomas Becket', in Wilks (ed.), *World*, pp. 427–38.
26 J. Barrau, 'La *conversio* de Jean de Salisbury: La Bible au service de Thomas Becket?', *Cahiers de civilisation médiévale X$^e$–XII$^e$ siècles*, 50 (2007), 229–44.
27 See C. N. L. Brooke, 'Aspects of John of Salisbury's *Historia Pontificalis*', in L. Smith and B. Ward (eds), *Intellectual Life in the Middle Ages: Essays Presented to Margaret Gibson* (London: Hambledon Press, 1992), pp. 185–95. See the case for John's authorship of the *Historia pontificalis* in J. McLoughlin, 'John of Salisbury (c. 1120–80): The Career and Attitudes of a Schoolman in Church Politics' (PhD dissertation, Trinity College, Dublin, 1988), pp. 129–47.
28 J. Coleman, *Ancient and Medieval Memories: Studies in the Reconstruction of the Past* (Cambridge: Cambridge University Press, 1992), pp. 285–94, 305–16; M. Chibnall, 'John of Salisbury as Historian', in Wilks (ed.), *World*, pp. 169–77; Monagle, 'John of Salisbury and the Writing of History'.
29 M. Staunton, *Thomas Becket and his Biographers* (Woodbridge: Boydell and Brewer, 2006), pp. 19–27. John's *Vita Thomae* can be found in *MHTB* II, pp. 299–352, and in translation in R. E. Pepin, *Anselm and Becket: Two Canterbury Saints' Lives by John of Salisbury* (Toronto: Pontifical Institute of Medieval Studies, 2009), pp. 78–95.
30 *Cartulaire de Notre-Dame de Chartres*, ed. E. de Lépinois and L. Merlet, vol. 3 (Chartres: Garnier, 1865), pp. 201–2.
31 The three biographies are Schaarschmidt, *Johannes Saresberiensis*; C. C. J. Webb, *John of Salisbury* (London: Methuen, 1932); and C. J. Nederman, *John of Salisbury* (Tempe: Arizona Centre for Medieval and Renaissance Studies, 2005).
32 C. Homer Haskins, *The Renaissance of the Twelfth Century* (Cambridge, MA: Harvard University Press, 1927), p. 225.
33 *Met.* III. 4, p. 116.
34 C. H. McIlwain, *The Growth of Political Theory in the West from the Greeks to the End of the Middle Ages* (New York: Macmillan, 1932), p. 320.
35 H. Liebeschütz, *Mediaeval Humanism in the Life and Writings of John of Salisbury* (London: Warburg Institute, 1950).
36 J. Martin, 'John of Salisbury and the Classics' (PhD dissertation, Harvard University, 1968). See also J. Martin, 'John of Salisbury's Manuscripts of Frontinus and of Gellius', *Journal of the Warburg and Courtauld Institutes*, 40 (1977), 1–26; J. Martin, 'Uses of Tradition: Gellius, Petronius and John of Salisbury', *Viator*, 10 (1979), 57–76; J. Martin, 'John of Salisbury as Classical Scholar', in Wilks (ed.), *World*, pp. 179–201.

37 On these terms see C. Condren, *The Status and Appraisal of Classical Texts: An Essay on Political Theory, its Inheritance, and the History of Ideas* (Princeton: Princeton University Press, 1985), pp. 106–7, 117.
38 H. J. Berman, *Law and Revolution: The Formation of the Western Legal Tradition* (Cambridge, MA: Harvard University Press, 1983), p. 280.
39 Poole, *Medieval Thought and Learning*, and R. L. Poole, *Studies in Chronology and History* (Oxford: Clarendon Press, 1934), pp. 248–86.
40 M. Kerner, *Johannes von Salisbury und die logische Struktur seines Policraticus* (Wiesbaden: Franz Steiner Verlag, 1977).
41 Wilks (ed.), *World*.
42 A. Duggan, *Thomas Becket: Friends, Networks, Text and Cult* (Aldershot: Ashgate, 2007); *Thomas Becket* (London: Bloomsbury, 2004); *The Correspondence of Thomas Becket, Archbishop of Canterbury 1162–70*, ed. and trans. A. Duggan (2 vols; Oxford: Oxford University Press, 2000); *Thomas Becket: A Textual History of his Letters* (Oxford: Clarendon Press, 1980).
43 Many notable articles by Nederman are collected in C. J. Nederman, *Medieval Aristotelianism and its Limits: Classical Traditions in Moral and Political Philosophy, 12th to 15th Centuries* (Aldershot: Ashgate, 1997). Individual articles will be referred to throughout this volume, when relevant. See also C. J. Nederman, 'John of Salisbury's Political Theory', in Grellard and Lachaud (eds), *Companion*, pp. 258–88.
44 McLoughlin, 'John of Salisbury'; McLoughlin, '*Amicitia* in Practice'; J. McLoughlin, 'The Language of Persecution: John of Salisbury and the early phase of the Becket dispute (1163–66)', in W. J. Sheils (ed.), *Persecution and Toleration: Papers Read at the Twenty-Second Summer Meeting and Twenty-Third Winter Meeting of the Ecclesiastical History Society* (Oxford: Blackwell, 1984), pp. 73–87; J. Barrau, 'Jean de Salisbury, intermédiaire entre Thomas Becket et la cour capétienne?', in M. Aurell and N.-Y. Tonnerre (eds), *Plantagenêts et Capétiens: Confrontations et héritages* (Turnhout: Brepols, 2006), pp. 505–16; J. Barrau, 'Ceci n'est pas un miroir, ou le *Policraticus* de Jean de Salisbury', in F. Lachaud and L. Scordia (eds), *Le Prince au miroir de la littérature politique de l'Antiquité aux Lumières* (Rouen: Publications des Universités de Rouen et du Havre, 2007), pp. 87–111; Barrau, 'La *conversio* de Jean de Salisbury'.
45 C. Grellard, *Jean de Salisbury et la renaissance médiévale du scepticisme* (Paris: Les Belles Lettres, 2013).
46 Grellard and Lachaud (eds), *Companion*.
47 J. van Laarhoven, '"Thou shalt NOT slay a tyrant!" The So-Called Theory of John of Salisbury', in Wilks (ed.), *World*, pp. 319–41; K. L. Forhan, 'Salisburian Stakes: The Use of "Tyranny" in John of Salisbury's *Policraticus*', *History of Political Thought*, 11 (1990), 397–407; R. H. Rouse and M. A. Rouse, 'John of Salisbury and the Doctrine of Tyrannicide', *Speculum*, 42 (1967), 693–709. John's views on tyranny will be discussed in detail in Chapter 6, while the model of the body politic comes under investigation in Chapters 3 and 4.
48 *The Statesman's Book of John of Salisbury: Being the Fourth, Fifth and Sixth Books and Selections from the Seventh and Eighth Books of the Policraticus*, trans.

J. Dickinson (New York: Knopf, 1927); John of Salisbury, *Policraticus: Of the Frivolities of Courtiers and the Footprints of Philosophers*, trans. C. J. Nederman (Cambridge: Cambridge University Press, 1990).

49 J. Hosler, *John of Salisbury: Military Authority of the Twelfth-Century Renaissance* (Leiden: Brill, 2013); Bloch, *John of Salisbury on Aristotelian Science*.

50 A. Somfai, 'The Eleventh-Century Shift in the Reception of Plato's *Timaeus* and Calcidius's *Commentary*', *Journal of the Warburg and Courtauld Institutes*, 65 (2002), 1–21; M. Gibson, 'The Study of the *Timaeus* in the Eleventh and Twelfth Century', *Pensamiento*, 25 (1969), 183–94. For the Calcidian commentary see Calcidius, *Timaeus a Calcidio translatus commentarioque instructus*, ed. J. H. Waszink (London: Warburg Institute, 1975).

51 Somfai, 'The Eleventh-Century Shift', p. 1; on the differences between the preservation of the text in the two translations see pp. 4–5. On the fragmented Ciceronian translation of the *Timaeus* see L. D. Reynolds (ed.), *Texts and Transmission: A Survey of the Latin Classics* (Oxford: Clarendon Press, 1983), pp. 124–8.

52 Bernard of Chartres, *The* Glosae super Platonem *of Bernard of Chartres*, ed. P. E. Dutton (Toronto: PIMS, 1991); William of Conches, *Glosae super Platonem*, ed. E. Jeauneau (CCCM 203; Turnhout: Brepols, 2006); P. E. Dutton, 'The Uncovering of the *Glosae super Platonem* of Bernard of Chartres', *Mediaeval Studies*, 46 (1984), 192–221.

53 See B. G. Dod, 'Aristoteles Latinus', in N. Kretzmann, A. Kenny and J. Pinborg (eds), *The Cambridge History of Later Medieval Philosophy* (Cambridge: Cambridge University Press, 1988), pp. 45–79. E. Jeauneau, 'Jean de Salisbury et la lecture des philosophes', in Wilks (ed.), *World*, pp. 77–108, notably pp. 103–8, where Jeauneau suggests that John the Saracen could have been the translator of the edition of the *Posterior Analytics* used by John. C. Burnett, 'John of Salisbury and Aristotle', *Didascalia*, 2 (1996), 19–32 (24–5), notes the intimacy of Robert of Torigni and Richard l'Évêque. Robert may have served as an intermediary between Richard and James of Venice and, thus, as a source for John's access to James's translations. John requested Aristotelian glosses from Richard to be made 'at my expense (and no cost spared here on my account, I beg)'; see Letter 201, *Letters* II, pp. 294–5. See *Met*. IV. 6, p. 145, on the *Posterior Analytics*.

54 A useful summary of the *Metalogicon* can be found in Haseldine, 'Introduction', pp. 54–76.

55 *Met*. IV. 7, pp. 145–6. Bloch, *John of Salisbury on Aristotelian Science*, especially pp. 83–186.

56 For examples of such overstatement see the following articles by C. J. Nederman: 'The Aristotelian Doctrine of the Mean and John of Salisbury's Concept of Liberty', *Vivarium*, 24 (1986), 128–42; 'Aristotelian Ethics before the *Nichomachean Ethics*: Alternate Sources of Aristotle's Concept of Virtue in the Twelfth Century', *Parergon*, 7 (1989), 55–75; 'Aristotelianism and the Origins of "Political Science" in the Twelfth Century', *Journal of the History of Ideas*, 52 (1991), 179–94. The case for regarding Nederman's views as an overstatement will be conveyed in Chapter 5. His implication that John's writing took place in a

near-vacuum, in which classical models of political writing were almost absent, as found in Nederman, 'John of Salisbury's Political Theory' (pp. 260, 288), must be rejected, as this belies the significance of intermediary witnesses, as well as ignoring the value of texts such as Cicero's *De officiis* and Seneca's *De clementia*, which can, *contra* Nederman, clearly be regarded as 'major political works'.

57 A. R. Dyck, *A Commentary on Cicero, De officiis* (Ann Arbor: University of Michigan Press, 1996).

58 K. Nothdurft, *Studien zum Einfluss Senecas auf die Philosophie und Theologie des zwölften Jahrhunderts* (Leiden: Brill, 1963).

59 Selected studies include: J. Martin, 'Cicero's Jokes at the Court of Henry II of England: Roman Humour and the Princely Ideal', *Modern Language Quarterly*, 51 (1990), 144–66; B. Munk Olsen, 'L'humanisme de Jean de Salisbury, un Cicéronien au 12ᵉ siècle', in M. de Gandillac and E. Jeauneau (eds), *Entretiens sur la renaissance du 12ᵉ siècle* (Paris: Mouton, 1968), pp. 53–69; C. J. Nederman, 'Nature, Sin, and the Origins of Society: The Ciceronian Tradition in Medieval Political Thought', *Journal of the History of Ideas*, 49 (1988), 3–26; C. J. Nederman, 'Beyond Aristotelianism and Stoicism: John of Salisbury's Skepticism and Moral Reasoning in the Twelfth Century', in I. Bejczy and R. Newhauser (eds), *Virtue and Ethics in the Twelfth Century* (Leiden: Brill, 2005), pp. 175–95; K. Guilfoy, 'Stoic Themes in Peter Abelard and John of Salisbury', in J. Sellars (ed.), *The Routledge Handbook of the Stoic Tradition* (London: Routledge, 2016), pp. 85–98 (pp. 93–6), acknowledges the influence of Seneca on John, but does not dwell in sufficient depth upon John's Stoic debt.

60 S. Ebbesen, 'Where were the Stoics in the Late Middle Ages?', in S. K. Strange and J. Zupko (eds), *Stoicism: Traditions and Transformations* (Cambridge: Cambridge University Press, 2004), pp. 108–31 (p. 108). On the Stoic tradition in the Middle Ages see also M. Colish, *The Stoic Tradition from Antiquity to the Early Middle Ages* (2 vols; Leiden: Brill, 1990); G. Verbeke, *The Presence of Stoicism in Medieval Thought* (Washington, DC: Catholic University of America Press, 1983). See also M. Lapidge, 'The Stoic Inheritance', in Dronke (ed.), *A History of Twelfth-Century Western Philosophy*, pp. 81–112; M. Spanneut, *Permanence du Stoïcisme: De Zénon à Malraux* (Gembloux: Duculot, 1973).

61 A. MacIntyre, *After Virtue: A Study in Moral Theory* (3rd edition; London: Duckworth, 2007), pp. 170–3.

62 C. J. Nederman, 'Freedom, Community and Function: Communitarian Lessons of Medieval Political Theory', *American Political Science Review*, 86 (1992), 977–86.

63 Q. Skinner, 'Meaning and Understanding in the History of Ideas', *History and Theory: Studies in the Philosophy of History*, 8 (1969), 3–53 reprinted with some additions/changes in Q. Skinner, *Visions of Politics*, vol. 1: *Regarding Method* (Cambridge: Cambridge University Press, 2002), pp. 57–89; J. G. A. Pocock, 'A History of Political Thought: A Methodological Enquiry', in P. Laslett and W. G. Runciman (eds), *Philosophy, Politics and Society*, 2nd series (Oxford: Basil Blackwell, 1962), pp. 183–202.

64 J. G. A. Pocock, Virtue, *Commerce and History: Essays of Political Thought and*

*History Chiefly in the Eighteenth Century* (Cambridge: Cambridge University Press, 2002), p. 9.

65 See also J. Dunn, 'The Identity of the History of Ideas', in P. Laslett, W. G. Runciman and Q. Skinner (eds), *Philosophy, Politics and Society*, 4th series (Oxford: Basil Blackwell, 1972), pp. 158-73 (p. 165), where the history of political thought is defined as 'the set of argued propositions in the past which discuss how the political world is and ought to be and what should constitute the criteria for proper action within it, and the set of activities in which men were engaging when they enunciated these propositions'.

66 Pocock illustrates the levels at which a text can be considered 'authoritative'; the contextual specificity of the environment in which a text is read is actually influenced by the 'authority' of the text itself. See *Virtue, Commerce and History*, p. 29. Cf. S. Fish, *Is There a Text in this Class? The Authority of Interpretative communities* (Cambridge, MA: Harvard University Press, 1980), pp. 15-17.

67 Cf. Ross, who suggests in his study of Seneca's influence on the medieval period that the 'best evidence' for 'influence' consists of 'any instance in which Seneca's views are explicitly approved', although he acknowledges that 'more is really needed to establish that knowledge of them had any formative effect'. G. M. Ross, 'Seneca's Philosophical Influence', in C. D. N. Costa (ed.), *Seneca* (London: Routledge and Kegan Paul, 1974), pp. 116-65 (p. 116).

68 Skinner, 'Meaning and Understanding in the History of Ideas', p. 26; see also propositions to this effect in P. Weiner, 'Some Problems and Methods in the History of Ideas', *Journal of the History of Ideas*, 22 (1961), 531-48.

69 On the style of John's writings see R. Pepin, 'John of Salisbury as a Writer', in Grellard and Lachaud (eds), *Companion*, pp. 147-79.

70 *Entheticus de dogmate philosophorum*, or *Entheticus maior*, will be referred to simply as the *Entheticus* throughout; reference to *Entheticus in Policraticum*, or *Entheticus minor*, will be cited specifically as such. The edition used is *John of Salisbury's Entheticus Maior and Minor*, ed. and trans. J. van Laarhoven (3 vols; Leiden: Brill, 1987).

71 J. van Laarhoven, in *Entheticus*, ed. Van Laarhoven, pp. 15-16.

72 *Ioannis Saresberiensis Policraticus I–IV*, ed. K. S. B. Keats-Rohan (Turnhout: Brepols, 1993), p. xi, notes that the texts were separated in the late twelfth century and from then on had a separate history of transmission. For the later transmission of the text see R. E. Guglielmetti, *La tradizione manoscritta del Policraticus di Giovanni di Salisbury: Primo secolo di diffusione* (Florence: Sismel-Edizioni del Galluzzo, 2005); A. Linder, 'John of Salisbury's *Policraticus* in Thirteenth-Century England. The Evidence of MS Corpus Christi College 469', *Journal of the Warburg and Courtauld Institutes*, 40 (1977), 276-82; A. Linder, 'The Knowledge of John of Salisbury in the Late Middle Ages', *Studi medievali*, 3rd series, 18 (1977), 315-66; F. Lachaud, 'Filiation and Context: The Medieval Afterlife of the *Policraticus*', in Lachaud and Grellard (eds), *Companion*, pp. 375-438.

73 *Letters* I; *Letters* II.

74 Barrau, 'Ceci n'est pas un miroir', pp. 101-6.

75 Guglielmetti, *La tradizione manoscritta*, p. 16. M. Winterbottom, 'Review of *La tradizione manoscritta del* Policraticus *di Giovanni di Salisbury: Primo secolo di diffusione* by Rossana E. Guglielmetti', *Journal of Theological Studies*, 58 (2007), 740–2.

76 'Soissons, BM, MS 24 – Notice par Patricia Stirnemann (IRHT), décembre 2013', www.manuscrits-de-chartres.fr/sites/default/files/fileviewer/documents/notices-detaillees/soissons-bm-ms-24_policraticus_pstirnemann_2013-12.pdf (accessed 15 August 2014). See also the summary of Stirnemann's research provided in John of Salisbury, *Metalogicon*, trans. Hall, pp. 105–6.

77 I have examined a digital facsimile of the manuscript and agree that it can be dated to the third quarter of the twelfth century on palaeographical grounds.

78 Note the *ex libris*: fo. 7: '*Hunc librum fecit dominus Symon abbas sancto Albano quem qui ei abituerit aut titulum deleuerit uel mutanerit. Anathema sit amen amen amen.*'

79 R. Thomson, *Manuscripts from St Albans Abbey 1066–1235* (Woodbridge: Boydell and Brewer, 1982), pp. 66–7.

80 John describes the *Policraticus* as a '*libellus*' in *Entheticus in Policraticum*, 4, p. 231. Odo is referred to at line 191, p. 242.

81 Barrau, 'Ceci n'est pas un miroir', p. 106.

82 The sign appears in three out of the four manuscripts alongside: '*Est autem dux usquequaque inutilis apud quem disciplina non uiget*'. *Pol.* VI. 14; 2, p. 38. CCC 46, fo. 90v; Soissons MS 24, fo. 163r; BL Royal MS 13 D IV, fo. 82v.

83 CCC 46, fo. 91r; BL Royal MS 13 D IV, fo. 83r; Soissons MS 24, fo. 164r-v; Oxford, Bodleian Library, MS Lat. misc. c. 16, p. 147.

84 There is some variation among the manuscripts. These annotations are absent in Bodl. MS Lat. misc. c 16. CCC 46, fo. 90v contains reference to '*De coetaneis nostris*'; BL Royal MS 13 D IV, fo. 83r ('*De coetaneis nostris*'), fo. 83v ('*De Brehno*'); Soissons MS 24, fo. 164v ('*De coetaneis nostris*'), fo. 165v ('*De Brenno*').

85 CCC 46, fo. 92r: '*De Cnudo; De rege ruffo; de rege henrico primo*', fo. 92v: '*De rege henrico ii; de rege Stephano; Item de rege henrico secundo*', fo. 93r: '*De Eustachio*'; BL Royal MS 13 D IV, fo. 84r: '*De Cnudo; De Rege Ruffo; De Rege Henrico primo*' (a further annotation, in a distinct and smaller hand, refers to '*De duce Roberto*'), fo. 84v: '*De rege henrico ij; De rege stephano; Item de henrico secundo rege*; *De eustachio*'; Soissons MS 24, fo. 166r: '*De Cnudo*', fo. 166v: *De rege ruffo; de rege henrico primo; de rege henrico secundo*', fo. 167r: '*De rege stephano*', fo. 167v: '*Item de henrico secundo; De eustachio*'; Bodl. MS Lat. misc. c. 16, p. 149: '*De rege ruffo; De rege henrico i; De rege henrico ij; De rege stephano*'), p. 150: '*Item de henrici rege ij*'.

86 It is worth noting, however, that there are there are distinctive commonalities between BL Royal MS 13 D IV and Soissons MS 24 – for example, both manuscripts contain the annotation '*Contra sodomitos*' to III. 13 (BL Royal MS 13 D IV, fo. 46r; Soissons MS 24, fo. 89r) – and that Bodl. MS Lat. misc. c. 16 does not contain as many annotations as the other manuscripts. A late twelfth-century English manuscript, BL Royal MS 12 F VIII, contains a number of thirteenth-century annotations, including some that respond to the text. On fo. 84r of this

manuscript, for example, the annotator has added a schematic diagram itemising the list of vices provided in *Pol.* VIII. 1. At that point of the text John refers to Gregory the Great's depiction of '*hanc pestiferam arborem*'; the shape of the divisional diagram provided echoes the reference to the tree in the text, indicative of close reading.

87 E. g. fo. 41v: '*Quid princeps*'. This textual annotation in IV. 1 appears in all four early manuscripts (CCC 46, fo. 52v; BL Royal MS 13 D IV, fo. 48v; Soissons MS 24, fo. 94v; Bodl. MS Lat. misc. c. 16, p. 87).

88 G. Duby, *The Three Orders: Feudal Society Imagined*, trans. A. Goldhammer (Chicago: University of Chicago Press, 1980), pp. 263-8.

# 1

# The Roman inheritance

In his seminal study, *The Gothic Idol: Ideology and Image-Making in Medieval Art*, Michael Camille identified two ways in which the pagan content of classical material forms was 'neutralised' in the Middle Ages. The first was through an appreciation of the material legacy of the antique in a purely 'aesthetic' manner, reducing its representational significance. The second involved an 'allegorical reclassification' of the purpose of an object, so that sites of temples became sites of Christian worship, and antique gems retained a high-status function by being incorporated into bishops' rings.[1] This chapter investigates, in part, the relevance of Camille's modes of neutralisation for John of Salisbury's attitudes towards antiquity, particularly with regard to the apparent paradox between John's interest in the classics as a mode of authority and his relative lack of interest in the material culture of the classical age. In line with the methodological approach favoured by Skinner and Pocock, which was outlined in the Introduction, this chapter will also consider what John 'was doing' at the points of composition of his texts, notably the clues found in his own writings regarding his visits to Rome and the evidence we can glean from them regarding the sources to which he had access. It will conclude by summarising the classical sources available to John, and examine where he would have accessed them, and in what form.

## John's visits to Rome

A cleric affiliated to the episcopal court of Theobald of Canterbury and a scholar, John is a prime example of the cosmopolitan traveller of the twelfth century. He provided an account of his travels in the prologue to the third book of the *Metalogicon*: 'Leaving England, I have crossed the Alps ten times, journeyed through Apulia twice, often negotiated the affairs of my superiors and friends at the Roman Church, and as various cases emerged, travelled many times through not only England, but also Gaul.'[2] That said, it is difficult to be precise about the number of times John had visited Rome by 1159, the likely date of completion of the *Metalogicon*. When John mentions Rome in his writings he sometimes uses the place name as symbolic shorthand for meetings of the papal curia – at Benevento or Ferentino, for example.[3] Thus, John's occasional mentions of his business at the curia in his letters and works by no means constitute a precise account of his purpose or time in Rome. In addition, there is a persistent confusion in scholarship about whether his ten journeys across the Alps constituted ten individual trips or five there-and-back trips. In their introduction to *A Companion to John of Salisbury*, Grellard and Lachaud prefer the first interpretation, suggesting that from 1149 to 1159 John would have travelled to Italy 'on average once a year'.[4] Given Christopher Brooke's reasoned speculation that John was resident with the curia (in Italy) for most of the period from 1150 to 1153, combined with the evidence about his career that can be drawn from the *Historia pontificalis*, Lachaud and Grellard seem unduly optimistic about the number of times John could have travelled in subsequent years.[5] Reginald Poole preferred the second interpretation, that is, that John's ten journeys across the Alps were five independent return journeys, although as Brooke has noted, Poole's datings of these supposed trips do not concur with the evidence.[6] Brooke refers to 'four crossings' made in about 1149, in early 1154 and in 1155 and 1156, and conjectures that John may have been travelling in 1153 or in 1158–59, but concludes that 'we can only be certain of four out of the ten', implying that he too is referring to ten independent trips.[7] That John is referring to five back-and-forth crossings of the Alps seems to coincide more clearly with the available evidence. Either way, as Brooke has established, it is clear that on at least two of those visits John was definitely in Rome: between November 1149 and February 1150, during the visit of Henry of Blois, Bishop of Winchester, and in December 1153 when Anastasius IV granted a privilege to the abbey of Celle, an occasion on which it is likely that John acted as Peter of Celle's representative.

## Antiquity as example

What did John think of Rome? At the opening of the *Policraticus*, John alludes briefly to the city's triumphal arches, noting that they 'benefit the glory of illustrious men because the writing upon them teaches for what cause and for whom they have been inscribed', and commenting that the inscription is the key to understanding the significance of the Arch of Constantine; it identifies the emperor as 'liberator of his country and promoter of peace'.[8] Herbert Bloch regarded this reference to the Arch as exemplifying 'an unusual awareness of the monuments of ancient Rome'.[9] Michael Camille, on the other hand, saw it as an example of how classical material forms were neutralised for a medieval audience: 'only a scholar brought up in a tradition of monastic scriptural record and the logocentric culture of the cloister would make the arch of Constantine an aesthetic object as a text rather than an image of power'.[10] It is likely that John saw the Arch on one of his trips to Rome, but a mention alone does not satisfy Bloch's statement that John was showing here 'an unusual awareness' of the value of antiquity. On the other hand, John's words do not fully support Camille's claim that he rejected the 'representational language' of the monument by focusing only on its 'narrowly verbal communication'.[11] What it demonstrates, however, is that John viewed the residual heritage of ancient Rome instrumentally, seeking whatever moral lessons it could offer. In the context of the opening passages of the *Policraticus*, the message the Arch conveys is that a good ruler must rule by promoting peace. The Arch preserves Constantine's memory in the same fashion as Scripture preserves the lives of the apostles and prophets – as *exempla* worthy of emulation.

In *Policraticus*, Book II. 15, John also uses the remnants of antiquity as a source for a moral message. He describes a statue that was built by the city fathers to honour the majesty of Rome. The sculptor assured his patrons that the statue, a figure of a woman holding a globe in her right hand, would not collapse until a virgin gave birth. Upon the birth of Christ, however, the statue fell. The lesson to the reader is that 'the kingdom of man contracts as the kingdom of the divine expands'.[12] Two parallels to this account are found in Master Gregory's *Narracio de mirabilis urbis Romae*, a text composed in the late twelfth or early thirteenth century which describes the monuments of Rome's pagan past.[13] In one tale Gregory refers to a flame that was kept perpetually burning in a great hall. When asked if it would ever go out, the artificer responded that it would be extinguished only when a virgin gave birth. According to Gregory, on the day Christ was born the flame went out and the hall in which it was lit collapsed.[14] At another point, Gregory describes the destruction of the statue of the Colossus, which he claims was burned by Pope Gregory I. Master Gregory ends his account of this legend by noting that 'The head, and the right hand holding the sphere, did however survive the fire, and these make a wonderful sight for onlookers, elevated on two marble columns in front of the papal palace.'[15] John's story seems to be a conflation of the two narratives later presented by Gregory, adding to the likelihood that he was reporting a tale in common circulation. Given that both John and Gregory recount how the statue held a sphere in its right hand, it is probable that they were referring to the same bronze, displayed at that point outside the Lateran – a location with which John was likely to have been familiar.[16] Once again, the symbolism of John's account is striking; far from demonstrating an aesthetic appreciation of the antique, it is instead a tale of the moral triumph of Christianity over paganism. We must conclude that John perceived the remnants of ancient Rome – the Arch of Constantine and the statues outside the papal palace – without a sense of historical distance. His anachronistic tendency to reshape the lessons of the past to serve the needs of a medieval present is also apparent in his treatment of classical texts, as will be shown later in this chapter.

In Master Gregory's account, Gregory the Great is responsible for the fiery destruction of the Colossus. Pope Gregory I is also associated with the eradication of the pagan past of ancient Rome in John's writings, where he is linked to the destruction of classical books and notably of the Palatine Library, the public library founded by Octavian in 28 BC in the temple of Apollo.[17] John offers two accounts of the burning of the Palatine Library, and in so doing propagates a myth that would persist throughout the Middle Ages.[18] In the first account, John describes how Gregory proscribed the use of astrology in the court, but also burned books that claimed to offer insights into planetary movements and heavenly secrets.[19] In the second account John notes that some believe that the library was destroyed when the Capitol was struck by lightning – divine retribution for the sins of the reign of Commodus – but ultimately claims, rather prosaically, that Gregory burned its contents so as to make more room for works of Scripture and to encourage their study.[20] In an instance of historical elision, John comments that 'the two stories are not incompatible, however, since they might have happened at different times'.[21] John ascribes different motivations to Gregory in each account. In the first, Gregory is engaged in an explicit act of condemnation – an act that neatly coincides with the broader theme of this section of the *Policraticus*, that is, the rejection of astrology and other methods of prognostication, so-called sciences which surpass the boundaries of what we should know. In the second, Gregory is championing Scripture over pagan texts. In neither instance is the act regarded as regrettable, nor the destruction of the books considered in any way a loss. It is odd that Gregory is associated in these narratives with destruction, given that in one of his letters composed about 600 to Serenus, Bishop of Marseilles, Gregory says that pagan images should not be destroyed as their representations could be useful for teaching Christian faith to the gentiles.[22] It is likely that John was drawing on a common *topos*; Benedict of St Peter's, author of the *Mirabilia urbis Romae* composed in the 1140s, associated Pope Sylvester with the destruction of Roman temples, showing that a link was consistently drawn between the papacy and the decaying monuments of pagan Rome.[23]

While the stories of the destruction of the Palatine Library serve an argumentative function for John in the context of the broader themes of the *Policraticus*, they also serve to reinforce his view that the authority of antiquity must rest in the value of its message, not in its antiquity *per se*. In the prologue to the third book of the *Metalogicon*, John comments that 'old opinions are accepted, because they are old, while the far more probable and faithful opinions of our contemporaries are rejected because they are of our time'.[24] Antiquity alone does not confer an inherent value on a text. The authority of ancient writers rests in their words, but the careful reader will know how to select 'only what is edifying to faith and morals'.[25] As John recounts in the prologue to the fifth book of the *Policraticus*, 'Virgil was permitted to acquire the gold of wisdom from the clay of Ennius'; therefore it is also permissible for the careful reader of pagan texts to take Seneca's advice to Lucilius and 'imitate bees' by practising discrimination.[26] Reading from multiple sources is described as a transformative act: in the same fashion as honey is improved by the gathering of nectar from multiple flowers, so too the combination of intellectual 'flavours' can be regarded as a positive.[27] As we shall see, this does not imply that sources are simply quarried for applicable material, but that they should be read with careful attention, as 'it is certain that the faithful and prudent reader who spends time lovingly over his books always rejects vice and comes close to life in all things'.[28]

### Medieval interpretations of classical schools of thought

In evaluating the landscape of the medieval reception of the classics, we must resist the temptation to create anachronistic distinctions between individual schools of thought, distinctions that may not have existed in practice in the mind of the medieval scholar. We must consider not only what we regard as the tenets of Stoicism now, but what Stoicism was thought to consist of in the Middle Ages. What did it mean to be a Stoic, or an Aristotelian, or a neo-Platonist for that matter, in this period? John's poetic work *Entheticus* offers a discussion of the principal philosophical schools of the period and merits a closer examination prior to looking at the classical texts to which he would have had access. Near the opening of the poem John presents a scathing account of scholars of the time who 'read little to learn much', who praise Aristotle while scorning Cicero and rely on reputation rather than learning.[29] After praising the primacy of Scripture, '*pagina sacra*', a lengthy section (of over 800 lines of verse) describes the different philosophical schools in turn, all of whom are subordinate to the claims of Scripture, as 'Philosophy has given the citadel of her sacred empire [to her].'[30]

John starts with the Stoics, noting in particular their reluctance to fear death, a '*meditatio mortis*' that must be conducted with moderation so as to avoid despair: 'the constant meditation of death benefits the good man, through it the fool who fears without moderation perishes'.[31] He describes the Stoic attitude towards fate, a mechanistic understanding of how the causes of all that occurs in the world are interrelated, which he criticises by demonstrating the futility of soothsaying (a view consistent with similar expressions in Book II of the *Policraticus*).[32] John then refers to one of the paradoxes of the Stoic position: if all things are determined, what, then, is the place of free will? The Stoics did not believe, according to John, that fate necessarily implied 'forced obedience' but rather argued that man maintained responsibility for his actions.[33] He notes that 'rewards are due to no one for his merits, all crimes are devolved on the author of the fate itself', thereby ceding to the claim that we maintain some form of free will in the face of determinism.[34] John concludes his survey by referring to the paradoxical Stoic theory of the equality of vice: 'The Stoic makes guilts equal and balances them by the same punishment, but Scripture does otherwise.'[35] Proportionate punishment for sins is a better solution, in John's mind, than that offered by the Stoic. In spite of these criticisms, John recognised the proximity between some of Stoic teachings and Christianity: 'He [the Stoic] agrees, then, in many matters with the law ... Faith accepts his dogma unless manifest law rejects it or a stronger reason can condemn it.'[36]

After rejecting the lustful doctrine of Epicureanism, John turns to the Peripatetic school.[37] He discusses its belief that all things have potentiality, a potential that is actualised in causation: 'Reason precedes the birth of all things whatever, and once they are born the same reason carries them forward and moves them.'[38] Aristotle, according to John, believed 'that the supreme good is to know the causes of things'.[39] John, in turn, relates the Peripatetic version of man's rationality to that of God: 'The reason of man is an image of the supreme reason, it grasps truths inwardly under God's teaching.'[40] John then catalogues the views of Greek philosophers, Arcesilas, Zeno, Pythagoras, Socrates and Anaxagoras, before returning to the views of Aristotle, *'magnus Aristotiles'*, noting his expertise in physics, ethics and logic.[41] Despite claiming that 'if anyone is not of the opinion that Aristotle is to be considered as the first, he does not render the tribute worthy to his merits', John points out a deficiency in Aristotle's theory of free will, namely that 'he believed that the sublunary things were operated by chance [*casus*] and the more remote things by the fates', a view that limits 'true freedom of will for created beings'.[42] Aristotle's rejection of determinism and emphasis on the role of chance suggests that our capacity to assume full moral responsibility for our freely willed actions is not within our control. Finally, John turns to the Academics, who in placing emphasis on doubt note that 'the usual course of events makes probable what you see always under a similar pattern'; the Academic sceptic will not assert that something is true in the absence of definitive evidence, but will agree that it is probable, if it is the likely thing to happen in a particular context.[43] This lengthy section comparing the philosophical schools concludes with an assessment of the work of Cicero and Seneca, who are, at least within the structural context of the poem, given the final word on the part of the philosophers.[44] Again, free will and fate take centre stage, with John noting that one of Cicero's principal concerns is 'how free will may exist in harmony with fate, for if fate remains, free will perishes', one of the principal threads of Cicero's fragmentary *De fato*.[45]

John's treatment of the various philosophical schools is united by the common theme of free will versus determinism. However, his answer to what is the appropriate understanding of free will is found prior to his exposition of the views of the schools, in the context of an earlier discussion of grace.[46] Here John states that 'True free will requires the help of two things ... namely that reason should rightly discern and that affection should be enamoured of that which pious rights approve.'[47] Grace permits the reconciliation of divine foreknowledge with human free will, as (in seemingly Augustinian terms) we can do good (what reason should direct us towards) only with God's help in the form of grace, which 'frees free will'.[48] Therefore the purpose of the comparison of the philosophical schools is to compare their views with an already forwarded proposition, and not necessarily to prefer one perspective over another. Further support for this position rests in the fact that John concludes the whole section by saying: 'But why do I enumerate pagans whom error has driven away? For all reason fails without faith.'[49] Using this part of *Entheticus* to demonstrate which of the philosophical schools was preferred by John misleads, therefore, as the object of John's discussion in this context is the nature of free will, with the various schools marshalled as examples of differing opinions, all of which prove to be mistaken when compared with the Christian perspective. That said, this section enumerates the principal characters on the stage of John's intellectual theatre: Cicero and Seneca, but also Aristotle, Plato, Epicurus and other minor Greek philosophers.

In fact, this discussion of interpretations of free will and fate ably demonstrates the variety of sources used by John, as well as a further distinctive feature of classical reception in the medieval period. John draws subtle distinctions between the philosophical schools, but the contrast between the individual schools is less sharp than that drawn between *all* of them and the Christian perspective. In seeing the philosophical schools as an ensemble to be treated in opposition to Christianity, John casts the philosophers as an 'other'. Although he identifies key tenets of each of the schools (the probabilism of the Sceptics, the equality of vice in the minds of the Stoics and so on), the ideological overlap between the different schools means that clear points of distinction are difficult to identify.[50] Such perceived ideological overlap is not an exclusive feature of the medieval period; indeed, Cicero himself depended on a mélange of ideas drawn from Platonic, Aristotelian and Stoic thought. Therefore, it is challenging to think of medieval classical reception in clear categories and even anachronistic to try. As Stephen Rigby notes, 'it is rather difficult to make a clear distinction between Ciceronian/Stoic and Aristotelian notions of virtue or – what is more important for our purposes here – between medieval conceptions of them'.[51] We must, therefore, look for evidence of what medieval thinkers thought of as characteristic of these schools, while being aware that clear distinctions may be difficult to draw. This does not render the project of establishing lines of influence moot – far from it. It does suggest, however, that we must be circumspect in drawing distinctions between schools of thought, and open to the legitimate fact that ideas are transmitted through many channels, often simultaneously.

Nevertheless, despite his criticisms of pagan philosophy, John does, at various points of his work, express allegiance to a particular philosophical school, namely the Academy, and to its doctrine of scepticism.[52] By the time of the late Republic, the Academy, the school of which Cicero was a member, combined Platonic views with a new scepticism that permitted criticism of all philosophical doctrines. It was a philosophical position without positive doctrines, engaged in a continuous quest for knowledge and truth. Cicero's teacher Philo (159/158–84/83 BC) was a known adherent of probabilism, determining that one should weigh up all sides of a position and provisionally accept that which seems most persuasive.[53] In a similar vein, John describes how he also favours the Academic perspective: permitting doubt, rather than defending that which is still uncertain.[54] He specifically credits Cicero with holding this position, stating that the sage, whom he describes as the 'author of Roman style', turned to the school in his later life, as attested by *De natura deorum*.[55] Much of John's knowledge of the tenets of the Academy was derived from Augustine's *Contra Academicos*, although occasional insights into Cicero's position are also found in *De officiis*.[56]

In *Jean de Salisbury et la renaissance médiévale du scepticisme*, Christophe Grellard advises that the sceptical position claimed by John should be taken at face value. Grellard regards the testing and questioning of premises as fundamental to John's methodology, and identifies his scepticism as at its most explicit in two contexts: the prologues found throughout his works and his discussions of the history of philosophy.[57] The contribution of scepticism to John's historical writing is also noted by Matthew Kempshall, who points out that it has a critical role in John's assessment of the veracity of historical events and narratives. Indeed, as Kempshall clearly brings to the fore in his discussion of John's application of probable opinion, it often leads John to augment his presentation of historical 'truth' with argumentation and testimony from others, a rhetorical technique intended to make a narrative plausible and convincing. Although his discussion is necessarily short, as Kempshall is looking at John within the broader comparative context of twelfth-century history writing, his intervention makes an important point: that John's adoption of a sceptical position is in part due to his concern with appropriate rhetorical argumentation, a technique honed by his study of Cicero's *Topica* and Boethius's *De topiciis differentiis*. In this light, therefore, scepticism is one, albeit very important, aspect of a classically influenced rhetorical battery of arguments employed by John.[58] This offers a necessary corrective to Grellard's otherwise highly valuable survey of John's use of Ciceronian scepticism, that is, that the implications of John's employment of probable logic must be seen against a background of classical and Ciceronian appropriation and must not be unduly emphasised by being studied in isolation.

As noted, the disciplinary boundaries between philosophical schools were diffuse in the Middle Ages, even for an author who defined himself as an Academic, like John. Furthermore, John's use of probable logic must be examined in conjunction with his use of other philosophical theories – including those emanating from Christian discourse – as partially reflected by Grellard in his labelling of John's scepticism as 'Christian scepticism'.[59] Yet Grellard's account is explicitly confined to the 'non-political' parts of John's work, a distinction that seems artificial, given the present necessity to examine John's writings from a holistic perspective.[60] A broader position that sees John's scepticism as one among several significant philosophical borrowings from Cicero permits us to look at the implications of these borrowings within the wider context of inherited ideas from other Roman thinkers, such as Seneca. Taking this approach also permits us to look at classical reception in this period as necessarily hybrid, fused as it was with Christian thinking. No single medieval iteration of a philosophical doctrine can claim a true identity with its classical roots. Bearing this in mind, we must look to how classical ideas were accessed in this period and examine the sources available to John.

### Where did John access the classics?

Writing in 1977, Janet Martin pointed out that, despite a series of significant works on John of Salisbury, 'studies of his knowledge of ancient literature as a rule have failed to take into account the precise nature of the exemplars he used'.[61] In her study of the transmission of the writings of Frontinus and Gellius to John, and in other works, Martin provided a valuable reassessment of John's knowledge of the classics, establishing that he used intermediary sources, including excerpt collections and florilegia, alongside complete works.[62] Martin's study of John's access to Frontinus's *Strategemata* and to Aulus Gellius's *Noctes Atticae* pointed to the significance of the library at Christ Church, Canterbury, as a resource for his classical learning; she notes, 'typically he draws his classical citations not from venerable, authoritative continental manuscripts ... but rather from recently copied books of English provenance'.[63] We know that John did own some books in manuscript form, not least because he left a number of titles to the library of Chartres upon his death in 1180, which were recorded in the cathedral necrology.[64] Alongside a collection of biblical and patristic works, the following classical works are recorded: Valerius Maximus's *Facta et dicta memorabilia*, Vegetius's *De re militari*, Eutropius's *Breviarium historiae Romanae*, Seneca's *Naturales quaestiones* and Cicero's *De officiis* and *De oratore*. The bequest of books, while it reflects perhaps the best part of John's collection (and also included items such as his '*bibliotheca integra*', a one-volume Bible, and a copy of Isidore's *Etymologiae* – a text that could stretch to over 150 folios in manuscript form) – may not, however, have included all the books he owned. We are privy to other evidence of his accumulation of books from his letters. In the summer of 1165, for example, he debates whether to return from exile in a letter to Bartholomew of Exeter, writing, 'If God opens the path of return to me, please write back whether I should come with my books and all my baggage. If so, I shall need more horses and many other things I lack as yet.'[65] This passage suggests that John already possessed a number of books at this point. There are also rare references to his means of obtaining and copying books; around 1168, for example, he composed a letter to Azo, a monk of Canterbury, requesting 'the Quintilian I asked for, written and corrected'.[66] These fragments of evidence offer brief insights into John's collection of books, but remain unreliable sources for reconstructing the titles to which he would have had access in the 1150s, when he was composing his major works. Possession of a book at the point of death does not necessarily imply its possession more than twenty-five years earlier, particularly bearing in mind the privileged nature of private book ownership in this period.

We must, therefore, return to the other contexts within which John may have accessed his sources, notably twelfth-century English library holdings. As Martin pointed out, John frequently makes use of intermediary sources, notably florilegia – collections of textual excerpts arranged either by author or by theme – as a means of accessing the classics.[67] In his study of John's scepticism, Grellard suggests three criteria for evaluating John's employment of sources. For a source to be properly termed so, according to Grellard, it must be demonstrated that John directly cites from it (rather than simply alluding to it), it must be cited multiple times (to exclude the possibility that John is picking pithy quotations from florilegia), and it must be demonstrated that it could not have come from another, more accessible, intermediary source.[68] Grellard's method sits at the most rigorous end of the process of determining a source base. Nonetheless, it is open to critique as it does not mirror the actualities of the ways in which classical learning was most frequently accessed in this period. While it is clear that John placed an emphasis on the accuracy of the received text – requesting, on occasion, better translations than those at his disposal – and is seen to have expressed interest in acquiring new copies of old texts, he was also a man of his time, at the mercy of the material available to him.[69] Taking this into account, it seems harsh to criticise his use of florilegia and intermediary sources, and to render something that was an acceptable – even fashionable – means of reading and study in his time as somehow unworthy by modern standards.

While we cannot assume from his naming of Aulus Gellius's *Noctes Atticae* that John had access to a complete copy (instead, he knew the text through a florilegium also used by William of Malmesbury in his composition of the *Polyhistor*, as well as through mentions of it in Augustine's *De civitate Dei*), his references to it illustrate his desire to build a classical base of authority.[70] Even if by some standards, such as those of Grellard, such mentions fall short of it constituting a source, *per se*, it is clear that John himself would not necessarily have made such a distinction. The same pertains to texts which were accessed through an intermediary source; continuing with the example of the *Noctes Atticae*, we recollect that John could have accessed stories from this text through various routes.[71] Again, drawing a firm line between what is regarded as a legitimate source in contemporary terms and what constituted a source in the eyes of a medieval reader proves problematic. Accepting that intermediary sources played an important role in the transmission of the classics in the Middle Ages means that Grellard's other criteria (that a source must be cited multiple times, and that only citations, not allusions, are of relevance) are also moot. A re-evaluation of the pertinent research question is required; at issue is an understanding of *how* John and his contemporaries read the classics, not only *what* they read. Therefore, intermediary sources are of key relevance to our treatment as they make possible an accurate reconstruction of how John accessed classical texts and his interests; this is by no means a dilution of rigour in determining his source base, but a recognition of the realities of textual transmission in this period. Thus, recognising that John could have accessed the *Noctes Atticae* through multiple routes, without ever knowing the complete text, does not lessen the significance of the observation that what he knew of the text, steeped as it was in anecdotes of the classical age, was of interest to him. De-emphasising the 'whole text' as the only legitimate category of influence also means that any temptation to ascribe knowledge of rare texts to John without caution is lessened.

## Canterbury as a source for John's learning

Where, then, might John have gained access to classical texts at the point of composition of the *Policraticus* and the *Metalogicon*? John was based at Canterbury for much of the time during which he composed his major works. Our two main sources for reconstructing the library in this period are its twelfth-century fragmentary catalogue (now Cambridge, University Library, MS Ii.3.12, fos 135–7) and the first part of the fourteenth-century catalogue of Henry of Eastry (now London, BL, Cotton Galba E. IV, fos

128–47), which replicates much of the information of the earlier list, while offering some extensions.[72] The fragmentary catalogue, added at the end of a copy of two works by Boethius dating from the first third of the twelfth century, has a *terminus post quem* of 1176. A reference is made to the '*Enteticus Iohannis Carnotensis*', John's *Entheticus*; John did not become Bishop of Chartres, and so '*Carnotensis*', until 1176.[73] The fragmentary catalogue contains a number of works by Roman classical writers, including books explicitly attributed to 'Tullius' (Marcus Tullius Cicero), namely *De senectute* and two copies of *De amicitia* (items 102–4). Six books entitled '*Rethorica*' are also present (items 30–5); it is likely that these included copies of Cicero's *De inventione* and the pseudo-Ciceronian *Rhetorica ad Herennium*. The pseudo-Senecan epistles to Paul are named (item 178), as are '*Seneca de declamationibus*' (item 220) – the *Controversies* of Seneca the Elder, believed in this period to be by Seneca himself.[74] Named, but unattributed here to Seneca, is the pseudo-Senecan '*Forma vite honestae*' (item 184). A number of other classical works, including titles by Virgil, Terence, Horace and Lucan, are also listed.

The catalogue of Henry of Eastry, prior of Christ Church from 1284 to 1331, was divided into a first and a second '*demonstratio*', probably corresponding to the contemporary physical layout of the library.[75] The first *demonstratio* comprises a section arranged alphabetically that mainly consisted of theological books (items 1–274), followed by a section loosely arranged by subject (items 275–514), before concluding with a list of books from donors (items 515–782). The second *demonstratio* opens with a list of books of Thomas Becket (items 783–853), followed by those of Herbert of Bosham (items 854–8), and continues to list books by donors throughout (to item 1831). It is likely, as James suggests, that the Eastry catalogue is copied from earlier catalogue(s); indeed, James assumed that the first *demonstratio* recorded books received before the bequest of Thomas Becket, and thus offered a more complete record of the mid-twelfth-century library than the fragmentary catalogue could.[76] However, the first *demonstratio* may have postdated Becket's death by some distance. For example, item 233 of the alphabetically arranged part of the first *demonstratio* is the '*Visiones monachi Eyneshamensis*', the *Vision of the Monk of Eynesham*, which records an event that happened in 1196, while the section arranged by subject includes item 294, a martyrology accompanied by '*Constituciones domini R. de Wynchelese Cant. Archiep.*' – Robert Winchelsea was archbishop from 1305 to 1313 – so this volume, and in turn the source catalogue from which the list may derive, cannot predate this period. Similarly, the second *demonstratio* refers at the start of the list of Becket's books to *'Libri Sancti Thomae'*, so the list of names by donor must have been started after Becket's canonisation in 1173.[77]

Despite the fact that there is no way of being certain what texts were in the library in Canterbury during John's time there, a survey of the Senecan and Ciceronian texts listed among the alphabetical (and earliest) part of the first *demonstratio* of the Eastry catalogue, when combined with titles already identified in the fragmentary catalogue, gives a sense of the maximal range of texts by these authors which could plausibly have been available to John. Item 128 in Eastry's catalogue, *'Epistole Senece prime'*, contains the letters of pseudo-Seneca and Paul, along with other works of Seneca, namely the *Letters to Lucilius* and *De clementia*, while item 133, *'Epistole Senece et Pauli secunde'*, contains the pseudo-Senecan correspondence along with the apocryphal correspondence between Alexander the Great and Dindimus, and other titles. Other pseudo-Senecan works are present, namely *De moribus* (item 105; item 132: *'Liber Senece de institucione morum'*); the *Proverbia*, a collection of maxims largely derived from *De moribus* (in item 105: *'Prouerbia Senece secundum ordinem Alphabeti'*, also in item 616); *De remediis* (item 541: *'Seneca de remediis fortuitorum'*) and the *Formula vitae honestae* (also in item 105: *'Liber Martini episcopi de iv uirtutibus principalibus'*, and attributed to Seneca in item 541: *'Liber Senece de iv uirtutibus principalibus'*). Item 105, a miscellany bearing the title *'Parabole Salomonis Thodoricii'*, may have belonged to Thidricus, a scribe associated with Anselm, and if so, can be placed in the library from the early twelfth century.[78] It is likely that this volume was a collection of booklets or short texts; in its contents list *De moribus*, *Prouerbia*, and *Formula vitae honestae* take their place alongside Cicero's *Paradoxa Stoicorum* and other short biblical and grammatical texts. In addition to this work of Cicero and those listed in the earlier fragmentary catalogue, a *'Tullius Tusculanarum'*, Cicero's *Tusculanae disputationes*, is included among the books of Thomas Becket (item 813).

A further significant aspect of John's engagement with Roman sources at Canterbury concerns his knowledge of Roman law, which is demonstrated by his use of legal vocabulary and references to practice throughout his prose works and letters. How did John become acquainted with the study of Roman law?[79] The credit for bringing Justinian's *Corpus* to England is conventionally given to Vacarius, a *magister* at Bologna (Robert of Torigny describes him as *'gente Longobardus'*) who came to Canterbury in around 1149.[80] John, who was an episcopal *familiaris* at the same time as Vacarius, refers directly to him in the *Policraticus*, in a section steeped with criticism of King Stephen. John describes how

Stephen, whom he compares to the Greek tyrant 'Antiochus', forbade the study of Roman law, which had been introduced into the court of Theobald in Canterbury and so into the rest of England: 'It was forbidden by royal edict to keep the books, and our Vacarius was silenced.'[81] The principal target here is Stephen's impiety, and while Southern is right in claiming that John's implication of 'book-burning' is at best a 'flight of rhetoric', the passage provides evidence of an acquaintance between John and Vacarius.[82] Southern suggests that Vacarius was a 'mainstay of the archbishop's administration', noting that John's letter-writing on behalf of Theobald increased after 1154, a date that Southern connects with the departure of Vacarius from Canterbury.[83] Although it is unlikely that John read Vacarius's *Liber pauperum*, which may not have been composed until the 1180s, it seems from John's account that Vacarius was already known for his expertise in Roman law during his time in Canterbury.[84] As Yves Sassier noted, the frequency of John's juridical references (particularly in the *Letters*, but also in the *Policraticus*), and the fact that he often modifies and twists his references to suit the point at hand, make it challenging to identify the sources of John's Roman legal knowledge.[85] Quotations and allusions suggest that John knew and used the *Digest*, the *Institutes* and the *Code* of Justinian (including the *Tres libri*, which contained substantial information about Byzantine law), as well as an influential summary of the *Code*, the *Summa Trecensis*. While John's knowledge of Roman law is not a focal point of our study here, it should be noted that the legal codes provided, at times, important information to John about the norms of the classical world and were also a resource for legal vocabulary, a vocabulary rendered even more prestigious by its association with the Roman world.[86]

While our survey of the existing evidence for the library holdings at Canterbury illustrates that a concrete reconstruction of the texts available there in the period of the composition of John's work is impossible, a few points must be noted. First, it is clear that certain texts, such as Cicero's *De inventione* and the pseudo-Ciceronian *Rhetorica ad Herennium*, achieved their popularity in the library on account of their capacity to be used for the study of Latin argumentation, as well as their inherent value as classical texts – a reminder that we must bear in mind the context within which texts were used. Secondly, it is clear that many texts which are now regarded as apocryphal were considered authentic works in the twelfth century, notably Martin of Braga's *Formula vitae honestae*, which is explicitly attributed to Seneca in one instance in the Canterbury book-list. Finally, even though these book-lists fail to make possible a precise reconstruction of the twelfth-century library of Canterbury, they still provide an important illustration of how classical texts were read alongside a heterogeneous collection of patristic and contemporary texts and theological and liturgical materials. Attempts to sharply delineate classical learning as an independent discipline in the Middle Ages must necessarily fail on account of this heterogeneity. Our brief discussion of John's acquaintance with Vacarius at Canterbury, and so with the incipient context of development of the study of Roman law in England, illustrates another means of access to information about the classical world – that is, personal social networks – although our knowledge of the details of such networks must, by virtue of the passage of time, remain shadowy.

### Other sources for John's knowledge of the classics

Bearing these points in mind, it is also important to consider earlier contexts within which John may have encountered the classics. We do not know what John's standard of education was by the time he moved to study in France in 1136, but it was obviously sufficiently strong enough for him to be able to profit from the advanced curriculum to which he was exposed.[87] Classical holdings at the secular cathedral of Exeter, a place which John had a strong association with throughout his life, were sparse.[88] We can assume, therefore, that initial study at Salisbury provided the major part of his basic grounding in the *trivium* and *quadrivium*. As Tessa Webber notes in her study of the intellectual environment at Salisbury in the late eleventh and early twelfth centuries, the canons seemed to have an unusually strong interest in classical and secular texts.[89] For example, an early twelfth-century copy of Cicero's *Tusculanae disputationes* is attested to in Salisbury (now BL, Royal MS 15 C XI, fos 1–58).[90] Webber also provides a detailed description of Cambridge, Trinity College, MS R. 16.34 (which seems to have been copied from a Norman exemplar, as it contains a summary of the provisions of one of the reforming synods of the province of Rouen, the synod of Lisieux in 1064). This volume contains the earliest known English copy of Cicero's *De officiis* (I–II. 19), extracts from Seneca's *De beneficiis* and an anthology of works by Valerius Maximus and Aulus Gellius.[91] Whether John was acquainted with these selections is disputed; we know he used a different florilegium of extracts from Aulus Gellius's *Noctes Atticae* at the point of composition of his works, as has been proved by Martin, Marshall and Rouse.[92] However, this does not preclude the possibility that John gained some of his initial acquaintance with such classical works at Salisbury.

While the *Metalogicon* recounts the teachers with whom John studied (as detailed in the Introduction), it does not provide us with specific information about what he read during his studies in France or during his later travels. As a result, it is worth taking account of general trends of transmission of classical texts in the twelfth century. Birger Munk Olsen's magisterial multi-volume study *L'Étude des auteurs classiques latins aux XI<sup>e</sup> et XII<sup>e</sup> siècles* surveys surviving classical manuscripts from the eleventh and twelfth centuries. In the summary material accompanying this study, Munk Olsen tabulates the twenty-five texts that survive in the most copies from the ninth to twelfth centuries in turn.[93] While these lists must be read with caution – given varied circumstances of survival, and the fact that the presence of older copies in a library may have precluded the making of new exemplars without indicating cessation of use – they give an insight into the kinds of texts that were most popular in this period and, in turn, the kinds of texts John was most likely to have encountered. While Horace and Virgil led the way in the eleventh century, Cicero's *De inventione* and the pseudo-Ciceronian *Rhetorica ad Herennium* survive in the greatest numbers in the twelfth, with over 120 copies of each text extant. Ninety-four copies of Cicero's *De somnium Scipionis* survive from the twelfth century, while forty-two copies of *De officiis* are extant. Seneca's apocryphal *Epistles to Paul* survive in twelve copies from the eleventh century, but in sixty-seven from the twelfth, while the first part of the *Epistulae morales ad Lucilium* survive in fifty-five twelfth-century copies, and *De beneficiis* in forty-six from the same period. These figures demonstrate the general rise of interest in both of these authors, particularly in Seneca. Munk Olsen notes that the twelfth-century catalogue of the library at Pontigny even contained a special section entitled '*De Libris Senecae philosophi*' containing his known works, as well as some of the more unusual Ciceronian works, notably *De finibus* and the *Posterior Academics*.[94] In considering the specifics of John's access to Ciceronian and Senecan works, therefore, we must bear in mind the general modalities of transmission of the classics in this period; while John was undoubtedly unusual in the extent to which he employed the classics, many of the texts which he accessed and used were ones which were popular and circulated widely in his time.

## John's access to Cicero

As noted, John explicitly aligned himself with Academic scepticism at several points in his writings, singling out Cicero as an example of the teaching of this school. In *Entheticus*, John devotes a section of his discussion of ancient philosophers to Cicero, opening with these words: 'The Latin world held nothing greater than Cicero; compared to his eloquence, Greece was dumb.'[95] Despite his praise for Cicero's eloquence and his adherence to the Academic School, John is cagey about his personal virtues. He twists a maxim from Cicero's *De amicitia*, that one should follow 'nature, the best guide of life', by saying that without true knowledge of God, Cicero cannot claim to be truly following nature: 'Only faith perceives Him [God] and true love; and to follow nature is worship and love of God.'[96] He concludes by saying that 'if Cicero's life had been in harmony with his words he could have been the greatest among excellent men', but as it is, we are obliged to admire his 'mouth' ('*os*') and 'tongue' ('*lingua*') but not his 'heart' ('*pectus*').[97] John uses this critique of Cicero as an opportunity to introduce his own take on the key tenets of philosophy, namely that to 'live honestly' is the best part of philosophising, while an eloquent tongue is useless without being accompanied with the prudence of wisdom.[98] As Martin has noted, it is likely that John's opinions on Cicero's character were shaped by their presentation in the intermediary sources to which he had access; she draws attention to Augustine's account of reading Cicero's *Hortensius* for the first time, where the patristic writer noted that the author's eloquence, but not his heart, was admired by nearly all.[99] She also notes the influence of the account of Cicero found in the *Saturnalia* of Macrobius (395-423), a text heavily used by John, where Cicero is presented as 'a man thoroughly implicated in the push-and-shove of Roman politics' whose gibes and jokes are criticised as being of a type not appropriate to a wise man.[100] Martin suggests, therefore, that there is a tension in John's writings between his use of Cicero's works and his apparent difficulties in coming to terms with 'the extratextual reality of the historical Cicero'.[101] Bearing in mind the comments made earlier in this chapter regarding the apparent distance between John's interest in the moral lessons of ancient Rome and what could be accessed of the historical remains of the Roman empire in the Middle Ages, it is perhaps no surprise that John found it difficult to reconcile Cicero the ascetic moralist with Cicero the scheming statesman. It is notable, however, that on most occasions John chooses to gloss over this tension, and this is, in part, a reflection of the Ciceronian sources of which John made most use.

Rodney Thomson asserts: 'John makes heavy use of Cicero's writings in absolute terms, and in proportion to his first-hand acquaintance with them.'[102] Upon his death, as noted, John bequeathed his personal copies of *De officiis* and *De oratore* to Chartres cathedral. It is certain that he had access to the first of these titles at the time of composition of his major works, as is demonstrated by the number of occasions upon which he refers to it and his adaptations of the ideas it contains.[103] John's use of the second of these books in his works, however, is more difficult to reconstruct. While recorded in a number of eleventh- and twelfth-century library inventories, *De oratore* circulated in significantly fewer numbers than other rhetorical works by and attributed to Cicero, notably *De inventione* and the *Rhetorica ad Herennium*.[104] In a study entitled 'What the Middle Ages Missed of Cicero, and Why', John Ward discusses John's alleged use of *De oratore* in some detail.[105] Ward suggests that 'the Cicero references discussed … will be less than those that could be assembled by a more extended search', a statement that may not hold water in the case of John's use of this text.[106] Webb's edition of the *Policraticus* cites three possible uses of *De oratore*, two of which are found in Pike's translation of the *Policraticus* and discussed by Ward, and it has been generally accepted that John used the text.[107]

This position requires closer examination. In the first example (Book VIII. 14), John uses the phrase '*poetica licentia*', which Webb claims is derived from *De oratore*, III. 153. Given the context, a discussion of Virgil's presentation of Dido, which John describes as using poetic licence to 'pervert faithfulness to history', a more likely source for the phrase is Servius's *Commentary on the Aeneid*.[108] While John draws attention to the disparity between the supposedly chaste Dido and the lustful version found in Virgil, he also draws attention to the fact that the historical Aeneas and Dido could never have met, '*ex ratione temporum*', a point raised by Servius.[109] Servius uses the phrase '*poetica licentia*' on a number of occasions, and given the context and the fact that his commentary was 'universally available', it is far more likely that this is the source used here by John, not *De oratore*.[110] The same goes for the second reference referred to by Ward and Pike – that is, the reference to the eloquence of a certain 'Curio' in *Entheticus minor*: 'if Curio should compete in words, he will be vanquished by him'.[111] Curio's eloquence is praised by Cicero in *De oratore*, II. 98. Curio's son, also called Curio, is documented in another classical text, Lucan's *Pharsalia*, where he is criticised as '*audax venali … lingua*' ('bold, with his tongue for sale', I. 269). Here Curio exhorts Caesar to march against Rome (I. 273–91), and is later accused of having sold out the city (IV. 824). While it is plausible that John is referring to the account of Curio-the-father given in *De oratore*, an equally plausible alternative is that he is referring to Curio-the-son, the reckless and glib speech-maker of *Pharsalia* who inspires Caesar to battle. We must not merely, on the mention of such a name, assume that John had a copy of *De oratore* in the 1150s, particularly given the rarity of this text in this period versus the comparatively broad circulation of the *Pharsalia*.[112]

Aside from the two texts mentioned in his bequest, to what other Ciceronian works did John plausibly have access? He refers explicitly in *Policraticus*, Book II. 16, to the 'dream of Africanus', that is to the final book of Cicero's *De re publica*, which circulated independently in the Middle Ages in tandem with a commentary by Macrobius.[113] He groups Scipio's vision alongside biblical examples of apocalyptic visions, including the dreams of Joseph and Pharaoh, and the oracles of Daniel and Ezekiel. Aside from this section of Cicero's text, John, like his contemporaries, had access to only the passages from the rest of *De re publica* which were preserved in patristic texts like Augustine's *De civitate Dei* and Lactantius's *Institutiones divinae*.[114] As noted, John refers to the maxim of *De amicitia* – that nature is the best guide of life – and quotes elsewhere from this popular and widely circulated work, even referring directly to Laelius, its protagonist.[115] John also used the *Rhetorica ad Herennium*, a work attributed to Cicero in this period, and his *De inventione*; this is unsurprising given their commonality in the medieval schools.[116] Christophe Grellard has illustrated that it is likely that John had at least partial access to *Tusculanae disputationes*, although he rejects that John had first-hand knowledge of *Academica*, suggesting that patristic intermediaries served as his source for this text.[117] As the survey of the holdings of the library at Canterbury showed, John may have had recourse to *De senectute* and to *Paradoxa Stoicorum*, a text of substantial relevance to our study. In his edition, Webb noted two possible references to the latter text; in Book II. 22, John refers to the 'surprising opinions' of the Stoics, 'which they call paradoxes', an apparent reference to the preface of the work where Cicero notes that the Stoics themselves use the term '*paradoxa*' to describe their teachings, while in Book VII. 16, John references a maxim from the text – 'he regards parsimony as of little importance, although it is more lucrative than revenue' – in the context of his critique of the avaricious courtier.[118] We have already noted John's reference in *Entheticus* to the paradox of the Stoic equality of the vices. As will be illustrated in the following chapters, John returns to a number of the six named paradoxes in his writings, which suggests that, although he does not refer to the text by name, he had knowledge of its contents.

It is unlikely that John knew Cicero's *De finibus*, as will be demonstrated in more depth in Chapter 3, while other texts such as his *De natura deorum* (despite being referred to by name in the *Policraticus*) and *De fato* were similarly unknown to him, except through the medium of intermediary authors, such as Augustine.[119] Cicero's letter collections had diverse patterns of circulation in this period. Despite not knowing the *Epistulae ad Atticum* or the *Ad Brutum* directly, Laure Hermand-Schebat has demonstrated the likelihood that John had access to the second half (Books 9 to 16) of the *Epistulae ad familiares*.[120] Cicero's speeches circulated rarely in this period. Even William of Malmesbury (*c*.1090–*c*.1142), who had a much broader knowledge of Cicero's works than John (as evinced by his *Polyhistor*), knew only four of the speeches.[121] John's limited knowledge of the corpus of speeches and letters affected the presentation of Cicero in his works, making it easier for him to elide the conflict between Cicero as moralist and cunning statesman. Despite the gaps in John's knowledge, the scope of his quotations from Cicero's works suggests that he did not rely on excerpt collections for access to this author.[122] While this is not universally the case for John's borrowings, on the basis of her study of the Becket correspondence, Duggan argued that John's letters show a stronger direct acquaintance with the classics than those of his contemporaries. She notes that only three or four of the seventeen or eighteen classical allusions and quotations in John's letters in the Becket collection can be located in either the *Florilegium Gallicum* or the *Collectanea* of Henry of Auxerre; with one exception, all quotations by correspondents other than John can be located in one or other of these collections.[123]

### John's access to Seneca

In *Entheticus*, John refers to Quintilian's critique of Seneca's style.[124] John responds to this critique by saying that Seneca should be commended for his virtue and for his 'gravity of life', explicitly identifying the Roman writer as 'an acute Stoic' who 'makes compendia of morals'.[125] In the *Policraticus*, John comments further: 'His [Seneca's] *Epistles* should be read; his works *De Beneficiis* and *[De] Clementia*; those books also in which he expressed the views of the ten orators in the form of imaginary discussions of scholars; those which he published under the title *De naturalibus questionibus*, and the works on philosophy which Quintilian argued were lacking in precision.'[126] This can be regarded as a list of the Senecan texts to which John claimed access and advised others to read. To establish the veracity of John's access to this list of texts, we must look both to internal evidence of his writings and to external evidence regarding the circulation of Seneca's works in the twelfth century. John refers by name to Seneca several times in the *Policraticus*. In the prologue to Book

I of the text, John compares Seneca's correspondence with Lucilius to the letters exchanged between Jerome, Oceanus and Pammachius, affirming his knowledge of the *Epistles*.[127] John later comments that 'our Seneca', '*Seneca noster*', 'won the friendship of the apostle and was placed in the catalogue of saints by the learned father Jerome'.[128] This statement sheds light upon an important aspect of Seneca's medieval transmission; as Leighton D. Reynolds noted, 'To form a true estimate of his [Seneca's] popularity one should remember that his reputation did not rest on genuine works alone: his fame grew fat on works he had never written.'[129] Most significant among these apocryphal texts is the widely circulated correspondence alleged to be between him and St Paul – the source of the 'friendship' between Seneca and the apostle to which John refers – numerous copies of which existed in the Canterbury library catalogue. Direct evidence of John's ownership exists for only one of the texts named in the *Policraticus*. One entry in the list of books bequeathed by John to the cathedral library at Chartres reads: '*Senecam de naturalibus questionibus*'.[130] We know for sure, therefore, that John had a copy of *Naturales quaestiones* – Seneca's work on the workings of the universe, a relatively rare text in this period – at least upon his death.[131] As for the other works, we must seek indirect evidence for his knowledge of them in his writings.

John's list refers to *De beneficiis* and *De clementia*, two texts that frequently circulated in tandem in this period; the archetypes of medieval copies of these texts, the Codex Nazarianus (Vatican Library, Pal. lat. 1547) and the Codex Reginensis (Vatican Library, Reg. lat. 1529), both dating from the ninth century, contained both works.[132] This physical connection was enhanced by a thematic one: both treatises were in the 'mirror for princes' genre, providing political advice for the virtuous ruler and paying particular attention to the claims of liberality and leniency. Webb's edition of the *Policraticus* does not note any references to *De clementia* in John's work, however, and identifies only three allusions to *De beneficiis*. However, this apparent paucity of reference is not an adequate reflection of John's use of these texts. As Peter Stacey has asserted, 'John's debts to *De clementia* have barely been acknowledged, but they are profound'; he notes especially the significance of this work for John's model of the body politic.[133] Furthermore, as Miriam Griffin's study of the afterlife of *De beneficiis* has established, quotations of this work often appear in veiled form; she describes it as a 'self-effacing work', saying 'it has rarely been quoted or cited by name by authors who have used it'.[134] John is no exception to this rule, and none of the allusions identified by Webb are direct quotations from the work. While John's tacit use of *De clementia* and *De beneficiis* will be examined in depth in the following chapters, let us look in detail here at two of the three allusions to *De beneficiis* identified in his edition by Webb, as, although they are by no means representative of the extent of John's use of the work, they prove that John did have access to, at the very least, an abbreviated version of *De beneficiis*.[135] Giancarlo Mazzoli has studied such abbreviated versions in depth, noting in particular a grouping he entitled the 'σ²' text, that circulated in the schools of continental Europe.[136] He identified Paris, Bibliothèque nationale de France (hereafter BnF), MS lat. 16592, a manuscript dating from the final third of the twelfth century, as an example of this abbreviated version.[137] The text of the *De beneficiis* found in that manuscript will be used here as a basis of comparison to the allusions identified by Webb, which will be compared, in turn, with the abbreviated versions found in the popular aphorism collections, the *Florilegium gallicum* and the *Moralium dogma philosophorum* (the latter is a summary of moral philosophy that borrowed heavily from the Ciceronian and Stoic tradition, and that some have claimed was composed by William of Conches for Henry II).[138]

In *Policraticus*, Book V. 10, John discusses the appropriate tone of voice to be used by one asking for a benefaction, noting that when requesting a favour one sacrifices a certain dignity and 'so cannot be said to receive gratis'.[139] The phrase used by John, '*nec gratis tulit qui cum rogaret accepit*', is very similar to that found in *De beneficiis*, II. 1: '*Non tulit gratis, qui, cum rogasset, accepit*'.[140] This particular phrase does not appear in the relevant section of the *Florilegium gallicum* (BnF MS lat. 7647, fo. 166r), although versions of the phrase are found in the *Moralium dogma philosophorum* and the abbreviated version of *De beneficiis* identified by Mazzoli as the σ² text.[141] Another allusion identified by Webb occurs in Book III. 11, where John notes that if a favour is granted with apparent reluctance, the appeal of the act is obscured.[142] Again the phrase used is not a direct quotation from *De beneficiis*, although the opening of *De beneficiis*, II. 1, may be an inspiration: there Seneca notes that a favour must be given without hesitation, as when it has rested too long in the hands of the giver it suggests reluctance.[143] If this is the source, it is likely again that either a complete or an abbreviated copy of *De beneficiis* was in use. The *Florilegium gallicum* provides only a limited version of this passage, referring to a favour remaining in the hands of the giver, but not to the apparent reluctance that this implies.[144] The abbreviated version of the text, on the other hand, as found in BnF MS lat. 16592 (fo. 97r), quotes the passage from the Senecan text in full.[145] That said, while John's words coincide here with those of Seneca, it may be an unconscious or coincidental allusion. The passage is followed by a verse, attributed by John to a '*versificator egregius*' (identified tentatively by Webb as Ovid), that is, in fact, a quotation from Bernard Silvestris's *Mathematicus*: 'Delay denigrates the merit of the giver; gifts quickly given carry more favour and praise.'[146] Indeed, this part of the *Mathematicus*, clearly inspired by *De beneficiis*, continues to praise prompt generosity, saying that reluctance in giving is most damning among friends, and that, if possible, generosity should anticipate a need, as 'a service quickly performed will bring more thanks'.[147] Patricia Stirnemann has suggested that John was the author of the *Florilegium gallicum*, although she admitted that it was striking that John does not appear to have used the work in the letters he composed on behalf of Thomas Becket.[148] If John was indeed the author of the *Florilegium gallicum*, it seems odd that these apparent borrowings from *De beneficiis* used in the *Policraticus* are not found in a similar form in the *Florilegium*, a fact that throws doubt on Stirnemann's claim. While based on a limited set of allusions, this survey suggests that John, at the very least, had access to one of the abbreviated versions of the *De beneficiis* at the point of composition of his major works, and may even have had access to the whole text.

What does John mean by 'those books also in which he [Seneca] expressed the views of the ten orators in the form of imaginary discussions of scholars'? There are two possible interpretations. The most likely is that John means the *Controversiae* by the Elder Seneca, which circulated in this period as works of Seneca the Younger.[149] Of the manuscripts of this work circulating in this period, one group, *Controversiarum excerpta*, contained excerpts from all the ten books of the *Controversiae* along with the prefaces to Books 1–4, 7 and 10.[150] Indeed, John quotes from the *Controversiae* and identifies his source as 'Seneca'.[151] The alternative, less likely, possibility is that John is referring to Seneca's *Dialogues*, as they also are ten in number. However, there is evidence of only one manuscript of these texts circulating at this time: that is, the copy recorded in the catalogues of the abbey of Monte Cassino, which appears to have been copied from an unrecorded exemplar in the late eleventh century.[152] It appears that the *Dialogues* were not generally available in northern Europe until after the date of composition of John's works. However, it is possible that John had indirect access to the content of at least one of the *Dialogues*; *De ira* was used as the basis for a popularly circulated text of the same title by Martin of Braga (*c.* 520–579).[153] We can presume that John had no access to Seneca's plays as these seem to have started to circulate only in the latter part of the twelfth century. As Reynolds remarks, 'they [Seneca's works] largely went their own way until the twelfth century when the demand for one work would help to promote the demand for others'.[154]

The case of John's access to Seneca's letters is more complex. Reynolds has examined the dissemination of the letter collection in the twelfth century. He has determined that at this juncture the letters were circulating in two halves. The first half comprised letters 1–88 and circulated mainly in France, though also in Norman England. The second half, letters 89–124, circulated primarily in south-west Germany.[155] Reynolds comments, 'His [John's] quotations are confined to letters 1–88. In both the *Metalogicon* and the *Policraticus* there is a possible reminiscence of letter 89 cited in Webb, but in both places John could easily have got his material from another source; the one refers to the distinction between *philosophia* and *sapientia*, the other to the divisions of philosophy.'[156] This finding prompts a reconsideration of earlier work on Seneca's influence on John, notably that of Liebeschütz, who derived some opinions regarding John's employment of Senecan material from his supposed use of the later letters.[157] Further attention must be paid to apocryphal works by Seneca: the spurious correspondence between St Paul and Seneca, and the *Formula vitae honestae* that sometimes circulated under the name of the name of Martin of Braga, being presumed to be an adaptation of a lost Senecan *De officiis*.[158] As it is a purported work of Seneca it is important to assess its influence as part of the Senecan corpus, interpreted in broad terms. Its influence on John's writings on virtue will be considered in detail in Chapter 5.

### Patristic sources

This survey of John's access to Cicero and Seneca, two of the principal figures in our study of John's use of Roman sources, illustrates the diversity of medieval means of access to the classics – through full works, apocryphal writings or excerpt collections. A final aspect to touch on before the conclusion of this chapter is the significance of patristic writings as a conduit for classical ideas in the medieval period. Four writers are of particular significance, namely Lactantius (*c.*250–*c.*325), Ambrose (*c.*339–397), Augustine (354–430) and Gregory the Great (*c.*540–604). The influence of these writers on specific aspects of John's work will be traced in the following chapters; our objective here is simply (and briefly) to consider the extent of John's knowledge of their works. Each of these four writers, aside from their significance in the history of the development of Christian doctrine, played an important role in the transmission of Roman philosophy, specifically Stoicism, to the medieval West. Lactantius provided a model for the employment of Stoic philosophy in Christian polemic. Ambrose illustrated how Roman philosophy could be imitated stylistically and materially in Christian writings. In spite of frequently not approving of Stoic tenets, Augustine cited significant excerpts from the works of Cicero, while Gregory the Great applied some of the social aspects of Stoicism to the practical and moral organisation of Christian society.

John's bequest to Chartres mentions a '*Lactencium*', which has been identified by Webb as a copy of the *Institutiones divinae* of Lactantius.[159] Lactantius's work was a potentially significant conduit for Stoic thought, given the fact that he commented extensively on the theological, physical and ethical theories of Stoicism, notably their perspective on providence and theodicy, their conception of the nature of the soul and their theory of the passions.[160] Lactantius rejected the claims of pagan philosophers, including those of the Stoics, to wisdom on account of the fact that without knowledge of God, and therefore of true virtue, pagans could not be truly wise.[161] Despite his rejection of Stoic authority, Lactantius quotes extensively from Stoic sources and had extensive knowledge of Stoic logic, attesting to the popularity of this philosophical school in the late antique period.[162] However, the *Institutiones* was a relatively rare text before 1300, although copies are attested to in the library catalogues of Cluny and Corbie, as well as in several Italian monasteries.[163] Although a 'Lactantius' was attested to in Alcuin's poem on the eighth-century library of York, no copy of the *Institutiones* survives from England until the later Middle Ages.[164] Indeed, Webb was unable to find any quotations from Lactantius in John's works.[165] Bearing in mind the reservations already stated concerning whether or not John possessed the books he left to Chartres at the point of composition of his major works, we must examine what evidence could lead us to assume John's knowledge of Lactantius in the 1150s. Writing in 1974, Braxton Ross noted that one surviving twelfth-century copy of the *Institutiones divinae*, now Oxford, Bodleian Library, MS Canon. Pat. Lat. 131, contained a number of annotations referring to a certain 'Thomas' and 'Henry', whom Ross identified as Thomas Becket and Henry II.[166] The annotations drew attention to certain passages on beneficence and avarice. Ross's situation of these annotations in the intellectual climate of the Becket conflict inspired Lynn Barker to suggest in 1990 that these annotations were actually by John of Salisbury, probably from between 1156 and 1164, speculating that John may have obtained a copy of the text from France by way of his friend Peter of Celle, and identifying this as the copy left by him to Chartres Cathedral upon his death.[167]

Barker's persuasive case reinforces the likelihood that this manuscript is actually John's own copy of the *Institutiones*, and we shall return to the significance of its annotations in Chapter 5 and Chapter 6. Although the annotations would seem to date from the late 1150s to early 1160s, it is impossible to establish precisely when John came into possession of this manuscript. Two potential clues to his ownership of the text at the point of the composition of the *Policraticus* must be noted, however. The first concerns a series of annotations found in this manuscript regarding the doctrines espoused by Epicurus; Max Kerner has already drawn a parallel between these and the account of Epicureanism given in the *Policraticus*.[168] The second regards a comment made in *Policraticus*, Book II. 29, concerning malpractice by doctors. The passage lists a number of supporters of the view that doctors frequently cause harm in the guise of doing good, including Seneca. A possible source for the use of Seneca's name here is *Institutiones divinae*, III. 15.11, which ascribes to Seneca the saying that for doctors 'there's a cure on the label, but there's poison in the bottle'.[169] In MS Canon. Pat. Lat. 131, this passage is highlighted not only with Seneca's name, but also with the phrase '*Contra medicos*', which is indicative of particular interest.[170] Despite the fact that it cannot be firmly established when he came into possession of it, the ultimate ownership of this manuscript by John, for which Ross and Barker have made a strong case, is clear evidence of his interest in this rare apologetic work that was valuable for the transmission of classical thought to the Middle Ages.

While Lactantius couched his Stoic borrowings in a critical, and often negative, context, Ambrose was more explicitly commendatory. Indeed, one of his prominent works, *De officiis ministrorum*, is stylistically and ideologically dependent on the themes of Cicero's *De officiis* and, like its exemplar, is arranged in three books, one dealing with the *honestum*, one with the *utile* and the third with occasions where the *utile* and the *honestum* intersect.[171] Ambrose's aim is primarily pedagogical; the work is a manual for the reform of the clergy.[172] While we can identify philosophical themes in the work, it is not an attempt to defend Christianity against philosophy, nor can it be conceived of as an explicit effort to synthesise Roman Stoic and Christian philosophy. In the context of Ambrose's work, Cicero's ideal republic and the Stoic cosmopolis are replaced by the visible community of the Christian Church: the Church is the institutional correlative of justice. Ambrose offers a Christianised interpretation of Cicero's work: for him the value of the *honestum* and the *utile* rests in the fact that they are a means to eternal life, a basis for a normative code for earthly behaviour that is, in itself, an imitation of Christ.

John's use of the Ambrosian *De officiis* is somewhat contested. In the edition of the *Policraticus* made by Webb in the 1920s only one quotation from Ambrose's text was noted. Smalley commented that this was unusual in view of the proliferation of the text in the twelfth century, commenting that 'since neither the author nor the title is mentioned, the assumption is that John did not know it directly. It seems that he made a deliberate choice in preferring the original *De officiis* to a patristic rehash.'[173] Is this a fair assessment? It is highly likely that John at least knew of the text as it was frequently excerpted in florilegia and canon law compilations.[174] Item 56 in the first *demonstratio* of Eastry's Canterbury catalogue is '*Ambrosius de officiis ministrorum, libri iii*', suggesting its presence in the cathedral collection (here the work is coupled with sermons of Cyprian).[175] Thomas Becket's donation to the library also included a copy. The popularity of the work in the twelfth century is further attested to by its influence on Bernard of Clairvaux's *Tractatus de ordine vitae*.[176] As examples in future chapters will demonstrate, a challenge in establishing the degree to which John used *De officiis ministrorum* rests in its similarity to its classical source text; at times it is difficult to determine to which text John is actually referring. However, these examples will show that John indubitably knew and used the text, and explicitly chose to depend on the patristic version rather than the classical original on several occasions.

While many of Augustine's works became mainstays of medieval libraries, *De civitate Dei* was the one used most frequently by John. A survey of the citations and allusions noted by Webb suggests that John found Augustine's text to be a mine of examples, especially for details about the ancient Roman world.[177] John also searched the text for information about philosophical schools and classical philosophers: particularly for testimonials on Plato, Socrates and Cicero.[178] Notably, the text provided a source for the transmission of Cicero's works to John, particularly of those that were not in circulation in this period, such as *De re publica* and *Pro Ligario*. The library at Canterbury was well stocked with Augustine's writings, and John also made significant use of his *Confessiones, De Genesi ad litteram, De libero arbitrio* and *De doctrina christiana*.[179] While John used Augustine as a source for information about the Roman world, his role as a transmitter of Stoic philosophy must be qualified. Augustine did not encounter the Roman classical works he read in a context that identified them as philosophically distinctive as 'Stoic'; rather they formed part of the standard knowledge of an educated man of his day. The fact that many Stoic ideas were silently absorbed into neo-Platonism complicates Augustine's role as a transmitter of them even further.[180] Augustine's use of the classical corpus is also uneven. As Hagendahl noted, 'Augustine mentions Seneca only a few times and in a way that does not show that he was well acquainted with him.'[181]

No survey of the influence of patristic literature on the medieval period would be complete without reference to the corpus of works of Gregory the Great. These staples of a twelfth-century clerical education hold an important place in John's works. The works of Gregory were extremely popular in England in the medieval period; Bede had presented an highly favourable opinion of Gregory, which had contributed to his popularity.[182] Gameson notes that copying of the texts of Gregory was largely a post-Conquest phenomenon, peaking between the end of the eleventh century and the middle of the twelfth, and points out that a large amount of English *Moralia* manuscripts have ended up in the bindings and wrappings of later manuscripts, attesting to the former ubiquity of the text.[183] Of Gregory's works, the *Moralia in Job* was the one most substantially employed by John, although he also used the *Dialogues* and the *Homilies*.[184] Webb noted two references to the *Regula pastoralis*.[185] However, this latter text may have been more useful as a model of rulership for John than has been previously recognised, as the survey of a number of possible allusions to it in future chapters will illustrate. Gameson notes that unlike the *Moralia*, the *Regula pastoralis* survives in only five copies from early Norman England, but he suggests, persuasively, that this text was probably already well represented in libraries before the Conquest.[186] It should be noted, moreover, that many compilations and abbreviations of Gregory's works, particularly of the *Moralia*, were in circulation in this period; William of Malmesbury, for example, made his own collection of extracts from Gregory, the *Defloratio Gregorii*.[187] There were also plenty of occasions for indirect transmission of Gregory's works; they were often referred to in exegetical texts, and even in the *Glossa ordinaria*.[188] The early catalogue of Canterbury library proves the existence of several copies of Gregory's *Homilies*, two copies of the *Regula pastoralis*, three copies of the *Dialogues* and a copy of Warner of St Victor's *Gregorianum*, a compilation of allegorical meanings of biblical themes, illustrated with excerpts from Gregory's writings.[189] As we shall see, John recommends Gregory's moral works to Thomas Becket as a guide to conduct; Becket's bequest to Canterbury would include Gregory's *Homilies* as well as a copy of '*Warnerius Gregorianus*', attesting to the readership of this text among the 'Becket circle'.

## Conclusion

John of Salisbury evidently had extensive access to, and interest in, the classical works of the Roman period. Although we cannot be precisely sure of its holdings, it is likely that the library at Canterbury along with the contacts he made during his studies abroad served as his principal means of access to these classical texts. We have pieced together the source base that contributed to John's knowledge of Stoic ideas: his direct use of the works of Cicero and Seneca as well as the significance of intermediary Christian works as a further source for his classical ideas. As illustrated, streams of classical philosophy in this period were not only in constant dialogue with Christian sources, but also interacted with each other. The fact that many of John's readings of the classics were filtered through those of his patristic forebears has significant implications for the ways in which he read and used his texts, and, as we shall see, is highly influential on his hybrid approach to political thought.

## Notes

1 M. Camille, *The Gothic Idol: Ideology and Image-Making in Medieval Art* (Cambridge: Cambridge University Press, 1991), p. 74.
2 *Met.* III. Prol., p. 101: '*Siquidem Alpium iuga transcendi decies egressus Angliam, Apuliam secundo peragraui, dominorum et amicorum negotia in ecclesia Romana saepius gessi, et emergentibus uariis causis, non modo Angliam, sed et Gallias multotiens circuiui.*'
3 See C. N. L. Brooke's discussion of John's travels in *Letters* I, pp. 253–6.
4 C. Grellard and F. Lachaud, 'Introduction', in Grellard and Lachaud (eds), *Companion*, pp. 1–28 (p. 8).
5 Brooke, in *Letters* I, p. xvii; pp. 253–6. If we accept Brooke's estimation of the amount of time John spent at the Curia in the early 1150s, Grellard and Lachaud are suggesting that John travelled to Italy nine times between 1153 and 1159! Cf. Haseldine, 'Introduction', who suggests that the ten crossings may be a figure of speech (p. 46).
6 R. L. Poole, 'John of Salisbury at the Papal Court', *English Historical Review*, 38 (1923), 321–30.
7 Brooke, in *Letters* I, pp. 253–6.
8 *Pol.* I. Prol.; 1, p. 13: '*Arcus triumphales tunc proficiunt illustribus uiris ad gloriam, cum ex quibus causis et quorum sint, inpressa docet inscriptio. Liberatorem patriae, fundatorem quietis, tunc demum inspector agnoscit, cum titulus triumphatorem, quem nostra Britannia genuit, indicat Constantinum.*' For the accuracy of John's description see H. Bloch, 'The New Fascination with Ancient Rome', in Benson, Constable and Lanham

(eds), *Renaissance and Renewal in the Twelfth Century*, pp. 615–36 (p. 632).
9   Bloch, 'The New Fascination with Ancient Rome', p. 631.
10  Camille, *The Gothic Idol*, p. 81.
11  Camille, *The Gothic Idol*, p. 80.
12  *Pol.* II. 15; 1, p. 92: '*quia humanum contrahitur ubi diuinum imperium dilatatur*'.
13  On this text see M. Campanelli, 'Monuments and Histories: Ideas and Images of Antiquity in Some Descriptions of Rome', in C. Bolgia, R. McKitterick and J. Osborne (eds), *Rome across Time and Space: Cultural Transmission and the Exchange of Ideas, c. 500–1400* (Cambridge: Cambridge University Press, 2011), pp. 35–51 (pp. 40–4).
14  Master Gregorius, *The Marvels of Rome*, trans. J. Osborne (Toronto: PIMS, 1987), VIII, p. 24. Osborne at p. 55 notes other parallels to this tale, noting that both the *Mirabilia* and the *Graphia aureae urbis* cite a similar story in connection with a golden statue of Romulus.
15  Gregorius, *The Marvels of Rome*, VI, pp. 22–3.
16  Osborne, in Gregorius, *The Marvels of Rome* (pp. 48–50), identifies it with the remains of a statue now in the Capitoline museum that consists of a head, hand and an orb.
17  Osborne, in Gregorius, *The Marvels of Rome* (pp. 50–1, 59), comments on Master Gregory's association of Gregory with the destruction of the pagan past.
18  T. Buddensieg, 'Gregory the Great, the destroyer of Pagan Idols: The History of a Medieval Legend concerning the Decline of Ancient Art and Literature', *Journal of the Warburg and Courtauld Institutes*, 28 (1965), 44–65.
19  *Pol.* II. 26; 1, p. 142.
20  *Pol.* VIII. 19; 2, pp. 370–1.
21  *Pol.* VIII. 19; 2, p. 371: '*Sed haec sibi nequaquam obuiant, cum diuersis temporibus potuerint accidisse.*'
22  C. M. Chazelle, 'Pictures, Books, and the Illiterate: Pope Gregory I's Letters to Serenus of Marseilles', *Word and Image*, 6 (1990), 138–53.
23  E. Gardiner and F. M. Nichols (eds), *The Marvels of Rome: Mirabilia Urbis Romae* (New York: Italica Press, 1986), pp. 9, 28–9.
24  *Met.* III. Prol., p. 102: '*Et haec quidem acceptae sunt opiniones ueterum, eo ipso quod ueteres, et nostrorum longe probabiliores et fideliores, eo quod nostrorum sunt reprobantur.*' Cf. *Entheticus*, 59–60 on the prevalence of the opposite attitude among teachers in the medieval schools.
25  *Pol.* VII. 10; 2, p. 132: '*ut quae nichil continent nisi edificationem fidei et morum*'.
26  *Pol.* V. Prol.; 1, p. 281: '*Si enim Virgilio licuit aurum sapientiae in luto Ennii quaerere, quae inuidia est ea, quae ad eruditionem nostram a gentilibus scripta sunt, nostris communicare?*'; *Pol.* VII. 10; 2, p. 133: '*apes quodammodo debemus imitari*'.
27  *Pol.* VII. 10; 2, p. 133.
28  *Pol.* VII. 10; 2, p. 134: '*Certum est quia fidelis lector et prudens et qui litteris ex amore inuigilat, uitia semper excludit et in omnibus accedit ad uitam.*'
29  *Entheticus*, 99, pp. 110–11: '*Pauca legas, ut multa scias.*'

30 *Entheticus*, 449–50, pp. 134–5: '*Arcem imperii sacri Philosophia dedit.*'
31 *Entheticus*, 489–90, pp. 136–7: '*Proficit ergo bonis iugis meditatio mortis, unde perit stultus, qui timet absque modo.*'
32 *Entheticus*, 501–14, p. 138.
33 *Entheticus*, 515, p. 138.
34 *Entheticus*, 517–18, pp. 138–9: '*praemia pro meritis nulli debentur; in ipsum auctorem fati crimina cuncta cadunt.*'
35 *Entheticus*, 521–2, pp. 138–9: '*Exaequat culpas, poenaque coaequat eadem Stoicus; at contra pagina sacra facit.*'
36 *Entheticus*, 523, 525–6, pp. 138–9: '*In multis igitur legi consentit … Dogma fides recipit, nisi lex manifesta repugnet, vel ratio potior hoc reprobare queat.*'
37 See *Entheticus*, 527–94 for John's views on the Epicurean School; these will be further analysed in Chapter 5. John's account of the Peripatetic School can be found in *Entheticus*, 595–726.
38 *Entheticus* 615–16, pp. 144–5: '*Praecedit ratio rerum quarumlibet ortum, et natas eadem provehit atque movet.*'
39 *Entheticus*, 671–2, pp. 148–9: '*Esse bonum summum rerum cognoscere causas, credit, quod docuit, magnus Aristotiles.*'
40 *Entheticus*, 629–30, pp. 146–7: '*Est hominis ratio summae rationis imago, quae capit interius vera docente Deo.*'
41 *Entheticus*, 821–62, pp. 158–61.
42 *Entheticus*, 851–2, pp. 160–1: '*Si quis Aristotilem primum non censet habendum, non reddit meritis praemia digna suis.*' *Entheticus*, 831–3, pp. 158–9: '*Sed tamen erravit, dum sublunaria casu credidit, et fatis ulteriora geri; non est arbitrii libertas vera creatis*'.
43 *Entheticus*, 1119–58; 1149–50, pp. 180–1: '*Nam solitus rerum cursus facit esse probanda, quae semper simili sub ratione vides.*'
44 *Entheticus*, 1215–68.
45 *Entheticus*, 1221–2, pp. 184–5: '*qualiter arbitrii libertas consona fato exstet, nam fatum si manet, illa perit.*'
46 *Entheticus*, 265–78.
47 *Entheticus*, 265–8, pp. 122–3: '*Exigit arbitrii libertas vera duorum subsidium … scilicet ut ratio recte discernat, ametque semper id affectus, quod pia iura probant.*'
48 *Entheticus*, 275, pp. 122–3: '*liberat arbitrium*'.
49 *Entheticus*, 1269–70, pp. 186–7: '*Sed cur gentiles numero, quos error adegit? Omnis enim ratio deficit absque fide.*' On contrasts between John's opinions on pagan philosophers in *Entheticus* and *Policraticus* see J. Marenbon, *Pagans and Philosophers: The Problem of Paganism from Augustine to Leibniz* (Princeton: Princeton University Press, 2015), pp. 99–103.
50 John offers a briefer comparison between the attitudes of the different philosophic schools to questions of fate and free will in *Met.* IV. 31, p. 168.
51 S. Rigby, *Wisdom and Chivalry: Chaucer's Knight's Tale and Medieval Political Theory* (Leiden: Brill, 2009), p. 81. See A. MacIntyre, *Three Rival Versions of Moral Enquiry: Encyclopedia, Genealogy, and Tradition* (London: Duckworth, 1990), p. 87, who suggests that such a mélange of classical views avoided being 'a

certain unprincipled eclecticism' on account of the fact that 'an overall framework of belief within which the different uses of different parts of ancient philosophy had to be put to work' existed.
52  For example, *Pol.* I. Prol.; 1, p. 17.
53  Cicero, *On Duties*, trans. M. T. Griffin and E. M. Atkins (Cambridge: Cambridge University Press, 1991), p. xxxvi.
54  *Pol.* I. Prol.; 1, p. 17; see also *Pol.* II. 22; 1, p. 122.
55  *Pol.* II. 22; 1, p. 122: '*Romani auctorem eloquii*'.
56  Augustine, *Contra Academicos*, III. 15–16; Cicero, *On Duties*, III. 20. See R. H. and M. A. Rouse, 'The Medieval Circulation of Cicero's *Posterior Academics* and the *De finibus bonorum et malorum*', in M. B. Parkes and A. G. Watson (eds), *Medieval Scribes, Manuscripts and Libraries: Essays Presented to N. R. Ker* (London: Scolar Press, 1978), pp. 333–67 (p. 352). For instances in other parts of John's work where he discusses probabilism note especially *Met.* II. 13; *Met.* III. 9; Letter 209, *Letters* II, p. 320.
57  Grellard, *Jean de Salisbury*, p. 17: '*un scepticisme chrétien, un scepticisme qui soit compatible avec une forme de fidéisme*'.
58  M. Kempshall, *Rhetoric and the Writing of History, 400–1500* (Manchester: Manchester University Press, 2011), pp. 408–27.
59  C. Grellard, 'John of Salisbury and Theology', in Grellard and Lachuad (eds), *Companion*, pp. 339–73 (p. 353).
60  Grellard, *Jean de Salisbury*, p. 225.
61  Martin, 'John of Salisbury's Manuscripts of Frontinus and of Gellius', p. 1.
62  See also Martin, 'John of Salisbury and the Classics'; 'Uses of Tradition: Gellius, Petronius and John of Salisbury'; 'John of Salisbury as Classical Scholar'.
63  Martin, 'John of Salisbury's Manuscripts of Frontinus and of Gellius', p. 16.
64  *Cartulaire de Notre-Dame de Chartres*, ed. Lépinois and Merlet, vol. 3, p. 202; C. C. J. Webb, 'Notes on Books Bequeathed by John of Salisbury to the Cathedral Library of Chartres', *Medieval and Renaissance Studies*, 1 (1941–43), 128–9.
65  Letter 150, *Letters* II, pp. 48–9: '*Si uero michi Dominus redeundi uiam aperuerit, rescribite, si placet, an me redire oporteat cum libris et tota sarcina. Nam si hoc fuerit, plures equi necessarii erunt et plura quae adhuc desunt.*'
66  Letter 263, *Letters* II, pp. 534–5: '*Quintilianum quem petii scriptum et emendatum*'.
67  For example, see Martin, 'John of Salisbury as Classical Scholar', pp. 193–5, on his use of Heiric of Auxerre's excerpts from Suetonius.
68  Grellard, *Jean de Salisbury*, p. 31.
69  See John's request for improved '*notulas*' on Aristotle's works from Richard l'Évêque, claiming 'that he does not all together trust the translator' in Letter 201, *Letters* II, pp. 294–5.
70  Martin, 'John of Salisbury's Manuscripts of Frontinus and of Gellius', pp. 5–16; R. Thomson, *William of Malmesbury* (Woodbridge: Boydell Press, 2003), pp. 189–98.
71  e.g. Augustine's *De civitate Dei*, IX. 4, paraphrases *Noctes Atticae*, XIX. 1.

72 M. R. James, *The Ancient Libraries of Canterbury and Dover* (Cambridge: Cambridge University Press, 1903).

73 The catalogue is edited in James, *Ancient Libraries*, pp. 7–12; images of it can be found on pp. 3–6. On various interpretations of its dating see P. Binski and P. Zutshi, *Western Illuminated Manuscripts: A Catalogue of the Collection in Cambridge University Library* (Cambridge: Cambridge University Press, 2011), pp. 22–3, who date it to xii$^{2/2}$ (p. 23); James, *Ancient Libraries*, pp. xxxi–xxxii, who claims the catalogue predates Becket's death; and Martin, 'John of Salisbury and the Classics', p. 11, who correctly points out that it must postdate John's elevation to the bishopric of Chartres.

74 Ker offered a possible identification of this volume with Oxford, Bodleian Library, MS Digby 5, fos 1–72, a twelfth-century Canterbury manuscript containing the *Controversiae*. See N. R. Ker, *Medieval Libraries of Great Britain: A List of Surviving Books* (2nd edn, London: Offices of the Royal Historical Society, 1964), p. 38. For a description of this manuscript see *Bodleian Library Quarto Catalogues IX Digby Manuscripts*, vol. 1: *A Reproduction of the 1883 Catalogue by W. D. Macray*, p. 6, and vol. 2: *Notes on Macray's Descriptions of the Manuscripts by R. W. Hunt and A. G. Watson*, p. 9 (published together; Oxford: Oxford University Press, 1999).

75 The catalogue is edited in James, *Ancient Libraries*, pp. 13–142.

76 James, *Ancient Libraries*, p. xxxix. James's opinion has largely been accepted by scholars. See, for example, M. Twomey, 'Medieval Encyclopedias in England before 1500', in P. Binkley (ed.), *Pre-Modern Encyclopedic Texts: Proceedings of the Second COMERS Congress, Groningen, 1–4 July 1996* (Leiden: Brill, 1997), pp. 329–62 (p. 352).

77 It is, of course, possible that the appellation of Thomas as 'saint' may simply reflect the fact that he was regarded as a saint at Canterbury, prior to being officially recognised as such.

78 I. Logan, 'Anselm and Thidricus: Revisiting MS Bodley 271', in G. E. M. Gasper and H. Kohlenberger (eds), *Anselm and Abelard: Investigations and Juxtapositions* (Toronto: PIMS, 2006), pp. 67–86 (pp. 76–8).

79 On John's knowledge of Roman law see M. Kerner, 'Römisches und kirchliches Recht im *Policraticus*', in Wilks (ed.), *World*, pp. 365–79; G. Miczka, 'Johannes von Salisbury und die *Summa Trecensis*', in Wilks (ed.), *World*, pp. 381–99.

80 Robert of Torigni, 'Chronicle', in *Chronicles of the Reigns of Stephen, Henry II and Richard II*, vol. 4: *The Chronicle of Robert of Torigni*, ed. R. Howlett (London: Rolls Series, 1889), pp. 158–9.

81 *Pol.* VIII. 22; 2, p. 399: '*Ne quis etiam libros retineret edicto regio prohibitum est et Vacario nostro indictum silentium.*'

82 R. W. Southern, 'Master Vacarius and the Beginning of an English Academic Tradition', in J. J. G. Alexander and M. T. Gibson (eds), *Medieval Learning and Literature: Essays Presented to Richard William Hunt* (Oxford: Oxford University Press, 1976), pp. 257–86 (p. 274).

83 Southern, 'Master Vacarius', p. 259.

84 On the composition of the *Liber pauperum* see P. Stein and F. de Zulueta (eds),

*The Teaching of Roman Law in England around 1200* (London: Selden Society, 1990), pp. xxxv–xxxvi, and L. E. Boyle, 'The Beginnings of Legal Studies at Oxford', *Viator*, 14 (1983), 107–32 (118–26), who propose that the work was composed in the 1170s, and R. W. Southern, 'From School to University', in J. L. Catto (ed.), *The History of the University of Oxford*, vol. 1: *The Early Oxford Schools* (Oxford: Oxford University Press, 1984), pp. 1–36 (p. 9), who suggests the 1180s as a more likely date.

85 Y. Sassier, 'John of Salisbury and Law', in Grellard and Lachaud (eds), *Companion*, pp. 235–57 (p. 237).

86 S. Reynolds, 'The Emergence of Professional Law in the Long Twelfth Century', *Law and History Review*, 21 (2003), 347–66 (351–2).

87 H. M. Thomas, *The Secular Clergy in England, 1066–1216* (Oxford: Oxford University Press, 2014), p. 330.

88 J. Willoughby, 'The Transmission and Circulation of Classical Literature: Libraries and Florilegia', in R. Copeland (ed.) *The Oxford History of Classical Reception in English Literature*, vol. 1: *800–1558* (Oxford: Oxford University Press, 2016), pp. 95–120 (p. 102), notes that the Exeter book-list of 1327 lists only four texts which could be termed classical (works by Boethius, Statius, Persius and Prudentius), all of which had been given to the church *c.*1072 by Bishop Leofric, with no subsequent evidence of augmentation of the classical holdings apparent in the intervening period. On John's connections with Exeter see Y. Hirata, *Collected Papers on John of Salisbury and his Correspondents* (Tokyo: Hakuho-do, 1996), pp. 157–81.

89 T. Webber, *Scribes and Scholars at Salisbury Cathedral, c.1075–c. 1125* (Oxford: Oxford University Press: 1992), p. 43.

90 Webber, *Scribes and Scholars*, p. 41.

91 Webber, *Scribes and Scholars*, pp. 41, 64–5.

92 Webber, *Scribes and Scholars*, p. 65; P. K. Marshall, J. Martin and R. H. Rouse, 'Clare College MS 26 and the Circulation of Aulus Gellius 1–7 in Medieval England and France', *Mediaeval Studies*, 42 (1980), 353–94 (369–70).

93 B. Munk Olsen, *L'Étude des auteurs classiques latins aux XI$^e$ et XII$^e$ siècles: La réception de la littérature classique. Manuscrits et textes*, vol. IV. 2 (Paris: CNRS, 2014), p. 33.

94 B. Munk Olsen, 'The Cistercians and Classical Culture', *Cahiers de l'Institut du Moyen-Âge Grec et Latin*, 47 (1984), 64–102; reprinted in B. Munk Olsen, *La réception de la littérature classique au Moyen-Âge IX$^e$–XII$^e$ siècles* (Copenhagen: Museum Tusculanum Press, 1995), pp. 95–131 (pp. 104–5).

95 *Entheticus*, 1215–16, pp. 184–5: '*Orbis nil habuit maius Cicerone Latinis, cuius ad eloquium Graecia muta fuit.*'

96 *Entheticus*, 1235–6, pp. 184–5: '*Illum sola fides capit, et dilectio vera; naturamque sequi, cultus amorque Dei est.*' Cf. Cicero, *De amicitia*, V. 19, in *De senectute; De amicitia; De divinatione*, trans. W. A. Falconer (LCL 154; Cambridge, MA: Harvard University Press, 1923), p. 128: '*naturam optimam bene vivendi ducem.*'

97 *Entheticus*, 1241–2, pp. 184–5: '*Et si vita foret Ciceronis consona verbis, in summis poterat maximus esse viris.*'

98 *Entheticus*, 1251, pp. 186–7: '*Vivere sincere pars optima philosophandi est*'.
99 Augustine, *Confessiones*, trans. C. J.-B. Hammond (LCL 26; Cambridge, MA: Harvard University Press, 2014), III. 4.7, p. 100: '*cuius linguam fere omnes mirantur, pectus non ita*'; Martin, 'Cicero's Jokes at the Court of Henry II of England', p. 157.
100 Martin, 'Cicero's Jokes at the Court of Henry II of England', pp. 162–3.
101 Martin, 'Cicero's Jokes at the Court of Henry II of England', p. 166.
102 R. Thomson, 'John of Salisbury and William of Malmesbury: Currents in Twelfth-Century Humanism', in Wilks (ed.), *World*, pp. 117–25 (p. 121).
103 On the influence and circulation of this text in the Middle Ages more generally, see N. E. Nelson, 'Cicero's *De Officiis* in Christian Thought 300–1300', *Essays and Studies in English and Comparative Literature*, 10 (1933), 59–160.
104 Reynolds (ed.), *Texts and Transmission*, pp. 102–9.
105 J. O. Ward, 'What the Middle Ages Missed of Cicero, and Why', in W. H. F. Altman (ed.), *Brill's Companion to the Reception of Cicero* (Leiden: Brill, 2015), pp. 307–26 (pp. 321–3). On p. 321, Ward describes Cicero as 'a decidedly secondary reference' for John, a statement which I think does not stand up to scrutiny, given the strongly Ciceronian character of John's work, as elaborated in subsequent chapters.
106 Ward, 'What the Middle Ages Missed of Cicero', p. 321, n. 60.
107 Ward's treatment of John's source base is flawed here as he depends to a large extent on the annotations given in the translations, referring to those in Dickinson's as 'not ideal', while seemingly being unaware of the fact that Dickinson explicitly chose only to include the direct quotations cited by Webb. See *The Statesman's Book of John of Salisbury*, trans. Dickinson, p. xii. On John's alleged knowledge of *De oratore* see L. Hermand-Schebat, 'John of Salisbury and Classical Antiquity', in Grellard and Lachaud (eds), *Companion*, pp. 180–214. Hermand-Schebat says on p. 197 that John 'probably knew' the text, and more strongly on p. 198 that he 'certainly knew [it] at first hand'. Liebeschütz, *Mediaeval Humanism* (pp. 88–9), argues that the content of *De oratore* III influenced the combination of subjects found in Books VII and VIII of the *Policraticus*.
108 *Pol.* VIII. 14; 2, p. 329: '*poetica licentia fidem peruertens historiae*'.
109 Servius, *Servii Grammatici qui feruntur in Vergilii Aeneidos Libros I–III commentarii*, ed. G. Thilo and H. Hagen (Leipzig: Teubner, 1887), I. 267, p. 98; Servius uses the phrase '*arte poetica*' in this instance. In his commentary on Book I of the Aeneid, he uses the phrase '*poetica licentia*' or its variants in four instances: I. 42, I. 59, I. 227, I. 550. On Servius's treatment of poetic licence see N. Zeeman, 'The Schools give a License to Poets', in R. Copeland (ed.), *Criticism and Dissent in the Middle Ages* (Cambridge: Cambridge University Press, 1996), pp. 151–80 (pp. 162–9).
110 On the circulation of Servius's *Commentary* in the medieval period see C. Baswell, *Virgil in Medieval England: Figuring the Aeneid from the Twelfth Century to Chaucer* (Cambridge: Cambridge University Press, 1995), pp. 12, 49.
111 *Entheticus minor*, 41, pp. 232–3: '*Curio si certet verbis, vincetur ab ipso*'.

112 The *Pharsalia* survives in over thirty copies from the eleventh century, and in over 100 from the twelfth century. See Munk Olsen, *La réception de la littérature classique. Manuscrits et textes*, vol. IV./.2, p. 33.
113 Macrobius, *Commentarii in somnium Scipionis*, ed. J. Willis (Leipzig: Teubner, 1970); *Commentary on the Dream of Scipio*, trans. W. H. Stahl (New York: Columbia University Press, 1952).
114 On the medieval transmission of *De re publica* see Reynolds (ed.), *Texts and Transmission*, pp. 131–2, and M. Kempshall, '*De Re Publica* 1.39 in Medieval and Renaissance Political Thought', in J. G. F. Powell and J. A. North (eds), *Cicero's Republic* (Institute of Classical Studies, 2001), pp. 99–135 (especially pp. 99–112, which deal with the fate of the text up to the fourteenth century).
115 An example of a direct reference to Laelius can be found at *Pol.* III. 4; 1 p. 177. Aelred of Rievaulx and Bernard of Clairvaux also make substantial use of the *De amicitia*.
116 John quotes from *Rhetorica ad Herennium*, IV. 24, at *Pol.* III. 8; 1, p. 191. See J. O. Ward, 'The Medieval and Early Renaissance Study of Cicero's *De Inventione* and the *Rhetorica ad Herennium*: Commentaries and Contexts', in V. Cox and J. O. Ward (eds), *The Rhetoric of Cicero in its Medieval and Early Renaissance Commentary Tradition* (Leiden: Brill, 2006), pp. 3–75 (pp. 23–50) on the twelfth-century use of these rhetorical texts. See also R. Taylor-Briggs, 'Reading between the Lines: The Textual History and Manuscript Transmission of Cicero's Rhetorical Works', in Cox and Ward (eds), *The Rhetoric of Cicero*, pp. 77–108 (pp. 96–100) on the manuscript tradition of *De inventione*.
117 Grellard, *Jean de Salisbury*, pp. 33–4.
118 *Pol.* II. 22; 1, p. 122: '*Efferant Stoici inopinabiles sententias suas, quas paradoxas uocant, ueras quidem praeclaras et admirabiles*'; *Pol.* VII. 16; 2, p. 158: '*Ut minimum locum parsimoniae facit, qua nullum uectigal utilius*'. Cf. Cicero, *Paradoxa Stoicorum*, VI. 49, in *De oratore III; De fato; Paradoxa Stoicorum; De partitione oratoria*, trans. H. Rackham (LCL 349; Cambridge, MA: Harvard University Press, 1942), p. 300: '*non intellegunt homines, quam magnum vectigal sit parsimonia!*'
119 John refers to Cicero's authorship of *De natura deorum* at *Pol.* II. 22.
120 Hermand-Schebat, 'John of Salisbury and Classical Antiquity', pp. 198–202.
121 Thomson, *William of Malmesbury*, pp. 51–6; Thomson, 'John of Salisbury and William of Malmesbury', p. 121.
122 See B. Munk Olsen, 'Les Classiques latins dans les florilèges médiévaux antérieurs au XIIIe siècle', *Revue d'histoire des textes*, 9 (1979–80), 47–121. For his assessment of the importance of the *Florilegium Gallicum* see pp. 75–7; for details of Ciceronian extracts in the copy of the *Florilegium* that is now Paris, Bibliothèque nationale de France, MS lat. 7647, see pp. 80–1. See J. Hamacher, *Florilegium Gallicum: Prolegomena und Edition der Exzerpte von Petron bis Cicero, De Oratore* (Frankfurt: Peter Lang, 1975), pp. 254–437 for Ciceronian excerpts in the *Florilegium*.
123 A. Duggan, 'Classical Quotations and Allusions in the Correspondence of Thomas Becket', *Viator*, 32 (2001), 1–22 (11–12). Duggan highlights the extensive

61

use of the *Florilegium Gallicum* among the 'Becket Circle', discounting the influence of both the *Florilegium Duacense* and the *Florilegium prosodiacum cum distinctionibus*, two other common florilegia, on the grounds of their provenance. She argues that the *Florilegium Angelicum* was not used by the 'Becket Circle': it is 'almost certainly too late in composition to have been a "school" textbook when the members of the Becket circle were learning their letters' (p. 10).

124  *Entheticus*, 1257-63, pp. 186-7, refers to Quintilian, *Institutio oratoria*, X. i.125-31; John also quotes Quintilian's critique at length at *Pol.* VIII. 13.

125  *Entheticus*, 1265-68, pp. 186-7.

126  *Pol.* VIII. 13; 2, p. 320: '*Legantur Epistolae eius, libri de Beneficiis aut Clementia, illi quoque quos decem Oratorum sententiis sub imagine declamationum scolarium illustrauit, et hii quos de Naturalibus Quaestionibus edidit et quos de philosophia parum diligentes arguit Quintilianus*'.

127  *Pol.* I. Prol.; 1, p. 15.

128  *Pol.* VIII. 13; 2, p. 319: '*Apostoli familiaritatem meruisse constat et a doctissimo patre Ieronimo in sanctorum catalogo positum.*'

129  L. D. Reynolds, *The Medieval Tradition of Seneca's Letters* (Oxford: Oxford University Press, 1965), p. 112.

130  Webb, *John of Salisbury*, p. 168.

131  See Reynolds (ed.), *Texts and Transmission*, pp. 376-8 on the circulation of the *Natural Questions*; see C. Picard-Parra, 'Une utilisation des *Quaestiones naturales* de Sénèque au milieu du XIIe siècle', *Revue du Moyen Âge Latin*, 5 (1949), 115-26, for the use of the *Natural Questions* in the writings of John's teacher William of Conches.

132  Reynolds (ed.), *Texts and Transmission*, pp. 359, 363-5. These texts frequently circulated in an abridged form: see B. Munk Olsen, 'Les Florilèges et les abrégés de Sénèque au Moyen Âge', *Giornale Italiano di Filologia*, 52 (2000), 163-83 (p. 165). On the significance of these texts, and other works by Seneca, for the elaboration of the idea of the medieval *princeps* see P. Stacey, *Roman Monarchy and the Renaissance Prince* (Cambridge: Cambridge University Press, 2007), pp. 75-89.

133  P. Stacey, 'Senecan Political Thought from the Middle Ages to Early Modernity', in S. Bartsch and A. Schiesaro (eds), *The Cambridge Companion to Seneca* (Cambridge: Cambridge University Press, 2015), pp. 289-302 (pp. 293-4). Seneca's influence on John's model of the body politic will be investigated further in Chapters 4 and 6.

134  M. Griffin, *Seneca on Society: A Guide to De Beneficiis* (Oxford: Oxford University Press, 2013), p. 164.

135  I exclude Webb's identification of a parallel between the conclusion of *Pol.* II. 29 and *De beneficiis*, VI. 36. If, in fact, this passage is the source of John's claim, he is deliberately misinterpreting Seneca, who, rather than claiming that doctors kill men, explicitly says that doctors should not make practice by making men sick. For a more likely source see the discussion below regarding John's knowledge of Lactantius.

136 G. Mazzoli, 'Ricerche sulla tradizione medievale del *De beneficiis* e del *De clementia* di Seneca, 3: Storia della tradizione manoscritta', *Bolletino dei classici*, series 3, 3 (1982), 165–223 (192–204).
137 Mazzoli, 'Ricerche sulla tradizione medievale del *De beneficiis* e del *De clementia*', p. 200. BnF MS lat. 16592, accessed via *Gallica*, http://gallica.bnf.fr/ark:/12148/btv1b9067195z (accessed 10 July 2017).
138 The manuscript of the *Florilegium Gallicum* used is BnF MS lat. 7647, fos 34r–185v, accessed via *Gallica*, http://gallica.bnf.fr/ark:/12148/btv1b9066488j?rk=21459;2 (accessed 10 July 2017). For considerations on the authorship of the *Moralium* see P. H. Delhaye, 'Un adaptation du *De Officiis* au XIIe siècle: Le *Moralium Dogma Philosophorum*', *Recherches de théologie ancienne et médiévale*, 16 (1949), 227–58 (236–57), and J. R. Williams, 'The Quest for the Author of the *Moralium Dogma Philosophorum*, 1931–56', *Speculum*, 32 (1957), 736–47. The edition of the text used is *Das Moralium Dogma Philosophorum des Guillaume de Conches*, ed. J. Holmberg (Uppsala: Almqvist and Wiksells, 1929).
139 *Pol.* V. 10; 1, pp. 325–6: '*Verbum, inquit, uerecundum supplici ac submissa uoce dicendum. Rogo; nec gratis tulit qui cum rogaret accepit.*'
140 Seneca, *De beneficiis*, in *Seneca: Moral Essays III*, trans. J. W. Basore (LCL 310; Cambridge, MA: Harvard University Press, 1935), II. 1, p. 52.
141 *Moralium dogma philosophorum*, p. 14: '*Non tulit gratis qui, cum rogaret, accepit; nulla enim res carius constat quam que precibus empta est*'; BnF MS lat. 16592, fo. 96r: '*Non tulit gratis qui cum rogasset accepit.*'
142 *Pol.* III. 11; 1, p. 206: '*Quod si ex interuallo promissi fidem impleuerit, liberalitatis decor et beneficii species ipsa fuscatur, eo quod qui distulit interim uisus est noluisse.*'
143 Seneca, *De beneficiis*, II. 1, p. 50: '*Ante omnia libenter, cito, sine ulla dubitatione. Ingratum est beneficium, quod diu inter dantis manus haesit, quod quis aegre dimittere visus est et sic dare, tamquam sibi eriperet.*'
144 BnF MS lat. 7647, fo. 166r: '*Ingratum est beneficium quam diu inter manus dantis hesit.*'
145 BnF MS lat. 16592, fo. 96r: '*Ingratum est quam diu inter manus dantis hesit, quod quis egre dimittere uisus est et sic dare tamquam sibi eriperet.*'
146 *Pol.* III. 11; 1, p. 207: '*Denigrat meritum dantis mora, nam data raptim | munera plus laudis plusque fauoris habent.*' Cf. Bernard Silvestris, *Le Mathematicus de Bernard Silvestris et la Passio Sanctae Agnetis de Pierre Riga*, ed. B. Hauréau (Paris: C. Klincksieck, 1895), p. 32: '*Denigrat meritum dantis mora, factaque raptim | Munera plus laudis plusque favoris habent.*' John also quotes from the *Mathematicus* in *Pol.* III. 8: see Bernardus Silvestris, *Cosmographia*, ed. P. Dronke (Leiden: Brill, 1978), p. 3.
147 Bernard Silvestris, *Mathematicus*, p. 33: '*Officio celeri gratia major erit.*'
148 P. Stirnemann and D. Poirel, 'Nicolas de Montiéramey, Jean de Salisbury et deux florilèges d'auteurs antiques', *Revue d'histoire des textes*, n.s., 1 (2006), 173–88 (179).
149 B. Munk Olsen, 'Les Florilèges et les abrégés de Sénèque', p. 164. For subsequent incorrect divisions of the 'composite Seneca' see L. Panizza, 'Biography

in Italy from the Middle Ages to the Renaissance: Seneca, Pagan or Christian', *Nouvelles de la République des Lettres*, 2 (1984), 47–98.
150 Reynolds (ed.), *Texts and Transmission*, p. 356; Munk Olsen, 'Les Florilèges et les abrégés de Sénèque', p. 163.
151 e.g. *Met.* II. 8, p. 67.
152 For description of this manuscript of the *Dialogues* see F. Newton, *The Scriptorium and Library at Monte Cassino, 1058–1105* (Cambridge: Cambridge University Press, 1999), pp. 109–10, 130–1. For a discussion of the transmission of the work see L. D. Reynolds, 'The Medieval Tradition of Seneca's *Dialogues*', *Classical Quarterly*, 18 (1968), 355–72. See, in addition, H. Bloch, 'Monte Cassino's Teachers and Library in the High Middle Ages', *La scuola nell'occidente latino del'alto medioevo 15–21 aprile 1971: Settimane di studio del centro italiano di studi sull'alto medioevo*, 19 (1972), 563–605 (583).
153 Reynolds (ed.), *Texts and Transmission*, pp. 367–8; C. W. Barlow, trans., *Iberian Fathers*, vol. 1: *Martin of Braga, Paschasius of Dumiun, Leander of Seville* (Washington, DC: Catholic University of America Press, 1969), p. 9.
154 Reynolds (ed.), *Texts and Transmission*, p. 359.
155 See Reynolds, *The Medieval Tradition of Seneca's Letters*, pp. 90–111, for palaeographical information, evidence from library catalogues and details of quotations used in determining the tradition of the circulation of the *Letters* from the Carolingian period through to the twelfth century.
156 Reynolds, *The Medieval Tradition of Seneca's Letters*, p. 118, n. 1.
157 Liebeschütz, *Mediaeval Humanism*. At pp. 48, 84 Liebeschütz refers to John's use of *Ep*. 90 for his writings on the primitive society; at p. 82 he considers that John gets his ideas on frugality from Seneca's *Ep*. 108; at p. 83 he refers to *Ep*. 108 as a source for John's views on the education of the courtier.
158 [Pseudo-] Seneca, *Epistolae Senecae ad Paulum et Pauli ad Senecam <quae vocantur>*, ed. C. Barlow (Rome: American Academy in Rome, 1938), p. 3. Note the testimony to the correspondence in the works of Peter Abelard, John's teacher at pp. 110–1. For the *Formula vitae honestae* see Martin of Braga, *Martini Episcopi Bracarensis Opera Omnia*, ed. C. Barlow (New Haven: Yale University Press, 1950), pp. 236–50; E. Bickel, 'Die Schrift des Martinus von Bracara: Formula vitae honestae', *Rheinisches Museum*, 60 (1905), 505–51.
159 Webb, *John of Salisbury*, p. 166.
160 J. Stevenson, 'The Life and Literary Activity of Lactantius', *Studia Patristica*, 1 (1957), 661–77; Lactantius, *Divine Institutes*, trans. A. Bowen and P. Garnsey (Liverpool: Liverpool University Press, 2003), pp. 1–6; Colish, *Stoic Tradition*, 2, pp. 37–47.
161 M. Perrin, 'L'image du Stoïcien et du Stoïcisme chez Lactance', in M. Soetard (ed.), *Valeurs dans le Stoïcisme: Du portique à nos jours* (Lille: Presses Universitaires du Lille, 1993), pp. 113–29 (pp. 114–17). Note some significant divergences made by Lactantius from Stoic ideas on the soul as observed by Verbeke, *The Presence of Stoicism*, pp. 26–7. See Lactantius, *Divine Institutes*, III. 28.
162 S. Casey, 'Lactantius's Reaction to Pagan Philosophy', *Classica et Mediaevalia*, 32 (1980), 203–19; Colish, *Stoic Tradition*, 2, p. 47.

163 W. B. Ross, 'Audi Thoma ... Henriciani nota: A French Scholar Appeals to Thomas Becket', *English Historical Review*, 89 (1974), 333–8 (334).
164 P. Godman, *Alcuin: The Bishop, Kings and Saints of York* (Oxford: Clarendon Press, 1982), pp. 124–5. On p. lxviii Godman suggests that it is likely that this is a reference to Lactantius's supposed authorship of *De ave Phoenice*. Note that the first, alphabetical, part of the Canterbury library catalogue composed during the time of Prior Eastry detailed above is missing letters K–N, so we cannot determine whether there were copies of Lactantius available in the collection: see James, *Ancient Libraries*, p. xl.
165 Webb, *John of Salisbury*, p. 166.
166 Ross, 'Audi Thoma ...', pp. 335–8.
167 L. K. Barker, 'MS Bodl. Canon. Pat. Lat. 131 and a Lost Lactantius of John of Salisbury: Evidence in Search of a French Critic of Thomas Becket', *Albion*, 22 (1990), 21–37. Note that Barker suggests that an alternative owner could be Peter of Celle (37). On the provenance of the MS see also W. B. Ross, 'Giovanni Colonna, Historian at Avignon', *Speculum*, 45 (1970), 533–63.
168 Kerner, *Johannes von Salisbury*, p. 97, n. 587.
169 Lactantius, *Divine Institutes*, III. 15.11, p. 195.
170 Bodl. MS Canon. Pat. Lat. 131, fo. 52r.
171 Following Testard, I shall refer here to Ambrose's work as *De officiis*, using the longer form, *De officiis ministrorum*, only when it is required to distinguish the work from its Ciceronian model. See introduction to Ambrose, *Sancti Ambrosii Mediolanensis, De Officiis*, ed. M. Testard (CCSL, 15; Turnhout: Brepols, 2000), p. viii. Throughout, the edition and translation used is Ambrose, *De officiis*, ed. and trans. I. J. Davidson (2 vols; Oxford: Oxford University Press, 2001).
172 Colish, *Stoic Tradition*, 2, pp. 48–70; G. Madec, *Saint Ambroise et la philosophie* (Paris: Études Augustiniennes, 1974); R. Markus, 'The Latin Fathers', in J. H. Burns (ed.), *The Cambridge History of Medieval Political Thought c.350–c.1450*, pp. 92–122 (pp. 92–102).
173 B. Smalley, *The Becket Conflict and the Schools* (Oxford: Blackwell, 1973), p. 93.
174 Davidson, in Ambrose, *De officiis*, pp. 96–104.
175 James, *Ancient Libraries*, p. 22, item 56.
176 Davidson, in Ambrose, *De officiis*, p. 100.
177 e.g. *Pol.* V. 3; V. 17.
178 e.g. *Met.* IV. 34; *Pol.* VII. 4; VII. 5, VII. 6.
179 For a survey of some of the applications to which John put these works see S. Sønnesyn, *'Qui recta quae docet sequitur, uere philosophus est*: The Ethics of John of Salisbury', in Lachaud and Grellard (eds), *Companion*, pp. 307–38.
180 G. Verbeke, 'Augustine et le stoïcisme', *Recherches Augustiniennes*, 1 (1958), 67–89.
181 H. Hagendahl, *Augustine and the Latin Classics* (2 vols; Gotenburg: Almqvist and Wiksell, 1967), p. 675–80 (p. 677); G. O'Daly, *Augustine's City of God: A Reader's Guide* (Oxford: Oxford University Press, 1999) largely agrees with this assessment (p. 250), but notes on p. 60 that the Senecan presentation of a cosmic city that coexists alongside actual societies (*De otio*, 4.1–2) is similar in theme to

the coexistence of the city of God alongside the earthly polity in Augustine, commenting that: 'The Stoic notion of membership of a group that is defined in terms of an ethical ideal, a community of rational and morally good being, has more in common with Augustine's concept of the city than is often recognised.'
182 Bede, *Ecclesiastical History of the English People*, ed. and trans. B. Colgrave and R. A. B. Mynors (Oxford: Clarendon Press, 1969), II. 1, pp. 122-35.
183 R. Gameson, *The Earliest Books of Canterbury Cathedral: Manuscripts and Fragments to c.1200* (London: Bibliographical Society, British Library, 2008), pp. 325-6.
184 Gregory the Great, *Moralia in Job*, ed. I. R. Gillet, A. de Gaudermaris, A. Bocognano, C. Straw and A. de Vogüé (Paris: Cerf, 1951-2003).
185 Gregory the Great, *La Règle pastorale*, ed. I. B. Judic, F. Rommel and C. Morel (2 vols; Paris: Cerf, 1992); Gregory the Great, *Pastoral Care*, trans. H. Davis (Westminster: Paulist Press, 1950).
186 R. Gameson, *The Manuscripts of Early Norman England (c.1066-1130)* (Oxford: British Academy, 1999), p. 36.
187 R. Wasselynck, 'Présence de S. Gregoire le Grand dans les recueils canoniques X$^e$-XII$^e$ siècles', *Mélanges de science religieuse*, 22 (1965) 205-19; R. Wasselynck, 'Les Compilations des *Moralia in Job* du VII$^e$ au XII$^e$ siecle', *Recherches de théologie ancienne et médiévale*, 29 (1962), 5-32; Thomson, *William of Malmesbury*, p. 42.
188 R. Wasselynck, 'L'influence de l'exégèse de S. Grégoire le Grand sur les commentaires bibliques médiévaux (VII$^e$-XII$^e$ s.)', *Recherches de théologie ancienne et médiévale*, 32 (1965), 157-204; E. A. Matter, 'Gregory the Great in the Twelfth Century: The *Glossa Ordinaria*', in J. C. Cavadini (ed.), *Gregory the Great: A symposium* (Notre Dame, IN: University of Notre Dame Press, 1995), pp. 216-26.
189 James, *Ancient Libraries*, pp. 32-3, items 145, 146, 149, 150, 151, 156, 157.

2

# Nature and reason

The *Metalogicon* (I. 1) opens with a portrayal of the enemy of reason – the so-called 'Cornificius' (the name of one of Virgil's detractors, repurposed by John to represent the ignorant scholar) – who is bound through hasty and overambitious scholarship to destroy the study of the liberal arts. The enemy of eloquence, he is described by John as a foe to human bonds, charity and the exercise of duties.[1] Implicitly contrasting his followers, the Cornificians, with the wise man described at the start of Cicero's *De inventione*, who through the exercise of eloquence brought about social coherence, John reviles the prospect of a descent into primeval society where men fail to be united by duties and friendship and live, instead, in a state of brutality, where community becomes nothing more than a paddock for livestock.[2] Countering the Cornificians' position, John posits that it is the 'sweet and fruitful coming together of reason and words' that has led to the creation of cities, conciliated and brought kingdoms together, and united people in charity. He who challenges this unity in the name of a supposed common good is rightly a public enemy, as such order is God-given: 'what God has brought together must not be thrust apart'.[3] Reason and the use of eloquence – that is, speech informed by reason – make man unique among living creatures.[4] The progenitor of such reason is *Natura*, the 'most loving parent of all'.[5] John refers to a threefold relationship between nature, grace, and reason, whereby nature is fertilised by grace, while reason serves to 'shake out the folds' of nature through observation and examination.[6] In so doing, nature, grace and reason inform the attainment of happiness, and become the foundation of social living. Throughout the *Metalogicon* and the *Policraticus* John comments further on the value of nature and reason (informed by grace) as critical necessities of social living. He codifies what nature is. He also rationalises why behaving according to the norms of nature, norms he regards as capable of objective isolation, is a valuable goal. Finally, he illustrates why acting sociably is the (necessary) epitome of such rational behaviour. We shall look in detail at each of these principles in this chapter.

## Defining nature in the Middle Ages

*Natura* in the Middle Ages was a polyvalent term. In the first instance, it incorporated what could be observed about the world, a world created by God. Secondly, it was used to refer to what could be distinguished as the essence of a created being, something that was permanent and specific about a particular individual.[7] The twelfth century was a period of flux for natural philosophy, in part owing to the influence of classical texts, such as Plato's *Timaeus*. Read alongside its late antique commentary by Calcidius, it was valuable for interpreting the natural causes underlying creation and, by extension, facilitating a rational narrative for physical phenomena that could be set alongside a symbolic, biblical one. John's teacher Thierry of Chartres, for example, posited an identification between the World-Soul of the *Timaeus* and the Holy Spirit of the Bible in his exegetical account of the Creation, the *Hexaemeron*.[8] Furthermore, as Tullio Gregory established, the study of natural philosophy at the 'school of Chartres' (whether we regard it as locatively or ideologically defined) permitted the adaptation of neo-Platonism to the goal of developing a mechanistic account of nature, whereby the initial creative activity of God could be distinguished from the secondary causes that continued to animate the world.[9] This achieved what Marie-Dominique Chenu termed the development of a mechanistic, as opposed to a symbolic, understanding of nature – in short, its desacralisation.[10]

Thus, Thierry would write in his commentary on *De inventione* that the study of nature should properly be divided into the study of the nature of divine things – the realm of the '*theologos*' – and the study of the nature of beasts, which pertained to the '*physiologos*'.[11] This comment is situated in the context of an examination of Cicero's account of the attributes of a person that explain or make a particular behaviour likely.[12] Such attributes include one's name, manner of life, fortune, habit, feeling, interests, purposes, achievements, accidents and speeches made, as well as the category of interest to Thierry: nature. While Cicero referred in this passage to nature, it was not the intended focus of his discussion; rather, he aimed to identify which characteristics of a person could be used to support or reject a rhetorical argument or proposition. Thierry, on the other hand, manipulates his source text to mount a discussion of nature in a deeper, more philosophical, sense.[13]

> [T]here are various and multiple ways one can speak of nature; whether as a cause of being, or as *naturalia*, or as lasting practices, or in other ways. The nature that we call *naturalia*, however, is that which one attributes to something due to its being, whether of the soul, the body, or of extrinsic features, such as age, sex, and the like. Also, *genera* and species and different essences and characteristics and accidents of nature, all fall under nature. So Tullius listed those that are required for rhetoric and proceeded to divide them into those natural things that pertain to man, and that pertain to character, as required by the orator.[14]

Meanwhile, in his *Hexaemaron*, Thierry advises a different means of approaching the subject of defining nature, explicitly saying that he shall leave aside allegorical and moral readings of nature, and examine it '*secundum physicam et ad litteram*'.[15] What is clear from these accounts is that for medieval scholars, like Thierry, what was at issue was not simply what nature consisted of, but also what the best way of interpreting it actually was.

Cicero followed up his list of personal attributes with the comment, 'It is hard to give a simple definition of nature.'[16] This remark was used as a prompt by medieval authors to create a framework for the comprehension of nature, with its lack of specificity permitting an appealing interpretative flexibility. Hugh of St Victor (*c.* 1096–1141) in the *Didascalicon*, for example, writes, 'the meaning of this word [nature] ought not to be passed over in complete silence, even though as Tully says, "Nature is difficult to define".' Hugh then refers to the three senses of nature proposed by 'men of former times': first, 'the archetypal Exemplar of all things which exists in the divine Mind' – 'the primordial cause of each thing'. This definition is characteristic of the neo-Platonic vision of nature. His second definition refers to nature as 'each thing's peculiar being (*proprium esse*)'. His final definition considers nature as 'an artificer fire [*ignis artifex*] coming forth from a certain power to beget sensible objects', a Stoic definition based on Cicero's *De natura deorum* – a text probably known to Hugh through the medium of the *Explanationes in Ciceronis Rhetoricam* of Victorinus (*fl.* fourth century).[17] This definition proposes a distinction between the primary creative power of nature and the animating fire that, linked with the element of water, is a secondary creative force. Although Hugh avoids the pantheistic implications of this Stoic definition, he was clearly inspired by it, as he also uses the term *ignis* and *artifex* in other contexts: for example, he casts the Holy Spirit as an artificer who uses the fire of love to inspire virtue, while working in cooperation with grace and the free will of man.[18]

Another teacher of John, William of Conches, was also provoked by Cicero's ambiguous comment, writing in his *Dragmaticon philosophiae*, 'As Cicero says, "it is difficult to define nature"; however, as the term is understood here, nature is a certain force implanted [*insita*] in things, producing similar from similar.'[19] For William, the four elements (fire, air, water, earth) result in four visible '*elementa mundi*', or elements of the world (hot and dry – of fire; hot and moist – of air; cold and moist – of water; and cold and dry – of earth). In turn, these '*elementa mundi*' combine in various permutations to result in the four forces of nature ('*vires naturae*') – attractive, retentive, digestive, and expulsive – and are active in all the workings of the observed world.[20] In his earlier work, *Philosophia*, William referred to the Platonic World-Soul, as described in the *Timaeus*, and compared it with the Holy Spirit, but this comparison is absent from the *Dragmaticon*, seemingly as a result of William's growing assurance in the consistency and dynamic order of the natural world.[21] William, along with other scholars such as Bernard Silvestris and Gilbert of Poitiers, distinguished between the initial creative work of God, who made the world from nothing, and the productive forces of nature, which are self-perpetuating but autonomously moderated and advanced by the continued participation of humanity.

### John of Salisbury's definition of *natura*

These varied interpretations of *natura* demonstrate the range of debates that developed around the term; they derived their inspiration from neo-Platonism and Stoicism, and were prompted by diverse sources, including the Bible, classical intermediaries and the contemporary classroom context. As noted, Cicero's 'non-definition' of nature was a popular prompt for the debate, despite the fact that it was frequently removed from its original rhetorical context. John of Salisbury initially applied it in a limited manner in his account of the modalities which invite reverence for a person; nature (sex, race, place of birth, family, age) is one among several features leading to reverence, alongside office, character, rank and fortune.[22] He notes that while defining nature is difficult, per Cicero, defining fortune is even harder. This is because nature has some substance ('*substantia*'), and fortune has none. He points out that 'Nature provides the origins of things, which could not be if, in truth, it did not exist. What does not exist at all, cannot provide existence to something else. As fortune does not exist it cannot be defined.'[23] While rank can, on occasion, proceed from nature, or from duty or character, fortune's origins are unpredictable. It would seem that the thrust of John's use of Cicero's comment on the vagaries of defining nature in this instance is to argue that fortune has no validity in determining whether a person is worthy of reverence or not; he does not aim to provide an explicit commentary on nature, but to criticise capricious '*fortuna*'. However, a corollary of his conclusions is the oblique implication that nature in itself has substance, and is in turn generative. Nonetheless, we must look to other parts of his work to find a more concrete analysis of what nature demands, and the degree to which it is of significance in determining the relationship of man to the world around him, and to his fellow human beings.

In the first book of the *Metalogicon*, John provides a more philosophical insight into his views on nature. He writes:

> Nature is, according to some (although it is difficult to explain this definition) a certain generative force, grafted in all things, whereby they can act or have the ability to do so. It is called generative, because everything obtains both its cause of being from it and its principle of existence. Everything obtains its suitability for this or for that from its composition, whether its composition is reckoned in name as 'of parts', whether it comes from an origin of matter and of form, as in simple things that do not permit an aggregation of parts, or whether the reason of its composition is solely constituted by the decree of divine goodness.[24]

John regards this final form of composition as the 'first nature' ('*prima natura*'), a Platonic perspective transmitted to John from Victorinus's *Explanationes in Ciceronis Rhetoricam*, which asserts that Plato claimed that 'nature is the will of god'.[25] Thus, all created things come ultimately from God. Meanwhile, the generative force that emanates from nature is secondary: 'That force which is originally implanted in each and every thing and constitutes the source of its activities or aptitudes is a nature, but a created one.'[26]

John notes that most definitions of *natura* provided by various authors refer to this 'created nature'. Even the '*ignis artifex*', which produces visible effects by invisible means, is created. The principal problem with this 'created nature' is that, while it can be powerful and effective, it is also mutable. It can as easily be corrupted and impeded by vices, as it can be helped or repaired by aid. Similarly, nature can be aided or abetted by care or neglect. Nature's gifts must be fully realised through study, and when aided by virtue may grow strong.[27] John's perspective has certain traits of neo-Platonism, but also has a Christian quality. As Gregory noted, a characteristic of the cosmological perspective associated with the scholars of Chartres was the limitation of the role of God in nature to the creation of the elements and the human soul.[28] The work of nature ('*opus naturae*') consisted of everything else; it was the product of secondary causes, of physical reason. God was not the continuing efficient cause throughout nature, rather God's initial role as creator facilitated the dynamism of the natural world, to the extent that it subsequently regulated itself. John conceded that the 'principle of movement [in created nature] traces back to God', a view he claims Aristotle would agree with.[29] This theory finds a parallel in Peter Abelard's *Hexaemeron*, where it is contended that 'nature is the power of things conferred upon them at the beginning which prepared them henceforth to give rise to anything, that is, sufficient to bring them about'.[30] It is a '*vis*' that continues the work of the creator, assuring a '*similitudo nascentium*' – a likeness of being: a force equated with the will of God.[31] This force of nature engenders man, implying the immanence of God in nature.[32] However, John also saw a continued role for nature as a creative impulse in the world; man, in cooperation with nature, works through reason for the perfection of the arts.[33] Indeed, no art could develop without nature, or if it did it would be sterile and useless, as 'the beginning of all things is in nature'. To work against nature – '*invita Minerva*', using the Ciceronian trope – would lead to negligible achievement.[34]

John writes that nature is 'a certain generative force, grafted in all things, whereby they can act or have the ability to do so'. Although Stephen Epstein does not refer directly to John in his analysis of the place of grafting ('*insitio*') in theories of nature in the Middle Ages, it is illuminating to examine John's definition in this context.[35] The botanic procedure of grafting, that is the joining of parts of two plants for the purpose of propagation, was influential for medieval notions of inheritability. It was also theologically significant: Hildegard of Bingen spoke of the creation of Eve as a grafting process, and grafting was also used as a metaphor in Romans 11:24 to convey to Gentiles and Jews their role in faith; they were as branches grafted from a wild olive tree to a cultivated one, supported by a common root.[36] Although an interventionist process, grafting was a way of improving and facilitating nature's activities. So by using this specific term, John suggests that nature is continually (and causally) active in the world; the term is also found in the writings of his teacher William of Conches, as observed above. To explore this causal efficiency further we must look to another of John's texts, *Entheticus*, where – in the context of a discussion of the beliefs of the Peripatetic school – John provides a further analysis of the causal power of nature. John, drawing on the Peripatetic view, identifies the 'idea of the good' (*'idea boni'*) as the 'source of truth' (*'veri fons'*), and as the active (first) cause of things. The 'causes of things' (*'rerum causarum'*), in John's words, emanate from this source. John calls this series of causes 'nature', and describes it as that which ensures that all things attain the fulfilment intended for them by their genus. It is, in other words, the 'final cause' of everything.[37]

John combines this important principle, that nature is essential to the ordering of all things in the world, and continually active in it, with a Stoic principle: that is, the concept of nature as a guide.[38] The concept of 'nature as guide' derives from Cicero's *De amicitia*, V. 19. In recommending nature as a guide to man, Cicero depended on a Stoic notion regarding the *seminales rationes* inherent in man, which continuously facilitated the pursuit of virtue. The Stoics believed that these seminal reasons (in Greek, *logos spermatikos*), emanating from God (*Logos*), were the source of all matter, and were the active cause of all that happened in the world. The causal capacity of such seeds stemmed from their materiality, which was infused in all things, and in turn gave humans the capacity to approximate the divine. Seneca identified nature with divinity in a similar manner in *De beneficiis*: 'For what else is nature but god and the divine reason that pervades the whole universe and all its parts?'[39] Nature serves to animate man through the constant presence of the creative impulse in the world. Seneca, understanding nature as at once created, and becoming in turn the generative force dictating all circumstances – expressed in Stoic terms as aethereal fire – presented a pantheistic, materialistic, interpretation of the role of nature.[40] He argued that one should act in accordance with the purpose that has been pre-ordained for each person since Creation. Man can only achieve his highest good if 'he has fulfilled the good for which nature designed him at birth' – what reason demands of him – that is, 'to live in accordance with nature'.[41] In *Naturales quaestiones*, Seneca made specific reference to the derivation of all things from seminal causes: 'Whether the world is an animated being, or a body governed by nature, like trees and plants, there is incorporated in it from its beginning to its end everything it must do or undergo.'[42] For Seneca, the validity of nature's guiding role was based on the principle that the world contains within its creation all the ingredients that determine its fate.

While these Roman texts may have offered a route for John into the Stoic theory of seminal reasons, it is more likely that he was influenced by the mediated version of the theory he would have read in the writings of Augustine. For Augustine, the fate of all things was established since primordial times and known to, and dependent on, God. To explain this, Augustine adapted the Stoic idea of the *rationes seminales*, seeing them as imitative of the form of the *rationes aeternae*, the eternal reasons in the mind of God. These created *rationes seminales*, which are the source of all matter, explain the continuation of God's purpose in a world created from nothing; they are causally active in the material world. But while the Stoics saw the *rationes seminales* as material particles of the divine, Augustine viewed them as simply created by God; they are not God themselves. However, as they are imitative forms of the *rationes aeternae*, they act by enabling humanity's potential knowledge of God's mind; they allow participation in the divine, rather than permitting man to actually *be* divine.[43] John incorporates some aspects of Augustine's theory of seminal causes to show the continued immanence of God in the world.[44] He reflects on Plato's view that nature can be equated with the will of God in *Policraticus*, Book II. 12: 'And so the wisdom and goodness of God, from which all things originate, is rightly called nature – against which nothing can be done, because nothing cancels the purpose of God, or deprives the causes which have existed from eternity in the mind of Him, whose understanding made the heavens, from accomplishment.'[45] John proceeds to refer directly to the '*res seminales*' that cause events and which, in a preordained time, produce their effects. John describes this process as 'miraculous', because the reason behind the process is hidden.[46] Nothing can, therefore, be contrary to the will of God, as God is nature.[47]

The influence of Augustine's interpretation of rationes *seminales* on John is clear when we consider the context of this discussion, that is, the role of phenomena and portents in human history. John notes that the portents surrounding the Day of Judgement 'will not be subject to the laws of nature', if 'by nature we mean the customary course of events and the hidden causes of events for which a reasonable explanation can be given'.[48] This echoes the Augustinian notion that 'portent, therefore, does not occur contrary to nature, but contrary to what is known of nature'.[49] John, like Augustine, suggests that the natural order of the world, although initially 'hidden' from humanity, can potentially be discerned through the ultimate knowledge of God. Everything, according to Augustine, follows the 'orderly scheme of nature'; the continuous development of the purpose inherent in nature, corresponding to God's will, leads to harmony.

John shares with Augustine the perspective that God's plan is worked out progressively throughout human history and believes that, when that is achieved, a harmony will exist among all created things.[50] While John noted, in his enumeration of the things that invited reverence for a person, that nature, unlike fortune, has *substantia*, a material existence, it is clear that his understanding of this materiality was dependent on Augustine, who saw *rationes seminales* as imitative of God's *rationes aeternae* but not in themselves material particles of the divine.[51] John, similarly, does not go so far as to adopt the Stoic position that material particles of the divine were inherent in nature. Nature imitates God, rather than being God – a definitive departure from Stoic pantheism. Nevertheless, the immanence of nature in the world gives it its character – as producer, facilitator and guide: roles that ensure its continued effectiveness as a causal force. In spite of the adaptations made, this study of the influence of the theory of *rationes seminales* illustrates how Stoic sources provided ample flexibility for patristic and medieval scholars, facilitating the identification of the 'god' of the Stoics with the 'God-creator' of the Bible.

### Reason

If following nature can be seen as a prescriptive recommendation on John's part, then reason is the tool that facilitates the perception and discernment of its rules.[52] In Book II of the *Policraticus*, John describes reason as allowing human consciousness to understand a range of experiences: first, 'matter', 'which sense perceives and which necessarily has form', which John considers to be the 'first and unique substance'. Secondly, the mind perceives 'that without which substance can neither exist nor be understood', which John terms a 'second substance'.[53] Reason 'defines what understanding had conceived' – what was first perceived through the senses.[54] John notes that this two-stage process of reasoning is generally more useful in the immaterial realm of the mind than in the physical world.[55] Reason, therefore, allows discernment between the different situational properties of being, and true nature.[56] According to John, man was solely selected by God to be a participant in divine reason, which distinguished him from the animals. This capacity resulted from God breathing life into man, imbuing him with a '*spiritus*', 'which comes from and will return to God', thus rendering him able to contemplate the divine, a description that has overtones of the Stoic idea of *seminales rationes*.[57] John even makes explicit reference here to Seneca's treatment of reason as 'a certain part of the divine spirit, immersed in human bodies'.[58] However, it is clear from John's critique of this position that he denies the corporeality of the 'divine spirit' to which Seneca referred.[59] On the one hand, he says that Seneca can be understood as suggesting that the *anima mundi* was divided into individual souls, an error that John identifies as shared by the 'Gentiles', who mistakenly equate the *anima mundi* with the Holy Spirit. On the other hand, John defends Seneca's interpretation by suggesting that in adding the term '*quaedam*', Seneca qualified his statement, demonstrating that he meant it as a 'figure of speech'. This second interpretation, which John describes as 'kinder', implies that reason is not a quantitative part of the Holy Spirit, but a part 'by virtue'. Reason holds status as a '*modo uirtus diuina*', a means of divine virtue, but cannot be literally interpreted as 'part of him whose simplicity is absolute', that is, God.[60] John's adoption of a non-corporeal interpretation of Seneca's words enables him to Christianise the Stoic notion of reason as diffused in man.

However, John does not entirely resist the notion of the corporeality of particles of reason in the mind. In his discussion of the Stoic position in *Metalogicon*, II. 20, John claims that the Stoics suggest that matter is coeternal with God but that God is the 'conciliator', not the 'creator' of matter. John claims that the Stoics posit three principles of existence: matter, form and god. The presumed source of John's reformulation of Stoic thought is Seneca's Letter 65, on the subject of causation; all things come into being, according to the Stoics, through 'cause' and 'matter', but as Seneca adds, cause is 'created reason', or god.[61] Cause/god, the active principle, identified here with reason, shapes matter. In referring to a triad of principles (matter, form, god), rather than simply matter and cause, John is not necessarily misinterpreting his source. In fact, John proceeds to comment that form and matter are intrinsic to each other. Both are created *ex nihilo* by God, and 'by this way form exists through matter, just as matter is discerned by form'.[62] One could not exist without the other. What is significant to John (and to the Stoics) is the primacy of the creator's role as the principal cause. Although Michael Lapidge terms the inclusion of a third principle of existence in this passage – that is, form – an 'error' on John's part, it is, rather, a recognition by him that matter cannot exist without form, a perspective consistent with his understanding of God's continued animating role in nature.[63] Thus, a third element is implicit and necessary in his reading of the Senecan dictum: it is neither superfluous nor fallacious.

That said, John denies that this implies the coeternity of matter and form with God. Contrasting the Stoics and the Epicureans in *Metalogicon*,

Book IV. 35, John comments that the Stoics believe that 'matter' and the 'Idea' are coeternal with God, while the followers of Epicurus reject the significance of providence and of the 'Idea' (in the sense of a Platonic 'form'). By contrast, John presents the case of Bernard of Chartres, 'the best Platonist of our time', who believed that neither 'matter' nor the 'Idea' should be regarded as 'coeternal' with God. According to Bernard, the 'Idea' is posterior to the triune divinity, as it does not require an external cause, and so is intrinsic to the divine, a view John appears to align with.[64] This is also apparent from John's discussion of forms in *Entheticus*, where he comments that God is *'informis'*: 'That which is truly simple, is altered by no motion, is not made old by time, always the same.'[65] This example underscores the necessity of reading John's works side by side in order to fully appreciate the blend of Stoic and neo-Platonic perspectives which he offers in order to explain the potential of reason in the world.

While John does not follow the Stoics in seeing material nature as coequal with God, he appropriates another Stoic perspective in order to validate the necessity of living in accordance with nature, that is, the Senecan suggestion that perfected reason (defined as virtue) is the appropriate end for man, and the source of honourable living.[66] The force of Seneca's assertion lies in its emphasis on the divine aspect of reason; it is a godly quality: 'What, then is the difference between our nature and the nature of god? In ourselves the better part is the mind, in god there is no part other than the mind. He is entirely reason.'[67] John, likewise, considers that 'reason is ennobled by its divine origin'.[68] Employing a metaphor that echoes some elements of his famous model of the body politic (especially in terms of the Roman imagery it evokes), he comments:

> Since reason examines our senses, which, because they often fail us, can be suspected, nature, the best parent of all, has made our head the location of all senses; reason holds dominion over the soul, akin to the status of the Senate on the Capitol, where it sits in the apex of the head between the chambers of imagination and memory and can examine the judgements of sensation and imagination.[69]

It is interesting to note a subtle distinction implied here by John, that is, that reason may be situated in the head, but the head is not necessarily the only location of the soul. In the *Policraticus*, John describes the soul as responsible for the animation of the body, stating that 'As long, therefore, as it [the body] is alive in all parts, it is disposed in accordance with a whole [the soul] which is not diffused part to part, but exists as a whole and operates in each and every part.'[70] The soul itself is indivisible, but this indivisibility does not prohibit its diffusion throughout the body, a perspective that John reinforces in the *Metalogicon* with reference to Cicero's *Tusculanae disputationes*, where the immortality of the soul and the divinity of reason are discussed.[71]

Reason, however, cannot act alone. It operates in tandem with grace. John speaks of the 'treasures of knowledge' that are accessed through two means: the exercise of reason, which allows the discovery of what can be known, and revealing grace, which allows things that are hidden to become known. Reason facilitates the opening of the 'book of knowledge ... carried in the heart' of all.[72] Reason, when aided by grace, exceeds the limits of sensory perception by investigating things that are incorporeal and spiritual; this is the basis of wisdom.[73] Furthermore, John distinguishes between reason as a 'spiritual force that examines the nature of things' and the 'primitive', or original, reason, which he considers to be a 'divine wisdom or power'.[74] Using the metaphor of a sphere, he describes this original reason as the 'nature of all things, their cause, process, and end': it encompasses everything that exists physically in the world as well as the species (particulars) and genera of all things. John notes that 'such a sphere can be seen as an image as well as an Idea of the world', expressing the conceptual value of viewing divine reason as immanent in nature, if not materially diffused in it.[75] Reason, therefore, is a 'power of the soul', and its understanding is based on what can be determined through the senses, or by intellect.[76] Grace, on the other hand, 'reveals what has been hidden by presenting it to our eyes'.[77] The implication of this perspective that the true reality of things can be accessed only through knowledge aided by reason, or revealed by grace, is that the universal qualities of all things are inferable only through an understanding of what is hidden from the visible senses.[78]

John's views on reason are significant for his understanding of universals, and worth exploring further. In seeing genera and species as mental representations of material specific things (that is, the basis of the knowledge of sensible reality), John departs from the Aristotelian perspective that sees universals as existing only in things. Instead, he suggests that universals facilitate the process of attaining knowledge by providing a sort of interpretative shortcut; however, true understanding can be achieved only through nature and grace: 'It is then through nature or through grace that each one can arrive at the recognition and knowledge of truth of those things that are necessary.'[79] In this sense, John's understanding of universals bears strong similarities to that of the Stoics, who considered them to be conceptual constructs informed by sense-perception; they may resemble reality, but are not to be confused with it. Universals, according to this interpretation, are figments of the mind, but they remain useful to John as conceptual tools of analysis; as Michael Wilks put it, they are a 'useful fiction'.[80] Introducing the debate on 'universals', John lists a number of contesting views: 'opinions which would identify universals with word sounds [*uocibus*], word concepts [*sermonibus*], sensible things [*sensibilibus rebus*], ideas [*ideis*], native forms [*formis natiuis*] or collections of things [*collectionibus*]'.[81] As noted, John distinguishes between two types of knowledge: that which is aided by the use of reason (which is already superior to simple sense perception) and that facilitated by the use of grace. The result, '*intellectus*' or intuitive understanding, achieves what reason investigates and is the source of wisdom ('*sapientia*').[82] Therefore, as Brian Hendley contends, 'Knowledge of a universal for John is not knowledge of a thing through its form (exact nature), but knowledge of the nature of a thing inferred from various sensibly manifested effects.'[83]

John's distinction between reason as a 'spiritual force that examines the nature of things' and 'primitive reason' is found in the context of a description of the perspectives on *ratio* held by different philosophical schools. After discussing the positions of the Stoics, the Peripatetics and the Epicureans, John turns to the sceptical position of the Academicians.[84] He notes that some deny that anything can be known (universal doubt), and some allow only for knowledge of things that are obvious to everyone (mathematical and logical knowledge); meanwhile, a third group 'of us' use doubt as a tool of enquiry, accepting probable knowledge in cases where absolute knowledge is not accessible.[85] This reference to the group 'of us' suggests that John identifies with the Academicians, but the thrust of this statement should not be read simplistically as an expression of John's philosophical affiliation, but in its appropriate context, that is, his investigation of Christian theories of providence and the nature of truth. Truth, for John, ultimately rests in God's purpose for the world – a loose echo of Stoic theories of *Logos* and providential causes. John considers that God's purpose, absolute perfect reason, is immutable, and can be equated with perfect truth.[86] In his exposition of this point in *Metalogicon*, Book IV. 37, John refers to the immutability and immortality of the Word. God's memory, wisdom, knowledge and word (here identified with reason) are one.[87] The truth of reason rests, therefore, in the truth of the Word of God: permanent, immutable and eternal.

### Living in accordance with nature: reason, virtue and intention

Living in accordance with nature, and according to rational principles, involves an understanding of the demands of virtue, a dominant theme in John's writings and those of the Stoics that will be fully assessed in Chapter 5. In brief, according to the Stoic perspective, the significance of a virtuous action lies in the agent's relation to it: the virtuous person will develop a conscience that conforms with rationality (for the Stoic, the rationality of nature, for John the rationality of God's purpose as expressed in nature). The intention behind an act, therefore, becomes the significant element through which its merit can be judged, and through which vice can be resisted. In this respect, the intention to follow nature is as important as the act of actually following nature. The Greek Stoics recommended the pursuit of *apatheia*, that is, the ability to reject the significance of the passions as true goods. The desired end was to avoid being ruled by morally indifferent externals, things that did not contribute to the cultivation of virtue, among which the passions were counted – even *eupatheiai*, 'good emotions' – and to regard only true goods as worthy, notably the rational adherence to virtue. Emotions, or passions, were problematic for the Stoics; they were maligned because they frequently acted in the place of reason as a basis for action, but they were also, as Plato and Aristotle argued, impossible to avoid because of their reactive spontaneity. In order to explain why spontaneous emotions existed, the Stoics distinguished between pre-emotions, or 'first movements', which are involuntary reactions to a situation, and true emotions which involve voluntary assent. A wise man may experience an affective involuntary response to a situation, but the Stoic sage will never rely on such responses in judging between what is good and what is bad (and will invariably reject indifferent passions).

The doctrine of 'first movements' in the Latin tradition is found in both Senecan work (especially *De ira*, which as we have noted received some attention in the medieval period in its redaction by Martin of Braga) and in Ciceronian work, with Richard Sorabji drawing particular attention to *Tusculanae disputationes*, III. 82-3.[88] It was also of interest to early Christian commentators, although, as Sorabji notes, from the time of Rufinus's translation of Origen, 'first movements' become conflated with genuine emotions, as they are incorrectly connected with bad thoughts, which in scriptural sources 'come from the heart'.[89] A prime example of this confusion, according to Sorabji, is found in a story of a shipwreck involving a Stoic sage that is borrowed by Augustine from Aulus Gellius's

*Noctes Atticae*, XIX. 1. In Augustine's retelling, the Stoic reacts to the shipwreck by becoming pale; he describes him as having 'shuddered [*perhorrescere*] with danger as to give witness to fear with pallor'. The shuddering and act of becoming pale, in Augustine's mind, demonstrated an involuntary consent on the part of the Stoic to fear – a consent, Augustine reasons, that shows that the Stoics are unable to reject the passions to the extent to which they claim.[90] Sorabji argues that Augustine's interpretation lies in the lack of clarity of his source. In his telling of the story, Aulus Gellius uses two verbs without distinction to describe the Stoic's reaction: *pallescere* (to pale) and *pavescere* (to tremble). The latter verb implies for Augustine that the Stoic is feeling more than an involuntary pre-emotion, an interpretation that Gellius did not necessarily intend to present. Regardless, Augustine's critique of Stoic first movements would prove to be highly influential for the medieval understanding of this Stoic doctrine.[91]

John discusses this story at length in *Policraticus*, Book VII. 3, and it is worth examining the way it fits into his broader views on intention. John introduces his adaptation of Augustine's presentation with a brief summary of Stoic doctrine:

> Now one of their [the Stoics'] widely accepted opinions was that there was no place in the mind of the sage for fear; as everything is the result of necessity it is folly to fear what cannot be avoided. On the contrary, the only remedy is that the man of prudence may equip himself with strength and fortitude and, by the power of endurance, may receive all the weapons of necessity as upon the solid shield of invincible courage.[92]

The word 'necessity' is used here in the Stoic sense of 'fate'. The account given by John of the value of fortitude as a remedy against fear bears similarities to that provided in Seneca's *Naturales quaestiones*, II. 59, where it is recommended that the soul should be strengthened, not so that the sage escapes the weapons of *necessitas*, but so that he can endure them bravely, claiming that 'We [the wise] can be unconquered, but not unshaken.'[93] After recounting the story of the ship at sea, John quotes the summary provided by Augustine of the doctrine of 'first movements': 'The difference between the mind of a sage and that of a fool is that the fool by mental consent yields to his passions while the sage, although he cannot help experiencing these emotions, retains unshaken a true and sound view with regard to things that it is reasonable to pursue and reject.'[94] However, while Augustine concludes his critique by noting that there are not many differences, save terminological quibbles, between how the Stoics and other philosophical schools deal with the passions, John concludes his discussion in a different vein. He argues that the Stoics are in error because they claim that they can resist the passions solely through their own volition, without the aid of God's grace. Even if the passions were to be 'turned to the use of justice', they would still be dependent on the mercy of God. He concludes by stating that 'Following Scripture, the *initium* of wisdom and the *finis* of humility is fear of God.'[95] John's denial of the validity of the Stoic position, unlike Augustine's, does not rest on a critique of its coherence but on the fact that the Stoics have a misplaced faith in their own capacities. Fear of losing riches, or even of death, does not provide a sound basis for the Stoic to make a rational decision, while for the Christian, fear of God and a will to conform to his teachings must work in conjunction with rationality to ensure correct action.

It is in the light of these considerations on what constitutes a true reaction to a situation that we must examine John's views on intentionality. He writes: 'An action becomes criminal not in itself but from its intention. No display of virtue gives an act distinction if its origin is derived from pleasure.'[96] An action is considered a virtuous one, therefore, only if it is undertaken for the right reasons, with the passions regarded as an inappropriate motivation. John notes later that if one intends to carry out an act, 'but does not have the power to do so, God will regard it as completed, and it will attain the same reward'.[97] An important corollary of this is John's contention that virtue cannot be feigned; the appearance of virtue must be matched by a genuine commitment to its precepts, that is, virtuous behaviour must be matched by virtuous intention. John claims that the very expression 'good faith' derives from the relation between correct intention and correct action, a perspective he attributes to the Stoics (and derives from Cicero's *De officiis*).[98] Following nature, therefore, necessarily requires a mind that is directed towards its pursuit, a mind that must be informed by virtuous intentions, not misled by external considerations. The mind informed by reason will necessarily align intention and action; this is the best way to follow nature – a perspective shared by John and the Stoics.

In a single case, John refers to the Stoic '*scintillula rationis*', the 'little spark of reason', a term that carries the sense of a superior natural goodness, innate and specific to man.[99] The context is John's discussion of self-indulgence and lust. Referring to Deuteronomy 32:15–17, John describes how the Israelites turned away from God, their saviour, and by engaging in gluttony and lust 'extinguished the spark of reason'. The term '*scintillula rationis*' has a significant twelfth-century heritage, notably on account of its conflation with the *scintilla conscientiae* described by Jerome as equivalent to *synderesis*, or a natural inclination to the good.[100] Peter Lombard, writing in the *Sentences*, refers to the 'superior spark of reason' (*'superior enim scintilla rationis'*), which, according to Jerome, remained unextinguished even in the murderous Cain. This 'spark', in Peter's interpretation, consisted of a natural desire on the part of man for the 'good', and remains extant even in the worst sinners.[101] The use of '*scintilla rationis*' by Peter is presumably inspired by Augustine's *De civitate Dei*, XXII. 24, where Augustine refers to the 'spark of reason' that remained in man after the Fall. It is intriguing that, despite the fact that most scholars in this period accept that the *scintilla rationis* is inextinguishable, John implies that the excess of the Israelites is sufficient to negate it. The consent of the Israelites to 'devote themselves to the spirit of Bacchanalians' is not, apparently, simply a flawed exercise of free will, contrary to the natural inclination towards the good; rather, their perversion leads to the total extinction of this natural inclination that is characteristically human. John's perspective is all the more striking in view of the fact that later scholars, such as Philip the Chancellor, would distinguish between conscience and *synderesis*, and argue that while conscience may err, *synderesis* is never mistaken; as it is non-deliberative, it does not entail the possibility of making a wrong choice.[102] Given the context of the remark, it is possible that John used the phrase without taking account of its implications for ethical causality, but, whether read simply as anti-Jewish polemic or not, it seems to indicate that a natural inclination towards the good is not necessarily a given and may be revoked. Broader implications aside, this passage underscores the necessity of grace working as an accomplice to reason in the pursuit of life in accordance with nature. Without grace, reason lacks efficacy. The Jews, subject to the 'Law' of the Old Testament, are excluded from the grace that facilitates access to the highest truths of nature.

## Conclusion

From this survey of the significance of nature and reason it is apparent that John built his political theory on the foundations of an account of rational, virtuous living. Man needs to be guided by the precepts of nature (innate in God's providential plan for the world) in order to live virtuously, a recommendation that can be achieved only through the development and application of right reason. By borrowing elements from Stoic doctrine, such as a modified version of the theory of seminal causality and the diffusion of rationality in all things, John elides 'living in accordance with nature' with 'living in accordance with God's purpose in the world'. The process is Stoic; the result is Christian. The mechanics of John's approach are apparent in this brief overview of his views on intention. Here, by conflating the Christian rejection of things unnecessary to God's purpose with the Stoic rejection of the indifferents, John suggests that any action undertaken for a purpose other than the pursuit of virtue (such as the accretion of external gains) is contrary to virtue, and to life in accordance with nature. In the next chapter it will be examined how this forms the basis of an account of appropriate exercise of duties, the best way of living in accordance with nature in the public sphere.

## Notes

1 *Met.* I. 1, p. 13: '*Et quamuis solam uideatur eloquentiam persequi, omnia liberalia studia conuellit, omnem totius philosophiae impugnat operam, societatis humanae foedus distrahit, et nullum caritati aut uicissitudini officiorum relinquit locum.*'
2 *Met.* I. 1, pp. 13–14: '*Brutescent homines si concessi dote priuentur eloquii, ipsaeque urbes uidebuntur potius pecorum quasi saepta quam coetus hominum nexu quodam societatis foederatus, ut participatione officiorum et amica inuicem uicissitudine eodem iure uiuat.*' Cf. Cicero, *De inventione*, trans. H. M. Hubbell (LCL 386; Cambridge, MA: Harvard University Press, 1949), I. 2–3.
3 *Met.* I. I, p. 13: '*Haec autem est illa dulcis et fructuosa coniugatio rationis et uerbi, quae tot egregias genuit urbes, tot conciliauit et foederauit regna, tot uniuit populos et caritate deuinxit, ut hostis omnium publicus merito censeatur quisquis hoc quod ad utilitatem omnium Deus coniunxit, nititur separare.*' Cf. Matthew 19:6.
4 *Met.* I. 1, p. 12: '*hominem priuilegio rationis extulit, et usu eloquii insigniuit*'. Cf. Cicero, *On Duties*, I. 50, pp. 21–2: 'First is something that is seen in the fellowship of the entire human race. For its bonding consists of reason and speech, which reconcile men to one another, through teaching, learning, communicating, debating and making judgment, and unite them in a kind of natural fellowship. It is this that most distances us from the nature of other animals.' John refers to eloquence as the 'gift of nature and grace' in *Met.* I. 7, p. 24.
5 *Met* I. 1, p. 12: '*natura clementissima parens omnium*'.
6 *Met.* I. 1, p. 12: '*Dum itaque naturam fecundat gratia, ratio rebus perspiciendis et examinandis inuigilat, naturae sinus excutit*'.
7 P. Delhaye, *Permanence du droit naturel* (Louvain: Nauwelaerts, 1967), pp. 10–21. See also A. Pellicer, *Natura: Étude sémantique et historique du mot latin* (Paris: PUF, 1966), pp. 143–9, and E. Dudley Sylla, 'Creation and Nature', in A. S. McGrade (ed.), *The Cambridge Companion to Medieval Philosophy* (Cambridge: Cambridge University Press, 2003), pp. 171–95 (notably pp. 173–7).

8 Dudley Sylla, 'Creation and Nature', p. 175.
9 T. Gregory, *Anima mundi: La filosofia de Guglielmo di Conches e la scuola di Chartres* (Florence: Sansoni, 1955); T. Gregory, 'L'idea di natura nella filosofia medievale prima dell'ingresso della fisica di Aristotele', in *La filosofia della natura nel medioevo: Atti del terzo congresso internazionale di filosofia medioevale* (Milan: Società Editrice Vita e Pensiero, 1966), pp. 27–65; T. Gregory, 'The Platonic Inheritance', in Dronke (ed.), *A History of Twelfth-Century Western Philosophy*, pp. 54–80; T. Gregory, 'La nouvelle idée de la nature et de savoir scientifique au XII$^e$ siècle', in J. E. Murdoch and E. Dudley Sylla (eds), *The Cultural Context of Medieval Learning: Proceedings of the first International Colloquium on Philosophy, Science and Theology in the Middle Ages – September 1973* (Dordrecht: D. Reidel, 1975), pp. 193–212. For an earlier interpretation of the 'Chartrian' vision of nature see J. M. Parent, *La doctrine de la création dans l'école de Chartres* (Paris: J. Vrin, 1938).
10 M.-D. Chenu, 'Nature and Man: The Renaissance of the Twelfth Century', in *Nature, Man and Society: Essays on New Theological Perspectives in the Latin West*, ed. and trans. J. Taylor and L. K. Little (Chicago: University of Chicago Press, 1968), pp. 1–48.
11 Thierry of Chartres, *Commentarius super Libros De Inventione*, in *The Latin Rhetorical Commentaries of Thierry of Chartres*, ed. K. M. Fredborg (Toronto: Pontifical Institute of Medieval Studies, 1988), pp. 49–215: 1.24.34, p. 131: '*Nam de naturis divinorum ad theologos, de naturis autem brutorum animalium, quae generali nomine bestias appellat, de his, inquam, tractare ad physiologos pertinet.*' For the dating of this commentary see J. O. Ward, 'The Date of the Commentaries on Cicero's *De Inventione* by Thierry of Chartres (*ca.* 1095–1160?) and the Cornifician attack on the Liberal Arts', *Viator*, 3 (1972), 219–73. See also K. M. Fredborg, 'The Commentary of Thierry of Chartres on Cicero's *De Inventione*', *Cahiers de l'Institut du Moyen-Âge Grec et Latin*, 7 (1971), 1–36; P. Delhaye, 'L'enseignement de la philosophie morale au XII$^e$ siècle', *Mediaeval Studies*, 11 (1949), 77–99.
12 Cicero, *De inventione*, I. 33.
13 Cicero, *De inventione*, I. 34, p. 71: 'All propositions are supported in argument by attributes of persons or of actions.'
14 Thierry of Chartres, *Commentarius super Libros De Inventione*, I. 24.34, p. 131: '*Naturam definire, etc., difficile, ideo quoniam vario et multiplici modo dicitur natura, sive causa nascendi sive naturalia sive diuturna consuetudo vel alio modo. Naturam autem hic appellat naturalia, id est ea quae alicui attributa sunt ab ipsa causa nascendi, sive animi sint sive corporis sive extrinseca, ut aetas, sexus et consimilia. Genera etiam et species et differentiae substantiales et propria et accidentia a natura attributa, omnia haec sub natura continentur, sed Tullius enumerat ea tantum, quorum indiget ad rhetoricum, et dividendo descendit ad illa naturalia, quae sunt in homine et quae ad personam pertinent, quibus indiget orator.*' Fredborg notes the dependence of Thierry on Victorinus and Boethius in 'Twelfth-Century Ciceronian Rhetoric: Its Doctrinal Development and Influences', in B. Vickers (ed.) *Rhetoric Revalued: Papers from the International*

Society for the History of Rhetoric (Binghampton, NY: Center for Medieval and Early Renaissance Studies, 1982), pp. 87-98 (p. 88).
15 Quoted in H. White, *Nature, Sex and Goodness in a Medieval Literary Tradition* (Oxford: Oxford University Press, 2000), p. 77. On the use of Aristotle's 'four causes' as the framework for Thierry's analysis see R. C. Dales, 'A Twelfth-Century Concept of the Natural Order', *Viator*, 9 (1978), 179-92 (183-4).
16 Cicero, *De inventione*, I. 34, pp. 70-1: '*Naturam ipsam definire difficile est; partes autem eius enumerare eas quarum indigemus ad hanc preceptionem facilius est.*'
17 Hugh of St Victor, *The Didascalicon of Hugh of St Victor: A Medieval Guide to the Arts*, trans. J. Taylor (New York: Columbia University Press, 1961), I. 10, pp. 56-7, 193-4; cf. C. Marius Victorinus, *Explanationes in Ciceronis Rhetoricam*, ed. A. Ippolito (CCSL 132; Turnhout: Brepols, 2006), I. 24, 124-7, p. 109: '*Denique sapientes quidam sic definiere naturam: 'natura est ignis artifex quadam uia uadens in res sensibles procreandas'; etenim manifestum est omnia principe igne generari.*' For the significance of 'fire' in Stoic doctrine see M. C. Horowitz, 'The Stoic Synthesis of the Idea of Natural Law in Man', *Journal of the History of Ideas*, 35 (1974), 3-16 (14-16).
18 B. Taylor Coleman, *The Theology of Hugh of St Victor: An Interpretation* (Cambridge: Cambridge University Press, 2010), pp. 207-10.
19 William of Conches, *A Dialogue on Natural Philosophy* (*The* Dragmaticon Philosophiae), trans. I. Ronca and M. Curr (Notre Dame, IN: University of Notre Dame Press, 1997), I. 7.3, p. 18. See William of Conches, *Dragmaticon philosophiae*, ed. I. Ronca (CCCM 152; Turnhout: Brepols, 1997), I. 7.3, p. 27: '*Vt ait Tullius, difficile est naturam diffinire: sed tamen, ut hic hoc nomen accipitur, natura est uis quedam rebus insita, similia de similibus operans.*' See S. A. Epstein, *The Medieval Discovery of Nature* (Cambridge: Cambridge University Press, 2012), p. 10 for some observations on William's definition.
20 D. Elford, 'William of Conches', in Dronke (ed.), *A History of Twelfth-Century Philosophy*, pp. 308-27 (pp. 311, 318-20). On the elemental balance of the soul see William of Conches, *Dragmaticon philosophiae*, VI. 25.4.
21 Elford, 'William of Conches', p. 327. For the development of William's natural philosophy see J. Cadden, 'Science and Rhetoric in the Middle Ages: The Natural Philosophy of William of Conches', *Journal of the History of Ideas*, 56 (1995), 1-24. See Spanneut, *Permanence du Stoïcisme*, p. 183 for the Stoic implications of William's description of the World-Soul in his *Philosophia*.
22 *Pol.* V. 4.
23 *Pol.* V. 4; 1, p. 292: '*Naturam diffinire difficile esse asserit Tullius. Ego difficilius credo diffinire fortunam, eo quod huius nulla, illius aliqua substantia est. Natura siquidem rebus originem praebet; quod nequaquam esset, si in ueritate ipsa non esset. Quod enim omnino non est, alicui praestare non potest ut sit. At fortuna cum non sit, non potest diffiniri.*'
24 *Met.* I. 8, p. 25: '*Est autem natura ut quibusdam placet, licet eam sit definire difficile, uis quaedam genitiua rebus omnibus insita ex qua facere uel pati possunt. Genitiua autem dicitur, eo quod ipsam res quaeque contrahat a causa suae generationis, et ab eo quod cuique est principium existendi. Res enim quaelibet*

*a componentibus contrahit unde ad hoc apta sit uel ad illud, siue componentia partium nomine censeantur, siue accedant ad originem materiae et formae ut in simplicibus quae coaceruationem partium non admittunt, siue ratio componendi ad solius diuinae bonitatis decretum accedat.*'

25 *Met.* I. 8, pp. 25–6: '*Nam et haec ipsa prima natura est auctore Platone, qui sicut Victorinus et alii multi testantur, certissimam omnium rerum naturam esse asseruit diuinam uoluntatem.*' Victorinus, *Explanationes*, p. 109: '*Plato autem sic definiuit: "natura est dei uoluntas".*'

26 *Met.* I. 8, p. 26: '*Vis itaque originaliter indita cuique, ex qua opus aut aptitudo procedit, natura quidem est sed creata.*'

27 *Met.* I. 8, pp. 25–7.

28 T. Gregory, 'Considérations sur ratio et natura chez Abelard', in R. Louis and J. Jolivet (eds), *Pierre Abelard et Pierre le Vénérable: Les courants philosophiques, littéraires et artistiques en Occident au milieu du XIIe siècle* (Paris: CNRS, 1975), pp. 569–84 (p. 576).

29 *Met.* I. 8, p. 26: '*Item principium motus secundum se a Deo habuisse initium, nec Aristotilem negaturum credo.*'

30 Quoted in Dales, 'A Twelfth-Century Concept of the Natural Order', p. 183.

31 Quoted in Gregory, 'Considérations sur ratio et natura chez Abelard', p. 574. Gregory notes the Boethian aspect of this definition. See J. Marenbon, *The Philosophy of Peter Abelard* (Cambridge: Cambridge University Press, 1997), pp. 125–7.

32 Cf. Marenbon, *Philosophy of Peter Abelard*, pp. 178–9.

33 *Met.* I.11, pp. 29–31.

34 *Pol.* VI. 19; 2, p. 58.

35 Epstein, *Medieval Discovery of Nature*, pp. 4–39.

36 Epstein, *Medieval Discovery of Nature*, pp. 10, 26.

37 *Entheticus*, 597–608, p. 145.

38 John claims that both Cicero and Plato would agree that 'life should imitate nature': *Pol.* VI. 21; 2, pp. 59–60.

39 Seneca, *De beneficiis*, IV. 7, pp. 216–17: '*Quid enim aliud est natura quam deus et divina ratio toti mundo partibusque eius inserta?*'

40 Seneca, *Naturales quaestiones*, trans. T. H. Corcoran (2 vols, LCL 450, 457; Cambridge, MA: Harvard University Press, 1971–72), VII. 2. The power of nature is also illustrated in I. Pref. 1, p. 3.

41 Seneca, *Ad Lucilium Epistulae Morales*, trans. R. M. Gummere, (2 vols, LCL 75, 76; Cambridge, MA: Harvard University Press, 1917–20), *Ep.* 41.9; 1, pp. 276–9: *Consummatur itaque bonum eius, si id inplevit, cui nascitur. Quid est autem, quod ab illo ratio haec exigat? Rem facillimam, secundum naturam suam vivere.*'

42 Seneca, *Naturales quaestiones*, III. 29; 1, pp. 228–89: '*sive animal est mundus, sive corpus natura gubernabile, ut arbores, ut sata, ab initio eius usque ad exitum quicquid facere quicquid pati debeat, inclusum est.*'

43 Augustine, *City of God: Concerning the City of God against the Pagans*, trans. H. Bettenson (Harmondsworth: Penguin, 1984), XII. 5, p. 477: 'No existence

which came from nothing can claim to be equal to him; nothing could exist in any way, if it had not been created by him.' See M. C. Horowitz, *Seeds of Virtue and Knowledge* (Princeton: Princeton University Press, 1998), pp. 49–51.

44 For other twelfth-century applications of this Augustinian idea see H. Häring, 'The Creation and Creator of the World according to Thierry of Chartres and Clarembaldus of Arras', *Archives d'histoire doctrinale et littéraires du Moyen Âge*, 22 (1955), 137–216 (205–8). The distinction between the Augustinian perspective and that of the Chartrian scholars is drawn out in Gregory, 'La nouvelle idée de nature', pp. 212–13.

45 *Pol.* II. 12; 1, p. 86: '*Et quidem sapientia Dei et bonitas, quae rebus omnibus originem praebet, natura rectissime appellatur; contra quam utique nihil fit, quia dispositionem Dei nihil euacuat, aut causas quae in mente illius, qui fecit celos in intellectu, ab eterno constiterunt, suo priuat effectu.*' Cf. Proverbs 3:19–20. Cf. *Met.* I. 8, pp. 27–9; Victorinus, *Explanationes*, p. 109.

46 *Pol.* II. 12; 1, p. 86: '*Insunt itaque rebus seminales euentuum causae et originariae rationes, quae praeordinato tempore in suos procedunt effectus, ex eo quidem mirabiles, non quod nullas sed quod occultissimas habeant rationes.*'

47 Spanneut, *Permanence du Stoïcisme*, p. 184 describes it as 'la définition stoïcienne adapté à une thèse créationniste'.

48 *Pol.* II. 11; 1, p. 85: '*naturae legibus minime subiacebunt, dum tamen naturam hic ... dicamus solitum cursum rerum, aut causas occultas euentuum, quarum ratio reddi potest*'.

49 Augustine, *City of God*, XXI. 8, p. 980.

50 *Pol.* II. 12; 1, p. 86.

51 Horowitz, *Seeds of Virtue and Knowledge*, pp. 49–51.

52 For the relationship between John's understanding of nature and his views on 'universals' see B. Hendley, 'John of Salisbury and the Problem of Universals', *Journal of the History of Philosophy*, 8 (1970), 289–302 (especially 295–8).

53 *Pol.* II. 18; 1, p. 105: '*Quod igitur sensus percipit, formisque subiectum est, singularis et prima substantia est. Id uero sine quo illa nec esse nec intelligi potest, ei substantiale est, et plerumque secunda substantia nominatur.*'

54 *Pol.* II. 18; 1, p. 104: '*Diffinit ergo ratio quod concipit intellectus*'.

55 *Pol.* II. 18; 1, p. 105: '*Quod forte facilius in intellectu quam in natura rerum poterit inueniri, in quo genera et species, differentias propria et accidentia, quae uniuersaliter dicuntur, planum est inuenire, cum in actu rerum subsistentiam uniuersalium quaerere exiguus fructus sit et labor infinitus, in mente uero utiliter et facillime reperiuntur.*'

56 *Pol.* II. 18; 1, pp. 105–6: '*Sin autem detracta specie, eam quasi formarum exuit uestimento, acumen quidem suum exercet, et rerum naturam, quid scilicet in se, quid in aliis sint, liberius et fidelius contemplatur, dum rerum substantiam, quantitatem, ad aliquid, qualitatem, situm esse, ubi, quando, habere, facere, pati, singillatim discutit et discernit.*' John uses Aristotle's list of ten categories to facilitate classification by genus or species, distinguishing between what is essential and what is accidental.

57 *Met.* IV. 16, p. 154: '*Hominis uero spiritus quoniam a Deo datus et ad Deum rediturus est, solus diuina meditatur*'.
58 *Met.* IV. 16, p. 154: '*Ratio est quaedam pars diuini spiritus humanis immersa corporibus.*'
59 Lapidge, 'The Stoic Inheritance', p. 110. See Coleman, *Ancient and Medieval Memories*, p. 56, for the distinction between the Ciceronian and Senecan positions: Cicero supports the Platonic idea of the soul outside the body, rather than the Stoic and Aristotelian position which suggests that that soul is trapped in the body. Seneca, *Ep.* 66 speaks of the soul as part of divinity (*pneuma*) in the body of man.
60 *Met.* IV. 16, p. 154: '*Licet enim ratio quodam modo uirtus diuina sit, nequaquam tamen pars eius est, qui absolutissimae simplicitatis est.*'
61 Seneca, *Ep.* 65.2; 65.12; 1, p. 450: '*Quaerimus, quid sit causa? Ratio scilicet faciens, id est deus.*'
62 *Met.* II. 20, p. 93: '*Quodam enim modo per materiam existit forma, sicut discernitur materia ipsa per formam.*'
63 Contrary to Lapidge, 'The Stoic Inheritance', p. 106. Lapidge sees John's threefold identification of the parts of existence as an 'error' for which 'certainly there is no excuse'.
64 *Met.* IV. 35, pp. 173-4.
65 *Entheticus*, 1037-8, pp. 172-3: '*Quod vere simplex, nullo motu variatur, non antiquatur tempore, semper idem.*'
66 Seneca, *Ep.* 76.10; 2, p. 152: '*Quid in homine proprium? Ratio. ... Haec ratio perfecta virtus vocatur eademque honestum est.*' See also 76.15 and 76.16.
67 Seneca, *Naturales quaestiones*, I. Pref.; I.14, pp. 11-13: '*Quid ergo interest inter naturam dei et nostram? Nostri melior pars animus est, in illo nulla pars extra animum est. Totius est ratio.*' See also III. 15.1, p. 233, on the relationship between nature in the world and the systems of the body.
68 *Met.* IV. 17, p. 155: '*ratio origine diuina nobilitetur*'.
69 *Met.* IV. 17, p. 155: '*Et quia sensuum examinatrix est qui ob fallendi consuetudinem possunt esse suspecti, natura optima parens omnium uniuersos sensus locans in capite, uelet quendam senatum in Capitolio animae rationem quasi dominam in arce capitis statuit, mediam quidem sedem tribuens inter cellam phantasticam et memorialem, ut uelut e specula sensuum et imaginationum possit examinare iudicia.*'
70 *Pol.* III. 1; 1, p. 171: '*Dum ergo totum uiuit, ad eam totum disponitur, quae se non per partes infundit partibus, sed tota est et operatur in uniuersis et singulis.*'
71 *Met.* IV. 20, p. 158. John refers to *Tusculanae disputationes*, I. 28-9, 70-1.
72 *Pol.* III. 1; 1, p. 173: '*Porro scientiae thesaurus nobis duobus modis exponitur; cum aut rationis exercitio quod sciri potest intellectus inuenit ... Quodque magis mirere, quilibet quasi quendam librum sciendorum officio rationis apertum gerit in corde.*'
73 *Met.* IV. 16, p. 154: '*Porro ratio transcendit omnem sensum, et iudicium suum, etiam incorporalibus et spirtualibus rebus immergit.*'

74 *Met.* IV. 31, p. 168. John refers to '*uis spiritualis naturae rerum examinatrix*' and to a '*primitiua ratio*'.
75 *Met.* IV. 31, p. 168: '*Quae quidem spera imago quaedam uidebatur, ideaque mundi.*'
76 *Met.* I. 11, p. 30: '*Ratio ... animi uis est*'.
77 *Pol.* III. 1; 1, p. 173: '*aut quod absconditum est reuelans gratia oculis ingerens patefacit*'.
78 John's ideas on the relationship between grace and nature are explored and compared with those of Augustine and Ambrose in Sønnesyn, 'The Ethics of John of Salisbury', pp. 321–30.
79 *Pol.* III. 1; 1, p. 173. '*Sic utique aut per naturam aut per gratiam ad ueritatis agnitionem et scientiam eorum quae necessaria sunt unusquisque potest accedere.*'
80 See D. Sedley, 'The Stoic Theory of Universals', *Southern Journal of Philosophy*, 23 (1985), 87–92 (89), on the implications of such an interpretation in Stoic thought. M. Wilks, 'John of Salisbury and the Tyranny of Nonsense', in Wilks (ed.), *World*, pp. 263–86 (pp. 268–9).
81 *Met.* II. 20, p. 85.
82 *Met.* IV. 18, p. 156: '*Nam intellectus assequitur quod ratio inuestigat.*'
83 Hendley, 'John of Salisbury and the Problem of Universals', p. 298.
84 *Met.* IV. 31, p. 168.
85 For an analysis of John's scepticism see Grellard, *Jean de Salisbury*.
86 *Met.* IV. 38, p. 178: '*diuina ratio immutabilis substantia est*'.
87 *Met.* IV. 37, p. 177: '*Memoria namque eius, aut uerbum, siue ratio, sapientia ipsius est.*'
88 R. Sorabji, 'Stoic First Movements in Christianity', in K. Strange and J. Zupko (eds), *Stoicism: Traditions and Transformations* (Cambridge: Cambridge University Press, 2004), pp. 95–107 (pp. 97–8). Seneca, *De ira*, II. 2–4, trans. in Sorabji, 'Stoic First Movements', pp. 95–6.
89 R. Sorabji, *Emotion and Peace of Mind: From Stoic Agitation to Christian Temptation* (Oxford: Oxford University Press, 2000), pp. 8, 343–56; Sorabji, 'Stoic First Movements', p. 99. For scriptural influences on Rufinus's misinterpretation see Mark 7:21, Matthew 15:19.
90 Sorabji, 'Stoic First Movements', pp. 104–6; Sorabji, *Emotion and Peace of Mind*, pp. 375–84.
91 Augustine, *City of God*, IX. 4, pp. 343–8; S. Rigby, 'Worthy but Wise? Virtuous and Non-Virtuous Forms of Courage in the Later Middle Ages', *Studies in the Age of Chaucer*, 35 (2013), 329–71 (345–6).
92 *Pol.* VII. 3; 2, p. 100: '*Illis autem ex magna parte in sententiam sedit timori locum non esse in animo sapientis, cum omnia ex necessitate proueniant stultumque sit timere quod uitari non potest, et e contra unicum sit remedium ut uir prudens fortitudinis uires praeparet et robore patientiae quasi solidissimo animi inuicti clipeo omnia tela necessitaties excipiat.*'
93 Seneca, *Naturales quaestiones*, II. 59.3; 1, pp. 192–3: '*Invicti esse possumus, inconcussi non possumus.*'
94 *Pol.* VII. 3; 2, p. 101: '*Hoc enim esse uolunt in potestate idque interesse censent inter*

*animum sapientis et stulti, quod stultus consensu mentis passionibus cedit; sapiens autem, licet eas nececessitate patiatur, retinet tamen de rationabiliter appetendis uel fugiendis ueram et firmam inconcussa mente sententiam.*' Cf. Augustine, *City of God*, IX. 4, p. 347.
95 *Pol.* VII. 3; 2, p. 101: *'Siquidem scriptum est quia initium sapientiae et finis modestiae timor Domini.'*
96 *Pol.* I. 4; 1, p. 33: *'Opus etenim non ex se sed ex causa fit crimen. Nec aliqua uirtutis ostentatione clarescit, cui uoluptas originem praebet'.*
97 *Pol.* V. 9; 1, p. 321: *'Hoc utique praetermittitur quod nec opere nec uoluntate impletur. Quicquid enim uis et non potes, factum Deus reputat, eo quod uoluntas plena totius operis mercedem consequitur.'*
98 *Pol.* III. 6; 1, p. 185. See Cicero, *De officiis*, trans. W. Miller (LCL 30; Cambridge, MA: Harvard University Press, 1913), I. 23, p. 24: *'Ex quo, quamquam hoc videbitur fortasse cuipiam durius, tamen audeamus imitari Stoicos, qui studiose exquirunt, unde verba sint ducta, credamusque, quia fiat, quod dictum est, appellatam fidem.*' Cf. *Pol.* III. 9.
99 *Pol.* VIII. 6; 1, p. 253.
100 Peter Lombard, *Commentaria in Ezechielem*, I. 1, PL 25, 22.
101 Peter Lombard, *Sententiae*, 2.39.3.
102 T. C. Potts, *Conscience in Medieval Philosophy* (Cambridge: Cambridge University Press, 1980), p. 96.

# 3

# Defining duties: the cooperative model of the polity

If, for John, 'following nature' has a normative role in how human sociability is best ensured – aided in this respect by the combined forces of grace and reason – then a key part of living according to nature is the responsibility it enjoins on man to carry out reciprocal services to others. This system of enacting duties is carefully calibrated in John's works, with every individual being obliged to carry out duties which are appropriate to their status within the polity. This theory of reciprocal political obligation underpins the relational model of the body politic sketched out in Book V of the *Policraticus*, a model that is informed by classical and Christian precedent. Indeed, the importance of the appropriate division of duties is clear from the prominence given to it in the opening chapters of the *Policraticus*. In Book I. 2, John draws a distinction between the derivation of certain obligations from nature, and those obligations that derive from one's duty. Obedience to natural law is a type of duty but, generally speaking, obligations that derive from duties are only applicable to certain individuals, whereas nature's prescriptions are applicable to all.[1] However, as John proceeds to demonstrate, many duties ultimately derive from natural conventions, and so extend beyond the sphere of personal concern. Book I. 3 demonstrates that such a position has its precedent among the 'philosophers' who recommend that everyone should be 'content with their own activities and interests', while – on both the level of the individual and that of the community – everyone should be solicitous of the requirements of public utility.

John refers here to the 'philosophers' and, as further investigation will show, his theory of duties is heavily dependent on classical ideas, particularly those of the Roman Stoics, transmitted to John through Cicero and Seneca. Most notably, as this chapter will demonstrate, John adapts a significant guiding principle from the Stoics for a Christian audience: that is, *oikeiôsis*. This term – essentially untranslatable from the Greek – is defined by Julia Annas as 'the tendency we have both towards developing self-concern and towards developing other-concern'.[2] According to Stoic theory, humans have a tendency to extend their initial feelings of self-preservation (common to animals and pre-rational humans) to care for others, as their sense of reason develops. By this account, correct actions are those that tend towards self-preservation and then extend to the preservation of others and, in their broadest conception, to the social whole. The virtuous individual will seek out such actions, choosing them on rational and altruistic grounds. *Oikeiôsis* is a process, therefore, by which the individual learns to distinguish between what is *oikeion* (appropriate, familiar or belonging to him) and what is *allotrion* (alien) and prefer the first. This is the basis of a binary division by which all societal goods and impulses can be classed. As Gretchen Reydams-Schils notes, a distinctive feature of the Roman adaptation of Greek Stoicism is its emphasis on social responsibility.[3] While the community was conceived by the Stoics to include gods and men, it started with the individual. Indeed, the term *oikeiôsis* itself derives from '*oikos*', the 'household' – the basic social unit. As the first step, self-preservation, is a natural impulse innate from birth, the progressive widening of the rational self's duty to care for others is also a natural impulse. It is, in the truest sense, the basis of living by nature and endearing oneself to all that is appropriate in nature. Gerard Vérbeke pointed out that the selective function of *oikeiôsis* also serves a role in the works of Aquinas, where it forms a basis for the development of his take on *synderesis*, discernment through reason.[4] John of Salisbury, however, provides an even earlier example of the coherent application of this Stoic concept.

## The Roman adaptation of *oikeiôsis*

In order to demonstrate that the exercise of appropriate duties in John's writings plays a role similar to that in Stoicism, we must examine the sources of this concept in more detail. It is important to acknowledge that the medieval process of assimilation of ideas about *oikeiôsis* is a complex one because of their reiteration in different contexts – Greek, Roman and Christian. On account of its Latinity, medieval uses of Stoicism were heavily dependent on the Romano-Christian tradition, while later appropriations would depend more heavily on the Graeco-tradition.[5] As noted, *oikeiôsis* in the Roman tradition places a special emphasis on social relations and their exercise in the community, emphasising the connection between parts of that community and its whole.[6] John of Salisbury's account of relationships within the body politic echoes this aspect of Roman theories of *oikeiôsis*; but which classical accounts of *oikeiôsis* were readily available to him in the twelfth century?

The most thorough account of the Roman Stoic process of *oikeiôsis* is found in Cicero's *De finibus bonorum et malorum*. Writing in *De finibus*, Cicero says: 'a living creature feels an attachment for itself, and an impulse to preserve itself and to feel affection for its own constitution and for those things which tend to preserve that constitution. ... This leads to the conclusion that it is love of self which supplies the primary impulse to action.'[7] A significant feature of Cicero's account is the focus it places on *oikeiôsis* as a 'developmental' process. Using Cato as a mouthpiece, Cicero explains how the primary basis of *oikeiôsis* is 'life in harmony with nature'. Nature provides the impulse for parental love of offspring – 'we derive from nature herself the impulse to love those to whom we have given birth' – and this concern for others then extends to all of society: 'parental affection is the source to which we trace the origin of the association of the human race in communities'.[8] The discussion in *De finibus*, III. 62, expresses the naturalness of society by referring to a metaphor of the body: the procreation of children is accommodated by the 'conformation of the body and its members'.[9] Just as 'some parts of the body, such as the eyes and the ears, are created as it were for their own sakes, while others like the legs or the hands also subserve the utility of the rest of the members', so too humans are designed to serve each other in bonds of mutual aid: 'it follows that we are by nature fitted to form unions, societies and states'.[10]

Throughout the discussion in *De finibus*, Cicero connects the development of *oikeiôsis* to the practice of 'appropriate acts' – translated from the Greek, *kathêkon*, to the Latin, *officium*: 'the first "appropriate act" (for so I render the Greek *kathêkon*) is to preserve oneself in one's natural constitution'.[11] With the attainment of wisdom, the Stoic sage will then be able to perform *katorthômata*, which Cicero translates as '*recte facta*'.[12] Such perfect actions will be performed with a deliberate intention to follow nature, resulting from a stable personal disposition.[13] *Kathêkonta*, or *officia*, span the whole range of acts by the wise man and the non-wise man; they are inclusive categories that include *katorthômata*.[14] An *officium* is an act-type that is neither good nor bad, but a particular *officium* will be materially good or bad depending on whether or not it is in conformity with nature.[15] If an act is both in conformity with nature and intentionally performed by a rational agent who aims towards such a conformity with nature, then it is a perfect *officium*: an action approximating a *recte factum*, a *katorthôma*.

The connection between the correct exercise of duties, reason and nature inherent in the idea of *oikeiôsis* is at the root of the Stoic assertion that 'living in accordance with nature' can be connected with 'choosing what is in accordance with nature'.[16] Thus, not only does *oikeiôsis* serve to provide the motivational basis for performing *officia* (that is, it is connected with a primary impulse of self-preservation), but it also links with a secondary 'objective' standard: attaining homology with nature. The acquisition of reason is, therefore, at the root of altruism. A rational person will self-reflectively notice that he has been caring for other beings all along because they 'belonged to him', but now that he is rational, every other thing that is rational will also 'belong to him'.[17] In viewing it as a normative determinant against which the content of duties can be evaluated, we move from the first element of *oikeiôsis* to its second element, from 'self-concern' to 'other-concern'.

As noted, Cicero translates the Greek terms *kathêkonta* and *katorthômata* as '*officia*' and '*recte facta*' respectively. Translating the Greek vocabulary of *oikeiôsis* and its related terms proved a challenge, then as now, but one that permitted a certain flexibility of interpretation. In some cases, the transliteration was straightforward; for example, '*allotrion*' is translated in the Latin tradition as '*alienum*'. '*Oikeiôsis*' was translated by Cicero as '*commendatio*' or '*conciliatio*', words which, while not direct translations of the term, have a similar personal quality.[18] Translations could be more flexible, however, and were often less technical.[19] In the case of the translation of '*kathêkonta*' as '*officia*', for example, such flexibility extended the potential application of the term. As Brunt points out: 'In common speech *officium* could mean both the kind of service which social conventions expected one man to render another, and the function of a magistrate, for example, or a senator. Its use in ethical theory suggested that such services and functions constituted moral obligations.'[20] Therefore, Cicero conflates the theoretical actions that can be performed in conformity with nature with the actual roles performed by people in political society, thereby connecting following nature with the performance of the duties appropriate to one's social position.

Although *De finibus* contains Cicero's most detailed discussion of *oikeiôsis*, the state of its manuscript transmission makes it unlikely that John of Salisbury had access to the text. Webb credited John with a number of quotations and allusions to *De finibus*, but it is likely that these echoes come from other intermediary sources, or are simply commonplaces.[21] However, other sources served perfectly well as conduits for the transmission of the theory of *oikeiôsis* and its associated implications for the performance of duties. For example, much of the material regarding the developmental nature of *oikeiôsis* expressed in *De finibus* can also be found in *De officiis*, Cicero's text on duties. Here virtuous living in accordance with nature is founded on the bonds of affection that develop between man, 'a sharer in reason', and his fellows:

> From the beginning nature has assigned to every type of creature the tendency to preserve itself, its life and body, and to reject anything that seems likely to harm them, seeking and procuring everything necessary for life, such as nourishment, shelter and so on. Common also to all animals is the impulse to unite for the purpose of procreation, and a certain care for those that are born.[22]

Cicero explains that the first obligations of this theory of care are towards one's family, but extend towards others:

> It [Nature] drives him to desire that men should meet together and congregate, and that he should join them himself; and for the same reason to devote himself to providing whatever may contribute to the comfort and sustenance not only of himself, but also of his wife, his children, and others whom he holds dear and ought to protect.[23]

The degrees of extension of care are carefully calibrated in *De officiis*, where they are an element of Cicero's two-part definition of justice. Justice involves, first, not doing harm to another, unless motivated by a wrongful action, and secondly 'that one should treat common goods as common and private ones as one's own'. These are the basis of 'the fellowship of men' and the rational foundation of the community.[24] Justice is inherently linked to *oikeiôsis* (expressed by Cicero here as '*commendatio*'); each person will wish to endear himself to others, not because this is intrinsically rational, but because it is the best possible manner to ensure the good of the political community. Correct exercise of duties in extending care from one's family to others can lead to reverence from other members of the polity, as expressed by Cicero in *De officiis*, II. 46:

> One wins commendation primarily, then, for modesty, along with reverence for parents and goodwill to one's family and friends. Young men become known most easily, however, and in the best way, by attaching themselves to such famous and wise men as concern themselves with the good of the political community. By associating with such as these,

they will inspire in the people the belief that they too will become like those whom they have chosen to imitate.[25]

*De officiis* even offers a discussion of the vocabulary of duties, whether 'middle' or 'complete':

> For a duty can be called either 'middle' or 'complete'. 'Complete' duty we may, I think, label 'right', as the Greeks call it *katorthôma*; while the duty that is shared they call *kathêkon*. They give their definitions in such a way as to define complete duty as what is right; while middle duty, they say, is that for which a persuasive reason can be given as to why it has been done.[26]

It is clear from this excursus that sufficient material to reconstruct Cicero's views on *oikeiôsis*, the validation of life in a community dependent on a shared notion of natural duties, was available in *De officiis*, a text we know that John had access to and used.

### Appropriate duties in the writings of John of Salisbury

John's application of the idea of *oikeiôsis* can be demonstrated in two ways: first, through his explicit use of its Latinised vocabulary; secondly, through its implicit echo in his discussion of duties, which he considers to be rationally underpinned by the extension of self-care. With regard to the first point, John does not refer to the specific terms used by Cicero to express *oikeiôsis*: *commendatio* and *conciliatio*. Instead, he refers to the opposite of what is *oikeion*: what is *allotrion*, Latinised as *alienum*. In *Policraticus*, Book I. 2, *alienum* is defined as 'that which does not follow from the principles of nature or duty'.[27] John means this in the sense of something that is contrary to what is appropriate, familiar or belonging to man, as is clear from the subsequent discussion.[28] He points out that 'natural law' is a part of duty. Any violation of the laws of nature ('the mother of all') can, therefore, be compared with parricide: those who defy the laws of their parents commit a 'sacrilege'. By creating a parallel between respect for one's parents and respect for natural law, John situates the latter in the context of the familial bonds upon which society depends. He proceeds to comment that in certain cases 'moderate humour' and a concern for what is 'useful' (rather than, presumably, what is honourable) are not contrary to nature, as long as no one is harmed by the act. However, that which is truly *alienum* will always be in conflict with either the demands of duty or those of nature, and is classed as an 'error or a crime'.[29]

John pursues this theme further in Book I of the *Policraticus*, distinguishing between the common obligations resulting from natural concern for oneself (the first manifestation of *oikeiôsis*) and those that result from the extension of rational self-concern to others (the exercise of *officia* in the social and political context). If an act is committed purely for the purposes of pleasure or necessity it is a violation of duty and nature: an act is good only if it is primarily aimed at following nature through the proper exercise of reason, even if it contains a component of self-gratification. Intention plays an important role: 'Another reason why an act can be decorous, whether it comes to a stop by necessity, or thrives through utility, or shines out through honour, is when the entire being of the deed is capable of being coloured by the intention of the mind.'[30] A similar emphasis on the role of intention in validating an activity is shown in his discussions of gambling (I. 5), music (1.6) and acting (I. 8). Indeed, the question of what constitutes an appropriate act is a constant preoccupation of Book I of the *Policraticus*. Although John does not use Cicero's positive vocabulary of *oikeiôsis*, he is clearly concerned with the rational motivations that underpin the exercise of duties.

As noted, one of the key features of the Roman presentation of *oikeiôsis* was the emphasis placed on social responsibility; one extended care of self to care for the community, broadly defined. Following the discussion of what is *alienum*, John proceeds to discuss the distribution of duties. John refers to the 'pagan philosophers' who considered that the *res publica hominum* functioned best when everyone, whether a city- or country-dweller, was content with his own belongings and pursuits. In this fashion, one and all were concerned for the utility of the polity. John presents an intriguingly meritocratic account of the distribution of property, which is to be divided according to the worth ('*ex merito*') of each person and safeguarded by '*caritas*', which ensures that no one appropriates the goods of others.[31] Kate Langdon Forhan posited that John's discussion of 'what could be termed *alienum*' set the scene for a possible conflict between the norm of natural law and obedience to natural duties, suggesting that John implies a 'separation of legality from morality' as 'it is within the context of *self*-knowledge and *self*-betrayal that the differences between obedience to duty and obedience to natural law are indicated'.[32] However, even if the Ciceronian definition of justice, 'to each his due', is calculated in material terms on the basis of one's worth and the fruit of one's industry, it is not solely a matter of the dry application of legal measure. Instead, *caritas* and bonds of affection between members of the political community are presented as correctives to the unjust distribution of goods. One's sense of self is necessarily linked to one's care of others within the community, when seen through the lens of the development of *oikeiôsis*. Conceptualising John's comments on what is *alienum* within the context of a broader discussion of what constitutes appropriate duties demonstrates that there cannot be a disjunction between individual duty and the exercise of natural law in his mind. Rather the opposite is the case; each guarantees the other. Just distribution rests, therefore, on the appropriate exercise of one's duties in the political system in a manner commensurate with one's specific function and role.

In Book V of the *Policraticus*, John develops the idea of duty further, linking the idea of *officia* as duty and *officia* as expressive of one's political role.[33] Referring to Cicero, John points out that we are obliged to honour our parents and those related to us, a precept followed by all nations, and one that also had precedent in the biblical commandments. John asserts that this is a natural impulse: children honour their parents, and when a man leaves his parents for a wife he and she become 'one flesh', and so are also motivated to honour each other. John notes that this is mandated by divine writings, but that such a mandate is hardly necessary, considering the strength of nature's motivation in enjoining man to honour his relations and acquaintances.[34] In line with the developmental aspect of Stoic *oikeiôsis*, John regards the first impulse supplied by nature as concern for one's bloodline, a concern that is then extended to others. John deliberately under-emphasises the role of divine law in this instance and implies that following nature is a sufficient guide in this case, a point reinforced in Book III of the *Policraticus*, where John demonstrates the power of bonds of affection: 'Affection is the more effective bond because it approaches what is familiar to nature, and whatever is joined by the knot of affection is united to the soul.'[35] It is worth noting that while this account focuses on Cicero as the source for John's Stoic interpretation of *oikeiôsis*, John could also have accessed some of these Stoic sentiments from other sources, notably Seneca's letters, which also provide an account of the development of the community of reason and the necessity to love one's neighbour.[36] What all these examples illustrate is that John borrowed not only some of the vocabulary of *officia* from his Roman sources, but also the philosophical doctrines upon which they depended.

His perspective on the reciprocal performance of duties is one of the main features of John's political theory that can be described as 'communitarian'. Communitarianism posits that the self is 'embedded' in the community: the community plays a vital role in shaping personal identity, values and purpose. Rejecting the individualist premises of liberalism, modern communitarians place emphasis on how humans enact their political roles in their social, cultural and historical context.[37] Communitarians also posit that the community should be intrinsically valorised, and that solidarity is a normative good that should be actively sought within political life. Communitarianism, although a broad church, fundamentally recommends that considerations of the 'common good' should motivate political life, although agreement on what this common good consists of is more challenging to reach. Writing in 1992, Cary Nederman described John as contributing to this tradition by exemplifying what he termed 'communal functionalism': 'the claim that the community is, in the first instance, composed neither of individuals nor of citizens but, rather of functional groupings or parts, arranged according to the nature of their contribution to the communal whole'. Nederman based his discussion upon an analysis of John's model of the body politic, which he described as 'the expression of a principle of cooperative harmony', noting John's references to the 'utility of all', 'public utility' and 'public advantage'.[38] Nederman correctly notes that the practice of justice motivates such cooperation, but suggests that each part of the polity is morally autonomous in choosing and acting upon the correct course, thus emphasising the role liberty plays in John's thinking. What is proposed here, instead, is that John's sense of liberty is a necessarily limited one, constrained by the fact that humans are obliged to feel a sense of duties towards one another, a sense that is not exclusively a matter of will, but develops naturally through the growth of a rational capacity to recognise that the good of the self is best achieved through respecting the good of all. Nederman regards Aristotle as the principal source for John's account of the 'common good' as a necessary feature of public life.[39] As this account shows, however, an alternative inspiration for his views must considered: John's appropriation of Stoic ideas of *oikeiôsis* offers a rational explanation for agreement upon, and action in coherence with, the common good.

## The Christian contribution

John proceeds to define duties in Book V. 4, investigating the means by which office holders become worthy of reverence. Duties are imposed on the individual '*ex institutis aut moribus*', by law or moral custom. Some duties are public, and some are private (pertaining to the private status of individuals). John notes that there are almost as many private duties as there are different types of person; meanwhile, those who exercise public duties will obtain reverence in proportion to the eminence of their role. Public duties are of two varieties: those that are decreed by divine law, and those that come from human law, a division that John claims derives 'from books of offices', noting that as well as being discussed in ethical writings, duties are also a subject of canonists and lawyers.[40] This implies that John is not solely dependent on Roman sources in his conceptualisation of duties, but draws on Christian ones too. As Thomas Osborne notes, medieval Christians were eudaimonistic in their ethical perspective; virtuous behaviour maximised the good of the individual.[41] Even so, a preference for the common good does not involve the sacrifice of the individual's good, as this is considered to be concomitant with the common good.[42] Thus, John's use of Christian sources in his account of duties should come as no surprise. Indeed, concern for others, expressed in Christian terms as *caritas*, is fundamentally linked with concern for oneself; this inspires each person to commend themselves to others, a view also evident in the epistles of Paul.[43]

The debt John owes to Christian sources in formulating how concern with oneself is linked with concern for others is clear from his discussion of the relationship between self-knowledge and the exercise of duties. All wisdom is dependent on self-knowledge, a perspective John may have borrowed from the writings of Bernard of Clairvaux: 'The first task of a man aspiring to wisdom is the consideration of what he himself is: what is within him, what without, what below, what above, what opposite, what before and what after.'[44] Self-knowledge is at the root of one's capacity to properly perform duties; this philosophical (rational) contemplation, available only to the rational being, 'bears fourfold fruit: benefit to self, charity for those close to one, contempt for the world, love of God'.[45] John further develops the relationship between self-knowledge and the exercise of duties in *Policraticus*, Book III. 1, where he points out that the truth of all things that are necessary can be accessed through either nature or grace. Awareness of duties is carried in a 'book of knowledge' in one's heart; nature and grace, as demonstrated in Chapter 2, provide access to its contents. John connects the resultant knowledge with the best interests of the polity: 'Therefore the recognition of truth and the cultivation of virtue is the general and universal safeguard of the individual, of the polity and of rational nature.'[46] Indeed, in Book VIII. 5 of the *Policraticus*, John describes how the desire for self-advancement is balanced by the love of justice, the first being a matter of necessity and the second being a matter of will. While the love of justice (described by John as acting as a soldier for charity) does not have bounds, seeking, as it does, that which is of God, the love of self-advancement needs to be made subservient to utility.

Good character, according to John, must involve a person doing for another what he would want done for himself, and refraining from doing to another what he would not have done to himself (Matthew 7:12; Luke 6:31).[47] From this comes 'love of freedom, love of country and, finally, love of those outside it'.[48] This closely echoes the developmental aspect of *oikeiôsis*, already familiar from the Stoic tradition.

However, John regards this as motivated not only by rationality, but by the Christian virtue of *caritas*, charity, writing: 'For he cannot fail to love freedom if he loves himself and his country and, by degree, those outside it, as whosoever loves his neighbour with sincere charity does, since, indeed, *caritas ordinata* consists in this.'[49] The term '*caritas ordinata*' was coined by Augustine in *De doctrina christiana*, and derived from Song of Songs 2:4, '*ordinavit in me caritatem*'. In I. 3–40 of *De doctrina christiana*, Augustine discusses how one can 'use' other people. They are correctly used when they are loved for God's sake, but incorrectly used when exploited for earthly or temporal ends. Correct use requires '*caritas ordinata*', that is, love that is properly directed towards appropriate ends.[50] Written in the mid-twelfth century, the *Summa decretorum* of Rufinus suggested that proximity, extending from the familial circle to incorporate strangers, was a guide to the appropriate exercise of charity. Rufinus described this system of discrimination as '*caritas ordinata*'.[51] Therefore, the notion of charity as a duty-system constructed on the basis of associative bonds was a familiar idea in medieval Christian writings. Indeed, the *Glossa ordinaria* on the *Decretum* would propose a hybrid scale of merit based in part on one's virtue and in part on one's relational proximity to the giver.[52] These examples demonstrate that in Christianising Stoic principles governing the performance of duties, John was inspired by contemporary discourse on Christian *caritas*.[53] Like Augustine, John sees justice as defined not only in Ciceronian terms of giving to each their due, but also as founded on the Christological precept of not doing to one's neighbour what one would not have done to oneself.[54]

## Ambrose's *De officiis ministrorum*

An important potential source for the Christian reformulation of Roman *officia* is Ambrose's *De officiis ministrorum*; indeed, this may have been among the volumes in John's mind when he referred to 'books of offices'. This text, strongly dependent on Cicero's *De officiis*, offers a discussion of two important aspects of the theory of *officia*, namely a distinction between 'perfect' and 'middle' duties and an account of the relationship between the exercise of appropriate duties and mechanisms of societal bonding. Furthermore, Ambrose provides a rationale for the consideration of *officia* by Christian thinkers, referring to the *officium* of Zacharias the priest, as described in Scripture.[55] Ambrose, drawing on Cicero, distinguishes between what he terms '*media officia*' and '*perfecta officia*', and provides a scriptural justification for this distinction, that is, Jesus' advice to the young man who wished to attain eternal life (Matthew 19:16-30). Ambrose identifies the '*media officia*' as consisting simply in observance of the commandments, duties 'in which there is something lacking'. In addition to telling him to follow the commandments, Jesus also advised the young man to give up his possessions and become a disciple. The total rejection of externals in pursuit of a life of virtue is described by Ambrose as a 'perfect duty', one which 'sets right any duties which may have fallen short of the mark in one way or another', what is 'called by the Greeks *katorthôma*'.[56]

Implicit in Ambrose's distinction is the idea that very few are able to achieve a lifestyle conducive to the exercise of perfect duties; this is akin to the Stoic idea that very few people are capable of achieving the status of the sage. By implying that the pursuit of perfect duty is a 'vocation for a select group who have consecrated themselves completely to the service of God's church', Ambrose, as Davidson has suggested, transforms the 'Panaetian-Ciceronian casuistry ... into a Christian ethic of a two-tier spiritual calling'. The result is that 'by making perfection the only acceptable standard for his men, and by presenting God and the eschaton, not the human consensus and this world, as the real reference points, A[mbrose] ends up obliterating the Ciceronian notion of "middle" duty as an appropriate measure of moral achievement for a spiritual elite'.[57] John's account of the difference between public and private duties operates in a similar fashion to Ambrose's distinction between 'middle' and 'perfect' duties, which are transposed in John's version to a politico-social setting. Just as Ambrose implies that the real challenge is not simply observance of the commandments, but a total surrender to a life of virtue, so too John describes private duties as a second-order obligation when compared with public duties, which are exercised not just for personal purposes, but for the good of the whole community.[58]

Because of the similarity between Ambrose's *De officiis ministrorum* and Cicero's *De officiis*, it is often hard to distinguish which of these sources John was using. It is likely, in fact, that he drew on both. A notable example of this is found in the discussion of *officia* in *Policraticus*, Book

I. 4, where John examines the merits and demerits of hunting. John, as noted, places a heavy emphasis on the role played by intention: 'Deeds are coloured by their result and purpose; an act is seemly if it is preceded by an honourable cause.'[59] John satirically points out that knowledge of hunting is the 'first element of virtue' according to contemporary students of the liberal arts – presumably the followers of Cornificius, reviled in the *Metalogicon* – who claim erroneously that it constitutes the *via* to the peak of happiness, a route that was previously ascended laboriously only by those who climbed the path of virtue.[60] John then considers whether hunting, classed among the '*curialium nugas*', can rightfully be counted as 'indifferent'. It is a source of 'immoderate pleasure' and 'subverts reason'. However, this does not necessarily mean that the fault lies in the act itself. John compares it to the intoxicating qualities of wine; a man may become drunk, but this is the fault of immoderate consumption by the man, not the fault of the wine. Similarly, hunting can, in certain circumstances, become 'useful and honourable', depending on 'place, time, manner, the individual and purpose'.[61] In the end, as John points out, 'what is most seemly for a man is the thing that is most his own', an aphorism borrowed directly from Cicero, who John refers to as the '*ethicus*'.[62] Within the same section, however, John remarks, 'Indeed, your intention, as the wise man [*sapiens*] says, gives its name to your deed', a reference to Ambrose's *De officiis ministrorum*.[63] Although this was a common aphorism in the Middle Ages used by, among others, John's correspondent Peter of Celle, its application in this context underscores the fact that, although John is discussing a worldly pursuit, his conclusions have implications for the inward-facing Christian.[64] It also attests to the simultaneous application on John's part of both Cicero and Ambrose's 'books of offices', refuting Beryl Smalley's conclusion that John 'made a deliberate choice in preferring the original *De officiis* to a patristic rehash'.[65]

## Duties: structuring the body model

One of the most innovative ideas found in the *Policraticus* is the comparison between the polity and the human body, with each organ or limb representing a different element of the *res publica*.[66] Introducing it in Book V of the *Policraticus*, John asserts that his metaphor is based on a Roman text called 'The Instruction of Trajan' by Plutarch, which he claims to follow in general, rather than specific, terms.[67] John's unwillingness to assert that he is reproducing his source accurately has led to claims that this so-called text of Plutarch was an invention – an argument that will be examined more fully in the next chapter. In this model, the prince is the head of the *res publica*. The religious community is situated in the soul. The senate is placed in the heart. The eyes, ears and tongue are the judges and governors of the *res publica*. The hands equate to officials and soldiers. Courtiers and assistants to the prince correspond to the flanks of the body. The digestive system is akin to the financial officers of the polity. Finally, the feet of the body are the peasants.[68] John summarises Plutarch's vision of the *res publica* thus: 'A *res publica*, according to Plutarch, is a certain body that is animated by the benefice of divine favour, acts at the nod of highest equity and is ruled by a type of rational management.'[69]

While the body metaphor offers an acute critique of the individual roles within political society, as will be investigated in depth in the next chapter, John also intended his metaphor to illustrate the exercise of appropriate duties. This is indicated by the content of the letter he sent introducing the text to his friend Peter of Celle. John writes:

> All things on earth derive their strength from mutual aid ... it is for this reason alone that all things go upon their way, because the same indwelling spirit of unanimity nurtures the concord of things dissident and the dissidence of things concordant, and arranges the diverse parts of the body of the universe as though they were its members, in order that they may be attuned together for mutual and reciprocal service. Thus it is that in the human body the members serve each other and the offices of each are allotted for the benefit of all. There are less of some and more of others according to the size of the body, but all of them are united to secure the body's health; they differ in their effects, but if you consider the health of the body, they are all working for the same end.[70]

This summary posits a relationship between mutual care ('*mutuis auxiliis*'), reciprocal public duties ('*singulorum officia publicis usibus*') and the common good ('*salutis omnia*'). Indeed, this is the conceptual crux of the body metaphor. Duties – *officia* – were, as noted, motivated by natural impulses, extending from the rational self-care of the individual to the individual's care for the family and subsequently for the whole community. The exercise of appropriate duties creates, and in turn depends upon, a web of rationally constructed reciprocal relationships. The body is a uniquely appropriate vehicle for the expression of such relationships, as it is an organic unity whose physical parts function together, each being capable of individual movement while remaining subservient to the whole.

While precedents for John's comparison between the microcosm of the body and the macrocosm of the polity will be assessed more thoroughly in the next chapter, the remainder of this section focuses on the value of the body model as an expression of the division of *officia* and their exercise. Yeager notes that John's discussion of the body politic starts with the assumption that there is already in existence a '*corpus* of human association'; John does not seem to see any great novelty in his use of corporeal language.[71] It is the manner, therefore, in which John appropriates the metaphor of the body to understand social roles and the nature of *officia* that is ultimately of concern. However, a brief look at antique precedent for the use of the body as an exemplar of associative links remains of value. Cicero serves as an important forerunner to John, with *De officiis* showing how the exercise of appropriate political duties is concomitant with the virtuous arrangement of the body and its activities. The basis of the analogy is found in Book I of *De officiis* where Cicero refers to the 'appropriate arrangement of the limbs' of the body, 'its parts in graceful harmony'. Its 'seemliness' is a product of 'the order and constancy and moderation of every word and action'.[72] Just as the body has been organised to allow optimal modest conduct, with 'sense of shame' hiding 'the parts of the body that are devoted to the necessities of nature', so too must the actions of those in the polity be rational and seemly.[73] Cicero describes how the body mirrors the polity in terms familiar from Platonic discourse, saying, 'let them [those who take charge of public affairs] care for the whole body of the republic rather than protect one part and neglect the rest'.[74] He further develops this theme in Book III, with reference to the 'limbs' of the body, which must not exceed their purpose, just as each man should avoid pursuing his own advantage at the expense of others, for fear that 'fellowship and community among men would be overthrown'.[75] This mutuality of dependence is necessary as 'the benefit of each individual and the benefit of all together should be the same'.[76] This is Cicero's guiding *formula* expressed in its clearest form; in the resolution of conflicts between what is honourable and what is useful, it must be ensured that the benefit accrued to one and the benefit accrued to all are not in contradiction.[77]

We find a similar application of the model to convey relational duties in John's near-contemporary Hugh of St Victor. In Hugh's *De institutione novitiorum*, the necessity that 'each part of the body performs it own function (*officium*) and does not usurp that of another, and then that each accomplish its task (*officium*) as decently as modestly, so that the eye is not offended by indiscipline' is emphasised. Hugh also recommends clear differentiation of roles, 'so that each part of the body confines itself to the functions (*officia*) for which it was created and does not confuse its role (*ministerium*) with another'.[78] Hugh extends his account of *offi-*

*cia* to make recommendations for the *res publica*, which he describes as 'a human body in which every member is assigned its own duty'. An emphasis is placed on staying within the bounds of one's prescribed role: 'while one member wrongfully claims for himself the duty of another member, how can the harmony of the body but be lessened? At any time such a movement impairs another movement, the arrangement that nature moderates has been disturbed.' In this fashion, 'neither the duties of the members are exchanged, nor confusingly mixed'.[79] Hugh's goal in using the body metaphor is different from John's (seemly and appropriate personal behaviour, rather than normative political recommendations, is his focus), but his comparison between the *officia* carried out by respective parts of the body and political *officia* demonstrates the facility of the body metaphor for understanding the role of duties, as well as attesting to the contemporary popularity of the analogy.

It is worth noting that the body metaphor ascribed to Plutarch is not the only corporeal analogy developed in the *Policraticus*. John also references the fable of Menenius Agrippa as recounted in the *History of Rome* of Livy (59 BC–AD 17).[80] The story describes the dissension of the other parts of the body against the stomach owing to their claim that all the members were working for the nourishment of the stomach with no return. Upon starving the stomach, however, the rest of the body lost its power, thus demonstrating the necessary interdependence of body parts. Livy says that Menenius Agrippa used this fable to 'show how like was the internal dissension of the bodily members to the anger of the plebs against the Fathers'.[81] John refers to this fable in Book VI. 24 of the *Policraticus*, but he ascribes it to Pope Adrian IV, saying that it was cited by the pope in conversation as a defence of the papacy's financial policy.[82] Several changes can be observed in the version attributed to Adrian; when reaching a resolution 'all took refuge in the counsel of the heart' (the heart is the seat of the Senate in John's model), and the members are described as 'persuaded by reason' in their solution.[83] The application of the tale in this context is particularly apt; John twists the point of the story to fit Adrian's case that the financial workings of the papacy should be respected, but he also plays on the metaphoric association between matters of finance and the less savoury aspects of digestion: the officers of the treasury are situated in the stomach and bowels of his corporeal model.[84] Thus, the story works on two levels – as an example of the necessity of cooperation, with each doing the duty appropriate to him for the favourable working of the whole, and as a satirical commentary on the money market of the papacy, tainted by its association with defecation.

On the basis of the reference to the fable of Menenius Agrippa found in Book VI. 24, another poem, entitled 'On the Conspiracy of the Members', has been attributed to John.[85] Regardless of its authorship, it is an interesting example of the twelfth-century popularity of Livy's story and, by extension, of the use of the body metaphor. Its take on the fable states that 'we ought to live not for the belly, but for reason; a good man wants to have her as leader, not him'. The poet allows the belly to speak, and it declares that its role is that given to it by Nature. The conclusion of the poem enforces the idea that all must do their respective duty:

> They rise, they set about their duties, they pay their debts,
> The individual members pay attention to their own work.
> Whom Nature made partners of life, mutual
> Care then makes all partners of toil.[86]

The implication is that 'mutual care' ('*mutua cura*') obliges all who are 'partners of life' ('*socios vitae*') to cooperate together. While it is unlikely that the poem is by John, its emphasis on the disaggregation of duties to individual members of the polity, who are also bound in a cooperative relationship founded on care, offers a striking contemporary parallel to the ideas present in the *Policraticus*.

## Conclusion

Existing scholarship on John's use of the body model has largely underestimated the subtleties of the relationships between different parts of the body, focussing instead on single aspects: turning from the role of the head to that of the feet, from the power of the soul to that of the army. Such analyses are primarily concerned, however, with seeking to identify a specific locus of power in medieval society, or with extrapolating conclusions about individual social classes. While these objectives are meritorious, they tend to isolate elements of John's theories indiscriminately without evaluating his perspective as a whole. By emphasising instead the role of duties and the reciprocal relationships between members of the polity that result from a natural extension of care from the self to others, the perspective presented here takes into account the subtleties of the individual relationships between different parts of the body (politic) and their contribution to the social whole. This investigation amplifies Kate Langdon Forhan's interpretation of John's work as 'polycratic', which suggested that the interdependence of the members of the bodies implied multiple centres of political rulership.[87] Emphasising the mutuality of the members, Forhan posited that John's use of the body metaphor 'stresses neither duality nor subordination but interdependence' between groups and individual political actors.[88] However, without an accompanying thesis on the significance of duty in John's model, Forhan's analysis is incomplete. It emphasises utility, not questions of mutual benefit or responsibility, and should be corrected by a more nuanced approach that does full credit to the sophistication of John's views. As will be demonstrated in the next chapter, John's corporeal model is innovative as it pays attention to the abstractly political on a micro-level; it examines the rationale behind the actions of political entities, and the diversity and agency of individual members, while situating such observations within the context of a society dominated by secular and divine powers. Certain ambiguities result from John's application of a bounded physiological metaphor to a political system whose limits remain open to negotiation. The next chapter will examine how the body metaphor works in practice to shape, as well as restrict, John's conclusions about political society.

## Notes

1 *Pol.* I. 2; 1, pp. 19–20: '*Quae uero naturae sunt, peraeque sunt omnium; quae officii, singulorum. Aliud itaque ex officio, aliud ex natura; licet naturae ius ex officio debeatur.*'
2 J. Annas, *The Morality of Happiness* (Oxford: Oxford University Press, 1993), p. 263; see J. Cooper, 'Eudaimonism and the Appeal to Nature in the Morality of Happiness: Comments on Julia Annas, *The Morality of Happiness*', *Philosophy and Phenomenological Research*, 55 (1995), 587–98, and J. Annas, 'Reply to Cooper', *Philosophy and Phenomenological Research*, 55 (1995), 599–610. See also C. Brooke, 'Grotius, Stoicism and "Oikeiosis"', *Grotiana*, 29 (2008), 25–50 (31–7) for a summary of the theory of *oikeiôsis* and details of Annas's position. Given the difficulties in finding an appropriate and succinct translation for *oikeiôsis*, I will continue to use the Greek term in the majority of cases when referring to the concept.
3 G. Reydams-Schils, *The Roman Stoics: Self, Responsibility, and Affection* (Chicago: University of Chicago Press, 2005), p. 3.
4 See Verbeke, *The Presence of Stoicism*, p. 55.
5 Such an assertion is, of course, contingent on noting that the Roman texts themselves heavily depended on Greek texts; for example, the third book of Cicero's *De finibus* is generally agreed to have derived from a handbook of Diogenes or Antipater. See S. G. Pembroke, 'Oikeiosis', in A. A. Long (ed.), *Problems in Stoicism* (London: Athlone Press, 1997¹), pp. 114–49 (p. 120). *De officiis*, in turn, draws heavily on a volume by the Stoic Panaetius: see Dyck, *A Commentary on Cicero, De Officiis*, pp. 17–29.
6 Reydams-Schils, *The Roman Stoics*, p. 53.

7   Cicero, *De finibus bonorum et malorum*, trans. H. Rackham (LCL 40; Cambridge, MA: Harvard University Press, 1931), III. 16, pp. 232–5: '*simul atque natum sit animal … ipsum sibi conciliari et commendari ad se conservandum et ad suum statum eaque quae conservantia sunt eius status diligenda, alienari autem ab interitu iisque rebus quae interitum videantur afferre. … Ex quo intellegi debet principium ductum esse a se diligendo.*'
8   Cicero, *De finibus*, III. 62, pp. 280–3: '*Pertinere autem ad rem arbitrantur intellegi natura fieri ut liberi a parentibus amentur; a quo initio profectam communem humani generis societatem persequimur.*'
9   Cicero, *De finibus*, III. 62, p. 283.
10  Cicero, *De finibus*, III. 63, pp. 282–5: '*Ut enim in membris alia sunt tamquam sibi nata, ut oculi, ut aures, alia etiam ceterorum membrorum usum adiuvant, ut crura, ut manus … Itaque natura sumus apti ad coetus, concilia, civitates.*'
11  Cicero, *De finibus*, III. 20, pp. 238–9: '*Primum est officium (id enim appello καθῆκον) ut se conservet in naturae statu*'. See T. Engberg-Pedersen, 'Discovering the Good: *Oikeiosis* and *Kathekonta* in Stoic Ethics', in M. Schofield and G. Striker (eds), *The Norms of Nature: Studies in Hellenistic Ethics* (Cambridge: Cambridge University Press, 1986), pp. 145–83, for the Greek tradition of *kathêkonta* as found in the works of Diogenes Laertius.
12  Cicero, *De finibus*, III. 24, p. 243.
13  G. Striker, 'Following Nature: A Study in Stoic Ethics', *Oxford Studies in Ancient Philosophy*, 9 (1991), 1–73 (39).
14  T. Engberg-Pedersen, *The Stoic Theory of Oikeiosis: Moral Development and Social Interaction in Early Stoic Philosophy* (Aarhus: Aarhus University Press, 1990), pp. 126–8.
15  Engberg-Pedersen, *The Stoic Theory of Oikeiosis*, p. 137.
16  Cicero, *De finibus*, III. 31. See G. Striker, 'The Role of *Oikeiôsis* in Stoic Ethics', *Oxford Studies in Ancient Philosophy*, 1 (1983), 145–67 (162).
17  For the mechanisms of this process in *De finibus* see Engberg-Pedersen, *The Stoic Theory of Oikeiosis*, pp. 123–6.
18  Pembroke, 'Oikeiosis', p. 120.
19  J. G. F. Powell, 'Cicero's Translations from Greek', in J. G. F. Powell (ed.), *Cicero the Philosopher: Twelve Papers* (Oxford: Oxford University Press, 1995), pp. 273–300 (p. 292).
20  P. A. Brunt, 'Stoicism and the Principate', *Papers of the British School at Rome*, 43 (1975), 7–35 (15). See F. Lachaud, *L'Éthique du pouvoir au Moyen-Âge: L'Office dans la culture politique (Angleterre, vers 1150–vers 1330)* (Paris: Garnier, 2010) for an interpretation of how John similarly uses the word *officium* to describe both a moral obligation, and an administrative or political function (p. 204).
21  Rouse and Rouse, 'The Medieval Circulation of Cicero's *Posterior Academics* and the *De finibus bonorum and malorum*', pp. 351–2. My own examination of Webb's attributions led to the same conclusion.
22  Cicero, *On Duties*, I. 11, p. 6; *De officiis*, I. 11, p. 12: '*Principio generi animantium omni est a natura tributum, ut se, vitam corpusque tueatur, declinet ea, quae nocitura videantur, omniaque, quae sint ad vivendum necessaria, anquirat et paret, ut*

*pastum, ut latibula, ut alia generis eiusdem. Commune item animantium omnium est coniunctionis adpetitus procreandi causa et cura quaedam eorum, quae procreata sint.*'

23 Cicero, *On Duties*, I. 12, p. 6; *De officiis*, I. 12, p. 14: '*ut hominum coetus et celebrationes et esse et a se obiri velit ob easque causas studeat parare ea, quae suppeditent ad cultum et ad victum, nec sibi soli, sed coniugi, liberis ceterisque, quos caros habeat tuerique debeat*'.

24 Cicero, *On Duties*, I. 20, p. 9; *De officiis*, I. 20, p. 22: '*Sed iustitiae primum munus est, ut ne cui quis noceat nisi lacessitus iniuria, deinde ut communibus pro communibus utatur, privatis ut suis.*'

25 Cicero, *On Duties*, II. 46, p. 80; *De officiis*, II. 46, pp. 214–16: '*Prima igitur commendatio proficiscitur a modestia cum pietate in parentes, in suos benivolentia. Facillime autem et in optimam partem cognoscuntur adulescentes, qui se ad claros et sapientes viros bene consulentes rei publicae contulerunt; quibuscum si frequentes sunt, opinionem afferunt populo eorum fore se similes, quos sibi ipsi delegerint ad imitandum.*'

26 Cicero, *On Duties*, I. 8, p. 5; *De officiis*, I. 8, p. 10: '*Nam et medium quoddam officium dicitur et perfectum. Perfectum officium rectum, opinor, vocemus, quoniam Graeci κατόρθωμα, hoc autem commune officium καθῆκον vocant. Atque ea sic definiunt, ut, rectum quod sit, id officium perfectum esse definiant; medium autem officium id esse dicunt, quod cur factum sit, ratio probabilis reddi possit.*'

27 *Pol.* I. 2; 1, p. 19: '*Alienum profecto est, quod ratio naturae uel officii non inducit, si tamen interdum recte dicitur alienum, quod rectius fuerat semper fuisse nullius.*'

28 Lachaud in *L'Éthique du pouvoir au Moyen-Âge*, describes *alienum* as meaning for John 'l'inadéquation entre la personne et son action' (p. 187). Note that, while Lachaud correctly notes that *officum* and *alienum* are opposing poles for John (pp. 186–92), she interprets *alienum* as meaning moral impropriety rather than my more extreme position, which views John (in line with the Stoics) as seeing *alienum* as something that is unnatural, as well as improper.

29 *Pol.* I. 2; 1, p. 20: '*Aliud itaque ex officio, aliud ex natura; licet naturae ius ex officio debeatur. Parricidii siquidem species est impugnare iura naturae, et sacrilegii instar parentis leges euacuare, et matri omnium honorem debitum non referre. Quod tamen ratio ex honestis causis admittit, non est simpliciter alienum. Si modesta forte iocunditas uel utilitas subest, et nemini noceatur, hoc etenim non aduersatur officio uel naturae; sin autem impugnat alterutrum, statim est et simpliciter alienum, et usquequaque non licet. Huius itaque contrectatio semper est aut erroris aut criminis.*'

30 *Pol.* I. 4; 1, p. 32: '*Causa quoque actum poterit decorare, si aut necessitate subsistat aut uigeat utilitate aut honestate splendescat, cum ex affectu mentis tota ualeat substantia operis colorari.*'

31 *Pol.* I. 3; 1, p. 20: '*Naturae, laboris, et industriae fructum unusquisque recipiebat ex merito. Nemo quod esset alterius usurpabat, manente in omnibus indiuiduo caritatis affectu.*'

32 K. L. Forhan, 'The Not-So-Divided Self: Reading Augustine in the Twelfth Century', *Augustiniana*, 42 (1992), 95–110 (106).

33 Note Lachaud's summary of the number of occurrences of the term *officium* in John's writings and the variety of meanings which he attaches to it in *L'Éthique du pouvoir au Moyen-Âge*, pp. 183-4.
34 *Pol.* V. 4; 1, p. 290.
35 *Pol.* III. 13; 1, p. 216: '*Affectio tamen efficacior est, eo quod ad naturam familiarius accedit, ipsique unitur animae quicquid affectionis federe copulatur.*'
36 Seneca, *Ep.* 48, refers to the need to live for one's neighbour as for oneself. *Ep.* 73 and *Ep.* 85 argue that the sage is rationally concerned with all mankind.
37 Classic modern accounts of communitarianism include MacIntyre, *After Virtue*; M. Sandel, *Liberalism and the Limits of Justice* (Cambridge: Cambridge University Press, 1998); C. Taylor, 'Atomism', in his *Philosophical Papers*, vol. 2: *Philosophy and the Human Sciences* (Cambridge, 1985), pp. 187-210; and R. Walzer, *Spheres of Justice: A Defense of Pluralism and Equality* (New York: Basic Books, 1983).
38 Nederman, 'Communitarian Lessons of Medieval Political Theory', p. 979.
39 Nederman, 'Communitarian Lessons of Medieval Political Theory', p. 985.
40 *Pol.* V. 4; 1, p. 290: '*Officium uero est debitum exequendi quae unicuique ex institutis aut moribus agenda sunt. Ex eo namque personis singulis proprii congruunt actus. In his autem quae sic agenda sunt, alia ad publicum, alia ad suum cuiusque pertinent statum. Ex quo liquet officiorum quaedam publica, quaedam priuata conuenienter dici. Priuatorum uero tanta multiplicitas est quanta fere est diuersitas personarum. Publica quidem omnia referuntur ad duas species; aut enim a diuino aut ab humano iure descendunt. Haec autem ex libris officiorum latius patent, sed pertinent ad praesentem articulum ut publicis officiis reuerentia impendatur.*'
41 T. M. Osborne, *Love of Self and Love of God in Thirteenth Century Ethics* (Notre Dame, IN: University of Notre Dame Press, 2005), p. 1.
42 Osborne, *Love of Self and Love of God*, p. 3.
43 2 Corinthians 3:1; 4:2; 5:12; 10:12, 18.
44 *Pol.* III. 2; 1, p. 174: '*Est ergo primum hominis sapientiam affectantis, quid ipse sit, quid intra se, quid extra, quid infra, quid supra, quid contra, quid ante uel postea sit, contemplari.*' Cf. Bernard of Clairvaux, De consideratione, in *Sancti Bernardi Opera Omnia*, vol. 3: *Tractatus et Opuscula*, ed. J. Leclercq and H. Rochais (Rome: Editiones Cistercenses, 1963), II. 6, p. 414: '*Iam quod ad considerationes attinet fructum, quatuor, ut occurunt, tibi consideranda reor: te, quae sub te, quae circa te, quae supra te sunt.*' On the history of the idea of self-knowledge since antiquity see P. Courcelle, *Connais-toi toi-même de Socrate à Saint Bernard* (3 vols; Paris: Études Augustiennes, 1974-75), which discusses in depth the relationship between the Graeco-Roman and Christian traditions.
45 *Pol.* III. 2; 1, p. 175: '*Haec etenim contemplatio quadripertitum parit fructum, utilitatem sui, caritatem proximi, contemptum mundi, amorem Dei.*'
46 *Pol.* III. 1; 1, p. 173: '*Agnitio igitur ueritatis cultusque uirtutis publica singulorum et omnium et rationalis naturae uniuersalis incolumitas est.*'
47 *Pol.* VIII. 5; 2, p. 244: '*Ab hoc duplici fonte mores oriuntur. Recti quidem, si faciat quis alii quod sibi uult fieri et ab eo abstineat alii inferendo quod sibi nollet ab alio*

*irrogari; distorti uero, si quis alium ledat uel non prosit, cum possit, quae quidem utrimque multipliciter fiunt.*'

48 *Pol.* VIII. 5; 2, p. 244: '*A priore quidem amor libertatis, amor patriae, et tandem extraneorum amor.*'

49 *Pol.* VIII. 5; 2, p. 244: '*Nam libertatem non amare non potest qui se ipsum et patriam amat et in gradu suo extraneum quicumque sincera caritate diligit proximum; siquidem in eo consistit caritas ordinata.*'

50 H. Chadwick, 'Frui-uti', in C. Mayer (ed.), *Augustinus-Lexikon*, vol. 3, fasc. 1/2 (Basle: Schwabe, 2004), pp. 70–5.

51 M. Rubin, *Charity and Community in Medieval Cambridge* (Cambridge: Cambridge University Press, 1987), pp. 69–70.

52 Rubin, *Charity and Community*, p. 69.

53 See T. Engberg-Pedersen, *Paul and the Stoics* (Edinburgh: T&T Clark, 2000) for the expression of Stoicism in the Pauline Epistles.

54 On the limits of potential applications of the Ciceronian account of duties to Christian *caritas*, see A. MacIntyre, *Whose Justice? Which Rationality?* (London: Duckworth, 1988), p. 148.

55 Ambrose, *De officiis*, I. 8.25, pp. 132–3.

56 Ambrose, *De officiis*, I. 11.36–7, pp. 136–9.

57 Davidson, in Ambrose, *De officiis*, p. 814. Cf. A. Coyle, 'Cicero's *De officiis* and the *De officiis ministrorum* of St Ambrose', *Franciscan Studies*, 15 (1955), 224–56 (229–30), who considers that the distinction in Ambrose's mind lies, rather, between absolute and relative duty; for Ambrose the root of this departure from Stoic ethics is his denial that the sage can ever possess absolute virtue as God alone is good.

58 *Pol.* V. 4; 1, pp. 290–1: '*Unde in constitutionibus principum, magistratuum edictis aut promulgationibus per prolemsim fit plurium conceptio personarum, ut non tam personae quam uniuersitatis tota constitutio uideatur esse uel quaeuis alia promulgatio.*'

59 *Pol.* I. 4; 1, p. 22: '*Opera singulorum ex euentu et proposito colorantur; res quippe decora est, si honesta causa praecesserit.*'

60 *Pol.* I. 4; 1, p. 23: '*Haec sunt prima elementa uirtutis, haec uia felices ad beatitudinis cumulum compendioso perducit tramite, quo maiores nostri non nisi laboriosae uirtutis gradibus docuerant ascendendum.*'

61 *Pol.* I. 4; 1, p. 31: '*Potest igitur uenatica esse utilis et honesta; sed ex loco, tempore, modo, persona, et causa.*'

62 *Pol.* I. 4; 1, p. 32: '*Id unumquemque decet maxime, quod est cuiusque maxime.*' See Cicero, *De officiis*, I. 113.

63 *Pol.* I. 4; 1, p. 32: '*Affectus etenim tuus, ut ait sapiens, operi tuo nomen imponit.*' See Ambrose, *De officiis*, I. 30.147.

64 Peter of Celle, *The Letters of Peter of Celle*, ed. and trans. J. Haseldine (Oxford: Oxford University Press, 2001), Letter 134, p. 498.

65 Smalley, *The Becket Conflict and the Schools*, p. 93.

66 By preference, the term *res publica* is untranslated throughout. On the history and inherent challenges of defining the term see L. Hodgson, *Res Publica and*

the Roman Republic: 'Without Body or Form' (Oxford: Oxford University Press, 2017), pp. 1–15.
67  *Pol.* V. 2; 1, p. 282: '*Sequuntur eiusdem politicae constitutionis capitula in libello qui inscribitur Institutio Traiani, quae pro parte praesenti opusculo curaui inserere, ita tamen ut sententiarum uestigia potius imitarer quam passus uerborum.*' A reconstruction of the *Institutio Traiani* can be found in [Pseudo-] Plutarch, *Die Institutio Traiani: Ein pseudo-plutarchischer Text im Mittelalter*, ed. H. Kloft and M. Kerner (Stuttgart: Teubner, 1992). The controversy surrounding the origin of this text will be discussed in the next chapter.
68  *Pol.* V. 2, p. 283.
69  *Pol.* V. 2, p. 282: '*Est autem res publica, sicut Plutarco placet, corpus quoddam quod diuini muneris beneficio animatur et summae aequitatis agitur nutu et regitur quodam moderamine rationis.*'
70  Letter 111, *Letters* I, p. 181: '*Mutuis auxiliis constant omnia ... et profecto ea sic uniuersa procedunt, quod tantam dissidentium concordiam et concordium dissidentiam idem unanimitatis 'spiritus intus alit' et, ut sibi inuicem uicario quodam ministerio consonent, mundani corporis partes uelut membra disponit. Sic sic in humano corpore sibi inuicem membra deseruiunt et singulorum officia publicis usibus deputantur. Absunt quidem haec magis illa minus pro mole corporis, sed in effectu salutis eius omnia uniuntur; uarios habent effectus, sed si usum salutis penses, in idem uniuersa concurrunt.*'
71  R. F. Yeager, 'The Body Politic and the Politics of Bodies in the Poetry of John Gower', in P. Boitani and A. Torti (eds), *The Body and Soul in Medieval Literature* (Cambridge: D. S. Brewer, 1999), pp. 145–65 (p. 149).
72  Cicero, *On Duties*, I. 98, p. 39; *De officiis*, I. 98, p. 100: '*Ut enim pulchritudo corporis apta compositione membrorum movet oculos et delectat hoc ipso, quod inter se omnes partes cum quodam lepore consentiunt, sic hoc decorum, quod elucet in vita, movet approbationem eorum, quibuscum vivitur, ordine et constantia et moderatione dictorum ominum atque factorum.*'
73  Cicero, *On Duties*, I. 126, p. 49; *De officiis*, I. 126, p. 128: '*quae partes autem corporis ad naturae necessitatem datae aspectum essent deformem habiturae atque foedum, eas contexit atque abdidit*'.
74  Cicero, *On Duties*, I. 85, p. 33; *De officiis*, I. 85, p. 86: '*ut totum corpus rei publicae curent, ne, dum partem aliquam tuentur, reliquas deserant*'.
75  Cicero, *On Duties*, III. 22, p. 108; *De officiis*, III. 22, p. 288: '*si unum quodque membrum sensum hunc haberet, ut posse putaret se valere, si proximi membri valetudinem ad se traduxisset, debilitari et interire totum corpus necesse esset, sic, si unus quisque nostrum ad se rapiat commoda aliorum detrahatque, quod cuique possit, emolumenti sui gratia, societas hominum et communitas evertatur necesse est*'.
76  Cicero, *On Duties*, III. 26, p. 109; *De officiis*, III. 26, p. 292: '*Ergo unum debet esse omnibus propositum, ut eadem sit utilitas unius cuiusque et universorum*'.
77  Striker, 'Following Nature: A Study in Stoic Ethics', p. 47.
78  M.-C. Pouchelle, *The Body and Surgery in the Middle Ages*, trans. R. Morris (Cambridge: Polity, 1990), p. 118.

79 Hugh of St Victor, *De institutione novitiorum*, in *L'Oeuvre de Hugues de Saint Victor*, vol. 1: *De institutione novitiorum*. *De virtute orandi*. *De laude caritatis*. *De arrha animae*, ed. H. B. Feiss and P. Sicard, trans. D. Poirel, H. Rochais and P. Sicard (Turnhout: Brepols, 1997), XII, p. 72: 'Est enim quasi quaedam respublica corpus humanum, in quo singulis membris sua officia distributa sunt. Dum ergo unum membrum alterius membri officium inordinate sibi vindicat, quid aliud quam concordiam universitatis pertubat? Cumque aliud suo motu alterius motum impedit, certe illi quam natura moderatur, dispositioni contradicit. Prima igitur est custodia disciplinae in gestu, ut unumquodque membrum in eo ad quod creatum est officia se contineat, neque alterius membri ministerium sui admistione confundat. Id est, ut oculi videant, aures audiant, nares olficiant, os loquatur, manus operentur, pedes ambulent, quatenus neque transmutentur officia membrorum neque inordinate permisceantur.'

80 Livy, *History of Rome*, ed. and trans. B. O. Foster (LCL 114; Cambridge, MA: Harvard University Press, 1919), II. 32, pp. 324–5. Cicero used a version of this story also: *De officiis*, III. 22.

81 Livy, *History of Rome*, II. 32, p. 325.

82 Note that John accessed Livy's *Histories* through a late first-century, or second-century, epitome of Roman history by Florus: see Martin, 'John of Salisbury as a Classical Scholar', p. 185; C. Kostick, 'William of Tyre, Livy and the Vocabulary of Class', *Journal of the History of Ideas*, 65 (2004), 353–68 (359–60).

83 *Pol.* VI. 24; 2, p. 72: '*Ad cordis ergo consilium omnia redierunt ibique habita deliberatione ratio patefecit*'; see L. Scanlon, *Narrative, Authority and Power: The Medieval Exemplum and the Chaucerian Tradition* (Cambridge: Cambridge University Press, 2007), pp. 98–100, for the rhetorical significance of the employment of this model by John: 'In this exemplum, as in Livy's before it, narrative is literally power. By telling a story Adrian defends not only his authority but also his practical exercise of power, and its possible oppressiveness' (p. 100).

84 A further example of a twelfth-century use of this fable is found in the work of Marie de France (*fl. c.*1180–*c.*1189), who concludes her rendition of 'The Fable of a Man, his Belly, and his Limbs' thus: 'What every free person ought to know: | No one can have honour | Who brings shame to his lord. | Nor can his lord have it either | If he wishes to shame his people. | If either one fails the other | Evil befalls them both.' In *Readings in Medieval Political Theory 1100–1400*, ed. and trans. C. J. Nederman and K. L. Forhan (Indianapolis: Hackett Publishing Company, 2000), p. 25. It should be noted that Nederman and Forhan's assertion at p. 24 that John of Salisbury could have heard Marie telling the fable at Henry II's court should be regarded as implausible. Although it is possible that Marie could have frequented Henry's court prior to the Becket controversy – as her work shows some influence of Chrétien de Troyes, so could feasibly have been composed in the 1160s – it is most likely that her works were composed in the 1170s-1180s. See 'Introduction to Marie de France', in *The Lais of Marie de France*, trans. G. S. Burgess and K. Busby (Harmondsworth: Penguin, 1999), pp. 7–20.

85 R. Pepin, '*On the Conspiracy of the Members*: Attributed to John of Salisbury', *Allegorica*, 12 (1991), 29–42 (31): '*De Membris Conspirantibus* is probably not by

John of Salisbury, or at least it is not a work of his mature years. Yet, these verses tell a charming, pointed story of wide appeal and utility in the schools during the late medieval period.'

86 R. Pepin, '*On the Conspiracy of the Members*', lines 195–8, p. 41.
87 K. L. Forhan, 'Polycracy, Obligation, and Revolt: The Body Politic in John of Salisbury and Christine de Pizan', in M. Brabant (ed.), *Politics, Gender, and Genre: The Political Thought of Christine de Pizan* (Boulder: Westview, 1992), pp. 33–52.
88 Forhan, 'Polycracy, Obligation and Revolt', pp. 34–5. On how the emphasis on social reciprocity in body metaphors facilitated the legitimation of social inequality see S. Rigby, 'Justifying Inequality: Peasants in Medieval Ideology', in M. Kowaleski, J. Langdon and P. R. Schofield (eds), *Peasants and Lords in the Medieval English Economy: Essays in Honour of Bruce M. S. Campbell* (Turnhout: Brepols, 2015), pp. 173–97 (pp. 184–9).

# 4

# Political relationships in context: the body politic

John's model of the body politic takes its place among a host of diffuse metaphorical interpretations of the body in the twelfth century, the contested nature of the metaphor being efficiently summarised by Caroline Walker Bynum:

> It would be no more correct to say that medieval doctors, rabbis, alchemists, prostitutes, wet nurses, preachers and theologians had 'a' concept of 'the body' than it would be to say that Charles Darwin, Beatrix Potter, a poacher, and the village butcher had 'a' concept of 'the rabbit'.[1]

Bynum's statement illustrates the wide variety of contexts within which bodily language and analogies were applied in the medieval period. The body was used pictorially, for example, as a literal 'map' upon which societal links could be illustrated; the diagram of the 'body-familial' traces kinship links, with the most distant agnate and cognate relations taking their places at the extremities of the body.[2] Some models were purely physiological, examining different parts of the body as sources of the humours which determined the well-being of a person.[3] Many body analogies derived their force from a tradition of reasoning from the microcosm to the macrocosm, where the physiology of the body represented larger entities, such as the natural structure of the universe – as seen for example in the Platonic parallel between the animation of the world by a World-Soul and the animation of the body by the soul.[4] Finally, there was also an influential stream of discourse emanating from Christian writings where the 'Church embodied' conveyed an image of unity.[5] Notable in this respect are the Pauline Epistles, where an analogy is drawn between the Church and the *corpus Christi*.[6] This chapter opens with a consideration of the commonality of the body metaphor in the medieval period, looking briefly at some of its iterations in biblical and contemporary discourse. It then turns to a detailed examination of the parts of the body discussed by John, before concluding with a study of the potential sources for one of the key elements of John's analogy: the requirement for moderation in the actions of the ruling head towards the members that make up its body.

## The body in medieval discourse

The Pauline Epistles offered an important precedent for the use of body metaphors in medieval discourse. Here, the metaphor of the body is used to imply unity; each member of the Church may play an individual role, but all are incorporated in a common goal, the formation of a unified *ecclesia*, just as the different parts of the body work together to form a physical whole.[7] 1 Corinthians 12:22 advocates the necessity for the body to work for the protection of the weak, while 1 Corinthians 12:25 requires 'that there may be no dissension within the body, but the members may have the same care for one another'. In addition, 1 Corinthians 12:26 recommends harmony between the members of the community: 'If one member suffers, all suffer together with it; if one member is honoured, all rejoice together with it.' Cooperation implies care in the Pauline model. A second level of interpretation of the metaphor regards the body not only as representative of the Christian community, but as expressive of the corporate body of Christ.[8] In *The King's Two Bodies*, Ernst Kantorowicz argued that the body metaphor in the Pauline tradition was simultaneously employed to refer to the binary nature of Christ (as both body and spirit) and to the '*corpus mysticum*' of the Church as the organised body of Christian society.[9] A hierarchical dimension of the metaphor is also developed, with Christ placed as the head of the body of the Church; Ephesians 1:22 describes how God 'put all things under his feet and has made him the head over all things for the church'. Ephesians 4:15-16 regards this ruling head as a source 'from whom the whole body, joined and knitted together by every ligament with which it is equipped, as each part is working properly, promotes the body's growth in building itself up in love'. Love is described as the binding force within the body of the Church: 'But speaking the truth in love, we must grow up in every way into him who is the head, into Christ' (Ephesians 4:15). While coherence is the dominant theme here, the body metaphor has additional uses; it encourages the protection of the weakest by the strong, but it also implicitly validates hierarchies within the Church. The Pauline Epistles, therefore, are an important source for the normalisation of the use of corporeal language in the medieval period; through their emphasis on the body as a unified whole, on the necessity of cooperation between all parts, and on the hierarchical dominance of the institutionalised Church over its members, they assert some of the principal ways in which the body metaphor could be manipulated for the expression of interrelationships.

An example of the continued relevance of the Pauline metaphor of the ecclesiastical body in the medieval period is found in the writings of the Cistercian abbot Isaac of Stella (d. late 1160s). Isaac's writings provide an interesting parallel to those of John, as he was writing within a similar political and intellectual context. We know, for example, that Isaac also came from England to study in the schools of France, and he appears to have had some association with Thomas Becket, although the strength of this association is disputed.[10] The metaphor of the body was frequently used by Isaac in his sermon collection. In Sermon 34, Isaac emphasises the indivisibility of the Church: 'All those under the influence of the ever so holy Head of this Body are described as its members. The Body is one, just as the Head is, but the members are many. All this is based on analogy with a human body, which has its head uppermost and stands upright.'[11] Isaac depends on the physiology of the body to stress the reciprocity of relations within the Church, whereby bearers of different functions complement each other: 'The eye cannot walk along the ground, nor can the foot give light to the body; yet both walking and seeing are necessary for the body, although both cannot be done by each part on its own.'[12] He also demonstrates how such reciprocity can aid both the strong and the weak. The weak benefit from care, but they also provide a 'spiritual harvest' for the strong: 'the lower help the higher parts and are helped in turn by them; the same holds for those on the same level, for everything without exception belongs to each and another'.[13] Isaac's sermon shows the continued perceived value of the comparison between the body and the Church, and also offers a demonstration of how the body metaphor can be used to express the diversity of functions within a unified association, an important aspect of the analogy.

While the examples examined so far have focused on the body as a metaphor for the Church, John's contemporaries also used it as a descriptive tool for society and its members.[14] An influential source in this respect was the summary of Plato's *Republic* preserved in the fourth-century commentary on the *Timaeus* by Calcidius, which was extensively studied, glossed and commented on by a group of scholars associated with the school of Chartres, among others.[15] The *Timaeus* recounted how

Socrates separated society into farmers, the military and the guardians of the republic.[16] This separation paralleled the macrocosmic order of the cosmos: the governing heavens, the angels and demons, the earthly domain. It also paralleled the motivating principles of the human body: reason, courage and appetite had their respective locations in the head, heart and genitalia.[17] The tripartite divisions proposed in the Platonic literature were highly significant in the Middle Ages.[18] An application of the Platonic model to political society is found in the *Glosae super Platonem* of Bernard of Chartres (d. after 1124), where the *res publica* is compared to a human body, with the principal citizens of the city living in its most prominent part, just as reason is found in the head of the body. Meanwhile, the soldiers defending the polity live in the heart – the source of vigour – while workers live on the outskirts, keen to maximise profit, just as the lower parts of the body are associated with desire.[19]

A quadripartite division, by contrast, is found in *Commentary on the First Six Books of the Aeneid* by Bernard Silvestris (fl. 1130–60), which compares Aeneas's city to the human body. Referring to the 'four types of dwellings in the city' and its 'four orders', Bernard finds four equivalent spaces in the human body. The head, 'the first and most distinguished dwelling', is the citadel – the place of the wise men, and the body's source of wisdom, perception, wit, reason and memory. The heart is the 'seat of spirit', while the 'seat of desire', the loins, is the 'home of the men of desire'. Finally, Bernard equates the outskirts of the city, where farmers are found, with 'the extremities of the body' – the hands and feet which produce action.[20] For Bernard, the body is one among a range of potential metaphoric comparators, with the four quarters of a city being used to similar effect at a later juncture.[21] In *Cosmographia*, a work demonstrably influenced by microcosmic and macrocosmic reasoning as the titles of its two books (*Megacosmus* and *Microcosmus*) suggest, Bernard provides a further variant on the Platonic tripartite division of the soul. He asserts that the head is the 'seat' of wisdom, where recollection, speculation and reasoning occur.[22] The heart is 'second in dignity to the brain, though it imparts to the brain the source of its vitality'.[23] The desirous aspect of man is found in the loins and lower parts of the body.[24] Here, however, the analogy between the division of the parts of the soul and the body functions as a means to understand the workings of the human body rather than society, reinforced by the fact that this description follows a discussion of the humours.[25]

A similarly body-focused approach is found in the *Glosae super Platonem* of William of Conches, who, like Plato, divides wisdom into intelligence, sense (meaning) and memory (signification).[26] William situates wisdom in the head, spiritedness in the heart and desire in the loins. On the basis of this, he presents a modified version of the Platonic societal model:

> According to this likeness, Socrates wanted there to be a senate in the citadel of the head, under it soldiers, as courage abides in the heart, and under the soldiers confectioners, as desire is in the loins. And as heavy feet in the lowest part of the body tread the earth, so farmers, hunters, and shepherds manage the land outside the walls of the city.[27]

Drawing particular attention to his extension of the body model to treat its 'feet', Dutton claims that William was a 'popularizer of ideas', who 'paved the way down which John of Salisbury was soon to walk'.[28] As with Bernard's model in the *Cosmographia*, however, the metaphor's primary function in this case is to serve as a tool for understanding the workings of the human body, as demonstrated by the fact that it is also found within the context of a discussion of the humours. These neo-Platonic accounts illustrate that there was a precedent for establishing parallels between parts of the body and specific social groups. However, it is important to note that John's application of the body metaphor does not depend directly on the Platonic model; while the *Timaeus* and its associated commentary tradition may have inspired John, his version is far more complex in terms of its divisions and parallels. Furthermore, while Bernard Silvestris and William of Conches used the comparison between the body and the city state to improve their understanding of how the former functioned, the opposite is the case in John's model; the physiological structure of the body is assumed, and the focus is placed instead on what the analogy reveals about the workings of the polity.

## Sources for John's model of the body politic

In an influential article composed in 1943, Hans Liebeschütz forwarded the idea that the 'Plutarchian tract' referred to by John in the opening of Book V of the *Policraticus* was a fiction, an assertion based on the fact that John was the first scholar to refer to the *Institutio Traiani*, while all later mentions of its content can be shown to trace back to the *Policraticus*, not to an antique source.[29] This idea has largely been accepted.[30] Liebeschütz contended that John made up the text to add authority to his model: 'the ideas which John expresses within the framework of the *Institutio Traiani* shows a belief in the hierarchical structure of society, combined with a desire to find sanction for this belief in classical writings and examples'.[31] Liebeschütz posited an alternative source for John's model, namely the *Book of Sentences* of Robert Pullen (d. 1146).[32] He argued that John, a pupil of Robert, followed the sequence of the classes of society provided in the *Sentences*. Furthermore, Robert used a body analogy in his discussion of the role of the prince, also referring to the priesthood-soul. That said, Robert's application of the metaphor is limited; as Janet Martin pointed out, Robert stops short of using the body analogy to describe the functions of all parts of society, as his focus is solely on the ruling classes.[33] Thus, his description of society is insufficiently detailed to be considered a direct source for John's divisions of the body politic; it is hardly the 'systematic order' that Liebeschütz claims it to be.[34] In addition, Liebeschütz's conclusion that John and Robert look at the classes in society in the 'same order' seems inadequate as a basis for comparison; the order in which John describes the polity is primarily dictated by the physiological structure of his metaphor: he treats first the body's internal organs, and then its external members.

From these observations it is apparent that Robert's primary contribution to John's model of the body politic may have been his popularisation of the metaphor. Even though there are undeniable similarities between John's ideas and those of Robert, it more is plausible to regard such similarities as the result of access to a common set of sources and discourse, rather than evidence of conscious imitation. Instead of focusing on identifying the source of John's body metaphor, we should, rather, seek to establish his motivations in choosing it. Whether or not we accept that the *Institutio Traiani* was invented by John or derived from an antique or medieval text now unknown to us, it is imperative to note that he chose to ground his invented analogy in Roman classical discourse, a technique consistent with the heavy use of Roman sources throughout his work. It is also clear that John used the structure of the body metaphor to great effect; while it was a popular analogy, it was also the one that best expressed the observations he wished to make about political life. Even weaknesses of the metaphor are worked to his advantage; for example, John exploits the lack of consensus on one single locus of power within the body to subtly analyse the relationship between the priesthood and prince. Further examples of analogical induction include the metaphoric significance of the spatial distance between the head and the feet, the duality behind the ascription of one hand to the army and the other to officials, and the manner in which John divides up offices between external 'limbs' and internal organs.

John suggests that 'nature, the most loving of parents' has arranged the body so that the inner parts are protected by the ribs and chest, saving them from violence. He recommends that the *res publica* copies nature by protecting its internal offices, while providing them with necessities for effective public ministry.[35] This implies a distinction in purpose between the roles represented by internal organs and those represented by the body's external parts. The body model is schematically effective for illustrating this distinction, as it permits the 'decision-making' roles to be located within the body, while the 'active' elements of the polity are compared to the external limbs. Both are equally important for the worship of God, which takes place either through 'affection of the mind' or by the 'display of works'.[36] Roles situated in the interior of the body comprise the heart as Senate, financial officers as the stomach, and the soul as the priesthood. Roles located in an intermediate position between the internal and external parts of the body include the characterisation of the prince as its head, and of the eyes, ears and tongue as the judges and governors of provinces. Roles that are unambiguously expressed externally are the representation of the hands as officials and soldiers, the sides as attendant officers to the prince, and the feet as the peasantry. In the following sections we shall look at each of these groupings of roles in turn.

### Heart, senses and sides: keeping the polity in check

John places the Senate in the heart of the body, describing it as the source of good and bad works.[37] John points out that the word '*Senatus*' derives from the term for old age, '*senectus*'.[38] Although he does not regard bodily age as the sole qualification for wisdom, maturity of the mind validates the dominant role played by the Senate in the body politic.[39] The principal purpose of the Senate is to counsel the ruler in wise decisions; it is the heart that provides lifeblood to the governing head. The heart of the tyrannical body politic is, by contrast, a 'senate of iniquity' dominated by 'impious counsellors', although John implies that even good senators were not immune to placing personal interest ahead of that of the polity; their needs had to be satisfied so that they did not covet other people's possessions.[40] By considering the heart the seat of wisdom, John departs from Platonic interpretations which see it as the seat of the spirited part of the soul. This redefinition of the role of the heart is derived from biblical precedents; the law of God is 'written on the heart' of the ruler. While the commandments, written on stone, were accessible through words, this 'second law' is learned through 'mystical insight'.[41] The Senate, a classical institution (and one that was memorably revived in the twelfth century during the Roman commune), is given a leading role in the polity: informing and guiding the prince. Its prominence contributes to a diffused model of governance, where multiple offices support the ruler in different ways.[42]

The eyes, ears and tongue are the perceptive organs of the body. John equates them with governors and judges. These roles must be aided by the prince, particularly in ensuring the adequate provision of resources necessary for the performance of their duties. Indeed, it is the fault of the prince if a governor wishes to act equitably, but does not have the resources to do so.[43] The close relationship between the prince, and the governors and judges is emphasised in John's model by the situation of all three in the head; the prince, governors and judges are all motivated by justice, and so share a metaphoric space, while the sensory organs of the eyes, ears and tongue serve as the instruments of justice for the prince. In a number of places in the *Policraticus*, John refers to the guiding role of the governing eyes and ears. When discussing the dependence of the prince on his governors, John references Job 29. This biblical account of virtuous life, which John describes as a '*formula regnandi*', emphasises the role of the senses: 'When the ear heard, it commended me, and when the eye saw, it approved.'[44] John explains that Job 'elegantly expresses' the bodily instruments that the soul depends on for sensory knowledge. Such perception 'most faithfully' takes place through the eyes and ears, whereas 'the reckless tongue can scatter the treasures of the heart'.[45] John also refers to a proverb from Sirach 25:9, 'Happy is ... one who speaks to attentive listeners', to further emphasise the link between the wise governors who perceive correctly and the wise prince who listens carefully.[46] In his recommendations for judges, John advises that they neither show anger nor sadness; they must avoid being moved by plaintiffs, as the eyes and tongue often seek to deceive.[47]

The importance of the discerning role of the senses is further emphasised in John's recounting of the story of Dido and Aeneas. The city of Carthage was initially regarded as 'fortunate'; it was built by all, and supervised by the eyes of its queen. However, Aeneas endeared himself not only to Dido, but also to her advisors, whose ears were corrupted by 'fabulous stories'; 'smooth words', according to John, permitted his access to the city.[48] The senses can serve, but can also mislead; they can guide, but can also leave the political agent open to subversion. As the title of Book VI. 22 implies, '*prudentia*' must be linked to '*sollicitudino*' in order to preserve the strength of the head of the '*res publica*'.[49] Such metaphoric layers illustrate the deeper purpose of John's employment of the body model; not only is it a metaphor for the polity, but it also serves as a prescription for an ideal-type of ruler who should remain wary of his senses and moderate in his emotions.[50]

Cooperation between the different parts of the body is further emphasised by John's introduction to the role of courtiers, who form its sides or flanks. According to the 'formula of nature', their duty is 'to assist the prince'.[51] John considers that they must be as virtuous as possible, as 'character is formed from association'.[52] The sides or flanks are external elements of the body, but John relates their role and responsibilities to those of financial officers, represented in John's model by the internal digestive system. Both courtiers and financial officers are obsessed with money and flattery. This is an example of how the physiology of the model permits analogical induction: the proximity of the sides of the body to the internal digestive organs suggests that the same flaws inhere in both offices. Courtiers may be tainted by their association with financial officers, just as 'one bunch of grapes is spoiled by another'.[53] As already mentioned in Chapter 3, in John's version of the fable of Menenius Agrippa the starved stomach that fails to perform its duties is used as a defence by Pope Adrian IV of the financing of the papal curia: the stomach must be fed to give energy to the rest of the body.[54] By associating financial advisors with a digestive system that 'retains tenaciously its accumulations', John is exploiting a contemporary trope, that is, the association between avarice and defecation.[55] The concept of greed and avarice as physical ailments is one that has biblical antecedents – for example, the story of Gehazi in the second book of Kings (2 Kings 5:20 ff.) – but also classical ones, with both Ovid and Horace describing avarice as a type of dropsy, an unnatural retention of bodily fluids.[56] The proximate locations accorded to courtiers and financial officers clearly illustrate how John plays on the physiological model to create associative links in the mind of the reader.

### Feet and hands: instruments of the polity

One of the most significant features of John's organological model is the prominence given to the feet of the body politic, which represent farmers (bound to the soil), but also cloth-makers, carpenters, metalworkers and all those engaged in menial occupations.[57] They require special care – 'shelter and support' from the head – because of their susceptibility to injury; they 'walk upon the earth doing service with their bodies', and may easily meet with injury in the process of keeping the body 'erect, sustained and moving'. Without the feet, even the most robust body would be obliged to crawl or move only with the assistance of 'brute animals'.[58] This is an important example of the reciprocity of duties at work; the head protects the feet from stumbling, while the feet serve the head in enabling the movement of the body. In his introduction to the extended account of the role of the feet found in Book VI. 20, John argues that the feet of the polity should be shod for their protection: 'Let us, therefore, follow him [Plutarch], and as he himself says, make a sort of shoe for the feet, so that they may not be wounded by stumbling against stones or other obstacles which are in many cases thrown upon them.'[59]

The concept of protecting the feet by making shoes to save them from stumbling has patristic precedents. Augustine's 'Exposition 2 of Psalm 90' employs similar imagery in its description of the Church. He writes, 'where the head has gone first, the members will follow', and states that God 'has his feet on earth; the head is in heaven, the feet on the ground'.[60] When discussing the role of the feet, Augustine equates them with the 'apostles' and 'all preachers of the gospel, for through them the Lord travels among all people'.[61] Elsewhere, Augustine, like John, describes the feet as prone to 'stumbling': 'these evangelists might stumble against a stone, for though the head was in heaven, a stone might easily trip the feet working hard on earth'. The stone upon which these preachers may stumble, according to Augustine, is the 'law', written on stone tablets, a stumble avoidable only with the aid of God's love.[62]

Another patristic source is likely to have influenced John's account of the feet of the polity, namely Gregory the Great's *Regula pastoralis*. The significance for John of this guidebook for the *rector* of a religious community has been under-emphasised; while the *rector* in Gregory's work is primarily a bearer of ecclesiastical office, he can also be regarded as a bearer of authority in general, and so may serve as a possible model for the political ruler. The similarity between John's account of the feet and that found in the *Regula pastoralis* is strong. Gregory similarly recounts how the feet may hamper the body, and so the ruler: 'For all rulers are the heads of their subjects, and surely the head ought to look forward from above, that the feet may be able to go onward on a straight path. Otherwise, if the body's upright posture becomes bent and the head stoops toward the earth, the feet will drag in the way of progress.'[63] The *rector* is obliged to put the community's interests before his own, and Gregory, like John, uses the metaphor of preparing shoes for the feet: 'If therefore, we have the care of our neighbours as well as of ourselves, we protect each foot with a shoe. But the man, who, thinking only of his own advantage, disregards that of his neighbours, loses with disgrace, the shoe, as it were, of one foot.'[64] Again, the emphasis in Gregory's account is on reciprocal care; the head protects the foot so that the feet can bear the body effectively. The parallel between the two texts is not exact, however; both refer to shoes made for the foot but Gregory uses the term *'calceus'* while John uses the word *'soccus'*. The only other instance where this word is used in the *Policraticus* is in a story borrowed from Jerome's *Adversus Iovinianus*. A 'certain Roman noble' – whom John calls Publius Cineaus Graceinus, while implying that this name is made up – describes why he divorced his wife by drawing a comparison with the shoe (*soccus*) on his foot, which looks good, but chafes badly.[65] John may have put the word, which, as this anecdote illustrates, he associated with Roman life, into the mouth of Plutarch in order to add verisimilitude to the fictive *Institutio Traiani*.

The subservient position of the feet is further emphasised in an introductory letter sent with a copy of the *Policraticus* to Peter of Celle. John describes how each part of the polity respects the duties of the other, just as the body is arranged to that end: 'The foot which moves in the mire does not aspire to the dignity of the head; but the head on the other hand does not, because it is erect to heaven, despise the foot for plodding in the mud.'[66] Tilman Struve claimed that John's approach to the feet was particularly novel: 'Giving the serving class of peasants and workmen their place in the functional relationship of the body politic certainly meant an improvement compared to the archaic division of the society into *oratores*, *bellatores* and *laboratores*, according to which the laity only exercised the auxiliary functions of the *Ecclesia*.'[67] Is the incorporation of the labouring feet a case in point of John's recognition of the realities of contemporary society? In spite of his inclusion of these lower classes, the model remains hierarchical; it validates the lowly position of labourers and workers by obliging each to do the work to which they are best suited or designated, even if that work is unprofitable and demeaning.[68] Nevertheless, John places a strong emphasis on reciprocity and mutual advantage, as is clear from the conclusion to *Policraticus*, Book VI. 20, which offers what could be regarded as a summary of John's reciprocal account of duties: 'The health of the whole *res publica* will be safe, as well as admirable, only if the superior members devote themselves to the inferior ones, while the lower respond in equal measure to the laws of their superior.'[69] The feet (artisans and farmers of the *res publica*) should be devoted to 'public utility', and 'should not exceed the limits of the law'. The reciprocity of the relationship is accentuated: 'For inferiors must serve their superiors, just as they should provide necessary protection in return.'[70] So the workers of the *res publica* are shod (*calcietur*) by the provisions of magistrates in order to protect them from injury.[71] John believed that superiors should treat inferiors fairly, although he never specifies what such attentions might translate to in practical terms; in the end, therefore, peasants must be satisfied with their lot.[72]

At a different extremity of the body, the hands of the body politic represent the magistrates and the army in John's model:

> The hand of the *res publica* is either armed or unarmed. The armed hand is that which performs the setting up of camps and the taking of blood; the unarmed is that which administers justice and in keeping holiday from arms, serves the law. ... For as some offices are of peace and others of war, so it is necessary that some are performed by one group, some by others.[73]

John clarifies the relationship between the hands and other parts of the body, primarily the princely head. The head is obliged to discipline the hands, as 'the hand of each army, namely armed and unarmed, is the hand of the prince; and unless he restrains both, he is lacking in continence'. Furthermore, 'the use of the hands testifies to the character of the head'.[74] Therefore, while a well-ordered polity will exercise power carefully through its hands, in the evil polity, where 'princes are infidels and associates of thieves', the hands also will be corrupted in their actions.[75] Judges in such lands obey 'Caesar', not Christ; 'they are all like parts of one body, fathered by the devil, as their manifest works demonstrate'.[76] Meanwhile, John refers to a Greek tradition of wearing a ring on the ring-finger of the left hand. The reason for choosing this finger is allegedly that a nerve ran from this part of the hand directly to the heart. Just as there is a special physical relationship between the hand and the heart, there must also be a close relationship between the seat of wisdom, the Senate, and the army.[77] Even the most brute force within the polity, the army, should be informed by wisdom and commanded by the heart.[78] This link between the heart and the hand demonstrates further how effectively the body model works in representing the complexities of political relationships. The hands are commanded by the head, according to a linear hierarchical structuring of power, while they are also commanded by the heart, in a concentric model of the diffusion of power.

## Modelling the polity and the model prince

One of the most significant treatments of the medieval body politic is found in Kantorowicz's seminal text, *The King's Two Bodies*.[79] Concentrating on the significance of the corporeal nature of the king, Kantorowicz argued that the medieval ruler possessed 'two bodies': the transient body-natural and the political body, which persisted from one holder of the role to the next. A major implication of his thesis is that a distinction was drawn between the personal actions of a ruler and his office. This suggests that normative codes of behaviour in the political realm need to be examined in a dual light, in terms of their social role and in terms of questions of personal conscience. With regard to John of Salisbury's model of the polity, Kantorowicz argues that John's 'prince' is 'not a human being in the ordinary sense', but rather is the 'idea of Justice'.[80] While the implications of this conclusion for John's treatment of law and justice require further evaluation, Kantorowicz's interpretation suggests that John's organological model does not simply describe the polity, but also serves as a means for identifying universal characteristics of rulers and states. As Scanlon notes, inductive reasoning from the basis of the body model plays a significant role in John's argument throughout the *Policraticus*.[81] To extend Kantorowicz's treatment further, it is clear that John's body metaphor serves not only as a composite of general characteristics of the ideal polity, but also as an account of the ideal prince.[82] By this reading, the body metaphor can also be read in a restricted sense as an expression of the ideal personal character of the prince and as a description of his responsibilities.

The dual nature of the metaphor as representative of the polity and of the ideal prince is reinforced in John's discussion of the relationship between the hands and the prince. John points out that the moderate prince exerts punishment reluctantly: 'For the prince has no left hand, and in subjecting to pain the members of his body of which he is the head, he is enslaved to the law with sadness and groans.'[83] Although physical force is an accepted element of political life, the prince himself is not encouraged to exercise it; in this manner he is akin to a cleric who is not allowed to wield a sword and is permitted only to delegate the responsibility of force to another. The division of duties within the body and, by extension, within the polity illustrates a complexity of governance that is at the root of a series of paradoxes in John's discussion of the relationship between the soul and the head, the priesthood and the prince.

## Head and soul: the prince and the priesthood

The most complicated relationships in John's model are those between the prince and the priesthood, and their respective interactions with the rest of the members of the polity. In an alleged borrowing from Plutarch, John writes: 'The place of the head in the body of the *res publica* is filled by the prince, who is subject only to God and to those who are representative of Him on earth, just as in the human body the head is animated and ruled by the soul.'[84] The soul, however, 'is, as it were, the prince of the body', and holds the role that 'prefects of religion' have in presiding over the whole body.[85] While this may seem to be a hierocratic interpretation of the structure of the polity, the manner in which John develops his metaphor is more complicated. By evaluating the relationship between the soul and the head, a clearer picture of the respective responsibilities of the prince and priesthood can be determined. The complexity of these relationships is provoked by the dual nature of John's metaphor. On the one hand, the body represents the totality of the polity; according to this reading the soul and head refer to two separate social entities, the priesthood and the principate. On the other hand, the model of the body can also be seen as specifically referring to an ideal-type of a ruler; in this interpretation the respective roles and responsibilities of the head and the soul can be read as a commentary on the dual character of the prince's personal role as simultaneously divinely ordained, while bound by his own humanity.

The prince 'is placed by divine disposition *in arce rei publicae*', on an 'apex which is exalted and made splendid with all the great and high privileges which he believes necessary for himself'.[86] However, his dominance is dependent on his effective execution of his role. Only if the prince faithfully performs his 'ministry' is he to be accorded the respect that the rest of the body shows to the head.[87] Therefore, the prince should act proportionally; his role obliges him to do the most for those who have the least, and to be most adversarial against those who wish to do harm.[88] In Book VI.25, John refers to Socrates as an advocate of such proportionality, as he pointed out that the humbler parts of the *res publica* should be lovingly cared for by those in greater offices.[89] John stresses this necessary interdependence of the prince and his subjects, and draws upon the corporeal metaphor to enforce his point. Just as parts of the body try to fend danger away from the head, so too the members of the polity will move to protect the prince; in return he is obliged to do all he can to protect his body and soul, 'skin for skin'.[90] An antecedent of this position is found in Seneca's *De clementia*, where it is argued that although men are primarily motivated by their own safety, they will happily rush into battle to protect their emperor as 'he is the bond by which the commonwealth is united, the breath of life which these many thousands draw'; if the *mens* of the empire was destroyed, they would also suffer. Interestingly, Seneca regards this as a logical extension of personal duty, as 'kings and princes and guardians of the public order, whatever different name they bear, are held more dear than those bound to us by private ties', an example of reasoning from the basis of Stoic *oikeiôsis* (as detailed in Chapter 3). Personal benefit is best served by cooperation with others, and therefore: 'while a Caesar needs power, the state also needs a head'.[91] Seneca identifies the emperor with the mind of the body, not its soul, but locates the mind in the head, implying its guiding role.

As previously argued, the body metaphor operates on two levels: it represents the polity, but also models the ideal ruler. Although the inferior limbs of the body are inextricably bound to the head, their obedience to the prince is contingent on the guarantee that religious freedoms are protected.[92] The prince's respect for religion legitimises his rule; this is a significant distinction between the prince and the tyrant. Just as the priesthood must play an important role in the polity, so religion must serve as a constant corrective to the faults of the prince's own soul. The emphasis placed on religion in John's account does not suggest that he wished for a hierocratic society, but, instead, that he regarded virtue in all parts of the polity as impossible to gain without the aid of religion. In Book VI. 25, John refers to the effect of sin in the polity: the sins of the people damage the princely head, while offences on his part are also detrimental to the good of the polity as they set as a bad example for the populace. The 'innocence' of the populace makes the prince merciful, while 'princely innocence' acts as its corrective.[93] John suggests therefore, that public utility is best served by personal attention to one's own character. 'If each were to work on the cultivation of themselves, regarding all external things as alien, then the status of each and all would be the best, virtue would flourish and reason prevail, while mutual charity would reign everywhere.' This is an approach best achieved by a subjection of the flesh to the spirit, and of the spirit to devotion to God.[94]

Being the '*potestas publica*', the prince draws strength from all and must protect all. By preserving the virtue and reputation of each duty or office of the *res publica* he preserves his own virtue and reputation; likewise, his corruption (through negligence or dissimulation, for example) is reflected by disease and injury to the polity. Sickness of the body impairs the head and vice versa.[95] In that respect, the prince has a role akin to a doctor, and is obliged to 'treat' the members of the polity when they overstep or fail in the duties allocated to them. John makes a comparison between the prince and a medical practicioner in *Policraticus*, Book IV. 8, referring to a passage from 1 Corinthians 10:24 that states that one should put the interests of all over personal interests. He then comments that the prince is obliged to 'keep within the limits of moderation', referring to the practice of doctors, who treat first with potions and mild medicines before applying 'fire and steel'.[96] John then asks, 'but who can amputate part of their body without sadness?'[97]

This discussion is of interest, as it is a further attestation to John's use of Ambrose's *De officiis*. In Book II of that text, the body metaphor is used to describe the *ecclesia*, with the bishop situated at its head.[98] The bishop must be protective of the members of the Church, and is obliged to act as a physician, curing weak members, or cutting them off (*'auferre'*) if healing proves impossible, while acknowledging the 'great distress' it will cause him. The excision of the member is the final resort and must be preceded by treatment of the sick and cauterisation by burning (*'adurere'*).[99] The list of punishments used by the bishop-doctor are identical in degree to those presented by John. The similarity between the two texts is further underscored by the fact that Ambrose also refers in his description to the same passage from 1 Corinthians used by John. The use of the same biblical reference in a similar context, the employment of comparable terms to describe the actions that should be taken by the ruler and the similar emphasis on the grief that will be experienced by the ruler if he is forced to take extreme action reinforce the likelihood that Ambrose is the source of John's comparison between the ruler and the doctor.[100] While Ambrose's advice is intended for an ecclesiastical figure, John may have wished to suggest that the political ruler has the same obligations towards his subjects as a bishop has towards his flock, thereby underscoring the pastoral obligations of the ruler.

What, then, is the role which John accords to the soul in the body? The most in-depth discussion, from a philosophical point of view, is found in the *Metalogicon*, where the capacity of the soul to animate the body is discussed.[101] Elsewhere, John demonstrates the similarities between the Platonic, Ciceronian (accessed through Augustine) and Christian perspectives; all emphasise the soul as the truest part of man's character:

> Plato, moreover, as well as Stoic and Peripatetic dogma, teaches that man is more correctly called a soul than a body. Marcus Tullius follows his meaning in his book on the republic, saying: 'You are not what the outward self designates, but the mind of each man which is that man.' The doctors of the Church, Augustine and others, agreed. If anyone doubts this, read Scriptures, which ascribe to the soul a certain rulership over the person, and compare the body to an inn or garment.[102]

If the soul is the defining organ of the self, per this account, where is it situated in the body? In the *Metalogicon*, John implies that the rational part of the soul is situated in the head, the seat of all senses. Just as the head is '*in arce rei publicae*', reason is '*in arce capitis*'; it is the 'senate on the soul's Capitoline hill', and holds this location by virtue of nature, 'the best parent of all'.[103] By situating reason, the primary part of the soul, in the head – the place of the prince in the body politic – John seems to imply that theocracy and monarchy should operate hand in hand. The principal elements of each type of rulership are situated in the same physical location; indeed, John may be suggesting that the priesthood should dominate the principate on account of its association with reason, the dominant sense of the body.

His position, however, is even more subtle; while the reasoning part of the soul is situated in the head, the other parts of the soul are diffused throughout the body – a diffusion that does not affect the essential coherence of the soul or dilute the effectiveness of the priesthood he associates it with. This is expressed in the opening chapter of *Policraticus*, Book III, where John discusses the universal public good. He asserts that the body fails if any of its parts cease to be animated by the soul: 'As long, therefore, as it [the body] is alive in all parts, it is disposed in accordance with a whole [the soul] which is not diffused part to part, but exists as a whole and operates in each and every part.'[104] If the soul represents the priesthood, then its presence in every part of the body demonstrates that religion should be relevant to every aspect of the polity.[105] However, if we return to the notion that the body metaphor simultaneously represents the ideal-type of ruler, a more restrictive picture emerges of the relationship between the soul and head. John is certainly not recommending that the ruler of the Church and the ruler of the polity should be one and the same. Instead, he is implying that the prince has a dual character: his nature is both secular and divine. In this respect, John's analogy takes on a more formulaic tone; in acknowledging that power comes from God, John sees reason as the manifestation of the divine in the mind of the prince.

A notable parallel to John's claim that the parts of the soul are diffused throughout the body is found in the writings of Seneca. Seneca used the metaphor of the body as a microcosmic representation of relations in the world: just as 'world matter corresponds to our mortal body', so the 'lower serve the higher' within the body.[106] In *De clementia*, Seneca compares the soul of the body (situated in the head) to the spirit, which animates and is innate in all parts of the world: 'it is from the head that comes the health of the body; it is through it that all the parts are lively and alert, or languid and drooping according as their animating spirit [*animus*] has life or withers'.[107] Thus, 'the whole body is the servant of the mind'; although the latter 'remains invisible', 'the hands, the feet, and the eyes are in its employ'. Seneca paints a picture of a body in the service of wisdom and reason.[108] While Seneca's account of the dominance of the soul in the body depended heavily on the Stoic conception of the *animus* that pervades the world, the analogy he drew between the role of the soul and the role of the ruler politicised the Stoic position. Seneca tells the addressee of the text, Nero, that 'if you are the soul of the state, and the state your body', then mercy is a necessary attribute: 'you are merciful to yourself when you are seemingly merciful to another'.[109] This should limit the ruler in taking punitive action towards members of the polity, permitting clemency to pervade the polity: 'That kindness of your heart [*tui animi mansuetudo*] will be recounted, will be diffused little by little throughout the whole body of the empire, and all things will be moulded into your likeness.'[110] While Cicero's treatment of the metaphor of the body politic also used the physiology of the body to metaphorically visualise the interdependence of duties, Seneca exploited its natural facility for representing an hierarchical system to enforce the idea that the ruling head has a natural guiding role. It is likely that Seneca's writings appealed to medieval writers, like John, as their imperial context eased their application to the monarchical context of the medieval period.

John's body analogy, while functionally useful for determining the relationship between different elements of the polity, is inherently ambiguous when it comes to an examination of the correspondence between the priesthood and the prince. In part, this is due to the fact that John does not sufficiently develop the discussion of the priesthood-soul in the *Policraticus*. Conclusions about its nature must be extrapolated from discussions found elsewhere regarding the role of reason, or from ancillary information on the nature of the soul found in the *Metalogicon*, where descriptions tend more towards the philosophical than towards the political. Further ambiguity is introduced by the fact that John sees the body analogy as representative not only of the polity, but also of the ideal prince. By creating an additional layer of metaphor, John is able to establish that that prince should be guided by the reasoning, divine, part of his soul, and so creates the normative expectation that the prince must respect religion. On a macrocosmic level, however, both priests and rulers are bearers of an authoritative role. Their collocation in the physical head of the body politic seems to suggest an uneasy cooperation in rulership, an ambiguity that would find further expression in John's commentary on contemporary politics, as explored in Chapter 6.

## Conclusion

The body metaphor has two functions for John. It serves, first, as a descriptive tool, with each element of the polity equated to a different member of the body. However, it is also a prescriptive tool, describing a certain kind of political order, a certain kind of prince. John's selection of metaphor, while no doubt influenced by its commonality in contemporary political discourse, proves particularly effective in forwarding the kinds of ideas he wishes to espouse. John aims to present a model of a polity that functions on the basis of a series of interrelationships and reciprocal exchanges of duties. The body, a confined system, serves to illustrate the necessary interdependence of the members of the polity who are engaged in pursuing the public good, the health of the body politic. As the discussion of the sources he used to describe the responsibilities of particular parts of the polity has shown, he also wished to situate his political discourse in a particular environment, one informed by a dialogue between Roman philosophical and Christian antecedents, a desire most forcibly expressed in his presumed invention of a manual for a Roman ruler, the *Institutio Traiani*, as the claimed source of his analogy. The body metaphor sets the scene for John's other statements on the responsibility of the ruler. In the opening of Book IV of the *Policraticus*, John rationalises the place of the prince as head of the polity; nature, the 'best guide of life', enshrines man's senses in his head, and so on a macrocosmic level the polity must be subject to a prince guided by rationality.[111] If the prince proves to be irrational – the hallmark of the tyrant – the body politic will be corrupted. Tyranny and irrationality are combatted by the emphasis John places on virtue and by his recommendations for moderate rulership, aspects of his political thought that shall be examined in the next two chapters.

### Notes

1 C. Walker Bynum, 'Why All the Fuss about the Body? A Medievalist's Perspective', *Critical Enquiry*, 22 (1995), 1–31 (8). On John's model see T. Struve, 'The Importance of the Organism in the Political Theory of John of Salisbury', in Wilks (ed.), *World*, pp. 303–17; T. Struve, *Die Entwicklung der organologischen Staatsauffassung im Mittelalter* (Stuttgart: Anton Hiersemann, 1978), pp. 123–48; C. J. Nederman, 'The Physiological Significance of the Organic Metaphor in John of Salisbury's *Policraticus*', *History of Political Thought*, 8 (1987), 211–23; Duby, *The Three Orders*, pp. 264–7. See also A. H. Chroust, 'The Corporate Idea and the Body Politic in the Middle Ages', *Review of Politics*, 9 (1947), 423–52.

2  Pouchelle, *Body and Surgery*, figure 2: Grenoble, Bibliothèque Municipale, MS 34, fo. 185; see G. Duby (ed.), *A History of Private Life*, vol. 2: *Revelations of the Medieval World* (Cambridge, MA: Belknap Press, 1993), p. 90 for a similar image from Auxerre, Biblothèque Municipale, MS 269.
3  For example, William of Conches, *Philosophia mundi*, ed. G. Maurach (Pretoria: University of South Africa, 1980), IV. 13, p. 98: '*Cuius est, quod frigidum et siccum est, in frigida et sicca membra (ut sunt ossa) mutare, quod frigidum et humidum, in flegmatica (ut est pulmo), quod calidum et siccum, in colerica (ut est cor), quod calidum et humidum in sanguinea (ut hepar).*'
4  For a general survey of this concept see R. Allers, 'Microcosmos from Anaximandros to Paracelsus', *Traditio*, 2 (1944), 319–407. John was clearly familiar with techniques of reasoning from microcosm to macrocosm; see *Pol.* IV. 1, p. 235, where he refers to the body as a 'microcosm', or 'little world'.
5  Yeager, 'The Body Politic and the Politics of Bodies', p. 146.
6  1 Corinthians 12:12-27 and Ephesians 4:25 emphasise the reciprocity of offices of the different parts of the body. Colossians 1:18 refers to Christ as the head of the Church.
7  See E. M. Atkins, 'Domina et Regina Virtutum: Justice and Societas in *De Officiis*', *Phronesis*, 35 (1990), 258–89 (271) on the metaphoric coherence of the Pauline model.
8  1 Corinthians 12:12: 'As a body is one though it has many parts, and all the parts of the body, though many, are one body, so it is with Christ.' See also 1 Corinthians 12:27 ('You are Christ's body, and individually parts of it') and Romans 12:5 ('We, though many, are one body in Christ').
9  E. Kantorowicz, *The King's Two Bodies: A Study in Medieval Political Theology* (Princeton: Princeton University Press, 1957).
10  B. McGinn (ed.), *Three Treatises on Man: A Cistercian Anthropology* (Kalamazoo: Cistercian Publications, 1977), p. 47; see E. Dietz, 'When Exile is Home: The Biography of Isaac of Stella', *Cistercian Studies Quarterly*, 41 (2006), 141–66 (150-1) for Isaac's connection with Becket.
11  Isaac of Stella, *The Selected Works of Isaac of Stella: A Cistercian Voice from the Twelfth Century*, ed. D. Deme (Aldershot: Ashgate, 2007), Sermon 34.4, p. 90.
12  Isaac of Stella, *Selected Works*, Sermon 34.9, p. 92.
13  Isaac of Stella, *Selected Works*, Sermon 34.11, p. 92.
14  Lachaud, *L'Éthique du pouvoir au Moyen-Âge*, discusses the variety of metaphors employed in this period to describe the polity, and the success of the corporeal metaphor among medieval thinkers (pp. 193–5, 200–3).
15  Calcidius, *Timaeus a Calcidio translatus*. For the Chartrain Platonic commentaries see Bernard of Chartres, *Glosae super Platonem*; William of Conches, *Glosae super Platonem*; Dutton, 'The Uncovering of the *Glosae super Platonem* of Bernard of Chartres'.
16  Calcidius, *Timaeus a Calcidio translatus*, 17 c, p. 8.
17  Gregory, 'The Platonic Inheritance', p. 62. Gregory quotes the gloss found in Oxford, Bodleian Library, MS Digby 23, fo. 5r, which describes the relationship: 'He [Socrates] saw in man some intermediate qualities such as courage,

whose seat is in the heart, and concupiscence, whose seat is in the kidneys or the loins; and low things such as feet, hands, etc. According to this disposition, he disposed the republic, instituting high officials such as senators, intermediate ones such as soldiers on active service, and low ones, such as the specialists in the mechanical arts – furriers, cobblers, apprentices, and outside the city, farmers.' See P. E. Dutton, '*Illustre ciuitatis et populi exemplum*: Plato's *Timaeus* and the Transmission from Calcidius to the End of the Twelfth Tentury of a Tripartite Scheme of Society', *Mediaeval Studies*, 45 (1983), 79–119 (98) for further discussion of this gloss. Note that this gloss places the senators in the heart, as does John.

18 Dutton, '*Illustre ciuitatis*', p. 85; A. Murray, *Reason and Society in the Middle Ages* (Oxford: Oxford University Press, 1978), pp. 97–9; Duby, *The Three Orders*; for a summary of the hierarchical implications of the tripartite model see D. E. Luscombe, 'Conceptions of Hierarchy before the Thirteenth Century', in A. Zimmerman (ed.), *Soziale Ordnungen im Selbstverständnis des Mittelalters* (Berlin: De Gruyter, 1979), pp. 1–19.

19 Bernard of Chartres, *Glosae super Platonem*, 7.138–54, p. 206: '*Potest uero notari in regione humani corporis dispositio rei publicae, quia sicut in eminentiori loco ciuitatis habitant maiores, ita in capite maior uis anime, id est ratio. Et sicut in medio ciuitatis milites habitant qui defendunt ciuitatem, ita in medio hominis, id est in corde, est naturalis uigor animae, scilicet ira per quam malis irasci debemus. Et sicut in ciuitate circa extremos habitant opifices, id est sellularii et ceteri seruiles, qui semper cupiunt adquirere, ita in homine circa posteriora habitant concupiscentiae.*'

20 Bernard Silvestris, *The Commentary on the First Six Books of the Aeneid of Virgil*, ed. and trans. E. G. Schrieber and T. E. Maresca (Lincoln, NE: University of Nebraska Press, 1979), Book 3, pp. 17–18. See also Dutton, '*Illustre ciuitatis*', pp. 105–7.

21 Cf. Bernard Silvestris, *Commentary on the Aeneid*, Book 6, p. 102: 'Just as the world has four regions, and each has its own adornment, so the city is divided into four areas by politicians; and just as in the highest region are the rational substances and in the lowest region are the brutes, likewise in the city. The philosophers Plato and Socrates are in the citadel, the soldiers are in the second quarter, the merchants are in the third, and the farmers are in the suburbs.'

22 Bernard Silvestris, *Cosmographia*, trans. W. Wetherbee (New York: Columbia University Press, 1990), II. 14, p. 123.

23 Bernard Silvestris, *Cosmographia*, II. 14, p. 125. Bernard's description of the heart continues thus: 'It is the animating spark of the body, nurse of its life, the creative principle and harmonizing bond of the senses; the central link in the human structure, the terminus of the veins, root of the nerves, and controller of the arteries, mainstay of our nature, king, governor, creator. It is a noble lord journeying abroad through all the state of the body, to the limbs and the ministering senses, each of whom it maintains the function assigned to it.'

24 Bernard Silvestris, *Cosmographia*, p. 126. Bernard concludes his discussion by noting that 'in creating man Physis had to bestow limbs of which the universe

has no need: eyes to keep watch in the head, ears for sound, feet to bear him, and all-capable hands' (p. 127).
25 Bernard Silvestris, *Cosmographia*, II. 13, pp. 120–3.
26 See Dutton, '*Illustre ciuitatis*', p. 93 on the relationship between this model and that of Constantinus Africanus; see Coleman, *Ancient and Medieval Memories*, pp. 11–12, for this division of wisdom in Plato.
27 Trans. in Dutton, '*Illustre ciuitatis*', p. 93. William of Conches, *Glosae super Platonem*, XV, p. 75: '*Ad hanc vero similitudinem voluit Socrates in arce civitatis esse senatum ut in arce capitis est sapientia; sub isto esse milites ut in corde animositatem, sub quibus sunt cupidinarii ut in lumbis est concupiscentia. Et ut pedes bruti in inferiori parte calcant terram, ita agricole et venatores et pastores extra muros terrram exercent*' (gloss on *Timaeus*, 17 c). See Dutton, '*Illustre ciuitatis*', p. 94, n. 56, on the dual meaning of the word *cupidinarii* as used by William of Conches: 'Because of the similarity of the words cuppedium (confection), from which the cupedenarii of William's gloss on Macrobius derives, and cupido (desire or longing), it seems likely that William wanted the cupidinarii of his gloss on the Timaeus to stand for the entire class of desirous men. In addition, the orthography of the second usage draws it closer still to cupiditas (desire).' For the relationship between this passage and the humours see William of Conches, *Glosae super Platonem*, XV, p. 75: '*Quia ergo ista tria que faciunt perfecte sapientem habent sedem in capite, merito in eo dicitur esse sedes sapientie. Sub capite vero est cor, quedam pirea substantia calida et sicca, cuius est semper dilatari et constringi, ex quo ira est in homine. Sub corde sunt renes in quibus est sedes concupiscentie.*'
28 Dutton, '*Illustre ciuitatis*', pp. 93–4. On pp. 91–2, Dutton draws attention to William's *Glosae super Macrobium*, which provides a comparable quadripartite division of the body and the city state.
29 H. Liebeschütz, 'John of Salisbury and Pseudo-Plutarch', *Journal of the Warburg and Courtauld Institutes*, 6 (1943), 33–9.
30 Martin reinforced Liebeschütz's argument, pointing out that John's unwillingness to quote directly from the supposed text is telling. She suggests that the mention of Plutarch in Aulus Gellius's *Noctes Atticae* caught John's attention; from there it was a small step to turn Plutarch into a political philosopher and associate him with Trajan. See Martin, 'John of Salisbury and the Classics', pp. 184–6. See also Martin, 'John of Salisbury as Classical Scholar', pp. 195–6. However, there has been some dissension. Kerner believes that the text came from a genuine 'Pseudo-Plutarchian' text, possibly an anonymous medieval text that incorporated antique elements: see M. Kerner, 'Die Institutio Traiani und Johannes von Salisbury: Ein mittelalterlicher Autor und sein Text', in [Pseudo-] Plutarch, *Die Institutio Traiani*, pp. 93–124. See also Struve, 'The Importance of the Organism', p. 305: 'But it is made evident alone by the manner in which the *Institutio Traiani* was inserted into the thematic context of the *Policraticus* that John must have used a text in which the *officia* of the late Roman empire had been compared to the members of the human body.' A summary of recent scholarship can be found in M. Pade, *The Reception of Plutarch's Lives in Fifteenth-Century*

*Italy* (2 vols; Copenhagen: Museum Tusculanum Press, 2007), pp. 62–6. My thanks to Fred Schurink of the University of Manchester for facilitating my access to Pade's work.

31 Liebeschütz, 'John of Salisbury and Pseudo-Plutarch', p. 38; Liebeschütz, *Mediaeval Humanism*, pp. 23–4, 26.

32 John's account of his study under Robert is found in *Met*. II. 10. For information about Robert's life and works see F. Courtney, *Cardinal Robert Pullen: An English Theologian of the Twelfth Century* (Rome: Universitatis Gregorianae, 1954); Smalley, *The Becket Conflict and the Schools*, pp. 38–50.

33 Martin, 'John of Salisbury and the Classics', p. 179.

34 Smalley, *The Becket Conflict and the Schools*, p. 43: 'Pullen is neither conclusive nor original on the subject of *regnum* and *sacerdotium*. The important point is that he published views which could be discussed and interpreted.' Smalley points out that Robert, like John, considered that nature as reason was best guide to life (p. 50). Courtney, *Cardinal Robert Pullen*, p. 262, noted that both John and Robert emphasise the prevalence of venality and corruption in the exercise of ecclesiastical and civil power.

35 *Pol*. V. 9; 1, p. 322: '*Et forte ideo crates pectoris costarumque soliditatem et extremae cutis claustrum natura diligentissima parens circumposuit intestinis, quo aduersus omnem exteriorem uiolentiam fierent tutiora, et eis quod necesse est ministrat, nec umquam sine salutis suae dispendio exterioribus exponuntur. Oportet autem in re publica hanc naturae opificis seruari imaginem et his necessariorum copiam de publico ministrari.*' Cf. Lactantius, *De opificio Dei*, VII, on the enclosure of the inner organs by the exterior limbs and skin, and Ambrose, *De officiis*, I. 18.77.

36 *Pol*. V. 3; 1, p. 286: '*Colitur ergo Deus aut affectu mentis aut exhibitione operis.*'

37 *Pol*. V. 2; 1, p. 283: '*Cordis locum senatus optinet, a quo bonorum operum et malorum procedunt initia.*'

38 *Pol*. V. 9;1, p. 318.

39 *Pol*. V. 9; 1, pp. 318–19.

40 *Pol*. VIII. 17; 2, p. 348: '*cor consiliarii impii, quasi senatus iniquitatis*'. See also *Pol*. V. 9; 1, p. 322.

41 *Pol*. IV. 6; 1, p. 251: '*Describet ergo Deuteronomium legis, id est, secundam legem, in uolumine cordis: ut sit lex prima, quam littera ingerit; secunda, quam ex eo misticus intellectus agnoscit. Prima quidem scribi potuit lapideis tabulis; sed secunda non imprimitur, nisi in puriore intelligentia mentis.*'

42 T. Ricklin, 'Le Cœur, soleil du corps: Une redécouverte symbolique du XII$^e$ siècle', *Micrologus*, 11 (2003), 123–43; J. LeGoff, 'Head or Heart? The Political Use of Body Metaphors in the Middle Ages', in M. Feher, R. Naddaff and N. Tazi (eds), *Fragments for a History of the Human Body*, vol. 3 (New York: Zone Books, 1989), 12–27; see T. Shogimen, '"Head or Heart?" Revisited: Physiology and Political Thought in the Thirteenth and Fourteenth Centuries', *History of Political Thought*, 28 (2007), 208–29.

43 *Pol*. V. 11; 1, p. 330.

44 Job 29:11.

45 *Pol.* V. 6, 1, p. 302: '*Instrumenta corporis eleganter expressit, quibus sensus animae maxime conualescit; exteriorum namque notitia oculi et auris obsequio fidelissime transit ad animam, et thesauros cordis saepius lingua incauta dispergit.*'
46 *Pol.* V. 6; 1, p. 302: '*Beatus qui loquitur in aure audientis.*'
47 *Pol.* V. 15; 1, p. 345.
48 *Pol.* VI. 22; 2, pp. 63-4.
49 *Pol.* VI. 22; 2, p. 62: '*Quod sine prudentia et sollicitudine nullus magistratus subsistit incolumis, nec uiget res publica cuius caput infirmatur.*' Note that although these titles may not have been added by John, but by an early reader, such chapter headings still provide a means of navigating the themes of the text. See J. van Laarhoven, 'Titles and Subtitles of the *Policraticus*: A Proposal', *Vivarium*, 32 (1994), 131-60 (136-8).
50 See B. Yun, 'A Visual Mirror of Princes: The Wheel on the Mural of Longthorpe Tower', *Journal of the Warburg and Courtauld Institutes*, 70 (2007), 1-32 (15-19) on the five senses and microcosmic and macrocosmic analogies; see p. 21 for John's use of the metaphor of the ears, eyes and tongue.
51 *Pol.* V. 10; 1, p. 323: '*Sed et in lateribus, his scilicet qui principibus debent assistere, haec naturae formula seruanda est.*'
52 *Pol.* V. 10; 1, p. 323: '*Constat enim quia a conuictu mores formantur.*'
53 *Pol.* V. 10; 1, p. 323: '*uuaque contacta liuorem ducit ab uua*': here John quotes from Juvenal, *Satire* 2.14.
54 *Pol.* VI. 24; 2, p. 72.
55 *Pol.* V. 2; 1, p. 283; L. K. Little, 'Pride Goes before Avarice: Social Changes and the Vices in Latin Christendom', *American Historical Review*, 76 (1971), 16-49 (37-8).
56 R. Newhauser, 'The Love of Money as Deadly Sin and Deadly Disease', in K. H. Göller, J. O. Fichte and B. Schimmelpfennig (eds), *Zusammenhänge, Einflüsse, Wirkungen: Kongressakten zum ersten Symposium des Mediävistenverbandes in Tübingen, 1984* (Berlin: De Gruyter, 1986), pp. 315-26.
57 *Pol.* VI. 20; 2, p. 58.
58 *Pol.* V. 2; 1, p. 283: '*Pedibus uero solo iugiter inherentibus agricolae coaptantur, quibus capitis prouidentia tanto magis necessaria est, quo plura inueniunt offendicula, dum in obsequio corporis in terra gradiuntur, eisque iustius tegumentorum debetur suffragium, qui totius corporis erigunt sustinent et promouent molem. Pedum adminicula robustissimo corpori tolle, suis uiribus non procedet sed aut turpiter inutiliter et moleste manibus repet aut brutorum animalium ope mouebitur.*'
59 *Pol.* VI. 19; 2, p. 58: '*Sequamur ergo eum et, sicut ipse ait, quasi soccos pedibus faciamus ut non offendantur ad lapidem obicemue alium quem multiplex ingerit casus.*'
60 Augustine, 'Exposition 2 of Psalm 90', in *Expositions of the Psalms, 73-98*, ed. J. Rotelle, trans. M. Boulding (New York: City Press, 2002), pp. 329-44 (p. 334); *Enarrationes in Psalmos*, ed. E. Dekkers and J. Fraipont (CCSL 39; Turnhout: Brepols, 1956), XC, s. II. 4, pp. 1254-78 (p. 1270): '*quo caput praecessit, et membra sectura sunt*'. 'Exposition 2 of Psalm 90', p. 335; *Ennarationes*, XC,

s. II. 5, p. 1270: '*Longe est super omnes caelos, sed pedes habet in terra; caput in caelo est, corpus in terra.*'
61 Augustine, 'Exposition 2 of Psalm 90', p. 340.
62 Augustine, 'Exposition 2 of Psalm 90', p. 340; *Enarrationes*, XC, s. II. 8, p. 1275: '*Metuendum erat ne euangelistae offenderent in lapidem: illo enim in caelo posito capite, pedes qui in terra laborabant, possent offendere in lapidem. In quem lapidem? In legem in tabulis lapideis datam. Ne ergo legis rei fierent, non accepta gratia, et in lege rei tenerentur; ipsa est enim offensio reatus ... ne illi qui in terra laborabant in corpore eius, peragrantes totum orbem terrarum fierent rei legis, subtraxit ab eis timorem, et impleuit eos amore.*' Cf. Ephesians 6:15.
63 Gregory the Great, *Pastoral Care*, II. 7, p. 69; *La Règle pastorale*, II. 7, p. 222: '*Caput namque subiectorum sunt cuncti qui praesunt; et ut recta pedes ualeant itinera carpere, haec procul dubio caput debet ex alto prouidere, ne a prouectus sui itinere pedes torpeant, cum curuata rectitudine corporis caput sese ad terram declinat.*'
64 Gregory the Great, *Pastoral Care*, I. 5, p. 31; *La Règle pastorale*, I. 5, pp. 146–8: '*Si ergo ut nostram, sic curam proximi gerimus, utrumque pedem per calceamentum munimus. Qui uero suam cogitans utilitatem, proximorum neglegit, quasi unius pedis calceamentum cum dedecore amittit.*'
65 *Pol.* V. 10, p. 328. The story is borrowed from Jerome (PL 23, 279c).
66 Letter 111 to Peter of Celle (autumn 1159), *Letters* I, pp. 181–2: '*Pes enim qui uersatur in coeno nequaquam aspirat ad capitis dignitatem; sed et caput quod in caelum erigitur non aspernatur pedem qui inuersatur in coeno.*'
67 Struve, 'The Importance of the Organism', pp. 309–10.
68 Rigby, 'Justifying Inequality', pp. 175–7.
69 *Pol.* VI. 20; 2, p. 59: '*Tunc autem totius rei publicae salus incolumis praeclaraque erit, si superiora membra se impendant inferioribus et inferiora superioribus pari iure respondeant, ut singula sint quasi aliorum ad inuicem membra et in eo sibi quisque maxime credat esse consultum in quo aliis utilius nouerit esse prospectum.*'
70 *Pol.* VI. 20; 2, p. 59: '*Verumtamen quod generale est omnibus et singulis procuratur, ut legis scilicet limites non excedant et ad publicam utilitatem omnia referantur. Debent autem obsequium inferiora superioribus quae omnia eisdem uicissim debent necessarium subsidium prouidere.*'
71 *Pol.* VI. 20; 2, p. 59.
72 Rigby, 'Justifying Inequality', p. 192.
73 *Pol.* VI. 1; 2, p. 2: '*Manus itaque rei publicae aut armata est aut inermis. Armata quidem est quae castrensem et cruentam exercet militiam; inermis quae iustitiam expedit et ab armis feriando iuris militiae seruit. ... Sicut enim alia sunt officia pacis, alia belli, ita eadem necesse est per alios et alios expediri.*'
74 *Pol.* VI. 12; 2, p. 3: '*Manus tamen utriusque militae, armatae uidelicet et inermis, manus principis est; et nisi utramque cohibeat parum continens est.*' '*Vsus quoque manuum capitis sui protestatur imaginem*'.
75 *Pol.* VI. 1; 2, p. 6: cf. Augustine, *City of God*, IV. 4, p. 139: 'Remove justice and what are kingdoms but gangs of criminals on a large scale? A gang is a group of men under the command of a leader, bound by a compact of association, in

which the plunder is divided according to an agreed convention.' Cf. Cicero, *De re publica*, III. 24.
76 *Pol.* VI. 1; 2, p. 7: '*Omnes enim sunt quasi corpus unum quod, sicut manifesta conuincunt opera, ex patre diabolo est, cuius isti sunt membra.*'
77 *Pol.* VI. 12; 2, p. 30.
78 Cf. William of Conches's representation of the army as the heart and hands of the polity, as discussed in his gloss on Macrobius. J. Flori, *L'Essor de la chevalerie: XI$^e$–XII$^e$ siècles* (Geneva: Droz, 1986), p. 240.
79 Kantorowicz, *The King's Two Bodies*.
80 Kantorowicz, *The King's Two Bodies*, p. 96.
81 Scanlon, *Narrative, Authority and Power*, pp. 88–104.
82 A similar conclusion is reached by F. Lachaud, 'Corps du prince, corps de la *res publica*': Écriture métaphorique et construction politique dans le *Policraticus* de Jean de Salisbury', *Micrologus*, 22 (2014), 171–99 (191), although she refers to the conflation of the body of the prince and the body of the *res publica* on John's part as a 'confusion' (pp. 175, 183–6), whereas I regard it as an intentional aspect of John's metaphoric construct.
83 *Pol.* IV. 8; 1, p. 262: '*Sinistram namque non habet princeps et in cruciatu membrorum corporis, cuius ipse caput est, legi tristis et gemens famulatur.*'
84 *Pol.* V. 2; 1, pp. 282–3: '*Princeps uero capitis in re publica optinet locum uni subiectus Deo et his qui uices illius agunt in terris, quoniam et in corpore humano ab anima uegetatur caput et regitur.*'
85 *Pol.* V. 2; 1, p. 282: '*Porro, sicut anima totius habet corporis principatum, ita et hii, quos ille religionis praefectos uocat, toti corpori praesunt.*'
86 *Pol.* V. 6; 1, p. 298: '*dispositio diuina in arce rei publicae collocauit*'; *Pol.* IV. 1; 1, p. 235: '*Tot ergo et tantis priuilegiis apex principalis extollitur et splendescit, quot et quanta sibi ipse necessaria credidit.*'
87 *Pol.* IV. 3; 1, p. 241.
88 *Pol.* IV. 2; 1, p. 238.
89 *Pol.* VI. 25; 2, p. 73. Note Scanlon's observation in *Narrative, Authority and Power*, p. 101: 'If his scheme represents a step forward when compared to Carolingian notions of sacral kingship, or to the feudally inspired notion of the Three Estates, it is only as a rationalisation of existing privilege, and certainly not as a shift in the fundamental distribution of power.'
90 *Pol.* IV. 4; 1, p. 246.
91 Seneca, *De clementia*, in *Seneca: Moral Essays I*, trans. J. W. Basore (LCL 214; Cambridge, MA: Harvard University Press, 1928), 1.4.1, 3, pp. 368–9: '*Ille est enim vinculum, per quod res publica cohaeret, ille spiritus vitalis, quem haec tot milia trahunt nihil ipsa per se futura nisi onus et praeda, si mens illa imperii subtrahatur. … Ideo principes regesque et quocumque alio nomine sunt tutores status publici non est mirum amari ultra privatas etiam necessitudines … nam et illi viribus opus est et huic capite.*'
92 *Pol.* VI. 25; 2, pp. 73–7.
93 *Pol.* VI. 29; 2, pp. 86–7: '*Mansuescit itaque princeps ab innocentia populi et populares motus reprimit innocentia principalis.*'

94 *Pol.* VI. 29; 2, p. 86: 'Si enim in sui ipsius cultu quisque laboret et quae exteriora sunt reputet aliena, profecto optimus erit status singulorum et omnium, uigebitque uirtus et ratio praeualebit, regnante undique mutua caritate, ut sit caro subiecta spiritui et spiritus plena deuotione Domino famuletur.'
95 *Pol.* IV. 12; 1, pp. 278–9: 'Cum enim potestas publica sit, ut praediximus, omnium uires exhaurit, et, ne in se deficiat, incolumitatem omnium debet procurare membrorum. Quot autem in administratione principatus extant officia, tot sunt principalis corporis quasi membra. Dum autem singulorum officia in integritate uirtutis et suauitate opinionis conseruat, quandam quasi membris sanitatem procurat et decorem. Cum uero ex negligentia aut dissimulatione potestatis circa officia sit uirtutis aut famae dispendium, quasi in membra eius morbi et maculae incurrunt. Nec diu subsistit incolumitas capitis, ubi languor membrorum inualescit.'
96 *Pol.* IV. 8; 1, p. 262: 'Medicorum utique consuetudo est ut morbos, quos fomentis et leuioribus medicinis curare nequeunt, grauioribus adhibitis igne puta uel ferro curent.'
97 *Pol.* IV. 8; 1, p. 262: 'Sed quis sine dolore proprii corporis membra ualuit amputare?'
98 For Ambrose, the body model is employed as an expression of Acts 4:32: *De officiis*, II. 27.134, p. 343: 'If we wish to commend ourselves to God, let us possess love for one another, let us be of one mind, and let us strive to show humility, each of us regarding his neighbour as better than himself.'
99 Ambrose, *De officiis*, II. 27.134–5, pp. 342–3; cf. III. 3.17–18, pp. 363–4. T. Shogimen and C. J. Nederman, 'The Best Medicine? Medical Education, Practice, and Metaphor in John of Salisbury's *Policraticus* and *Metalogicon*', *Viator*, 42 (2011), 55–74 (71–2), regard these observations on surgical practice as 'based on knowledge of common practice rather than any form of specialist knowledge', but do not make a link with Ambrose's text.
100 W. Summers, 'John of Salisbury and the Classics', *Classical Quarterly*, 4 (1910), 103–5 (104).
101 *Met.* II. 4, p. 61: 'ut quodam modo sicut corpus ad uitam uegetatur ab anima'.
102 *Met.* III. 7, p. 124: 'Plato autem, et tam Stoicorum quam Peripateticorum dogma, hominem rectius animam quam corpus dici declarat. Quam secutus sententiam Marcus Tullius, in libro de republica, ait. Tu non es is quem exterior figura designat, sed mens cuiusque is est quisque. Doctoribus quoque ecclesiae Augustino et ceteris, id ipsum placuit. Siquis hinc dubitat, legat Scripturas quae principatum personalem quodam modo animae tribuunt, et corpus hospitio comparant aut indumento.'
103 *Met.* IV. 17, p. 155: 'natura optima parens omnium uniuersos sensus locans in capite, uelut quendam senatum in Capitolio animae rationem quasi dominam in arce capitis statuit'. See Chapter 2, pp. 77–8.
104 *Pol.* III. 1; 1, p. 171: 'Dum ergo totum uiuit, ad eam totum disponitur, quae se non per partes infundit partibus, sed tota est et operatur in uniuersis et singulis.'
105 C. Nederman, 'The Physiological Significance of the Organic Metaphor', p. 212, claims that the clerics are not 'strictly speaking' part of the polity as the soul is not

coextensive with the physical organism. While John does not consider that the soul is a corporeal entity, he by no means implies that the priesthood is outside the body. Nederman's argument (p. 212) that John's 'organic metaphor expresses a primarily secular political theory which excludes religious offices from a place within the metaphor itself' must be rejected.

106 Seneca, *Ep.* 64.24; 1, pp. 458–9: '*Quod est illic materia, id in nobis corpus est; serviant ergo deteriora melioribus.*'
107 Seneca, *De clementia*, II. 2.1, pp. 432–3: '*A capite bona valetudo: inde omnia vegeta sunt atque erecta aut languore demissa, prout animus eorum vivit aut marcet.*'
108 Seneca, *De clementia*, I. 3.5, pp. 366–7: '*Quemadmodum totus corpus animo deservit ... ille in occulto maneat tenuis et in qua sede latitet incertus, tamen manus, pedes, oculi negotium illi gerunt.*'
109 Seneca, *De clementia*, I. 5.1, pp. 370–1: '*tu animus rei publicae tuae es, illa corpus tuum vides ... quam necessaria sit clementia; tibi enim parcis, cum videris alteri parcere*'.
110 Seneca, *De clementia*, II. 2.1, pp. 432–3: '*Tradetur ista animi tui mansuetudo diffundeturque paulatim per omne imperii corpus, et cuncta in similitudinem tuam formabuntur.*'
111 *Pol.* IV. 1, p. 235: '*In quo quidem optimam uiuendi ducem naturam sequimur, quae microcosmi sui, id est, mundi minoris, hominis scilicet, sensus uniuersos in capite collocauit, et ei sic uniuersa membra subiecit, ut omnia recte moueantur, dum sani capitis sequuntur arbitrium.*'

5

# Moderation and the virtuous life

It is no accident that John of Salisbury is preoccupied with the question of the character of a statesman. What yet has to be invented in the twelfth century is an institutional order in which the demands of divine law can more easily be heard and lived out in a secular society outside the monasteries. The question of the virtues thus becomes inescapable: what kind of man can do this? What type of education can foster this type of man?[1]

Politics can be regarded as a process through which relationships between individual human beings are regulated by a series of public values, which supersede the place of individual desires. Given that the definition of the 'political' changes according to historical context, the content of such public values remains open to negotiation; but when they are institutionalised the question is no longer personal – 'what ought I do?'– but public: 'what ought I to do, taking into account the needs of those surrounding me?' As illustrated in the previous chapter, John expressed his version of a solution to this problem by means of the corporeal metaphor, demonstrating how political roles were distributed among members of the polity and describing the reciprocal obligations that facilitated its healthy functioning. That said, such a model still begs the question, as posed by Alisdair MacIntyre in the passage quoted at the opening of this chapter, of what *kind* of man is best suited to exercising particular political roles.[2] The success of modern political systems is perceived as the degree to which they allow the individual to maintain personal liberties vis-à-vis the state, while still ensuring the maintenance of civic society. However, for pre-modern political systems a further index of success was the degree to which they allowed their citizenry to lead as virtuous a life as possible. In a pre-modern political system the questions 'what ought I do?' and 'what is the virtuous thing to do?' theoretically have identical answers, making the exercise of the virtues intrinsic to political action. This impetus to align normative and virtuous codes can be seen in action in what can be termed the ethical components of John's political thought. This chapter will look, first, at John's account of the *summum bonum*, or highest good, and what constituted 'virtue' in his writings. It will then examine the significance of moderation for John, a safeguard placed on all actions that can be regarded as intrinsically Stoic in its presentation. The final sections will treat a number of examples of moderate virtue in practice. Throughout, the chapter will identify the personal characteristics that he considered to be necessary for life in the political realm.

## The pursuit of the *summum bonum*

In Book VII. 8 of the *Policraticus*, John offers three different definitions of the *summum bonum*, or highest good. The chapter opens by recognising that, despite the multiplicity of interpretations of various philosophical schools, all men are travelling towards a single goal, namely 'true happiness', '*vera beatitudo*'.[3] Although there are many paths to this goal, one route is recommended: 'virtue', as 'virtue is what happiness deserves and happiness is the reward of virtue'.[4] Happiness and virtue are described as two '*summa bona*', one of the way, the other of the homecoming. In defining the pursuit of virtue as a journey towards a destination, John plays upon the metaphor of exile; the exile needs virtue while travelling (John uses the verb *peregrinor*), and is ultimately happy when he 'rejoices with God'.[5] In his choice of words, John echoes Augustine's description of the citizens of the City of God as 'alien [*peregrinatur*] among the ungodly' while on earth, as well as the Pauline concept of man as distanced (*peregrinamur*) from the Lord when in the physical body.[6] His use of this vocabulary suggests a distinction between what can be regarded as an attainable *summum bonum* on earth, happiness, and the ultimate reward that men should strive to achieve through the practice of virtue (in itself a *summum bonum*). Happiness is the 'one unique *summum bonum*', but this is inferior to 'enjoyment of Him who is supremely good and is the *summum bonum*', that is God, the third, and ultimately superior, *summum bonum*.[7] John implies, therefore, that in the context of the necessarily limited life of men on earth, virtuous happiness is a sufficient 'highest' good, but that in the ideal salvific context, God is the ultimate good. This passage highlights a persistent tension in John's writings between the immaterial value of ultimate salvation and the concomitant necessity to achieve such salvation through virtuous behaviour in the material world.[8] Examining this passage in the broader context of Book VII. 8 reveals a secondary purpose: it must also be read an attempt to place the contributions of pagan philosophers within a Christian account of the *summum bonum*. The pagans, according to John, found the *summum bonum* in virtue as they had not learned of the true eternal life, despite believing in the immortality of the soul.[9] But, as John reiterates, virtue is a route towards happiness, not ultimate happiness in itself: 'one is not happy in order to do right, but one does right in order to live happily'.[10] Just as advanced philosophers sought 'justifications', so the Christian must also seek to 'know God' to the best extent possible in the earthly domain.[11]

But what precisely does doing right in order to live happily consist of? John concludes Book VII. 8 with a survey of the 'paths' taken by various philosophical sects: 'The Stoic, to show his contempt for goods, meditates upon death; the Peripatetic investigates truth; Epicurus wallows in pleasure'.[12] If we are, as John implies, sojourners in a realm of imperfect peace, what can we do to live appropriately? In the subsequent chapters (VII. 9–10) John expands on the contribution of knowledge to beatitude. Presenting a scathing critique of his contemporaries, who dwell on 'a small number of questions chosen as apt for dispute, on which to exercise their craft and consume their life', John advises that one should read extensively, but critically, paying particular attention to 'those matters which concern political life, whether of civil law or ethical principles, or [those matters] which manage the health of body and soul'.[13] Borrowing a metaphor from Seneca, John compares the wise man to the bee which collects choice pollen to make honey, implying that the writings of pagan philosophers must be read with care so as to facilitate the rejection of their errors.[14] The mark of wisdom is this capacity for discernment, but, of course, the knowledge that is gained through reading is not the only, nor even the best, type of knowledge that the philosopher should aspire to; grace remains the principal source of wisdom.[15]

John's elaboration of how this higher type of knowledge is attained is found in the first chapter of Book III of the *Policraticus*. John writes here that 'the acknowledgement of truth and the cultivation of public virtue is the general safeguard of one and all, and of rational nature; its contrary is ignorance and her hateful and hostile offspring, vice'.[16] Here 'truth' is knowledge of God, accessible through grace and nature; it is this truth (manifested in reason) that opens the 'book of knowledge' that John describes each individual as holding within their heart.[17] 'Knowledge of self ('*scientia sui*') is, as John demonstrates, an aspect of this greater knowledge, and lies in part in 'following nature', which, as illustrated in Chapter 2, is a necessarily rational activity.[18] John elaborates on what such 'knowledge of self' must consist of in Book III. 2, by way of a quotation from the *Satires* of Persius (III. 66–72), where Persius (who John refers to as '*ethicus*') advises that one must 'learn ... what God has commanded you to be, and what is your place in the business of mankind'.[19] This quotation is also employed by Augustine in *De civitate Dei*, II. 6, where the same passage is used to illustrate the empty morality of traditional Roman religion when compared with Christianity.[20] John may have used Augustine as the source for this passage, but may also have accessed the text through one of the numerous copies of Persius's works available at the library of Canterbury; given that John does not situate the passage in a comparable polemical context to that found in Augustine's work, the latter scenario is the more likely.[21]

John suggests that the contemplation of the self leads to four 'fruits': 'benefit to self, love for close ones, contempt for the world, love of God'.[22] John elaborates on this metaphor of the fruit-producing tree, asking, 'Is it not a good tree that brings forth such sweet fruit as well as bringing forth benefits?', while offering a comparison in Book III. 3 to the diseased plant which has pride as its root and whose branches thrive when cultivated with arrogance.[23] John warns that 'love of self' is innate in everyone, but that when this exceeds the 'mean' (*modus*), it becomes a fault: 'Every virtue is limited by its bounds, which consist of its mean; if you are excessive, you are off the path, not on the path.'[24] The placement of this discussion prior to John's description of the flatterer, 'the enemy of all virtue', suggests that self-love, and its associated vice of concupiscence or excessive desire, leaves one vulnerable to the type of self-aggrandisement that flattery encourages.[25] Meanwhile, the reference to the 'path' recalls the emphasis on virtue as the best route to happiness. But what does virtue consist of in practice, and how it can be best expressed in this world? Moderation, adherence to the mean, is an essential aspect of living virtuously, and one with fundamental ramifications for John's recommendations for life in the political realm; therefore the question of what John purported to be 'the mean' deserves a detailed examination.

## Life in accordance with the mean

Moderation is a major theme of John's writings and is duly emphasised from the beginning of the *Policraticus*. Book I looks at a number of pursuits favoured by members of the court: hunting, music, gaming, acting and magic. In each instance, John emphasises the necessity of moderation. As noted in Chapter 2, John regarded the intention with which an action was performed as an essential indication of its worth; actions which are motivated by the pursuit of pleasure are inappropriate, while those which are rationally considered and motivated by a desire to live virtuously are appropriate. As briefly illustrated in Chapter 3, John did not condemn hunting outright but used Ciceronian language to suggest that, 'depending on the place, time, manner, the individual and purpose', hunting could be 'useful and honourable'.[26] In *Policraticus*, Book I. 4, he recounts examples of famous hunters from classical and biblical sources, ranging from Hannibal to Ulysses, Nimrod to Esau, but notes that no philosophers or Christian fathers have engaged in such '*insania*'.[27] In his discussion, John considers whether hunting can be regarded as an '*indifferentia*', but discounts any grounds for this argument because 'the immoderate pleasure it causes agitates manly minds and undermines the foundation of reason'.[28] John's use of the term '*indifferentia*' is a deliberate reference to the Stoic notion that some things, such as health and wealth, are to be regarded as morally neutral – neither good nor evil in themselves (that is, not essential for the pursuit of the human good, virtue) – but may be preferred depending on one's circumstances and orientation towards them. As established in Chapter 3, it is unlikely that John had access to Cicero's *De finibus*, where Cicero offers an extensive discussion of the Stoic interpretation of the indifferents.[29] A plausible source for John's use of the term is Letter 82 of Seneca to Lucilius, where Seneca describes indifferent things as 'neither good nor evil – sickness, pain, poverty, exile, death', a definition with which John, although he does not offer a similar list of indifferents here, is clearly consistent.[30] A further echo of this letter is found in *Policraticus*, Book VIII. 15, where John writes (in the context of a critique of avarice), '[Therefore] the use of things is praiseworthy [*laudabilis*] or blameworthy; things themselves, strictly speaking, are indifferent', noting that 'other things are praised and not foolishly desired, such as good health, noble blood, an abundance of things, but none of these makes a disagreeable or dishonourable man praiseworthy'.[31] John clearly displays an understanding of the Stoic notion of the indifferents in line with that promulgated by Seneca.

The Ciceronian criteria that John uses to assess the value of a task – that it should be honourable and useful – are essential to his account of moderation, and necessary in establishing whether an action is done for the right reasons. This is illustrated by a comment made in Book I. 4, where

John claims that 'Truly the mean is praiseworthy, when applied prudently and with moderation and, if it is possible, wielded usefully, according to the command of the comic [Terence]: "nothing in excess".'[32] Hunting may, therefore, be a legitimate pursuit for some – for example, those who seek food – but it is always inappropriate for those in certain occupations, namely clerics and judges, for whom the activity cannot even be 'indifferent', but is to be regarded as a vice. John's critique of hunting clearly has a double purpose. On the one hand, it is a focus of his disapproval of the useless pursuits of the court, while on the other hand he uses it to reinforce his argument that everyone should attend to the occupation to which they are best suited. As it stands, in John's opinion, those who should be carrying out public duties prefer to hunt instead, perverting the appropriate distribution of roles.[33] In Book I. 5, John applies the same method to gambling. He regards it as *'inutilis'* on the grounds that it requires a lot of work for little profit, although admits, again, that it may be justifiable under certain circumstances, such as when it is used to relieve stress. Again 'moderation' is the guiding principle: a 'licence of moderation' (*'licentia moderationis'*) is given only to acts which are accomplished according to favourable circumstances.[34] Similarly, in Book I. 6, when John turns to music, he advises that it should be limited by the 'formula of moderation' (*'moderationis formula'*), so as to avoid excessive emotional arousal.[35] An example of this 'formula of moderation' in action is the use of music for the worship of God, while an example of excess is described in Book I. 7, where he criticises the conduct of Nero, whose uncontrolled obsession with music (recounted in Suetonius's *De vita Caesarum*) is rendered even more distasteful on account of the fact that he squandered his money on mimics and actors.[36] Acting, moreover, is an inherently dishonourable pursuit, in John's mind, as it permits indulgence in frivolity and cultivates vanity. The honourable man will permit *'modesta hilaritate'*, but will judge the value of plays or stories by whether they are 'instruments' of 'virtue and honourable utility', that is, the criteria of decorum established by Cicero in his *De officiis*.[37]

In each instance, John establishes that these pursuits can never be regarded as ends in themselves, nor as contributing in any real way towards the good that is appropriate for man. They are solely permissible according to circumstance, and while they may be accessories to good living, they are never its source. In this respect, John is consistent with the Stoic position on the indifferents; they may facilitate 'living in accordance with nature' as they can allow one to pursue their appropriate duty in certain circumstances (the hungry hunter must hunt to find food, the Christian musician may make music to praise God), but they cannot be regarded as intrinsic to the pursuit of the *summum bonum*. The eudaimonistic position of the Stoics, which equates virtue with happiness, denies the indifferents an instrumental role in the pursuit of virtue, while simultaneously (and somewhat paradoxically) regarding them as things worth pursuing.[38] As noted, John also struggles with accommodating the value of material goods in his writings, but elides this tension somewhat by positing two *summa bona*, the happiness of the virtuous life on earth and the happiness of eternal life with God in heaven. Material goods do not enhance a life of virtue, but one's disposition towards them – that is, pursuing them moderately in accordance with the demands of nature – can be seen as indicative of such a life. In this respect, John's enterprise of demonstrating the importance of the mean in discerning appropriate duties in the *Policraticus* is not dissimilar to that outlined by Cicero at the start of *De officiis*: 'The whole debate about duty is twofold. One kind of question relates to the end of good things; the other depends upon advice by which one ought to be fortified for all areas of life.'[39] That is, there is a distinction between a theoretical understanding of the relationship of duty to the final end or *telos* of life and practical questions about how to perform one's duties from day to day.

### Virtue as craft: the Stoic perspective

In Letter 76 to Lucilius, Seneca summarises the Stoic perspective on the particular good appropriate to man as 'perfect reason', that is, 'virtue'. He equates this with what is 'honourable', and describes it as the particular end intended for man by nature.[40] That said, there is a disjuncture in the Stoic account, generally speaking, between the anticipated result of the exercise of virtue – becoming virtuous and achieving the end intended for man by nature – and the point of practising it in the material world. The intention with which a duty is exercised is the defining quality determining its worth – not its ultimate accomplishment – while the material results of exercising duties, as already noted, should not matter in the broader scheme of pursuing virtue. Why, then, act virtuously? As discussed in Chapter 3, the Stoics posited a distinction between 'appropriate acts', *kathêkonta*, and 'perfect acts', *katorthômata*.[41] The first category involves the exercise of duties which aim to obtain a preferred indifferent, such as health. The second category also concerns the pursuit of preferred indifferents, but the distinction lies in the moral orientation of the agent towards the act: only the virtuous person can perform a 'perfect act', as only they are aware of its ethical justification. As Julia Annas puts it, 'The person who has become virtuous, then, will still do the same thing as he did before, but will stand in a different relation to it.'[42] Annas identifies this distinction between 'appropriate acts' (or 'due actions' in her terminology) and 'perfect acts' as a critical component of the Stoic conception of virtue as a craft, or skill.[43] The comparison between the pursuit of virtue and the attainment of a skill (*technè*) is one common in ancient ethical theories, but by making this distinction between *types* of duties, the Stoics emphasise above other theories the systematic aspect of becoming virtuous. The beginner embarking on a life of virtue will carry out the first type of actions, without being cognisant of their ethical implications. Over time they will internalise the sense of what it is to act virtuously, and in due course they will develop the practical intelligence (*phronesis*) to determine what is the virtuous action in all situations, regardless of their personal preferences. Annas identifies this as a distinctive aspect of the rules-based approach to virtue endorsed by the Stoics. By emphasising 'the *kinds* of action which are such that there is good reason for the ethical beginner to perform them', the Stoics imply that the acquisition of virtue is a systematic process, with stages through which the would-be-sage must progress.[44]

The early Stoics regarded the virtues as the 'shape' of a single virtue, the health of the soul; while this view was rejected by later Stoics such as Chrysippus, the thesis of the unity of the virtues remained a keystone of Stoic philosophy. In Cicero's *De officiis*, the connection of all the virtues to the virtue of justice and, by extension, to what is honourable demonstrates this unity: they are all manifestations of a fixed inner intention towards the good.[45] For twelfth-century Christians, the debate over what the virtues consisted of had its own set of intellectual parameters, both theological and philosophical; classical texts in this context served a function beyond their 'donor role': they were also valuable stimulants to discussion, discussions facilitated in part by existing modifications to classical texts made by patristic writers.[46] An illuminating example of this tendency to adapt Stoic theses to Christian contexts is found in John's take on the Stoic doctrine of the 'unity of the virtues'. In *Policraticus*, Book V. 3, John describes how the virtues are interrelated, regarding them as expressions of a single substance – namely the grace of God. He recounts how the sun's rays are diffused in different ways when viewed through different precious stones, while still emanating from the sun itself. He then compares this physical observation with the virtues: 'prudence is in some, fortitude in others, in others temperance or justice, in some faith, and, in others again, forbearance of hope; in some is the passion of charity, in others endurance of work, here consolation for grief, there perseverance in good works; all of which are separate qualities in separate individuals, but one and the same God.'[47] For John, the virtues demonstrate the omnipresence of God, with faith and grace as their common denominator.[48] Referring to 1 John 3:2, 'we shall see him as he is', John describes God as *'plenitudo virtus et cumulus beatitudinis'*, 'the fullness of virtue and culmination of happiness'.[49] While pointing to a future in which complete knowledge of God will be possible, John acknowledges that in the meantime, the 'worship displayed by external works requires a medium', namely the senses which are given to man by God. Thus, John exploits the idea of the interrelated virtues as a rationale for the pursuit of virtue in the present, imperfect, world; God created the senses which enable man to live virtuously, while the virtues themselves are aspects of his grace, and so although 'no bodily approach to the spirit is accessible to us', behaving virtuously still has merit as an expression of Christian love.[50]

### Virtue as craft: the Aristotelian perspective

How, though, does one become virtuous? The notion of *habitus*, first propagated by Aristotle in his *Nicomachean Ethics* (as *hexis*), was transmitted to the Middle Ages through a number of intermediaries, including Boethius and Cicero.[51] At the root of Aristotle's idea was the notion that virtue was a habit, state or condition, resulting from the repeated exercise of human capacities. Virtue is acquired through application; it is a gradual process facilitated by the exercise of virtuous conduct: 'we become just by doing just acts, temperate by doing temperate acts, brave by doing brave acts'.[52] Thus, virtue is a product of human activity and rational choice – essentially a matter of external conduct. The presence of Aristotelian ideas regarding *habitus* in the twelfth century, before the re-circulation of the *Nichomachean Ethics*, has been extensively examined by Cary Nederman, who suggests that twelfth-century philosophers absorbed a large number of Aristotelian ideas despite having no direct knowledge of this part of the Aristotelian corpus, positing this as evidence of 'an "underground" tradition of learning'.[53] He points to the contribution of the Aristotelian doctrine to a 'fundamentally anthropocentric perspective on moral theory', and explicitly regards John as one of the forebears of this Aristotelian tradition, suggesting that he 'employed Aristotle's concepts as tools to evaluate the personalities and courses of action with which he was immediately confronted'.[54] Nederman looks at several passages from

John's *Metalogicon*, *Policraticus* and *Letters* where the term *habitus* is used, noting instances where John emphasises the importance of repeated activity as a way of engendering knowledge and ensuring the replication of good acts in the future.[55] While Nederman acknowledges that 'John's investigations do not represent the pinnacle of twelfth-century thought about *habitus*', noting that they are 'neither systematic nor rigorous', he still regards him as an important way-marker on the route towards the full absorption of Aristotelian ethics into the medieval curriculum.[56]

However, it must be contended that, contrary to Nederman's position, the use of the term *habitus* by John does not situate him by default within an Aristotelian tradition; the term is commonly used by his contemporaries and is transmitted through a variety of classical sources which are not solely Aristotelian. Cicero's *De inventione*, II. 159, for example, offered an easily accessible version of Aristotle's position in its definition of virtue as habit, but placed this definition alongside an emphasis on the Stoic norm of conformity with reason and nature: 'Virtue is a habit of the mind in harmony with reason and the order of nature.'[57] In his commentary on this passage of *De inventione*, John's teacher Thierry of Chartres presented a similarly naturalistic interpretation of virtue: 'The definition of virtue is to be understood thus: virtue is a habit of the mind by which the mind is made to return to the mean of nature through following reason. Vice exceeds the mean of nature; virtue, through following reason, produces a return to this mean.'[58] While the Aristotelian interpretation sees virtue as a *habitus* produced by practice (albeit in conformity with an innate aptitude for the good), the Stoics regarded *habitus* as a fixed ethical intentionality – in accordance with nature – that the moral agent must display towards virtue or vice. According to the Aristotelian construct, we will begin to be virtuous by doing the right thing for the wrong reason; we will act as though we already have virtue in order to gain it by habituation. The Stoic, on the other hand, believes that virtuous action requires the attainment of a fixed will in conformity with the right attitude of mind (*habitus animi rectus*); practice alone is not sufficient.[59] As noted, the Stoic beginner on the route to virtue will start by doing the right things without fully understanding why they are right, but it is only when they understand the place of their action in the scheme of ethical rationality that their acts will become truly virtuous. Given the emphasis placed in John's writings on the dependence of virtue on faith and grace, it seems misguided to over-emphasise the suggestion, per Nederman, that John truly believed that virtue resulted from repeated action in the Aristotelian sense.

Nederman's argument focuses on Book V. 4 of the *Policraticus*, which he describes as 'the fullest exposition of John's adaptation of the doctrine of *habitus* to specifically ethical matters'.[60] The relevant passage is worth close examination: 'Character [*mos*] is a habit of mind [*mentis habitus*] from which the repetition of single acts proceeds. For if an act is done once or more often, it does not immediately become part of character, unless by being done steadily it passes into usage [*in usum*].'[61] Contrary to Nederman's interpretation, this passage seems to suggest that John explicitly contrasted *habitus* with *usus*, whereby the interiority of *mos* as a *mentis habitus* is distinguished from what is done in practice, its *usus*. If this reading is correct, John is not being particularly Aristotelian with regard to his treatment of *habitus* in this instance.[62] Furthermore, Book V. 4 concludes with a brief analysis of an issue that Marcia Colish has noted as critical for the medieval understanding of *habitus*, namely the issue of baptismal grace. John describes how we 'become friends of God' through 'grace, without merit', 'through merit from grace' or 'through a difficult and happy death'. Some are 'sanctified before they were born', while some rely on 'good works', facilitated by grace. St Nicholas of Myra, for example, is singled out as having begun his practice of fasting while still in the cradle, something that John ascribes to his innate grace.[63] Some of John's contemporaries use the term *habitus* to signify the latent baptismal grace of infants; Colish, however, notes that the use of the terminology of *habitus* in this case is generic rather than Aristotelian; a *habitus* by this reading is simply something that a person possesses that is not yet activated.[64] John does not use the term *habitus* in this part of his discussion, but it is clear from his emphasis on grace as the efficient factor facilitating proximity to God (the goal of the virtuous life) that his views are inconsistent with the Aristotelian idea of acquiring virtue through application. Contrary to Nederman, the Stoic concept of *habitus* – acts in consonance with a fixed ethical intentionality towards the good, systematically developed by the moral agent – seems to offer a better framework within which to understand the theories of the acquisition of virtues held by John and his contemporaries than the Aristotelian version, which seems to be applied inconsistently here, at best.

Nederman regards the 'mean' frequently referred to in John's writings as essentially Aristotelian. We recall that the Aristotelian perspective held that virtue required a developed disposition, a grasp of virtuous principle which leads to the agent choosing an action most in conformity with the mean, a mean that is identified through an examination of the agent's emotions. The mean, for Aristotle, is determined by practical wisdom (*phronesis*) and acted upon, as Julia Driver puts it, when 'The virtuous agent picks up on, and responds to, the ethically significant factors present in various contexts and tailors her actions accordingly', using a type of 'ethically sensitive perception'.[65] However, it is a mistake to identify this 'mean' with 'moderation'; Jean Porter suggests, rather, that 'it is better understood in terms of the degree and kind of passions appropriate to a particular situation': it recommends a proportionate response rather than a necessarily balanced one.[66] Nederman believes that, like Aristotle, John considered that the 'virtuous mean arises out of circumstantial determinations', claiming in particular that a lengthy passage in *Policraticus*, Book IV. 9, exemplifies an adherence to the Aristotelian concept of the mean, a precept that Nederman regards as 'the basis of the doctrine of individual and political liberty espoused by John'.[67] However, Nederman arguably conflates 'mean' with 'moderation' in his interpretation of this passage, resulting in a flawed analysis.[68] The passage reads:

> The next [commandment] is, 'He shall not turn aside to the right side nor to the left.' To turn aside to the right is to insist too vehemently on the virtues themselves. To turn aside to the right is to exceed the bounds of the mean [*modum excedere*] in the work of virtue, which consists in the mean [*quae in modo consistit*]. For truly all such vehemence is the enemy of health and all excess is a fault; nothing is worse than the practice of good works! ... To turn aside to the left means to break away or deviate from the way of virtue towards that of vice. So, one who is too quick to punish the faults of his subjects turns aside to the left, while one who is too quick to indulge their faults out of kindness turns aside to the right. Both deviate from the path [of virtue] but that which bends to the left is more destructive.[69]

While John uses the term '*modo*', 'mean', the tenor of the passage as a whole suggests that this is a discussion of the practical obligations of moderation, rather than of the content of the mean itself. Nederman's interpretation of the passage seems to rest in part on a misreading, as is evident from his translation of this passage in his partial edition of the *Policraticus*: 'To stray to the right is to insist vehemently on the virtues themselves. To stray to the *left* is to exceed the mean in the work of virtue, which consists in the mean.'[70] By introducing a polarisation between 'right' and 'left', absent in the original Latin, at the opening of the passage, Nederman undermines the subtlety of John's argument. John, rather, intends the passage to be read in two parts: the first section relates to excesses of virtue (straying to the right), and the second section concerns the excessive pursuit of vice (straying to the left). Through his mistranslation of the first part, Nederman understands this passage as a unitary commentary on the 'mean' and, thus, renders it more Aristotelian than it actually is. Rather, this passage is more persuasively read as a commentary on 'moderation' – the internal activities of the mind which ensure that virtue adheres to a rationally accessed 'mean' – and, as such, echoes the pre-eminence accorded to restraint and seemliness in the Stoic tradition. This latter interpretation is more persuasive, and reinforces John's concern with the internal constancy of the moral agent towards the mean of the good.

### Virtue: the personal and the political

Cicero's *De officiis* is highly influential for John's account of virtue, as it offers a rationale for virtuous behaviour in the political realm. In his treatise, Cicero adopts a Stoic idea: 'they hold that everything that is honourable is beneficial, and nothing beneficial that is not honourable'.[71] Referring to this as 'the rule', he suggests that the wise man will 'calculate' what is appropriate on each occasion.[72] The traditional Stoic position stated that to live virtuously was to choose the things which were in accordance with nature – a position that does not permit virtue and nature to be independently defined.[73] Cicero modified this slightly: 'Indeed, when the Stoics say that the greatest good is to live agreeably with nature, this means, in my view, the following: always to concur with virtue; and as for other things that are in accordance with nature, to choose them if they do not conflict with virtue.'[74] The 'good life' for humans, by this account, has two aspects: that it is a life in accordance with nature, and that the good life is necessarily a life of virtue.[75] Natural impulses towards self-preservation and fellowship are shared by humans and animals alike, but only humans will have the rational power to identify appropriate duties, and only the sage will be consistent in always choosing what is beneficial and honourable over what is personally advantageous.[76] Although 'certain kinds of duties have their origin in each individually', 'the chief place is accorded to the class of duties grounded in human fellowship'; Cicero denies that a wise man could do something that is useful for the *res publica* without it also being honourable.[77] In so doing he redefines the content of the *honestum*. In opposition to conventional Roman interpretations of honourableness, Cicero sees the *honestum* as having value in itself; he 'alters the term's denotion from its link with actual honour to what is honourable whether or not anyone is looking'.[78] The significance of this transformation lies in its blurring of the boundaries between public and private performance of duties: the good man will act virtuously in private as well as in public, in the personal domain as well as in the political.

The coincidence between one's personal and one's social role makes Stoic philosophy relevant to political thought, in spite of the fact that Stoicism in its purest ideological form did not promote one particular form of government over another (although individual Stoic thinkers did). It was not a depoliticised ideology, however, as the intrinsic value of the polity was recognised.[79] As Seneca put it: 'The advantage of the state and that of the individual are yoked together; indeed it is as impossible to separate them as to separate the commendable from the desirable.'[80] Such ideas were also diffused through a number of patristic intermediaries. Macrobius's *Commentarii in somnium Scipionis* – John's means of access to the final book of Cicero's *De re publica* – discusses four types of virtues, the political being the first type.[81] Macrobius defines a 'political' version of each of the cardinal virtues and notes that 'By these virtues, the good man is first made lord of himself and then ruler of the state, and is just and prudent in his regard for human welfare, never forgetting his obligations.'[82] Macrobius read Cicero through a neo-Platonic lens, permitting a reformulation of the scheme of virtues and allowing a distinction to be drawn between the virtues as good in themselves and the abstract potential of a further ultimate good, attainable in an other-worldly context.[83] He writes:

> Now if the function and office of the virtues is to bless, and, moreover, if it is agreed that political virtues do exist, then political virtues do make men blessed. And so Cicero is right in claiming for the rulers of commonwealths a place 'where they may enjoy a blessed existence forever'. In order to show that some men become blessed by the exercise of virtues at leisure and others by virtues exercised in active careers, he did not say with finality that nothing is more gratifying to that supreme God than commonwealths, but added a qualification, 'nothing that occurs on earth is more gratifying'.[84]

Macrobius offered medieval readers a reinterpretation of Cicero's writings that was favourable for use in a Christian context, whereby the value of political systems and the active life was emphasised, but only in terms of their contribution to material happiness in a finite world.[85] Moreover, as Maurizio Viroli has noted, Macrobius is an important conduit for the Roman philosophical ideal of 'the idea of the political man, as defined by the possession of a specific set of virtues'.[86]

Another patristic text that can be argued to be of greater significance to John's recommendation of the moderate application of the virtues in the political realm than previously acknowledged is Martin of Braga's pseudo-Senecan *Formula vitae honestae*, written in the 570s.[87] The influence of this text on John's writings has been neglected, despite the fact that several copies of the short work existed in the library at Canterbury.[88] Regardless of whether John believed that the treatise was by Seneca or not, it is of particular relevance to our study as the work is explicitly addressed to a king (named in some copies as Miro, king of the Sueves), and so directly applicable to a medieval monarchical context.[89] The work goes through each of the four cardinal virtues in turn – prudence, fortitude, temperance and justice – and may have been copied in part from a lost *De officiis* written by Seneca. The king is described as 'already possessing the sagacity of natural wisdom', but the prologue concludes with the comment that virtue is not only accessible to the faithful, as this book 'gives advice which, even without the precepts of the divine Scripture, may be fulfilled under the natural law of human intelligence, even by the laity if they will live rightly and honourably'.[90] The syncretic status of the text is explicit from this opening; the text provides moral advice derived from traditional classical models intended for use by a Christian king. Each of the virtues is accorded a single chapter describing its qualities and instances of application (chapters 2 to 5). These chapters are followed by a further four which describe the necessity of keeping each of these virtues within their appropriate bounds (chapters 6 to 9): 'these four forms of virtue will make of you a perfect man, if you keep them righteously and in due measure and set proper bounds to your life'.[91] The emphasis throughout, therefore, is on moderation. Prudence can be ensured 'if you first judge and weigh everything in advance', while 'if prudence exceeds its bounds' one will become over-cautious.[92] Fortitude must not 'be carried beyond its limits', but a balance kept between being timid and bold.[93] Continence or temperance must keep desires within the limits set by nature, and be observed 'with this aim of moderation'.[94] Finally, 'justice', 'a silent agreement of nature invented for the aid of many', 'must be controlled by holding fast to the mean'.[95] The treatise concludes by explicitly emphasising the social context of the virtues: 'If anyone would honourably devote his life to the advantage, not only of himself, but to that of many, he must observe the rules for the practice of the aforementioned virtues according to the mean, giving attention to considerations of time, place, persons, and circumstances.'[96]

Virtue, according to Martin, must accord with a mean, and must be practised with moderation and executed within certain limits – sentiments shared by John. Other arguments made by Martin are similar to those found in the *Policraticus*. In his discussion of the virtue of prudence, Martin emphasises the value of prudence as a virtue which guards against flattery by curbing excessive pride. Continence also mitigates against flattery: 'The most difficult task of continence is to ward off the pleasantries of flatterers, whose words unnerve the mind by a kind of pleasure. Do not win friendship by agreeing with someone, nor let any approach you easily in order to win your favour.'[97] Continence and prudence facilitate discernment and guard against deception. The prudent man will 'examine counsels', the treatise recommending a degree of scepticism: 'Do not make up your mind on doubtful matters, but reserve your judgement. Do not swear that anything is so, for not everything that appears to be true is immediately true ... As a matter of fact, the truth often retains the appearance of a lie, while a lie is frequently hidden by the appearance of a truth. Just as a friend sometimes wears a stern countenance and a flatterer a pleasant expression, so verisimilitude puts on ornaments and makes itself attractive in order to deceive or rob.'[98] Continence, in turn, also guards against deception: 'Do not pretend to be what you are not, nor desire what you are to seem greater than you are.'[99] These recommendations are akin to those found in the *Policraticus*, where deception is criticised and flattery condemned. Despite the fact that John does not appear to quote the text directly, the fact that the *Formula vitae honestae* was widely available in this period made it a ripe candidate for emulation, and a viable model for the performance of the virtues within a political arena.

## Moderation in action: prudence

John describes the classical virtues in *Policraticus*, Book IV. 12, by relating them to their contraries. He distinguishes between deception and fortitude, between contumely and prudence, between causing injury to another and temperance, and between injustice and justice. While he catalogues the cardinal, not the theological, virtues, he ascribes them a divine origin, asserting that they sprang from the '*fonte honestatis*', the source of all good things, and equating the virtues with the four rivers of paradise, a metaphor he may have borrowed from Gregory the Great's *Moralia in Job*.[100] Although he regarded the four virtues as interrelated, John places a particular emphasis on justice, which he describes as 'the queen of the virtues' (an adage borrowed from Cicero's *De officiis*), and on prudence, which he describes as 'the root of all the other virtues'.[101] In the next chapter, the virtues of fortitude and justice will be examined in detail, with particular reference to their importance for the prince. In the sections that follow, the virtues of prudence and temperance – the regulatory virtues – will be investigated through a series of case studies regarding frugality, beneficence and avarice.

John explicitly credits Cicero as the source for his emphasis on prudence in the *Metalogicon*, where it is noted that Cicero believed 'enquiry into the truth' to be the subject of prudence.[102] Cicero accorded prudence a prime position owing to its connection with wisdom; if prudence is 'the knowledge of what is good, what is bad, and what is neither good nor bad', then it is the principal virtue permitting discernment, and so works in association with wisdom in attaining knowledge of all things.[103] In the same passage of the *Metalogicon*, John provides another account of the relationship between the virtues: 'Prudence consists entirely in insight into the truth, together with a certain skill in examining the latter. Furthermore, justice embraces the truth, and fortitude protects it, while temperance moderates the exercise of the aforesaid virtues.'[104] Later, he extols prudence with reference to Cicero again: 'Prudence, according to Cicero, is a virtue of the soul, concerned with the investigation, perception and skilful use of the truth.'[105] One of the principal purposes of the *Metalogicon* is to defend the arts of the *trivium*, particularly the claims of dialectic, against those who wish to find shortcuts to wisdom.[106] As prudence is connected to the practice of dialectic and the pursuit of wisdom, establishing its role as a principal virtue may also be regarded as a subsidiary aim of the *Metalogicon*. Prudence is similarly emphasised in the *Policraticus*, where John describes its value to the *res publica*: 'For without prudence and vigilance not only will a *res publica* not progress, but nor can a house remain sturdy.'[107] Thus, prudence for John is a virtue with both personal and political implications.

John is distinctive in the role he accords to prudence, a virtue which held a less significant place in other twelfth-century accounts. In part, as Alexander Murray noted, this is to do with the double meaning of 'prudence' in the twelfth century: 'The word prudence could basically have two meanings. One was the Stoic meaning, as heavily elaborated by the scholastics. For them prudence was the virtue which distinguished aids and obstacles to the love of God. It was the recognition of the moral course of action. ... But there was another meaning: another set of presuppositions, that is to say, beside the Christian, for interpreting the chief Stoic virtue. In modern English the word prudent implies "worldly-wisdom" ... So it did commonly in both Latin and the main vernaculars throughout the period when we have testimonies of these languages.'[108] Thierry of Chartres, for example, describes prudence simply as a virtue consisting of the capacity to choose one thing and reject another.[109] William of Conches's *Moralium dogma philosophorum* presented a similar interpretation.[110] Abelard's Philosopher in the *Collationes* employed a definition akin to that found in *De inventione* ('the ability to distinguish between these things – between evil and good things'), but argued that prudence cannot be a virtue, because the wicked also have the capacity to distinguish between good and evil; it is not a power limited to the good.[111] Instead, the Philosopher suggests that it could be regarded as 'the mother or origins of virtue rather than a virtue itself'.[112]

A potentially influential source for John's emphasis on prudence is the place held by the virtue in Ambrose's *De officiis ministrorum*. While Ambrose provided a substantial examination of the virtues from a theological perspective in his exegetical work *De Iacob et beata vita*, in *De officiis ministrorum* the Roman virtues come to the fore, indicating its Ciceronian inspiration. Ambrose's principal contribution to John's understanding of the virtues is his recasting of Ciceronian prudence as a Christian virtue, whereby its facility in attaining knowledge of the truth is equated with the knowledge of God through faith.[113] Like John, Ambrose also regards prudence as 'the source from which all the other duties derive'.[114] Ambrose adapts the connection between prudence and justice posited by Cicero, making it depend not only on the capacity of prudence to determine what is just, but also on faith: 'For justice cannot exist without prudence, since it takes no small measure of prudence to determine which is the just course of action and which is the unjust: a mistake on either side is equally serious. ... But similarly, prudence cannot exist without justice, since piety towards God is the beginning of understanding.'[115] A similar relationship between justice and piety is posed by John, as we shall see in Chapter 6.

## Avarice and frugality

An area that serves as an illustration of John's treatment of temperance and prudence is his account of the politics of money. Money became of increasing importance in the twelfth century, a period when the 'Commercial Revolution' gathered pace, and the use and availability of money increased.[116] This increase in the availability of fluid cash sources facilitated social liquidity: as Alexander Murray puts it, 'liquidity in wealth makes for social liquidity; abstraction in wealth makes for an abstraction of power'.[117] As noted in Chapter 4, John's association of the financial officers of the polity with the sides of the body, and so with the digestive system, exploits a popular trope, that is, the association between avarice and defecation. It is unsavoury connotations such as these that lead John to dismiss avarice as the worst and most execrable vice, particularly among those who hold public office. Money is the fuel and progenitor of avarice; as John ironically notes, money is held in high value, since if such value was not placed on it there would be no need for money.[118] At a later juncture, John points out that praise and favour derive 'from deeds and from money' but that the route of gaining praise through money is easier, although not as impressive.[119] To this end, he recommends that the prince should be no pauper king; he is allowed to be wealthy, although his money must be not considered a matter of personal profit, but as belonging to the people at large.[120] Indeed, John recommends that one way to avoid the avarice of courtiers is to ensure that officials are adequately provided for out of public funds – 'so as to go about removing all occasion for malice'.[121]

To paraphrase John's conundrum in modern parlance: it is clear that even if 'money is the root of all evil', it is also 'money that makes the world go round'. Even Pope Adrian IV, in response to John's questioning on the avarice of the curia, suggested that John should 'not seek to measure our [the papacy] austerity or that of temporal princes, but attend rather to the utility of all', using, as we saw in Chapter 3, the fable of the starved stomach to argue that the curia be sufficiently funded.[122] The contradiction in this debate between Adrian and John is acute; it is, in essence, a debate between the value of spiritual poverty, as preached by the apostles, and the material demands of the hierarchy of the Church and polity.[123] Concern over the politics of money is not simply the disaffected theoretical response of morally minded clerics, but a real attempt to articulate new requirements of contemporary society, the need to formulate a code of practice for a hierarchical power structure which is no longer exclusively bound by land or kinship. The connection between avarice and ambition is one frequently made by John: 'Wealth is poured out in wooing power; and the more power is lusted after, the more easily money is spent. But when power is attained, one exalts oneself into a tyrant, and, spurning equity, does not scruple in the sight of God to oppress and humiliate the equals of one's rank and nature.'[124] Avarice, therefore, is not simply a perversion of Christian virtues, but a very perversion of the Christian order. Just as the money economy threatened to overturn conventional societal rankings, so too the elevation of money as a thing of worship threatened to overturn God's rightful position. John, quoting Horace, comments that the wealthy man is thought to be the wise man, as '"birth and beauty are gifts of Queen Money, and the goddesses Persuasion and Venus grace the man who is well-to-do", so that man who is rich, who prospers in his own ways, is [wrongly] judged as wise and happy'.[125] '*Regina Pecunia*' rules in the place of God.[126]

Avarice is not, of course, limited to the ruler, but is found on all levels of the court, indeed on all levels of society. John points out that the trade among court officials is not purely material, but extends into the immaterial: 'No act, no word, nothing is to be had without payment, not even silence; silence itself is for sale.'[127] Quoting from Juvenal, John comments: 'Everyone's credit matches the amount of coins he keeps in his treasure chest': character does not matter as much as money.[128] Indeed, it is the dissimulation of liberality and beneficence – virtues which oppose avarice – that seems to annoy John the most. But refraining from hoarding is not sufficient; the man who seeks to avoid avarice must be as consistent in his internal actions as he is in his external behaviour. It is illuminating to look at John's commentary on contemporary clerical orders in this light. John is particularly scathing about orders that do not practise what they preach. He points out that the Carthusians are known for their rejection of material goods and 'triumph over avarice', while the Cistercians follow the 'precepts and footsteps of blessed Benedict precisely'.[129] Nonetheless, there are worthy and unworthy men among them, and in some instances their claim to virtue is solely made on account of their association with their order, and cannot be seen as evidence of a genuine commitment to frugality; these wolves-in-sheep's-clothing are like the hypocritical Pharisees criticised in the Bible who flaunt their fasting and piety over others.[130]

How then *should* we live? John recommends moderate frugality as a counter-balance to avarice. Roman sources provide the grist for his argument, with the satires of Juvenal and Horace offering a literary precedent, while Stoic accounts of moderation provide a philosophical framework. Murray has contended that such dependence on Roman sources demonstrates a recognition on the part of medieval scholars of the fact that Horace, Juvenal and Seneca lived in a commercial world and so could serve as the source of old ways to understand new problems.[131] Frugality is described as a 'moderating virtue that is ignorant of use and misuse' by John, who even asserts, drawing on Cicero, that 'Acceptable are the vices of him who compensates faults of character by being sparing in expenditure. As Cicero says, "economy is the best revenue".'[132] John comments that 'philosophy does not enjoin us to flee from riches, but to inhibit our appetite for them. It demands a sane mind, which is satisfied with itself in every twist of fortune, in such a way, nevertheless, that its satisfaction is from God.'[133] Avarice, on the other hand, demonstrates the opposite characteristics: 'The madness of avarice consists in these two things: an immoderate appetite for what is not one's own combined with a tenacious protection of what is; whoever makes immoderate demands for what they do not have exceeds the law of necessity and utility.'[134] John counters his description of avaricious clergy with reference to clerics who do not dissimulate, notably the Carthusians and the Grandmontines, whom he praises as they 'have fixed limits to their desires, even to their necessities, and restrain avarice with the reins of moderation'.[135] John's commentary, therefore, aligns with the Stoic theory on the indifferents; wealth and material goods are superfluous to the pursuit of virtue and must always be treated with moderation and with an eye towards the Ciceronian principle of decorum, choosing what is in line with honour and utility.

### The Epicurean

The foil to the frugal man is the Epicurean, who epitomises the futility of excess. While the 'four rivers of virtue' stem from divine grace, the four rivers of vice, namely 'the love of possession', 'self-indulgence', 'tyranny' and 'excessive ambition', stem from 'the garden of the Epicureans', with lust as their common source.[136] John provides a relatively extensive treatment of the Epicurean School, whose views he regards as pervasive in contemporary courtly society. Epicureans pursue physical gratification, and prioritise self-indulgence in the ruthless pursuit of what they mistakenly regard as happiness. John generalises the category of Epicurean to apply not only to the 'horde' who followed Epicurus, but also to 'the multitude of men who are slaves to lust' and 'devotees of pleasure'.[137] It is intriguing to note that John's critique of Epicureanism depends on a subtle distinction that he makes between the Epicureans and the founder of the School, Epicurus (341–270 BC). The Epicureans are doubly mistaken, not only because they pursue self-indulgence, but also because they have deliberately misinterpreted the views of Epicurus. Epicurus recommended the 'happy life', but his followers interpreted this as legitimising unbridled physical pleasure. Epicurus himself, on the other hand, prized frugality and temperance, according to John: 'Seneca and many other distinguished philosophers, not to mention our own writers, testify that his [Epicurus's] works are replete with references to vegetables, fruits and other inexpensive foods.'[138] In *Policraticus*, Book VIII. 11, John explicitly defends Epicurus against the charge that he recommended carnal pleasure as a means of satiating lust, reiterating the claim that Seneca praised his virtue and that his views were corrupted by those of his followers.[139] In Book VIII. 25, towards the conclusion of the *Policraticus*, John returns to the distinction between Epicurus and his followers; pointing out that the appropriate route to happiness is the life of virtue, he says that this 'true dependable road' leads to 'the condition to be attained that Epicurus desired'.[140] John, therefore, does not deny the legitimacy of Epicurus's aim – happiness is the ultimate goal – although he believes that this happiness is not to be found in earthly rewards. It is, therefore, the hypocrisy of the pleasure-seeking Epicureans that he reviles.

A comparable valorisation of Epicurus is found in Abelard's *Collationes*, where the Philosopher suggests to the Christian that 'the happiness which Epicurus calls "pleasure", your Christ calls "the Kingdom of Heaven." What does a thing's name matter, so long as the thing stays the same, and neither the happiness nor the aim in living justly differs between philosophers and Christians?'[141] Abelard's Philosopher, like John, cites Seneca as a source for this positive perspective on Epicurus: 'Otherwise … Seneca – that greatest teacher of good behaviour, whose life, as you yourself have acknowledged, was very continent – would not have frequently brought the views of Epicurus, as if he were his master, into his moral teaching. He would not have done so if, as it is said, Epicurus had gone away from the path of restraint and worthiness.'[142] As David Luscombe has noted, John's critique of Epicureanism can also be read as an attempt to 'search for a compromise between renunciation of the world and reform of society and of courtly life'.[143] His elevation of Epicurus as a model of frugality offered a corrective to prevailing negative tendencies towards avarice, observed particularly in courtly life, where courtiers were the new Epicureans. Hans Liebeschütz recognised that Seneca was 'the foremost authority for John's argument that frugality is the key to the right life', but while the sentiment of this pronouncement may be true, he based this statement on a perceived similarity between John's writings and Seneca's Letter 108, a letter that John is unlikely to have accessed.[144] It is probable, however, that the letters served more generally as a source for John's positive remarks on frugality.[145] For example, Seneca comments in Letter 5 to Lucilius, 'Philosophy calls for plain living, but not for penance. … This is the mean of which I approve.'[146] This statement is comparable to John's claim that philosophy does not prohibit riches, but simply the excessive desire for them.[147] Furthermore, John could have accessed Seneca's views on frugality in *De beneficiis*, where Seneca states that it consists in 'knowing how to avoid unnecessary expenditure, or the art of applying moderation to the use of private means'.[148]

## Beneficence

Frugality counteracts avarice to a degree, but a further counteracting practice emphasised by John is beneficence. The primary source for John's recommendations on just benefaction was Seneca, notably his *De beneficiis*. This text posits that the bond that joins humanity together in its pursuit of living in accordance with nature is beneficence: 'What we need is a discussion of benefits and the rules for a practice that constitutes the chief bond of human society.'[149] As Griffin points out, for Seneca, beneficence is often associated with the gods and 'is a model from which correct human conduct can be inferred'.[150] Like Seneca, John sees beneficence as a matter of good character, a practice that requires integrity; for example, one needs to make promises that one can keep and efficiently act on.[151] John notes that the character of the giver and the recipient is influential, or as Seneca puts it: 'what counts is, not what is done or what is given, but the spirit of the action, because a benefit consists, not in what is done or given, but in the intention of the giver or doer'.[152] Therefore, the act of giving does not in itself suffice; it must also be done in good faith. John comments that 'the case and the person' should be the determinants of appropriate giving. 'Gifts should not be accepted from a dishonourable giver nor under dishonourable circumstances' but should be determined by 'the time, the place and the manner'; a gift is rendered honourable if it is given in honourable circumstances, but sordid if it is not.[153] Furthermore, benefaction must correspond to need, not to avaricious desire, and must not be given with the expectation of return, as the best form of liberality is that which does not take into account the prospect of remuneration.[154] The frugal man is the worthy recipient of benefaction because he does not lust after riches for his own advancement, unlike the avaricious man. John extends his treatment of just beneficence, and its contraries, rapaciousness and feigned generosity, into a critique of contemporary society. The dissimulation of false liberality is, in John's mind, among the principal flaws of the court:

> Among all the triflers of the court, the ones who harm most perniciously are those who gloss over their miserable follies under the pretext of honourableness and liberality, those handsome men who strut about, who dine splendidly, who often urge strangers to join them at table, who are kindly at home, friendly in public, affable in speech, liberal in their opinions, generous in caring for those who are close to them and famous for their imitation of all the virtues.[155]

In spite of such critiques, John does not deny the value of true liberality when practised by the wealthy man. Indeed, he comments that a king may be wealthy, provided that he looks upon his wealth as belonging to all.[156] Furthermore, liberality should not be limited to material goods, but also extends to good deeds: 'For those who are liberal with the industry and works of virtue will be of use to many; in benefiting others they will have the help of many. Therefore, the practice of doing good prepares them to be better so as to make them deserve the good of many.'[157] Like Seneca, John sees just beneficence as having an implication beyond its immediate context of gift and receipt; instead, it is a template for living well in a social and political community.

An intriguing application of this advice is found in the annotations appended to Oxford, Bodleian Library, MS Canon. Pat. Lat 131. As noted in Chapter 1, it has been suggested that the annotations to this manuscript, a copy of Lactantius's *Institutiones divinae*, were written by John himself, probably between 1156 and 1164, and that this was the copy of Lactantius' text left to the cathedral library at Chartres upon his death.[158] A number of annotations are found in the margins of Book VI. 12, fos 107r-108r, the section where Lactantius discusses beneficence and poverty. The annotator highlights multiple passages with *nota* signs, which extend alongside the length of the passages of interest. The first passage reads: 'it needs to be fully understood that hope of a return must be absolutely missing from the exercise of mercy: only God may look for reward from this particular work'; the second notes, 'distinguished and powerful men cannot be in need of anything, since their wealth protects them as well as distinguishing them'.[159] The third points out that 'it is benefactions to the outsider that truly deserve praise, because such acts come of humanity alone'.[160] The annotator accompanies the next *nota* sign with a exhortation: '*Audi Thoma*', which is interpreted by Barker and Ross as a direct plea to Thomas Becket. The passage it highlights reads: 'the giving of people who waste their inheritance on shows is trivial and futile, and has nothing to do with justice at all. Gift shouldn't even be the word when the only recipients are wholly undeserving.'[161] The annotator marks six further sections within this chapter. The first three relate to the end of life: accepting death without regret, the obligation to bury strangers and paupers, irrational fear of poverty.[162] The fourth and fifth *nota* signs situate such obligations in the context of religious observation, noting that 'a man rich with God can never be poor' and that 'despising and trampling on mortal things is the mark of a soul that rides high'.[163] The sixth passage reads, 'if you cannot manage great deeds on your own, practise justice as best as you can, but do it so that your effort compared with the rest matches your means compared with the rest'.[164] Two further passages are marked with both *nota* signs and textual annotations. '*Audi Thoma*' appears again alongside the following passage: 'What you buy wild animals with, free captives with; what you feed the animals with, feed the poor with; what you buy gladiators with, bury the innocent dead with.'[165] The next marginal *nota* sign is accompanied by the word '*Henriciani*', a reference to the supporters of Henry II, and marks this passage: 'What is the point of making rich men out of animal fighters, and of equipping them for crime? They are hopelessly wicked anyway. Turn what is about to go to awful waste into a great sacrifice, so that these true gifts may win you the eternal gift from God.'[166] Finally, in the next chapter, a further passage is marked '*Caute*' – encouraging its reader to take heed – and remarks that the penitent man should try even harder to be generous, for virtue's sake.[167]

If these annotations can be associated with John, which seems highly plausible given their theme and the provenance of the manuscript, then they clearly demonstrate the emphasis placed by him on the role of beneficence. Benefaction, particularly to outsiders, the poor and those who do not expect any return, is a mark of good rulership, whether in an ecclesiastical or royal context. Frugality, in turn, clearly edifies one's character. Exhortations in the vein of those highlighted in the Lactantius manuscript are frequently found in the letters composed by John during his exile. In Letter 188, addressed to Nicholas of Mont-Saint-Jacques at Rouen and composed around the end of 1166, for example, John compares the poverty of the exiles to that of Christ himself. He commends Nicholas's generosity, saying that 'Gratitude should be all the greater when frequent and substantial benefits have come, not to answer desert or a deserving case, but from a rich vein of inborn generosity.'[168] A further example of this sentiment can be found in Letter 194 to John Saracen, also composed around this period (1166–67). In this letter, John regards his poverty in exile as a virtue. Exile, according to John, could be termed a 'friend' as it 'drove away courtly trifles and alluring pleasures'; he reflects how it 'urged me on the path of virtue, and numbered me among the throngs of the philosophers'.[169] John writes, 'I am far freer than when burdened by worldy chattels and fardels gained by chance', noting that 'for the Christian, too, the whole world is exile, a pilgrimage apart from God, so that he is never exalted by prosperity'.[170] Given that true happiness cannot be found in this world – a perspective partly shaped by the Augustinian notion of the separation of the Christian from God in the earthly city, and partly by the Stoic contention that money and material goods were to be counted among the indifferents – true satisfaction cannot be found in either wealth or honour.

## Conclusion: ruling with moderation

Moderation is a key concept in John's work: it is his solution to the conundrum of how the prince could simultaneously be a figure of great economic power, a practitioner of public virtue and one obliged to be free with his generosity. The good prince is the one who is willing to give when required, but knows when to be restrained in his liberality. As John puts it, 'There are some however whose frugality must be inhibited, since they are by nature inclined to avarice. Then there are others upon whom it must be enjoined with greater precision, since they are prodigal, in contempt of a budget and wasteful; they do not discern between use and abuse.'[171] Balance is vital. John's most extensive discussion of tyranny is situated in the context of his observations regarding money and wealth: the necessity of moderation in the bestowal of gifts, the dangers of self-indulgence and avarice, and the politics of the Roman laws concerning food. The critique of avarice and the money market in John's work provides an important analogy to his comments on corrupt kingship; the fact that John saw the two as linked is exemplified most strongly in Book VIII of the *Policraticus*, where they are discussed in tandem. John criticises the avaricious and excessive – those who do not practise moderation in their lives – but excess in the pursuit of power is also a feature of the tyrant: 'Therefore respect for the honorable and the just is hardly or not present in the face of tyrants; and whether they are ecclesiastical or temporal, they want to be able to do all things, despising what should precede and follow the exercise of power.'[172] The next chapter will trace the role played by excess in defining the tyrant.

### Notes

1 MacIntyre, *After Virtue*, pp. 170–1.
2 MacIntyre, *After Virtue*, pp. 170–1.
3 *Pol.* VII. 8; 2, p. 118.
4 *Pol.* VII. 8; 2, p. 118: '*Virtus ergo felicitatis meritum est, felicitas uirtutis praemium.*'
5 *Pol.* VII. 8; 2, p. 118: '*Nichil enim uirtute praestantius, dum exul peregrinatur a Domino, nichil felicitate melius, dum ciuis regnat et gaudet cum Domino.*'
6 On Augustine's use of the term *peregrinatio* see the brief discussion in G. O'Daly, *Augustine's City of God*, p. 68. Augustine, *City of God*, I. Pref.,

pp. 5–6; cf. 2 Corinthians 5:6: 'while we are at home in the body we are away from the Lord': *'dum sumus in corpore, peregrinamur a Domino'*.

7   *Pol.* VII. 8; 2, p. 119: *'Unum igitur et singulare summum omnium bonorum beatitudo est'*; *Pol.* VII. 8; 2, p. 122: *'nichil melius est nisi frui eo qui summe bonus et summum bonum est'*. On the Augustinian precedents for John's view, particularly for the concept of 'enjoyment of God', *'Deo frui'*, see Sønnesyn, 'The Ethics of John of Salisbury', pp. 319–23.

8   P. Delhaye, 'Le Bien suprême d'après le *Policraticus* de Jean de Salisbury', *Recherches de théologie ancienne et médiévale*, 20 (1953), 203–21 (217–18).

9   *Pol.* VII. 8; 2, pp. 121–2.

10  *Pol.* VII. 8; 2, p. 118: *'Non enim felix est quis ut recte agat, sed recte agit ut feliciter uiuat.'*

11  *Pol.* VII. 8; 2, pp. 120–2.

12  *Pol.* VII. 8; 2, p. 122: *'Stoicus enim, ut rerum contemptum doceat, in mortis meditatione uersatur; Peripatheticus in inquisitione ueri; uolutatur in uoluptatibus Epicurus'.*

13  *Pol.* VII. 9; 2, p. 123: *'aut ut multum pauculas quaestiones aptas iurgiis elegerunt, in quibus ingenium suum exerceant et consumant etatem'*; 2, p. 125: *'sed prae omnibus maiori diligentia insistendum est quae aut politicam uitam siue in iure ciuili siue in aliis ethicae praeceptis instituunt aut procurant corporis aut animae sanitatem'.*

14  *Pol.* VII. 10; 2, p. 253. See Chapter 1, p. 29.

15  *Pol.* VII. 9; 2, pp. 128–9.

16  *Pol.* III. 1; 1, p. 173: *'Agnitio igitur ueritatis cultusque uirtutis publica singulorum et omnium et rationalis naturae uniuersalis incolumitas est. Contrarium uero eius ignorantia et odibilis et inimica propago eius uitium est.'*

17  *Pol.* III. 1; 1, p. 173: *'quilibet quasi quendam librum sciendorum officio rationis apertum gerit in corde'.*

18  *Pol.* III. 1; 1, p. 174. See Chapter 2, p. 78.

19  *Pol.* III. 2; 1, p. 175: *'Discite ... quem te Deus esse iussit, et humana qua parte locatus es in re.'*

20  Augustine, *City of God*, II. 6, p. 54.

21  James, *Ancient Libraries*, p. 10, items 141–9.

22  *Pol* III. 2; 1, p. 175: *'utilitatem sui, caritatem proximi, contemptum mundi, amorem Dei'.*

23  *Pol.* III. 2; 1, p. 175: *'Annon est arbor bona, quae tantam fructuum dulcedinem affert, tantam affert utilitatem?'*

24  *Pol.* III. 3; 1, p. 176: *'Omnis enim uirtus suis finibus limitatur et in modo consistit; si excesseris, in inuio es et non in uia.'*

25  *Pol.* III. 4 ff.

26  *Pol.* I. 4; 1, p. 31: *'Potest igitur uenatica esse utilis et honesta; sed ex loco, tempore, modo, persona et causa.'*

27  *Pol.* I. 4; 1, pp. 29–30.

28  *Pol.* I. 4; 1, p. 31: *'nisi quia immoderato uoluptatis incursu uirilem animum concutit et fundamentum subuertit rationis'.*

29 Cicero, *De finibus*, III. 50 ff. See Chapter 3, pp. 000-00.
30 Seneca, *Ep.* 82.10; 2, p. 246: '*id est nec bona nec mala, morbum, dolorem, paupertatem, exilium, mortem*'.
31 *Pol.* VIII. 15; 2, p. 341: '*Usus ergo rerum laudabilis aut culpabilis est, rerum dumtaxat indifferentia est*'; 2, p. 336: '*Laudantur cetera et non insipienter optantur, ut bona ualitudo, clarus sanguis, rerum copia, sed nichil istorum turpem aut inhonestum hominem facit esse laudabilem.*'
32 *Pol.* I. IV; 1, pp. 33-4: '*Is uero modus laudabilis est, cum moderatione adhibita prudenter et, si fieri potest, utiliter exercetur, ut mandato comici adquiescas, "Ne quid nimis."*'
33 *Pol.* I. 4; 1, p. 35.
34 *Pol.* I. 5; 1, p. 37.
35 *Pol.* I. 6; 1, p. 42.
36 *Pol.* I. 7; 1, p. 45.
37 *Pol.* I. 8; 1, p. 48: '*dum uirtutis aut honestae utilitatis habeant instrumentum*'. Cf. Cicero, *De officiis*, III. 11-13.
38 Some indifferents, such as health, are regarded as 'preferred': see B. Inwood, 'Rules and Reasoning in Stoic Ethics', in K. Ierodiakonou (ed.), *Topics in Stoic Philosophy* (Oxford: Clarendon Press, 2001), pp. 95-127 (pp. 101-4).
39 Cicero, *On Duties*, I. 7, p. 4; *De officiis*, I. 7, p. 8: '*Omnis de officio duplex est quaestio: unum genus est, quod pertinet ad finem bonorum, alterum, quod positum est in praeceptis, quibus in omnis partis usus vitae conformari possit.*'
40 Seneca, *Ep.* 76.10; 2, p. 152: '*Haec ratio perfecta virtus vocatur eademque honestum est.*'
41 See Chapter 3, pp. 94-7.
42 Annas, *Morality of Happiness*, p. 97.
43 Annas, *Morality of Happiness*, pp. 96-8.
44 Annas, *Morality of Happiness*, p. 98.
45 Dyck, *A Commentary on Cicero, De Officiis*, pp. 243-50.
46 For an insight into such discussions see O. Lottin, *Psychologie et morale aux XIIe et XIIIe siècles*, vols 2-3 (Louvain: Abbaye de Mont-César; Gembloux: Duculot, 1948-49); I. P. Bejczy and R. Newhauser (eds), *Virtue and Ethics in the Twelfth Century* (Leiden: Brill, 2005); I. P. Bejczy, *The Cardinal Virtues in the Middle Ages: A Study in Moral Thought from the Fourth to the Fourteenth Century* (Leiden: Brill, 2011).
47 *Pol.* V. 3; 1, p. 287: '*Sic in aliis est prudentia, fortitudo in aliis, temperantia in quibusdam, in quibusdam iustitia, in nonnullis fides, longanimitas spei in aliis; in his feruor est caritatis, hic patientia laborum, illic dolorum consolatio, alibi perseuerantia bonorum operum; quae tamen singula in singulis est unus et idem Deus.*'
48 On the comparable Augustinian precedent for the reinterpretation of the Stoic idea of the unity of the virtues see J. P. Langan, 'Augustine on the Unity and Interconnection of the Virtues', *Harvard Theological Review*, 72 (1979), 81-95.
49 *Pol.* V. 3; 1, p. 287.

50  *Pol.* V. 3; 1, p. 289: '*Ille autem cultus qui in exterioris operis exhibitione consistit, medio indiget, eo quod ad spiritum corporalis nobis non patet accessus*'.
51  Bejczy, *The Cardinal Virtue*s, pp. 257-8.
52  Aristotle, *Nichomachean Ethics*, ed. and trans. R. Crisp (Cambridge: Cambridge University Press, 2000): II. i, 1103b, p. 23.
53  C. J. Nederman, 'Nature, Ethics, and the Doctrine of "Habitus": Aristotelian Moral Psychology in the Twelfth Century', *Traditio*, 45 (1989-90), 87-110 (109).
54  Nederman, 'Nature, Ethics, and the Doctrine of "Habitus"', pp. 88, 99.
55  Nederman, 'Nature, Ethics, and the Doctrine of "Habitus"', pp 100-3.
56  Nederman, 'Nature Ethics, and the Doctrine of "Habitus"', p. 103.
57  Cicero, *De inventione*, II. 159, p. 326: '*Nam virtus est animi habitus naturae modo atque rationi consentaneus.*'
58  Thierry of Chartres, *Commentarius super Libros De Inventione*, 2.253.159, p. 209: '*Nam virtus, etc. Definitio virtutis sic intellegenda est: virtus est habitus animi quo reditur in modum naturae consentiendo rationi. Nam modus naturae per vitium exceditur, ad quem modum per virtutem sequendo rationem fit reversio.*' Trans. Taylor in Hugh of St Victor, *Didascalicon*, p. 226, n. 2.
59  This position is famously expressed by Seneca in *Ep*. 94; 2, pp. 92-3. It is unlikely that John knew this letter, although it was known to some of his contemporaries, most notably William of Malmesbury. See Thomson, *William of Malmesbury*, pp. 56-7; Reynolds, *The Medival Tradition of Seneca's Letters*, p. 117, pp. 120-4.
60  Nederman, 'Nature, Ethics, and the Doctrine of "Habitus"', p. 101.
61  *Pol.* V. 4; 1, p. 291: '*Mos autem est mentis habitus ex quo singulorum operum assiduitas manat. Non enim si quid fit semel aut amplius, statim moribus aggregatur, nisi assiduitate faciendi uertatur in usum.*'
62  See other examples of the distinction between virtue *in habitu* and *in usu* given in M. Colish, '"Habitus" Revisited: A Reply to Cary Nederman', *Traditio*, 48 (1993), 77-92 (80-4).
63  *Pol.* V. 4; 1, p. 295: '*Amici quidem Dei fiunt aut gratia, cessantibus meritis, ut Hieremias et Iohannes sanctificati antequem nati et gemma sacerdotum Nicholaus quarta et sexta feria semel lactens in cunis; aut meritis ex gratia, ut qui facili uia bonorum operum, sicut penitens latro, uel difficili et felici transitu merentur regna celorum, uelut apostolorum chorus et martirum.*'
64  Colish, '"Habitus" Revisited', p. 82.
65  J. Driver, *Uneasy Virtue* (Cambridge: Cambridge University Press, 2001), p. 5.
66  J. Porter, 'Virtue Ethics in the Medieval Period', in R. Gill (ed.), *The Cambridge Companion to Christian Ethics* (Cambridge: Cambridge University Press, 2001), pp. 96-111 (p. 98).
67  Nederman, 'The Aristotelian Doctrine of the Mean', p. 138.
68  Nederman, 'The Aristotelian Doctrine of the Mean', pp. 134-5.
69  *Pol.* IV. 9; 1, pp. 266-7: '*Sequitur: Neque declinet in partem dextram uel sinistram. Ad dextram declinare est uirtutibus ipsis uehementer insistere. Ad dextram declinare est in uirtutis operibus, quae in modo consistit, modum excedere. Omnis uero uehementia salutis inimica est, et excessus omnis in culpa; bonarumque rerum consuetudo nimia pessima est. ... Ad sinistram declinare est per abrupta*

*uitiorum a uia uirtutum declinare uel deuiare. Item deflectitur ad sinistram qui in subiectorum culpis nimis pronus est ad uindictam; et ad dexteram gressum torquet qui delinquentibus ex mansuetudine nimis indulget. Iter autem utrumque deuium est; sed quod ad sinistram uergit perniciosius est.*'
70 John of Salisbury, *Policraticus*, trans. Nederman, p. 53 (italics mine).
71 Cicero, *On Duties*, III. 11, p. 104; *De officiis*, III. 11, pp. 278–80: '*quicquid honestum esset, id utile esse censerent nec utile quicquam, quod non honestum*'.
72 Cicero, *On Duties*, III. 81; I. 59.
73 Cicero, *On Duties*, III. 13, p. 105.
74 Cicero, *On Duties*, III. 13, p. 105; *De officiis*, III. 13, p. 280: '*Etenim quod summum bonum a Stoicis dicitur, convenienter naturae vivere, id habet hanc, ut opinior, sententiam: cum virtute congruere semper, cetera autem, quae secundum naturae essent, ita legere, si ea virtuti non repugnarent.*'
75 Striker, 'Following Nature', p. 3. As Striker notes in 'The Role of *Oikeiôsis* in Stoic Ethics', there is a probable circularity in the Stoic argument, namely: 'It is natural for man to be guided by reason, therefore we should follow nature, and let ourselves be guided by reason' (162).
76 Cicero, *On Duties*, III. 14. See also I. 16.
77 Cicero, *On Duties*, I. 15, p. 7; *De officiis*, I. 15, p. 16: '*tamen ex singulis certa officiorum genera nascuntur*'; I. 160, p. 162: '*in officiis deligendis id genus officiorum excellere quod teneatur hominum societate*'. See also I. 159.
78 A. A. Long, 'Cicero's Politics in *De officiis*', in A. Laks and M. Schofield (eds), *Justice and Generosity: Studies in Hellenistic Social and Political Philosophy* (Cambridge: Cambridge University Press, 1995), pp. 213–40 (p. 218).
79 Brunt, 'Stoicism and the Principate', pp. 16–20, 31–2.
80 Seneca, *Ep.* 66.10; 2, pp. 8–9: '*Bonum omne in easdem cadit leges: iuncta est privata et publica utilitas, tam mehercules quam inseparabile est laudandum petendumque.*'
81 Macrobius, *Commentary on the Dream of Scipio*, I. 8.5, p. 121. The other types are the 'cleansing virtues', 'the virtues of the purified mind' and 'the exemplary virtues'.
82 Macrobius, *Commentary on the Dream of Scipio*, I. 8.7–8, p. 122.
83 On Stoicism in Macrobius see Colish, *Stoic Tradition*, 1, pp. 319–20.
84 Macrobius, *Commentary on the Dream of Scipio*, I. 8.12, pp. 123–4.
85 R. Tuve, 'Notes on the Virtues and Vices', *Journal of the Warburg and Courtauld Institutes*, 26 (1963), 264–303 (269).
86 M. Viroli, *From Politics to Reason of State: The Acquisition and Transformation of the Language of Politics, 1250–1600* (Cambridge: Cambridge University Press, 1992), p. 15.
87 Martin of Braga, *Formula vitae honestae*, in *Martini Episcopi Bracarensis Opera Omnia*, pp. 236–50. On Martin's use of Stoic ideas see Colish, *The Stoic Tradition*, 2, pp. 297–30; on the background of the composition of the *Formula* see M. J. Violante Branco, 'St. Martin of Braga, the Sueves and Gallaecia', in A. Ferreiro (ed.), *The Visigoths: Studies in Culture and Society* (Leiden: Brill, 1999), pp. 63–98 (especially pp. 91–2).

88  See Chapter 1, pp. 00-00, 00.
89  On the preface and widespread circulation of the work see Barlow, trans., *Iberian Fathers*, 1, p. 12. English translations used here are taken from this volume; *Rules for an Honest Life* is found on pp. 87-97.
90  Martin of Braga, *Rules for an Honest Life*, Prologue, pp. 87-8. *Formula vitae honestae*, p. 237: '*cui naturalis sapientiae sagacitas praesto est*'; '*sed ea magis commonet quae et sine divinarum scripturarum praeceptis naturali tantum humanae intellegentiae lege etiam a laicis recte honesteque viventibus valeant adimpleri*'.
91  Martin of Braga, *Rules for an Honest Life*, 6, p. 95. *Formula vitae honestae*, p. 247: '*His ergo institutionibus hae quattuor virtutum species perfectum te facient virum, si mensuram rectitudinis earum aequo vivendi fine servaveris*.'
92  Martin of Braga, *Rules for an Honest Life*, 2, p. 88; 5, p. 95. *Formula vitae honestae*, p. 238: '*si omnia prius aestimes et perpenses*'; p. 247: '*nam prudentia si terminos suos excedat*'.
93  Martin of Braga, *Rules for an Honest Life*, 7, p. 96. *Formula vitae honestae*, p. 248: '*Magnanimitas autem si se extra modum suum extollat*'.
94  Martin of Braga, *Rules for an Honest Life*, 8, p. 96. *Formula vitae honestae*, p. 248: '*Continentia deinde his terminis te adstringat*'.
95  Martin of Braga, *Rules for an Honest Life*, 5, p. 94; 9, p. 96. *Formula vitae honestae*, p. 246: '*Quid est autem iustitia nisi naturae tacita conventio in adiutorium multorum inventa?*'; p. 249: '*Iustitia postremo eo mediocritatis tibi tenore regenda est*'.
96  Martin of Braga, *Rules for an Honest Life*, 10, p. 97. *Formula vitae honestae*, pp. 249-50: '*Si quis ergo vitam suam ad utilitatem non tantum propriam sed et multorum inculpabiliter adscisci desiderat, hanc praedictarum virtutum formulam pro qualitatibus temporum, locorum, personarum, atque causarum eo medietatis tramite teneat*'.
97  Martin of Braga, *Rules for an Honest Life*, 4, p. 93. *Formula vitae honestae*, p. 244: '*Difficillimum continentiae opus est adsentationes adulantium repellere, quorum sermones animum quadam voluptate resolvunt. Nullius per adsentationem amicitiam merearis nec hunc promerendi ad te aditum aliis pandas*.'
98  Martin of Braga, *Rules for an Honest Life*, 2, p. 89. *Formula vitae honestae*, pp. 238-9: '*De dubiis non definias sed suspensam tene sententiam. Nihil affirmes, quia non omne quod verisimile est statim et verum est ... Crebro siquidem faciem mendacii veritas retinet, crebo mendacium specie veritatis occulitur. Nam sicut aliquotiens tristem frontem amicus et blandam adulator ostendit, sic verisimile coloratur et ut fallat vel subripiat comitur*.'
99  Martin of Braga, *Rules for an Honest Life*, 4, p. 92. *Formula vitae honestae*, p. 243: '*Non tibi affingas quod non eris, nec quod es maius quam es videri velis*.'
100  *Pol.* IV. 12; 1, pp. 277-8. Gregory the Great, *Moralia in Job*, II. 76.
101  *Pol.* IV. 9; 1, p. 267: '*regina uirtutum iustitia*'; Cicero, *De officiis*, III. 28, p. 294: '*Iustitia ... haec enim una virtus omnium est domina et regina virtutum.*' *Met.* II. 1, p. 57: '*Unde liquet prudentiam uirtutum omnium esse radicem*'.
102  *Met.* II. 1, p. 57: '*Constat ergo exercitatio eius in scrutinio ueritatis, quae sicut Cicero in libro de officiis auctor est, materia est uirtutis primitiuae quam

*prudentiam uocant*'; Cicero, *De officiis*, I. 15, p. 16: '*quae prima descripta est, in qua sapientiam et prudentiam ponimus, inest indagatio atque inventio veri, eiusque virtutis hoc munus est proprium*'.
103   Cicero, *De inventione*, II. 160, p. 326: '*Prudentia est rerum bonarum et malarum neutrarumque scientia.*'
104   *Met.* II. 1, p. 57: '*Prudentia uero tota consistit in perspicientia ueri, et quadam sollertia illud examinandi. Porro iustitia illud amplectitur, fortitudo tuetur, temperantia uirtutum praecedentium exercitia moderatur.*'
105   *Met.* IV. 12, p. 150: '*Prudentia autem est ut ait Cicero, uirtus animae quae in inquisitione et perspicientia sollertiaque ueri uersatur.*'
106   Keats-Rohan, 'John of Salisbury and Education in Twelfth-Century Paris', pp. 4–5.
107   *Pol.* VI. 22; 2, p. 62: '*Nam sine prudentia et sollicitudine non modo res publica non procedit sed nec minima consistit domus.*'
108   Murray, *Reason and Society in the Middle Ages*, p. 134.
109   Thierry of Chartres, *Commentarius super Libros De Inventione*, 2.53.160, p. 209: '*Prudentia, etc. Scientiam hic vocat discretionem eligendi unum et detestandi aliud.*'
110   William of Conches, *Moralium Dogma Philosophorum*, p. 8: '*Prudentiam diximus esse discretionem rerum bonarum et malarum et utraumque. Hec namque uirtus discernit bona a malis et bona ab inuicem, mala ab inuicem. Hec quidem, cum sua ui nos trahat, sub honesto continetur.*'
111   Peter Abelard, *Collationes*, ed. and trans. J. Marenbon and G. Orlandi (Oxford: Clarendon Press, 2001), 117, pp. 132–3: '*Horum itaque discretio, tam bonorum scilicet quam malorum, prudentia dicitur.*'
112   Peter Abelard, *Collationes*, 115, pp. 130–1: '*Nonnulli uero prudentie discretionem matrem potius siue originem uirtutum quam uirtutem nominant.*' J. Marenbon, 'Abelard's Ethical Theory: Two Definitions from the *Collationes*', in H. J. Westra (ed.), *From Athens to Chartres: Studies in Honour of Edouard Jeauneau* (Leiden: Brill, 1992), pp. 301–14.
113   Ambrose, *De officiis*, I. 122–9, pp. 188–203; see especially the example of Moses' discernment at I. 123, pp. 188–9 and the manner in which man's rationality leads him to pursue understanding of God at I. 124–5, pp. 188–91.
114   Ambrose, *De officiis*, I. 126, pp. 190–1: '*Primus igitur officii fons prudentia est.*'
115   Ambrose, *De officiis*, I. 126, pp. 190–1: '*[N]eque enim potest iustitia sine prudentia esse cum examinare quid iustum, quidve iniustum sit, non mediocris prudentiae sit; summus in utroque error. ... Neque iterum prudentia sine iustitia est: pietas enim in Deum initium intellectus.*'
116   R. S. Lopez, *The Commercial Revolution of the Middle Ages, 950–1350* (Cambridge: Cambridge University Press, 1976).
117   Murray, *Reason and Society in the Middle Ages*, p. 60. Little, 'Pride Goes before Avarice'; L. K. Little, *Religious Poverty and the Profit Economy in Medieval Europe* (London: Paul Elek, 1978), pp. 119–41. J. Huizinga, *The Waning of the Middle Ages* (Harmondsworth: Penguin, 1976), p. 27, claims that the twelfth century provides a 'furious chorus of invectives against cupidity and avarice'. Cf.

R. Newhauser, *The Treatise on Vices and Virtues in Latin and in the Vernacular* (Turnhout: Brepols, 1993), pp. 199–200, where he points out that discourses on avarice were also common in the early Middle Ages before the expansion of the commercial economy.
118   *Pol.* IV. 5; 1, p. 250.
119   *Pol.* VIII. 4; 2, p. 241.
120   *Pol.* IV. 4; 1, p. 250: '*Praeterea esse regem expedit copiosum, ita tamen ut diuitias suas populi reputet.*'
121   *Pol.* V. 10; 1, p. 328: '*Refert itaque potestatis istorum cohibere malitiam et eisdem de publico prouidere ut omnis grassandi occasio subtrahatur.*'
122   *Pol.* VI. 24; 2, p. 73: '*Noli ergo neque nostrum neque secularium principum duritiam metiri, sed omnium utilitatem attende.*'
123   On John's critique of the avarice of the papacy see I. O'Daly, 'An Assessment of the Political Symbolism of the City of Rome in the Writings of John of Salisbury', *Medieval Encounters*, 17 (2011), 512–33 (528–31). On John's views on venality more generally see J. A. Yunck, *The Lineage of Lady Meed: The Development of Medieval Venality Satire* (Southbend: University of Notre Dame Press, 1963), pp. 115–16, who describes John's writings as indicative of 'the struggle between old feudal principle and new fiscal necessity'.
124   *Pol.* VII. 17; 2, p. 161: '*Inde est quod ad conciliandam potentiam effunduntur opes; et quanto quis potentiae cupidior est, tanto eas facilius expendit. Cum uero potentiam nactus est, erigitur in tirannidem et aequitate contempta naturae et conditionis consortes inspiciente Deo deprimere non ueretur.*'
125   *Pol.* V. 17; 1, p. 364: '*Cum genus et formam regina Pecunia donet, et bene nummatum decoret Suadela Venusque, qui diues est, qui prosperatur in uiis suis, sapiens et felix iudicatur.*' See Horace, *Satires, Epistles, The Art of Poetry*, trans. H. Rushton Fairclough (LCL 194; Cambridge, MA: Harvard University Press, 1926), *Ep.* i.6, 37–8, pp. 288–9.
126   I have developed these ideas further in 'Assessment of the Political Symbolism of the City of Rome', pp. 523–7.
127   *Pol.* V. 10; 1, p. 324: '*Non opus, non sermo gratuitus est, non tacetur nisi ad pretium; silentium namque res uenalis est.*'
128   *Pol.* V. 10; 1, p. 323: '*quantum quisque sua nummorum seruat in arca, tantum habet et fidei*'. See Juvenal, *Satires*, trans. S. M. Braund (LCL 91; Cambridge, MA: Harvard University Press, 2004), III. 143–4, pp. 178–9.
129   *Pol.* VII. 21; 2, p. 192: '*siquidem Cartuarienses quasi auaritiae triumphatores praecipui ubique clarescunt; Cistercienses beati Benedicti ... praecepta et uestigia sequuntur ad unguem*'. On these orders see Little, *Religious Poverty*, pp. 84–96.
130   e.g. Matthew 6:16.
131   Murray, *Reason and Society in the Middle Ages*, p. 75.
132   *Pol.* VIII. 13; 2, p. 318: '*Est autem frugalitas uirtus moderatrix utendi et abutendi ignara.*'; *Pol.* III. 12; 1, p. 210: '*Grata sunt uitia eius qui deformitatem morum sumptuum parcitate compensat. Optimum, ut ait Cicero, si nescis, uectigal parsimonia est.*' See Cicero, *Paradoxa Stoicorum*, VI. 49.
133   *Pol.* V. 17; 1, p. 365: '*diuitiarum non indicit philosophia fugam sed inhibet*

appetitum. Mentem sui compotem quaerit et quae in omni fortunae calculo sufficiat sibi, ita tamen ut sufficientia eius ex Deo sit.'

134 *Pol.* VII. 16; 2, p. 159: '*Nam in his duobus articulis furor totius auaritiae constat quod immoderatius appetit aliena aut sua tenacius seruat; et quidem immoderatius appetit quisquis quod deest, legem necessitatis excedens et usus, exposcit.*'

135 *Pol.* VII. 23; 2, p. 204: '*Siquidem Cartuarienses cupiditati suae immo necessitati limites praefixerunt et moderationis habenis omnem auaritiam cohibent*'.

136 *Pol.* VIII. 16; 2, p. 342.

137 *Pol.* VIII. 24; 2. pp. 412–13.

138 *Pol.* VIII. 8; 2, p. 276: '*Testantur enim, ut de nostris taceam, Seneca et multi alii clari inter philosophos quod ille omnes libros suos repleret oleribus et pomis et uilibus cibis.*' See Seneca, *Ep.* 21.10. See Jerome, *Adversus Jovinianum*, II. 1.1 for a description of Epicurus's frugality towards food.

139 *Pol.* VIII. 11; 2, p. 294.

140 *Pol.* VIII. 25; 2, p. 423: '*Ecce habes uiam uerissimam et fidelissimam, assequendum statum quem desiderat Epicurus*'.

141 Peter Abelard, *Collationes*, 92, pp. 112–13: '*Quam, ut arbitror, beatitudinem Epicurus uoluptatem, Christus uester regnum celorum nominat. Quid autem refert quo nomine uocetur, dummodo res eadem permaneat, nec sit beatitudo diuersa nec iuste uiuendi philosophis quam christianis intentio proponatur alia?*'

142 Peter Abelard, *Collationes*, 81, pp. 102–3: '*Alioquin ... Seneca, ille maximus morum edificator et continentissimus, sicut et uos ipsi profitemini, uite, nequaquam Epicuri tamquam magistri sui sententias tam crebro ad instructionem morum induceret, si ita ut dicitur sobrietatis atque honestatis iste tramitem excessisset.*'

143 D. E. Luscombe, 'The *Ethics* of Abelard: Some Further Considerations', in E. M. Buytaert (ed.), *Peter Abelard: Proceedings of the International Conference, Louvain May 10–12, 1971* (Louvain: Leuven University Press, 1974), pp. 65–84 (p. 70).

144 Liebschütz, *Mediaeval Humanism*, p. 82; see Chapter 1, pp. 00–00.

145 See, for example, Seneca, *Ep.* 30 and *Ep.* 66.

146 Seneca, *Ep.* 5.5; 1, pp. 22–3: '*Frugalitatem exigit philosophia, non poenam ... Hic mihi modus placet.*'

147 *Pol.* V. 17; see pp. 164–5.

148 Seneca, *De beneficiis*, II. 34.4, pp. 120–1: '*Parsimonia est scientia vitandi sumptus supervacuos aut ars re familiari moderate utendi*'.

149 Seneca, *De beneficiis*, I. 4.2, pp. 18–19: '*De beneficiis dicendum est et ordinanda res, quae maxime humanam societatem alligat.*' On the place of beneficence in Seneca's work see Griffin, *Seneca on Society*, pp. 25–9. Note that Cicero also posits that the exchange of benefits is vital to communal life: *De officiis*, I. 20–2.

150 Griffin, *Seneca on Society*, p. 26.

151 *Pol.* III. 11; 1, p. 206.

152 Seneca, *De beneficiis*, I. 6.1, pp. 22–3: '*Itaque non, quid fiat aut quid detur, refert, sed qua mente, quia beneficium non in eo, quod fit aut datur, consistit, sed in ipso dantis aut facientis animo.*'

153 *Pol.* V. 10; 1, p. 326: '*Verumtamen et causae ratio habenda est et personae, ut nec a*

*turpi nec turpiter accipiatur quod ex loco et tempore et modo latius oportet inquiri. Nam plerumque a manu, plerumque a causa, a tempore interdum, interdum a loco uel modo splendent munera uel sordescunt.*'

154 *Pol.* VIII. 13; 2, p. 321.
155 *Pol.* V. 10; 1, p. 325: '*Illi tamen perniciosius nocent inter omnes curiae nugatores, qui sub praetextu honestatis et liberalitatis miseriae suae solent ineptias colorare, qui nitidiores incedunt, qui splendidius epulantur, qui propriam ad mensam saepius extraneos compellunt accedere, humaniores domi, foris benigniores, affabiliores in sermone, liberiores in sententiis, in proximorum cultu munifici et omnium uirtutum imitatione praeclari.*'
156 *Pol.* IV. 5; 1, p. 250.
157 *Pol.* VIII. 4; 2, p. 241: '*Nam qui uirtutis opera et industria liberales erunt, quo pluribus profuerint, eo plures ad benefaciendum habebunt adiutores. Deinde benefaciendi consuetudine paratiores erunt et tamquam exercitatiores ad bene de multis promerendum.*'
158 Ross, 'Audi Thoma …'; Barker, 'MS Bodl. Canon. Pat. Lat. 131 and a Lost Lactantius of John of Salisbury'. See Chapter 1, pp. 00–00.
159 Oxford, Bodleian Library, MS Canon. Pat. Lat. 131, fo. 107r. Lactantius, *Divine Institutes*, VI. 12.2; VI. 12.6, pp. 355–6.
160 Bodl. MS Canon. Pat. Lat. 131, fo. 107v. Lactantius, *Divine Institutes*, VI. 12.18, p. 357.
161 Bodl. MS Canon. Pat. Lat. 131, fo. 107v; see Ross, 'Audi Thoma …', p. 335.
162 Bodl. MS Canon. Pat. Lat. 131, fos 107v–108r. Lactantius, *Divine Institutes*, VI. 12.23; VI. 12.25; VI. 12.33, pp. 357–9.
163 Bodl. MS Canon. Pat. Lat. 131, fo. 108r. Lactantius, *Divine Institutes* VI. 12.35–6, p. 359.
164 Bodl. MS Canon. Pat. Lat. 131, fo. 108r. Lactantius, *Divine Institutes*, VI. 12.38, p 359.
165 Bodl. MS Canon. Pat. Lat. 131, fo. 108r. Lactantius, *Divine Institutes* VI. 12.39, p. 359. See also F. Barlow, *Thomas Becket* (Berkeley: University of California Press, 1986), p. 62.
166 Bodl. MS Canon. Pat. Lat. 131, fo. 108r. Lactantius, *Divine Institutes*, VI. 12.40, p. 359; See Ross, 'Audi Thoma …', 337–8, for the term *Henriciani* and its relationship to John's letter to 'Peter the Scribe' (1167) (Letter 225, *Letters* II, p. 390).
167 Bodl. MS Canon. Pat. Lat. 131, fo. 108v. Lactantius, *Divine Institutes*, VI. 13.3–4, p. 360.
168 Letter 188, *Letters* II, pp. 250–1: '*Et quidem tanto uberior debetur gratia quanto cumulatius et frequentius ad nec meritum nec merentem a sola diuite uena liberalitatis innatae beneficia praecesserunt.*' See also Letter 207, *Letters* II, p. 310.
169 Letter 194, *Letters* II, pp. 270–1: '*Et fortasse rectius amicum dixerim, qui oculos meos phantasticis fortunae ludibriis praestrictos aperuit et, excussis curialibus nugis et illecebris uoluptatum, me in uiam uirtutis inpulit et philosophantium coetibus aggregauit.*'
170 Letter 194, *Letters* II, pp. 270–1: '*Longe ergo liberior quam cum mundana suppellectili et sarcinulis fortuitorum premerer, laeta quidem condicione, ne dicam*

paupertate, quod philosophia uetat ... et Christiano mundus totus exilium est dum peregrinatur a Domino, ut nunquam prosperis extollatur.'
171 *Pol.* VIII. 13; 2, p. 317: 'Sunt tamen quibus frugalitas est inhibenda, ut quorum natura procliuior est ad auaritiam. Sunt tamen quibus est indicenda calcatius, ut qui sua prodigunt et ratione contempta effundunt, non discernentes quid usus sit uel abusus.'
172 *Pol.* VIII. 17; 2, p. 347: 'Ergo respectus honesti et iusti minimus aut nullus est in facie tirannorum; et siue ecclesiastici siue mundani sint, omnia posse uolunt, contempnentes quid potentiam antecedat hanc et sequatur.'

# 6

# The princely head

The virtues of temperance and prudence, the regulatory virtues, aid the individual in the pursuit of moderation. The two remaining cardinal virtues, fortitude and justice, have particular relevance for the prince, however, as his position as head of the *res publica* means that he is uniquely placed to abuse these virtues on a scale that would be detrimental for the polity as a whole. Good leadership and its counterpart, tyranny, are a constant preoccupation in John's works. John's emphasis on virtuous living forms part of his attempt to identify the qualities of a good prince, while his account of moderation aims, in part, to illustrate the dangers of excess – a warning to the would-be tyrant. This chapter will show how the proper observation of fortitude and justice, alongside the other virtues, aids the properly-ordered polity. By extension, it will also examine the characteristics of the good and bad prince. If moderation and virtuous living are established as normative goals for ecclesiastical and secular rulers alike, how can immoderate and unvirtuous leaders be countered? To answer this question, we must examine John's political ideas within the historical context from which they emanated. The ecclesiastical and secular political events of which John was a first-hand observer are of particular relevance, and the chapter will close with an examination of three case studies: King Stephen, Frederick Barbarossa and Thomas Becket. Placing John's theoretical approach to bad rulership alongside his comments on contemporary bad rulers permits a deeper understanding of the implications of his views – particularly those regarding tyrannicide – while providing an insight into the practical connotations of John's writings for the political and social milieux of which he was a part.

## Fortitude and the 'two swords'

John viewed courage as the counter-virtue to deceit and timidity. While references to it are often oblique, courage or fortitude is a constant theme throughout John's works, from the extensive discussion of the military found in Book VI of the *Policraticus* to the chiliastic vitriol of the letters written during his period of exile. Much of John's commentary on practical matters relating to the activities of armies is pulled from Vegetius's *De re militari*, a Roman text on military strategy that he depends on heavily in Book VI of the *Policraticus* in the sections dealing with the 'armed hand' of the body politic.[1] As John Hosler's study of John as a military thinker has demonstrated, John illustrates his account of military proficiency through a series of *exempla* drawn from Roman sources and from the Old Testament. Many of these *exempla* share the common theme of arguing that war should be led by 'great men', namely princes and kings.[2] Hosler's focus is primarily on the extent of John's practical military knowledge, but it is also instructive to consider the implications of the elevated metaphoric language used in his discussions of power, as these reveal his theoretical views on the virtue of fortitude.

John made frequent use of the metaphor of the 'two swords', a metaphor that refers to the division of power between secular and religious authorities. The distribution of power between these two authorities was described by Pope Gelasius I (d. 496), who in an influential letter to the emperor Anastasius wrote, 'The world is chiefly governed by these two: the sacred authority of bishops and the royal power. ... For you know, most merciful son, that although you rule over the human race in dignity, you nevertheless bow the neck to those who are placed in charge of religious matters and seek from them the means of your salvation; and you understand that, according to the order of religion, in what concerns the receiving and correct administering of the heavenly sacraments you must be subject rather than in command.'[3] This 'Gelasian sentence' was adopted and adapted for purpose by polemicists in the Investiture Contest as a rationale for the dominance of the papacy in all spheres, including the temporal.[4] Meanwhile, the 'two swords' metaphor, used to signify the temporal and sacred spheres, developed from exegetical treatments of Luke 22:38: 'They [the apostles] said "Lord, look, here are two swords." He replied, "It is enough."' During the eleventh century the sentiment of the 'Gelasian sentence' was conflated with the metaphor of the two swords, so that by the twelfth century the sword became a powerful symbol for the execution of rulership by the Church, as demonstrated by Bernard of Clairvaux's *De consideratione*, a manual written for Pope Eugenius III (d. 1153).[5] In Book II of that text Bernard advises Eugenius to 'Put on your sword, the sword of the spirit which is the word of God.'[6] Similar advice is found in Bernard's letter to Eugenius exhorting him to launch a new crusade (1150), where Eugenius is encouraged to 'put forth both swords'; Bernard claims, 'both are Peter's, the one to be unsheathed at his nod, the other by his hand, whenever necessary'.[7] The subservience of temporal to sacral power is clearly implied by Bernard through his use of the metaphor of the sword: 'Both swords, that is, the spiritual and the material, belong to the Church; however the latter is to be drawn for the Church and the former by the Church.'[8]

Another text that illustrates the ubiquity of the metaphor of the sword in this period is the *Sentences* of the English scholar Robert Pullen, who is identified in the *Metalogicon* as one of John's teachers of theology.[9] Robert does not claim that both the spiritual and material swords belong to the Church, but asserts that they must be used in its defence.[10] He draws on the physical form of the sword, saying that as the hilt of a sword is in the shape of a cross, both swords should be used to defend the Cross of Christ:

> Without doubt, the Holy Church, that is the body of the head that, indeed, supports it against the world, needs two swords in attack, as the sign of the cross shows. Of course, it is lawful neither to defend nor to fight, except where it is made appropriate that you save that revered cross. Of the swords, the one is assigned to clerics, the other to the laity.[11]

By this reading, the king must protect the Church, acting in accordance with justice to be worthy of his title: 'The king due to his ministry cherishes the Church and its offspring, stands in equity, destroys by all means the true enemies of justice; if he does this call him king, otherwise he cultivates the false name of tyrant.'[12] Pullen elevates justice into a feature of perfect rulership; the tyrant who debases justice and persecutes the Church should be rejected as a false ruler, a perspective John would also promulgate.

John's most extended contribution to the fraught issue of whether the temporal sword was devolved to secular powers by the Church is found in *Policraticus*, Book VI. 8. Here, referring directly to Luke 22:38, John describes how 'two swords' are 'enough' for the Christian *imperium*, and states that those who usurp power through other means (by wielding weapons against the Church, or through illegitimate soldiery) constitute a direct attack on the Church.[13] John outlines the duties of legitimate soldiers; they should 'protect the Church, attack infidelity, venerate the priesthood, ward off offences of the poor, pacify the province, pour out their blood for their brother ... and, if needs be, lay down their lives'.[14] Their swords are 'two-edged'; physical swords are contrasted on several occasions in John's letters with the more powerful sword of the Holy Spirit.[15] In wielding the temporal sword, secular power is necessarily subservient to the stronger power of God. John describes how secular forces are obliged to follow, not their own judgement, but 'the decision of God, the angels and men, in accordance with equity and public utility'.[16] The strength of this statement is reinforced by the discussion found in the following chapter regarding the relative degrees of obedience owed to God and secular rulers. John asserts that a soldier does not necessarily have to serve a Christian ruler, but if he does not do so, he must serve 'without damage to his own faith'; his obedience to the prince and the *res publica* are of secondary importance to this obedience to God.[17] While John seems to starkly prioritise obedience to God over others, he also notes that the formula of the military oath (outlined in VI. 7), when followed correctly, does not permit a distinction between the aims of God and those of the prince and the *res publica*. Living virtuously, in pursuit of courage and fortitude, implies living faithfully.

A comparable treatment of this account of the 'two swords' is found in Letter 269, written to Nicholas, sheriff (*vicecomite*) of Essex, at some point between 1164 and 1169. In this letter John compares the office of *comites* to that of priests, who are 'called by the Pope to exercise pastoral care and wield the spiritual sword'. *Comites*, on the other hand, 'are summoned by the king into the fellowship of the temporal sword'; they are 'bishops of the law of the world'.[18] All *comites*, whether provincial or local, 'carry the sword, not to carry out the bloody sentences of the tyrants of old, but in obedience to the divine law to serve the public good according to its rule, to the punishment of evil doers and the praise of good men'.[19] This letter stresses the obligations that priests and secular rulers have towards their respective corporate communities. It also re-emphasises the obligation towards 'public utility' that secular rulers have, on top of their obligation to respect divine law. This combination of obligations is expressed by the frequent association in John's letters of the metaphor of the sword with the metaphor of the Church as the bride of Christ.[20] This mixing of metaphors evokes Bernard of Clairvaux's letter to Eugenius III encouraging him to 'take out both swords in defence of the Eastern Church' and the 'bride' of Christ, in this case the Holy Land.[21] In his exploitation of such motifs, John appeals to a powerful rhetoric that had a considerable exegetical and polemical heritage. Armies have a dual responsibility: they must protect the Church as well as defending public utility. As Christopher Allmand has established, John's extensive discussion of Vegetius's military teachings was intended to reinforce the ruler's obligation to keep peace and protect society.[22] Maintaining the Church and respecting faith is an inextricable aspect of the preservation of the common good.

## Justice

What does the 'equity' with which military activity is supposed to conform consist of? This question brings to the fore the fourth and final cardinal virtue, justice. Justice (along with its opposing vice, injustice) is a recurrent theme in John's works. John discusses the meaning of equity and justice on several occasions in the *Policraticus*, while in the *Metalogicon* he offers a pragmatic distinction between civil law and natural justice: 'civil laws frequently acquire their power from human constitution, while what is believed to be expedient for the common welfare is equivalent to natural justice'.[23] A similar tack is followed in *Entheticus* where he focuses on the difference between divine and human law. Divine law is 'the only mistress of life for good men, not the rites of the ancients which are wanting in reason'.[24] Human law must conform with God's law.[25] Van Laarhoven suggests that the distinction made here between '*ius divinum et humanum*' is 'a theological statement in a "political theory": civil or royal rights are not at all independent, they have to fit into a higher system of divine justice'.[26] We must be careful not to overstate the case, however; John is not seeking to justify through this definition a practical sublimation of the civil or royal sphere into the ecclesiastical domain. Rather, he is simply acknowledging the debt that human law owes to divine law. John is dismissive of the claim of 'the rites of the ancients' to constitute an indisputable source of law: 'civil law' does not serve as an appropriate standard of justice in his eyes. Instead, divine law has the pre-eminent claim to act as the standard by which human laws are judged; divine law has the right 'reason' that the ancient laws, the human laws, lack. This perspective is reinforced by a comment made in the *Metalogicon* describing how civil law, like other branches of learning, 'has its own fictions', figments intended to aid reason, which are not to be confused with reason itself.[27]

John provides a definition of law in the *Policraticus* which does not differentiate between civil or human law, but appeals directly to theological principles: 'Law is the gift of God, the form of equity, a standard of justice, an image of the divine will, the guardian of safety, a binding and confirming unity between peoples, a rule of duties, an excluder and eliminator of vices, a punishment of violence and all offences.'[28] As already noted in Chapter 3, John opposes the virtue of justice to the desire for self-advancement; it is the foundational virtue that facilitates the extension of care outside one's immediate circle, to the community and ultimately to all.[29] Adapting a scriptural precept, he asserts that character (*mos*) 'is right, if one does for another what he would have another do for himself and refrains from imposing upon another what he would not wish another to impose on himself'.[30] John says too that 'one cannot wish too much for justice unless one can be too just or too happy'.[31] In *Policraticus*, Book IV. 9, John uses Ciceronian language to describe justice as the 'queen of the virtues', while noting that one must observe moderation in its practice, citing the biblical precept of Ecclesiastes 7:17: '*nolli esse justum multum*' – 'be not over just'. However, it would seem that John believes that certain aspects of justice can never be excessive; they have 'perpetual necessity, having legitimacy among all peoples', namely the maxims '"Do not do to others what you would not have done to yourself" and "Do to others as you would have them do to you."'[32]

The implication is that while one can go too far in one's performance of the other virtues, one cannot be overly just, provided that one recognises that the 'greater law' that forms the content of the virtue of justice is divine law. This is the logical conclusion of the study of the relationship between nature and reason outlined in Chapter 2. For John the ultimate aim of reason was knowledge of God; if reason aims towards 'following nature', then the 'law of nature' must be equivalent to the 'law of God'. At various points in his letters John stresses this relationship between law and reason. In a letter written to Thomas Becket in the first half of 1168, he writes that 'reason never leads to the perversion of justice'.[33] In another letter, written to his brother Richard in the early summer of 1166, in the wake of Becket's excommunications of a number of Henry's advisors and clerical supporters and the bishops' subsequent appeal, John advises on the conduct of the archbishop, saying, 'I would that in this conflict of power and justice he march with such moderation, with law going before him, with grace leading him by the hand, and reason in support, that he not seem guilty of rash folly against the power which God ordained, nor assent to wickedness to the Church's injury for fear of power or love of transitory goods.'[34] When this passage is picked apart, its most striking element is the conjunction of grace, reason and law as the triad guiding Becket's conduct along the path of moderation. Indeed, the letter proceeds to refer to the 'golden mean' (*aurea mediocritas*) as the criterion for proper conduct.[35] While the excommunicated bishops flout divine law, this does not give Becket unlimited licence in his actions against them; rather, he is still obliged to pursue a moderate course.

This relationship between law, grace and reason, and the apparent equation made between divine and natural law in John's work, puts personal morality at the heart of John's theory of justice. In describing injustice, John refers directly to the Stoics, saying that they see it as 'a habit of the mind which banishes equity from the realm of morals'.[36] If this passage is inverted, it could be suggested that John's interpretation of the Stoic definition of justice was that it was a habit of the mind which *enforced* the place of equity in the realm of morals. Given that the passage, which returns to the theme of avoiding harm to others, continues with a paraphrase of Cicero's *De officiis*, I. 23, there is no reason to doubt John's adherence to this interpretation: 'Now justice consists mainly in this: do not do harm and, out of a duty to humanity, prevent the doing of harm. When you do harm you agree to offence. When you do not impede the doing of harm, you serve injustice.'[37] In presenting justice as an individual virtue, with law as its physical expression, John de-emphasises the ethical worth of political institutions. Rather, their ethical significance (their justice) is appreciable only when the individual agency and quality of character of those involved in such institutions are considered. All politics is personal, so to speak. This emphasis on personal morality is in line with John's practical recommendations on just distribution (giving to each their due), already alluded to in Chapter 3. As illustrated, '*caritas*' is presented as an appropriate corrective to unjust distribution as it encourages the division of goods '*ex merito*', with no one claiming more than their fair and allotted share. John's views are evident in his reworking of a Roman legal norm, 'Justice is the constant and perpetual desire to give to everyone that to which he is entitled', to describe equity: 'Moreover, equity, as the experts of law assert, is an agreement of things, that rationally compares everything on the same footing, and seeks equal law for unequal things, being equitable to all by allotting to each that which belongs to him. Law is the interpreter of this, seeing as it makes known the will of equity and justice.'[38]

A further example of how justice, the common good and 'following duty' relate is found in the central chapters of Book IV of the *Policraticus*, which are, in part, a commentary on Deuteronomy 17:14-20. John provides a substantial exegesis on each of the precepts of this passage, commenting on their relevance for the role of the prince.[39] His commentary on

Deuteronomy 17:16, a passage that encourages the king to avoid excessive acquisition, is particularly instructive in this respect.[40] John argues that a prince should limit his desires: 'a legitimate quantity is that which necessity or utility begs by reason, provided that the useful is equated with the honourable, and that the art of government subscribes to the honourable'.[41] Indeed, John states here that 'the truest and most useful thought is that the honourable and the useful can always be converted into the other'.[42] This is an explicit use of the Ciceronian coincidence between the useful and the honourable found in *De officiis*.[43] John specifically comments on the prince's treatment of property, saying that he 'should count his wealth as the people's' and noting further that 'he is not his own [man], but his subjects'.[44] In his distinction between what belongs to the prince and what belongs to his subjects, John clearly echoes Seneca's *De beneficiis*: 'For I mean that, while all things belong to the wise man, each person, nevertheless, has the ownership of his own property, just as under the best sort of king everything belongs to the king by his right of authority, and to his subjects by their individual rights of ownership.'[45] John's interpretation of the virtue of justice – exemplified here in the necessary balance between the rights of the populace and the rights of the prince – has notable implications for the role of the prince.

## The prince and the tyrant

To fully understand the relationship between 'public utility' and justice in John's theory we must begin to look in detail at the figure of the prince. John concludes Book IV of the *Policraticus* by referring at length to the relationship between the prince and the members of the polity:

> For the prince holds all, and is seen to be the author of all, since being able to correct all, he is properly a participant in the things which he refuses to amend. For being, as we said, the public power, he draws power from all men, and, so as not to be wanting, he should procure the safety of all members. For as many offices as there are in the administration of a prince's government, so are there members, as it were, of the prince's body. Therefore, in conserving each office in the integrity of virtue and good reputation, he is procuring, as it were, the health and decorum of his own members.[46]

This passage demonstrates how the prince receives his power from the populace but is also obliged to ensure the common good.[47] The prince has the ability to correct everyone, that is, holds the power to enact justice. He is the public power; but as with every individual, his own character and temperament serve to facilitate or limit his capacity to be fully virtuous. Therefore, the good prince is defined not simply by his institutional capacity to be the just leader of the polity, but also by his personal attention to justice. This is expressed in this passage effectively through reference to the corporeal metaphor; this metaphor, as illustrated in Chapter 3, refers not only to the manner in which the polity must exemplify mutual concern, but also to the personal integrity of the prince himself. Kantorowicz drew attention to this dual role of the prince in John's account: 'as a public person he, the Prince, is at once *legibus solutus* [above the law] and *legibus alligatus* [subject to the law], is at once *imago aequitatis* [the image of equity] and *servus aequitatis* [the servant of equity]'.[48] Kantorowicz suggested that an antecedent for this presentation of the ruler as 'animate law' and an intermediary of divine justice can be found in Lactantius's *Institutiones divinae*, where Lactantius discusses the concomitant status of Jesus as 'a living law' and human being.[49] Kantorowicz concludes: 'the Prince as animate law or living Justice shared with *Iustitia* the duality which inheres in all Universals or "Ideas". It was this double aspect of Justice, human and divine, which was mirrored by her impartial vicar on earth who, in his turn, was mainly through *Iustitia* also the vicar of God.'[50]

John considers that a good prince is one who shows respect for justice and law, with justice expressed by its dedication to the common good. Law is the reason why the prince holds the 'first place in the management of the affairs of the *res publica*' and is responsible for all, while others are responsible only for their own affairs.[51] He holds the power of his subjects so that he can bring about the advantage of all, with the aim of ensuring that 'the state of the human *res publica* may be ordered optimally, as each is a member of the other'.[52] Indeed, for John, it is not right to speak of the will of the prince in matters of public affairs, as 'he may not lawfully have his own [will] unless law or equity prompts, or the calculation of common utility introduces'.[53] This is the necessary outcome of the fact that the prince, as already noted, belongs not to himself, but to his subjects. Given that the prince's role is identified with that of the lawgiver, 'his decision may not differ from the conscience of equity'.[54] To this end, the prince is 'the minister of the public interest and the servant of equity, and he bears the public persona as he punishes all offences, damages, and crimes with moderate equity'.[55]

The prince's role as lawgiver goes to the heart of John's views on tyranny, as brought out most clearly in *Policraticus*, Book III. 15, where John provides a justification for killing the tyrant. His justification is congruent with the theme of the early books of the *Policraticus*, which focus on the corrupting nature of the court and culminate in the statement that 'it is lawful to flatter him whom it is lawful to kill', a perspective that depends on a 'lesson from secular literature', namely the suggestion in Cicero's *De amicitia* that 'one lives one way with a friend, another with a tyrant'.[56] The subsequent passage is critical for understanding John's views on tyranny and deserves quotation in full:

> Furthermore, to kill a tyrant is not only lawful but also equitable and just. Whoever takes possession of the sword deserves to perish by the sword. 'To take possession of the sword' refers to he who usurps it by his own temerity, not to he who takes possession for wielding it from the power of God. In any case, he who takes possession of it from the power of God serves the laws and justice, and is a servant of the law. He who usurps it oppresses the law and places the laws under his own will. Therefore the laws rightly take arms against he who disarms the laws, and the public power cultivates [war] against he who is striving to make void the public hand. And while there are many crimes of treason, none are graver than that which is exercised against the body of Justice itself. Tyranny therefore is not only a public crime but, if this is in fact possible, more than a public crime. For if all persecutors undertake the punishment of crimes of treason, how much more punishable is that which suppresses the laws, the laws which must rule rulers? Certainly, no one will avenge a public enemy, and whoever is not prosecuting him commits an offence against himself and the whole body of the earthly *res publica*.[57]

As Van Laarhoven notes, John is original in stating that the worst type of treason is tyranny itself.[58] Usurping power is the ultimate form of injustice; for John, perversion of the legal order counts as a usurpation of power. This goes some way towards hinting at the complexity of the relationships between the prince as maker-of-laws and the 'greater law' binding the *corpus iustitiae* to which the prince (and the positive legal order) is necessarily subject.

Throughout, the *Policraticus* opposes two 'ideal-types' of rulers: the good prince and the tyrant. The tyrant is compared to the good prince in Book IV. 1: 'Between a tyrant and a prince there is this sole or principal difference, that the latter complies with the law and rules the people by its dictates, believing himself their servant.'[59] The subversion of the dictates of law is a feature of tyrants to which John draws frequent attention. By placing his own will ahead of that of the rest of the polity, the tyrant disobeys divine law and rejects the precepts of justice and equity, thus negating political liberty: 'For the will of a ruler depends on the law of God and is not prejudicial to liberty. But the will of a tyrant serves his desire and resists the law – which fosters liberty – striving to impose slavery upon his fellow slaves.'[60] Tyranny, whether private or public, is ubiquitous.[61] John expresses this pervasion of tyranny by comparing the tyrannical polity to a diseased body:

> The *res publica* of the impious also has its head and members, and strives to be like, as it were, the civil institutions of the legitimate *res publica*. Therefore, the tyrant, who is its head, is the image of the devil; its soul consists of heretical, schismatic and sacrilegious priests, and, to use the words of Plutarch, prefects of religion, who attack the law of the Lord; the heart of impious counsellors is like a senate of iniquity; its eyes, ears, tongue and unarmed hand are unjust judges, laws and officials; its armed hand is violent soldiers, whom Cicero calls brigands; its feet are those who among the humbler businesses oppose the precepts of the Lord and His lawful institutions.[62]

John pessimistically notes, 'but nevertheless, not only can he exercise his tyranny over the people, but he can exercise it from the lowest position'.[63] As there are degrees of tyrannical behaviour, 'the man who is fully immune from tyranny is non-existent or rare'.[64] John considers that, while there are tyrants on all levels of society, lack of respect for the law remains their defining feature: 'Therefore, respect for the honourable and the just is hardly or not at all present in the face of tyrants; and, whether they are ecclesiastical or temporal, they want the power to do all things, holding that which precedes and follows power in contempt.'[65] John points out that public office is a particular source of tyranny, however, as public roles are often attained through avaricious ambition, or bought for a price.[66]

This prompts the question: why does tyranny occur? If, as John asserts, all power comes from God, then, by necessity, tyrannical power must also have its source in God. In Book VIII. 18, John writes that 'all power is good' as it comes from God, and it remains good in spite of the fact that it may be misused by an individual or bring harm to someone.[67] While this may seem somewhat paradoxical, it is entirely consistent with John's views on the role played by personal character and intentionality in determining the value of an action. It is clear, however, that John does not view the political agent as entirely free, as he suggests that a populace may be punished on account of a 'divine dispensation' by God, who can use the tyrannical ruler as an implement to chastise sinners.[68] This creates a conundrum for John; the necessary implication of the fact that all power comes from God is that even power which is used unwisely serves a purpose: 'So the power of a tyrant is somehow good, although nothing is worse than tyranny. For tyranny is the abuse of power conceded by God to man.'[69] This makes, as Berman notes, the tyrant and the prince essentially species of the same genus.[70] This link is expressed by John in Book VIII. 17, where he comments that kings are rightly linked with tyrants because tyrants are commonly, if incorrectly, called kings: 'And so the tyrant is sometimes called a king and, conversely, the king is sometimes called a tyrant.'[71] Although the tyrant is opposed, by definition, to the law, this does not necessarily imply that a ruler who acts tyrannically should not be obeyed. In fact, John expressly notes that a ruler who fails in his virtues towards the populace should still be supported by it, as a bee supports its 'king'.[72] In part, the validation for this position rests on John's understanding that tyranny results from the sins of the members of the polity. Thus, even the tyrant can be a 'minister of God', sent, as it were, to teach the populace a lesson.[73]

What, then, can we make of John's advocacy of tyrannicide in *Policraticus*, Book VIII. 18? John revives his statement from Book III. 15: that as a tyrant can be flattered, a tyrant can also be killed. After recounting a series of biblical and Roman examples of poor rulership, and referring to a number of Roman historians to further bolster his case, John writes, 'From these [examples] it will easily be clear that it has always been permissible to flatter tyrants, and it has been permissible to deceive them and honourable to kill them if they cannot be bound in another way.'[74] John explicitly notes that this maxim applies only to tyrants who oppress the *res publica*, not to those in private life.[75] He supports his case with a series of Roman examples, starting with Cicero's account of the murder of Caesar, and then proceeds to detail several biblical examples of tyrannicide (including the murder of Abner Cinei by Jael and Judith's slaying of Holofernes).[76] Van Laarhoven has argued that this profusion of examples and qualifications in John's 'so-called theory' means that 'any practical application fades away'.[77] It becomes a history lesson, rather than a practical guide, or what Van Laarhoven describes as a 'tyrannology', not a 'theory of tyrannicide'. The tyrant assumes centre stage because he is 'an ideological resumé of inhuman, unnatural pride, of moral injustice, and of theological iniquity'.[78] John concludes his discussion in Book VIII. 20 by offering some caveats for those who may be tempted to follow the examples of their predecessors. He claims that, according to what 'the histories teach', no one should kill a tyrant to whom they are bounded 'by fealty or religious oath'.[79] Nor is it permissible to use poison, presumably because it is a deceptive measure. In sum, John concludes that tyrants can be removed only in cases where it can be done 'without loss of religion and honour'.[80] He offers an alternative solution, the power of prayer, noting that just as a tyrant can be raised to his position on account of the sins of the populace, he can also be removed by their repentance. John concludes that devout prayer is the 'most useful and safest' way to destroy a tyrant.[81]

John's ultimately moderate attitude towards a tyrant finds a precedent in the writings of Seneca. *De beneficiis*, VII. 20, provides an extended discussion of one's obligations towards a tyrannical ruler. Like John, Seneca believed that the tyrant's abuse of power served to negate any claims of reciprocity made by the exchange of duties that previously bound the ruler to the polity: 'For whatever the tie that bound him to me, it has been severed by his breach of the common bond of humanity.'[82] That said, Seneca also regarded the rule of a tyrant as a potential sign, or even punishment, for a populace: 'But so rare is such a degree of wickedness that it is always regarded as a portent.'[83] So while Seneca considers that the tyrant does not have to be obeyed, as 'from the moment when by violating all law he put himself beyond the pale of the law,' he recommends 'the observation of the mean': 'If my benefit to him is likely neither to increase his powers to work general harm, nor to strengthen what he already has, if, too, it shall be of such a character that it can be returned to him without being disastrous to the state, then I shall return it.'[84] Should 'the sanity of the tyrant be despaired of', then Seneca advocates tyrannicide: 'with the hand that returns a benefit to him, I shall bestow one on all men; since for such characters the only remedy is death, and if a man will probably never return to his sense, it is best for him to depart.'[85] Tyrannicide is the final recourse, but is permissible only in cases where the character of the ruler is proved to be utterly depraved.

The caveats which John places on tyrannicide have been interpreted as an about-turn by a number of scholars, including Richard and Mary Rouse, who are sceptical about his sincerity, suggesting instead that it is a response to his time and best read as a warning to Henry II: 'The doctrine of tyrannicide is purely theoretical in the sense that John was not proposing it as a plan of action. But it is theory with this practical purpose, that John hoped thereby to convince Henry that, for his own good, he must rule in accordance with the law.'[86] Kate Langdon Forhan suggests that tyranny is mainly a 'rhetorical device' for John, but notes that the corporate metaphor implies that anyone could be the agent of enacting divine justice towards the tyrant.[87] However, John's eventual rejection of tyrannicide, and his recommendation of the alternative route of prayer, can be seen as consistent with the thrust of his arguments throughout the *Policraticus*, namely his dependence on moderation as a normative guide. Just as the ruler must rule with 'tranquil moderation of mind' and respect the law, so too the populace must avoid rash action in favour of placing their trust in God.[88] As Van Laarhoven suggested, the accounts given of tyrants serve as an 'ideological resumé' of how not to rule. The account given of tyrannical power in the *Policraticus* evokes, as Michael Wilks argues, the corruption of learning on account of 'nimiety, too-muchness, and nonsense' in the *Metalogicon*.[89] Wilks points out that 'All three works [*Policraticus*, *Metalogicon* and *Entheticus*] share the common aim of denouncing those who would turn theoretical fictions into actual realities by only dealing with extremes, with one side or the other taken in isolation.'[90] By this reading, the tyrant serves as a foil, a counter-balance, to the good prince. If the hallmark of the bad ruler is immoderate behaviour, so too the mark of the good ruler must be moderation.

## Sources for John's account of the virtuous ruler

Moderation was a moral necessity for everyone, but it had specific implications for the ruler. This was, to a large degree, shaped by the sources John was using, sources which portrayed rulership as ethically significant, and politics as a potential arena for virtuous self-actualisation. An example of this attitude is found in Cicero's *Dream of Scipio* (the final section of his *De re publica*).[91] In this text the divine nature and reward of rulers are emphasised: 'nothing of all that is done on earth is more pleasing to that supreme God who rules the whole universe than the assemblies and gatherings of men associated in justice, which are called States. Their rulers and preservers come from that place, and to that place they return.'[92] Cicero claims that the earthly polity is a mirror of the divine cosmopolis. The relationship between the human and the divine is normative and aspirational, therefore; divine reward is the goal and the measure of human action. As noted in the previous chapter, Macrobius's commentary on this work points to a division in Cicero's work between those who 'become blessed by the exercise of virtues at leisure and others by virtues exercised in active careers'; Macrobius claims that this allows one 'to distinguish those who are primarily concerned with divine matters from the rulers of commonwealths, whose earthly achievements prepare their way to the sky'.[93] This interpretation prompted medieval scholars to consider how contemplation and action were linked in the virtuous rulership of the polity. Virtues became relevant, not only for the ruler, but also because they had ramifications for the correct exercise of power in the polity at large.

Seneca's *De clementia*, a commentary on correct monarchical rule, shares the *Dream of Scipio*'s obsession with the self-actualisation of the ruler through political conduct. As Peter Stacey puts it, 'In *De clementia*, Seneca makes Stoic *ratio* the governing principle of his political community, which thereby comes to share the same rationality, law and justice as the cosmic city. The two *res publicae* begin to be identified at a theoretical level.'[94] The defining characteristic of the just ruler for Seneca is mercy, which must be exercised with moderation. Mercy is described as 'restraining the mind from vengeance when it has the power to take it, or the leniency of a superior towards an inferior in fixing punishment'. It is the 'inclination of the mind towards leniency in exacting punishment'.[95] Moderation is especially evident in the exercise of proportional punishment, even though, as Seneca points out, 'no virtue gives to any man less than his due'.[96] In this respect, it is different from pardoning, which is 'the remission of punishment that is due'.[97] Mercy is the superior of these two traits; according to Seneca 'it sentences not by the letter of the law, but in accordance with what is fair and good. ... It does none of these things as if it were doing less than what is just, but as if the most just thing were that which it has resolved upon.'[98] Mercy allows the ruler to adjust power to the demands of 'Nature's law' and is a feature of good rulership that serves to distinguish the prince from the tyrant:[99]

> Mercy, then, makes rulers not only more honoured, but safer, and is at the same time the glory of sovereign power and its surest protection. ... What difference is there between a tyrant and a king (for they are alike in the mere outward show of fortune and extent of power), except that tyrants are cruel to serve their pleasure, kings only for a reason and by necessity?[100]

Seneca sketches a picture of the ideal ruler, highlighting the need for moderate punishment and the protection of all members of the polity. The ruler must seek to cultivate the admiration of the populace; a successful ruler is 'one the whole state loves, defends, and reveres'.[101] A comparable treatment of the role of mercy is found in *Policraticus*, Book IV. 8, where John emphasises the connection between mercy and justice, arguing that, as mercy can serve as a principle of moderation, it is a necessary corollary to justice. John says that a prince can moderate his acts by the 'rigour of justice or the leniency of clemency' and, in so doing, harmonise discordant positions, making all 'of one mind in one house'.[102] While recalling the account of the harmonious apostolic life found in Acts 4:32, John presents the ethical responsibilities of the prince, to act in the service of peace and charitable works – duties which require careful balance.[103] Mercy is a divine gift, an aspect of the power endowed on the prince from God (Book IV. 1), and so its exercise must be carefully moderated in line with the principles of virtue already described. Indeed, John suggests that the 'law of mercy' should always be on the tongue of the ruler and kept in balance with justice. This view is very similar in sentiment to the account of mercy found in Seneca's *De clementia*, and a reminder of John's earlier statement that the divine law should prove the greater part of the virtue of justice.[104]

While *De clementia* and Cicero's account of Scipio's dream presented a rationale for the pursuit of virtue by the ruler, patristic sources also demonstrated why a ruler's personal orientation towards virtue was important. Gregory the Great's *Regula pastoralis*, a manual written for the *rector* of a church community, is of particular significance. Like Cicero, Gregory also used a microcosmic and macrocosmic model, comparing the universal Church to man: the Church is a perfect reflection of the ideal internal ordering of man, while the hierarchy of the Church reflects the spiritual merit of the individual.[105] While classical thinkers regarded the polity as an optimal space for virtuous activity, Gregory viewed participation in the external affairs of the Church as a way of achieving the best kind of life for the individual. The *rector*, like the secular ruler, must achieve a moderate balance between contemplation and action; his role is that of a '*magisterium humilitatis*'.[106] The *rector* of Gregory's account is principally a bearer of an ecclesiastical office, but can also be seen more generally as a bearer of authority. Robert Markus's study of the genesis of the term '*rector*' in Gregory's *Regula* points out that Gregory sees the episcopal office as defined not only in the vocabulary of rulership and governance, but also within a framework of thought determined by the political relationship between the ruler and the ruled, the hierarchy of the superior and the inferior. John's account of the role of the prince is similarly multi-faceted; the prince has two roles: he has an authoritative role as a secular ruler, but also a quasi-ministerial role as a model Christian. This implies that similar qualities of character are expected from the prince and the prelate; both are obliged to live virtuously.

## The backdrop to John's works

In 1156 John suffered some kind of 'disgrace'. The evidence for John's fall from Henry II's favour is found in Letters 19 and 31 to Peter of Celle,

Letters 27 and 28 to Thomas Becket (at this juncture chancellor to Henry II) and to his secretary Ernulf, and Letter 30 to Pope Adrian IV – letters in which John describes himself as a victim of Fortune, *Fortuna*.[107] The context of John's disgrace was his time at the papal court of Adrian IV, when he played a role in the receipt of the grant of Ireland to Henry II as a hereditary fee from the pope. John may have been at the Curia as a representative of Theobald of Canterbury, but his visit coincided with that of envoys of Henry II, and so he may equally have been there under the auspices of the king. John was sent as the bearer of a gold ring signifying the investiture back to England, and so it seems that the pope, at least, viewed him as acting in some royal capacity.[108] Henry's personal displeasure with John seems to have been provoked by the terms of the grant; Henry wished to receive approval for his actions, not permission. John describes his experiences in the *Metalogicon*, reconsidering them in the light of Adrian's recent death. He describes how the grant to Henry took place 'in acquiescence to my petitions', and states that Adrian sent him (John) home with a 'golden ring, set with a beautiful emerald, whereby [the pope] invested Henry II with the right to rule Ireland'.[109]

As Duggan notes, the principal purpose of this passage is to establish John's intimacy with Adrian; she notes that it does not actually correspond to the terms of the bull *Laudabiliter*, as the latter does not mention the concession of hereditary rights in the case of Ireland, unlike John's account.[110] Duggan suggests that John's role may have been complicated by Canterbury politics, specifically the wish of Theobald to be established as primate over a subordinate Irish Church. Whether John was 'the clever agent of a clerical contrivance' or not, his actions seem to have provoked Henry II's wrath.[111] This is illustrated by Letter 19 to Peter, abbot of Celle, where John claims that he was 'accused of diminishing the royal dignity'. He complains that:

> The indignation of our most serene lord, our all-powerful king, our most unconquerable prince, has grown hot against me in full force. If you ask the reason, perhaps I favoured him more than was just, and worked for his advancement with greater vigour than I should; for I sighed for this with all my heart's longing, namely that I might behold him whom I deemed to be kept in exile by the malice of Fortune, reigning by God's mercy on the throne of his fathers, and giving laws to peoples and nations.[112]

In another letter to Peter, John explains his dilemma: 'to leave the island might suggest that I was a fugitive; to refuse to meet my calumniators might seem to argue a guilty conscience; not to await the sight of my sovereign might expose me to the laws of *lèse-majesté*.'[113] John does not provide details of his crime, claiming simply: 'I profess wisdom and defend the truth.' This seems to echo John 18:37 (unacknowledged in the edition of the letters); Jesus' defence against Pilate's cross-examination is that he came to the world 'to testify to the truth'.

In Letter 28 to Thomas Becket, John expresses the wish to retreat into philosophical asceticism; should he regain the favour of the 'most serene lord the king', he 'shall with greater freedom and more honourably to indulge my love of literature or occupy myself with some other study and thus withdraw from the great anxieties, toils, suspicions and perils which afflict me'.[114] This concept of withdrawal from the responsibilities of courtly life is a recurrent theme of the *Policraticus*, evident in John's criticisms of the avarice of the court. Furthermore, it bears resemblance to the Stoic idea of retreat into a productive *otium*, as referred to in the opening of the *Policraticus*, where John employs a Senecan quote to show the benefit of concentration on his literary rather than courtly life: 'However, while you [Becket] were besieging Toulouse I undertook this work and took myself away for a time from the frivolities of court life, turning over in my mind the thought that "leisure without letters is the death and burial of the living man."'[115] This period of alienation from the court could have afforded John the time in which to complete his masterwork. Assuming that he began composition of his works in this period, it is clear that this 'disgrace' could have sown the seeds in his mind of one of the principal themes of the *Policraticus*: the snares of courtly responsibilities and the delicate game of cultivating favour and avoiding royal criticism.

While the *Policraticus* and the *Metalogicon* were composed at approximately the same time, and so influenced by the same issues, there is some contention over the coherency of John's corpus of work as a whole. Given the time span within which it was composed, there are apparent disjunctions in content and language, which may seem at first glance to render comparisons across his works redundant. However, while it is impossible to claim that John's work is consistent in all respects, it would also be misguided to seek such coherency. It is true that John's language visibly changed in the letters he composed during his exile. McLoughlin terms this shift a move towards a 'language of persecution', which he sees typified in the range of examples used by John in letters written during his exile, especially the recurrence of tropes referring to biblical persecutions.[116] Julie Barrau also draws attention to this change in John's approach, noting the overwhelming dominance of biblical references in letters composed by John after 1163, especially his heavy use of the prophetic books of the Bible.[117] Barrau, like McLoughlin, notes the severity of John's language, commenting that the 'moderation' typical of the *Policraticus* is less evident in his later works, and suggesting that the Bible provides a source for the radicalisation of John's polemic.[118] In what remains of this chapter, we shall re-evaluate the case for positing a disjuncture between John's pre-exile and post-exile literary output, by suggesting that many of the precepts in John's theoretical works are replicated in his polemical letters; variation in means of expression does not necessarily imply thematic variation. Three case studies will be examined to illustrate the degree to which John applied the model of rulership sketched out in his theoretical works to contemporary society. First, we shall examine John's accounts of the Anarchy of Stephen (1135-54). Secondly, we shall turn to John's depiction of the emperor Frederick Barbarossa (1122-90). Thirdly, we shall look at John's lengthy correspondence concerning the conflict between Thomas Becket, the addressee of the *Policraticus*, and Henry II. These case studies will also reveal what the defining features of tyranny in practice were for John.

## King Stephen: tyranny and the Church

Our first case study concerns the period shortly before the composition of the *Policraticus*, namely the reign of Stephen. John refers to Stephen at several points during the *Policraticus* and *Entheticus*, masking his identity behind the pseudonym 'Hircanus'.[119] Stephen is criticised in *Entheticus* for his lack of respect for the law. Stephen/Hircanus 'believed falsely that kings were bound under no law and that whatever he fancied was pious'.[120] As well as for substituting his own desires in the place of divine law, Stephen is also reviled for his lack of respect for Roman law; he 'ordered the customs and laws of the ancients to be torn away', while 'under that king the Julian law slept in her tomb'.[121] In a loaded passage, John explicitly describes Stephen as a tyrant, but one who gives the appearance of being a good king:

> He who was a public enemy with the title of king,
> is put forward as a model of kings and of ruling a people,
> and he is given as a sure formula for living well.
> The cult of peace availed him, but in the manner of a tyrant,
> so that he might see all things subjected under his feet.[122]

Stephen dominated – in the language of the corporeal metaphor – by placing everything under his feet, inverting the proper obligations of the ruler to protect the feet of the polity. He also failed to respect the tenets of religious law:

> The peace of tyrants is this: that no one should protest, that, whatever they do, they should be able to do anything, the laws nothing. The laws are void, abuse subverts the sacred laws, they decree that their will should take the place of law.[123]

In what has been perceived as a change of tune, however, John does not explicitly describe Stephen as a tyrant in the *Policraticus*. Liebeschütz implied that the reason for this lay in a decline of interest in Stephen's reign by the time of composition of the *Policraticus*; *Entheticus* 'was written at a period when the anarchy was somewhat more present in men's mind'.[124] Cary Nederman suggests that the move away from describing Stephen as a tyrant stems from a change in how John used that term. He considers that tyranny in *Entheticus* is defined by excess; the prince rules by his own will, rather than by the will of God and the secular laws.[125] In the *Policraticus* tyranny is not found solely in government, nor is it simply coextensive with the abuse of ecclesiastical liberty, but is, rather, a general perversion of liberties. By this reading, John's account of Stephen as a weak ruler does not automatically make him a tyrant.[126] Nederman argues, therefore, that as John's parameters of tyranny changed, so did his desire to classify Stephen as a tyrant.[127] He draws attention to Book VIII. 21, where John recounts the 'tyranny' of Stephen's son Eustace and the dominance of the barons, who were 'not so much earls of the kingdom as public enemies', in order to demonstrate the emphasis placed in the *Policraticus* on private tyranny.[128]

Less emphasis is placed by Nederman on John's mentions of Stephen elsewhere in the *Policraticus*. In *Policraticus*, Book VI. 8, John draws an important comparison between Stephen and Henry I, claiming that Stephen's reign was the result of the sinfulness of the populace, a sinfulness and faithlessness that mirrored Stephen's own conduct towards the wishes of Henry I. He draws attention to the fact that Stephen – 'a man contemptuous of goodness and equity' – and the nobility broke their oath to make Matilda queen. This broken oath invited the wrath of God, who punished the populace for their lack of loyalty by elevating Stephen to king. In this passage John draws attention to one of Stephen's main deficiencies – he 'seemed not so much to rule the clergy and people as to bring them into conflict and clash them together' – noting in particular his attacks on the holdings of bishops.[129] Oddly, Nederman refers only in passing to Book VI. 8, in spite of the fact that it received particular attention from annotators in early copies of the *Policraticus*.[130] This account is important, nonetheless, as it illustrates a key argument of the *Policraticus*, that is, that the attitude of the ruler towards the Church can be used as a measure of the quality of rulership. The faithlessness of Stephen towards his oath and his machinations regarding the Church are grounds to regard him as a bad ruler, if not a tyrant. John uses more moderate language to describe Stephen's reign in the *Policraticus* than in *Entheticus*, not because his parameters of tyranny had changed, but because the focus of his discussion is different.

A reason for this changed emphasis may be found in the *Historia pontificalis*, a text composed during the time of John's exile that opens with an account of the Council of Rheims (1148). John describes how Theobald of Canterbury secretly journeyed to the council, despite the fact that he was forbidden to travel to it by Stephen.[131] In spite of Stephen's restrictions on Theobald, when the king was threatened with excommunication during the council, the archbishop came to his defence and begged for his mercy; Pope Eugene III subsequently agreed to suspend the sentence, although 'the king has by his effrontery deserved our wrath and the wrath of God's church'.[132] John presents a more negative impression of Theobald's attitude towards Stephen in chapter XLII of the *Historia*, where he notes that Theobald advised successive popes to do nothing to further the coronation of Eustace, Stephen's son, 'since the transfer of it [the throne] had been justly denounced, and the matter was still under dispute'.[133] In spite of this, in his account of the consecration of Gilbert Foliot as Bishop of Hereford, John provides a marginally more positive interpretation. Foliot, according to Theobald, was not to be criticised for vowing fealty to Stephen, as 'a bishop had no right to cause schism within the church by refusing fealty to the prince approved by the papacy'.[134] The implication of this statement is that, although the manner in which Stephen came to power was abhorred and although rights of succession were to be preserved for the Angevin line, the official Canterbury position was that Stephen was a rightful ruler as he had been approved by Pope Innocent II. This position is consistent with that of the *Policraticus*; John simply follows the line maintained by his archbishop, that Stephen is not a tyrant as his right to rule has been accepted by the pope.

Conduct, however, is a measure of good rulership for John. He refers to the magnates of Stephen as 'public enemies' ('*hostes publici*') in the *Policraticus*, ascribing to them the characteristics of tyrannical rulership. Eustace, for example, is derided for his fatal attempt to plunder Bury St

Edmunds.[135] Edmund King's study of the Anarchy notes that in most of the references to 'tyranny' made in the 1130s and 1140s two common points emerge: tyranny is associated with the lordship of castles and with the taking of arbitrary taxation.[136] Nederman refers to these conclusions, but argues that King's study is limited: 'all of the documents cited by King are strictly concerned with the treatment of the church and its servants by the great men of England'. He considers that the *Policraticus* 'opens up the field of application of the term "tyrant" to include those who suppress any legitimate liberty', implying that it presents a more secular position.[137] In fact, Nederman's distinction between the ecclesiastical nature of this documentation and the supposedly less ecclesiastical nature of the *Policraticus* is too strongly drawn. John, as we have seen, considers the protection of churches to be a primary function both of the ruler and of those holding lesser political positions, and, if we take the *Historia pontificalis* into account, he was also influenced by contemporary Church policy. This is an important observation to take into account as we turn to look at other examples of how John's theories about rulership relate to his contemporary political reality.

### Frederick Barbarossa: schism and the poisoned body politic

As noted, John placed a lot of emphasis on Stephen's relationship with the Church, firmly establishing that respect for the rights of the Church was a defining feature of the good ruler. This forms the basis of his frequent criticisms of Frederick Barbarossa, whose role in the papal schism is a dominant strand in John's post-exile correspondence.[138] Frederick is the figure most consistently referred to as 'tyrant' in John's letters. John's concern about Barbarossa predates his exile, as illustrated by a letter written in June or July 1160 to Ralph of Sarre, another member of Theobald's curia, concerning the schism of February 1160 that followed the recognition of the anti-pope 'Victor IV' at the imperial Council of Pavia. In this letter John recounts how he was present at Segni in 1152, when Frederick's embassy came to announce his election as King of the Germans to the pope. John accuses Frederick's embassy of pride, and says that Frederick himself 'promised to reshape the governance of the whole globe and would make the world subject to the City [Rome], saying that he would subdue all things with ease, if the favour of the Pope alone was on his side'. Frederick wished 'that so soon as any man was denounced an enemy, the emperor would wield the temporal sword against him, while the Roman Church should use the spiritual'.[139] To return to an earlier theme of this chapter,

John is clearly accusing Frederick of usurping the temporal sword that is rightly the pope's to delegate. Frederick's arrogance is not the only subject of his critique, however. In this letter, John returns to an element of his discussion of tyranny in the *Policraticus*, namely the notion that the tyrant is a punishment for a sinful populace and a test for the Church. Comparing the Germans to the Canaanites, John suggests that their behaviour may have been designed as a test for the Church, after which the Church will emerge even stronger – 'restored triumphant to the embraces of her spouse'.[140] Forcibly John describes schismatics as a 'footstool' ('*scabellum*') for the papacy: their overthrow gives glory to the Church.[141]

Among the letters to Henry II composed by John during the summer of 1160, under the auspices of his role as secretary to Theobald, several concern the schism and were used by John as an opportunity to present a summary of the obligations of good rulership. The first notes that 'never does the virtue of princes shine forth by any clearer sign than when their majesty brings peace to the people, quiet to the Church and to religion increase that is pleasing unto God'.[142] Another points out that 'the glory of a Christian prince is most vigorous and most effective, if he renders pious service to God from whom all princedoms come'.[143] John's concern, as Theobald's interlocutor, is to remind Henry of his obligations towards the Church and dissuade him from supporting the schismatic policies of Barbarossa. The emphasis on Henry's obligation to protect the Church does double duty as a pointed critique of Barbarossa's policies. That causing conflict within the Church is sufficient to negate Barbarossa's right to rule is clear from John's letter to his brother Robert in 1165, where he describes an inscription ('*Christus imperat*') on a ring gifted to him:

> It also shows that there is no emperor today so far as Christ is concerned, since a schismatic is striving by force and fraud and an epidemic of heretics to cleave the indivisible unity, corrupt integrity, defile chastity; and as much as in him lies he is plotting to overthrow God's design, to make nought Truth's promises and take the Roman imperial dignity from Christ. He is eager to abolish the name of Christ from his empire; but as the inscription of your gift tells us, Christ's name alone endureth for ever; the empire of the presumptuous and the honour of him who glories in a false name is drained to the dregs, and assuredly He who abideth of old will bring him down.[144]

Frederick is no longer a true emperor as he has failed to protect the Church. He is already '*ex-Augustus*', and is described as such in subsequent letters.[145]

John's descriptions of the schism and of Barbarossa's rule are emotive and rich in imagery and metaphor. He frequently uses language akin to the corporate metaphors found in the *Policraticus* in his post-exile letters, describing, for example, the crushing of the schism as the curing of a disease: 'A new dawn shows in the east: in the north schism's head is shattered, its sick limbs decay, its flanks are in pain, its scaly coils are loosed so that it is possible to take breath among them.'[146] In another letter John points out that the defeat of schism is not limited to punishment of the ruler, but extends to the populace at large: 'schism's head is now being shattered; and the limbs, which were once fully attached to – or rather rotted in its filth – must perish with it'.[147] John, in a letter written to Alexander III following the great losses suffered by the German troops in Rome in summer of 1167, describes Barbarossa as 'the schism's author', pointing out that just as God has taken action against Frederick, so the role of Alexander is to be 'God's helper': 'so that as you see God's sword drawn against the tyrants' heads you too may unsheathe Peter's'.[148] John's use of the corporeal metaphor throughout these letters reinforces his assertion that tyranny pervades every level of the polity and is particularly prevalent among public officials, the flanks of the body politic: 'What remains for us to look for from the Lord, save that his flanks may perish with him, and those who were his comrades in evil may be with him too in his fall?'[149]

As Timothy Reuter noted, letters concerning the German empire composed by John while he was in exile show a 'strange mixture of information and misinformation, interpretation and misinterpretation', which is inexplicable in view of the fact that John seems to have been well versed in the details of the schism and subsequent events.[150] Reuter suggests that the inaccuracies and exaggerations in John's rhetoric may result from an emotional response provoked by his exile.[151] It is also possible that these inaccuracies and exaggerations were the result of John's own theoretical perspectives on correct political behaviour. An example of such an inaccuracy is found in Letter 242 to William Brito, sub-prior of Christ Church, Canterbury, composed in late 1167, where John describes the 'deposition' of Frederick by Alexander:

> The Pope waited long and patiently for any sign that the German tyrant might even then be turned to repentance. But the schismatic abused his patience, constantly added sin to sin so that error might be turned into madness; and so Peter's Vicar, set by God over peoples and kingdoms, freed the folk of Italy and all who were tied to him by their oaths on

account of his imperial and royal authority from their fealty to him. At the Pope's instance almost the whole of Italy flew from the face of the raging tyrant even in his presence with delight and promptitude; and as a result he seems to have nothing left there but persecutors, whose clutches he has so far evaded, and constant adversity, which he cannot escape.[152]

No evidence of Frederick's formal deposition by Alexander survives, but Reuter points out that by absolving the Italian cities from allegiance to Frederick, Alexander, if not effectively deposing the emperor, carried out an analogous punishment.[153] John may have exaggerated the facts in this instance in order to reinforce the identification of Frederick as a tyrant; he is to be criticised not only on the basis of his treatment of the Church, but also because the bonds of fealty that previously bound the populace to him no longer held. John did not go so far as to recommend tyrannicide, despite the fact that according this account Frederick satisfies one of the criteria, namely that one can kill a tyrant if one is no longer bound to him by bonds of fealty. The attention paid to the negation of these bonds, given such prominence in the theoretical arguments of the *Policraticus*, clearly reinforced John's portrayal of the '*Teutonicus tyrannus*'.

## Thomas Becket: moderation in practice

The *Policraticus* was written with the whole court in mind, but it is specifically addressed to Thomas Becket, who was at this juncture Henry II's chancellor.[154] Becket is described in the introductory poem accompanying the work, *Entheticus minor*, as 'the light of the clergy, the glory of the English people, the king's right hand, the model of goodness'.[155] However, the immediate backdrop for this dedication is Thomas's participation in the siege of Toulouse (1159), a fact that, in the words of Hugh Thomas, 'elided some of the very tensions' of the *Policraticus*, given that John 'glossed over the fact that as a cleric Thomas was carrying out war'.[156] Evidence of John's somewhat ambiguous stance towards Becket is found at the conclusion of the book, where John writes that he does not wish to prevent Becket from wearing sumptuous clothing, eating elaborate meals or holding high office, but exhorts that he 'sees, speaks, and preaches justice' without leaving the '*via recta*' of virtue.[157] John took a more critical, if satirical, position in *Entheticus maior*, where he described the corrupting effect of the court in this period: 'drunk with the gift of Fortune the new court under a youthful king believes that all things are lawful for it'.[158] John terms Becket the 'defender of justice', but also says that 'he usually feigns many things, he simulates that he himself is also savage; he becomes all things to all people'.[159] Although John recognised that this was a ruse, he believed that it would never be a successful one given the degree of corruption of the court.[160] Indeed, given the contempt expressed by John at other points of his writings for dissimulation of character, this is hardly praise.

It is interesting to compare these ambiguous comments with John's later perspective on the siege of Toulouse by looking at a letter written to Bartholomew, Bishop of Exeter, in which he summarises Becket's early career (June 1166):

> I know at that time he [Becket] did not follow the counsel of greed, but the dictates of necessity; nonetheless I do not doubt that he was the servant of wickedness, and I judge him to have fully deserved to be punished, especially at the hands of the king whom he was putting before God, the author of all good things; and in return it is right for him to be a punishment to the king, whom he believed and claimed to be responsible for his wrongdoing.[161]

John sees Becket as having expurgated his sin through penance: 'now the archbishop does penance, sees and confesses his faults; once with Saul he attacked the Church, now he is prepared with Paul to lay down his life for it'.[162] Describing Becket and Henry as 'the princes of the people, of whom one regulates things spiritual and the other guides things temporal', he says that it is the responsibility of both rulers to guide and regulate their subjects.[163] However, if they are found to be failing in their duties they will be punished by God unless they 'return by the way of penance and follow more godly advice'.[164] John considers that Becket has already been punished for his role in the taxation of the church of Toulouse and has done due penance; Henry, however, has yet to repent. John is far more critical of Becket's role in the siege in this letter than in the *Policraticus*, clearly seeing it as grounds for divine punishment of both Henry and Thomas.

Doubtless, John regarded Becket's change in role from chancellor to archbishop as requiring a modification of behaviour.[165] Writing to Becket in early 1165, John advises that he takes careful counsel in exile, encouraging him to turn to prayer, 'lay aside all other activities' and desist from his study of canon and civil law, of which John considers he has 'no need at this moment'.[166] In lieu of philosophising, John recommends that Becket should 'ponder the Psalms and turn over the moral writings of St Gregory'.[167] Is this evidence of 'back-tracking' on John's part, a retraction of the value of secular learning? Another reading is potentially persuasive, namely to consider Letter 144 not as a change of heart on John's part but, rather, a modification of advice appropriate to Becket's change in status and the circles within which he is moving. In the *Policraticus* and *Entheticus*, John is prepared to recognise that Becket is obliged to wear fine clothing and mix with others in the court, as befits his role as chancellor, but in this letter his emphasis is on Becket's devotional character, as befits his role as archbishop. Prayer is recommended over expedient political rhetoric, as Becket is now a religious ruler with exclusive responsibility to the Church. This change in character is underlined further in Letter 187, written in late 1166 to Baldwin of Totnes, where John describes, with some irony, how Becket has changed in the eyes of others: 'while he was a mighty trifler in the court, while he seemed to despise the law and the clergy, while he followed low pursuits with the magnates, he was reckoned a great man, eminent, acceptable to all'. As archbishop, however, 'he became their enemy, because he spoke the truth to them and corrected their manner of life'.[168]

In both instances and with regard to both roles, John remains concerned with the quality of Becket's internal character. In fact, his comments on Becket's behaviour in the *Policraticus* and *Entheticus* could be framed as a test of Ciceronian *decorum*; Becket does what is advantageous, *utile*, in terms of maintaining his position at the court, but will ultimately fail if he does not also pursue what is morally right, *honestum*. As archbishop, Becket must pursue what is morally right and realise that that is the only route to true advantage. Throughout John's letters, moderation is frequently invoked as an appropriate normative standard for Becket to follow. Becket's moderation is 'known to all'.[169] John advises that he must answer his critics by 'showing moderation in deeds and words, in life and dress – which is not of much profit in God's eyes unless it comes from the depth of your conscience', advocating the coincidence between intention and action that is the mark of a truly virtuous action.[170] The account given by John of Becket's archbishopric in his *Vita*, although it is clearly written in eulogistic, hagiographical tones, describes Becket as the personification of many of the virtuous characteristics espoused in the *Policraticus*.[171] He is praised for avoiding avarice, shunning gifts and observing moderate abstinence in food and drink during his time in Canterbury. In a telling passage, John describes him as 'wearing costly garments' while being 'a pauper in spirit'.[172] Similar sentiments are found in a letter to John of Canterbury, composed following Becket's murder (early 1171), where Becket is described as having 'scorned riches and all the world's glory, set Christ's love before affectionate intercourse with friends and his whole family, submitted to exile, laid himself and his followers open to peril and poverty; he fought to the death to preserve his God's law and to make nought abuses which came from ancient tyrants'.[173] In so doing, according to John, Becket emulated Christ and the apostles by following the '*regia uia*', the 'royal road' of virtue.[174]

The previous chapter highlighted a number of notations found in a copy of Lactantius's *Institutiones divinae*, purported to be John's, including some addressed to Thomas and his adversaries, the '*Henriciani*'.[175] A number of other notes and remarks are scattered throughout the manuscript, written in the same slightly spiky hand and using a distinctive dark ink. Notably, eighteen passages are marked '*Caue*' or '*Caute*' – an invocation to the reader to take heed. These passages concern a number of themes, such as the nature of angels, the divine nature of Christ and the dangers of lust. Four warnings of this type are clustered towards the end of the manuscript, pointing to passages which refer to the signs indicating the end of the world. The first and last of these refer to the 6,000 years that followed the Creation, which would end with the Day of Judgment.[176] The second warns of the rise of a king who would become the destroyer of the human race, while the third warning is placed alongside the reference to the Sybilline prophecy of the Day of Judgment.[177] A further passage that refers to the rebellion of the evil nations against the Holy City at the end of the world is accompanied by the words '*Sanis Firmiane*', 'Wise Firmianus' – praise for Lactantius.[178] The emphasis placed on these points of the text suggests that the annotator felt himself to be in a time of crisis where such prophecies were of immediate relevance. Such a millenarian attitude is consistent with the pessimism of John's letters, and casts the advice given to Thomas and Henry's followers earlier in the manuscript in a new light: virtuous behaviour is not simply an abstract recommendation but, more critically, a necessity in the face of the last days of the world.

## Conclusion

Alisdair MacIntyre characterised the Becket controversy as a conflict between two bearers of 'an authoritative role' exercised in a shared framework of agreement on the content of human and divine justice.[179] As noted, John regards Becket and Henry as 'the princes of the people', one of matters spiritual and the other of matters temporal. It is clear that he considers both to be subject to the same normative code, namely moderate behaviour in the service of the Church. John never doubts the inherent value of a prince, even going so far as to suggest that the ruler is a necessary good for a polity by stating that even if a polity did not require a king it would maintain one anyway.[180] The mark of a good ruler, however, remains his respect for God's law. This is clear if we return to John's discussion of tyrannicide. John notes that 'to take the sword' refers to those who usurp it, not those who receive from God the right to use it. Those who receive the sword legitimately are 'the slaves of the law and the servant of right and justice', while those who usurp power 'make the laws slaves to his own will'. While Nederman has argued that John's metaphor of the body politic depoliticises the priesthood by representing it as the soul of the body politic, a soul that has an ambiguous location in the body, John clearly saw a role for the Church within the political hierarchy.[181] As our survey has demonstrated, Stephen received the right to exercise the sword, despite his usurpation, thanks to his approbation by Innocent II, which was validated by Theobald at the Council of Rheims. On the contrary, while his successor Henry II also received the approbation of the pope and so the right to wield the sword, he invalidated his right to rule by subjugating the laws of the land and the Church to his own will. The same applies to Barbarossa, who incited schism within the Church. While John may not go so far as to follow through on his advice that a tyrant deserves to be killed, it is clear that he expected rulers to protect the Church, act moderately, and in so doing, follow the rightful path of virtue; a ruler who does not observe these precepts does not deserve to rule.

## Notes

1 On the reception of this text in the Middle Ages see C. Allmand, *The De Re Militari of Vegetius: The Reception, Transmission and Legacy of a Roman Text in the Middle Ages* (Cambridge: Cambridge University Press, 2011). Allmand discusses John's use of the text at pp. 84–91, noting that John refers to Vegetius as '*Renatus noster*' (p. 85). John also referred to Vegetius in Letter 209, *Letters* II, p. 336.
2 Hosler, *John of Salisbury*, p. 91.
3 Quoted in I. S. Robinson, 'Church and Papacy', in Burns (ed.), *Cambridge History of Medieval Political Thought*, pp. 252–305 (pp. 288–9). For later interpretations of the 'Gelasian sentence' see pp. 289–300.
4 Gregory VII's reformulation of the Gelasian sentence (1081) read: 'that the priests of Christ are to be considered the fathers and masters of kings and princes and of all the faithful'; quoted in Robinson, 'Church and Papacy', p. 299. This version was incorporated into canon law and is referred to in *Distinctio* 96 of Gratian's *Decretum*.

5 For a summary of this conflation, particularly on the role played by Gottschalk of Aachen, see J. Canning, *A History of Medieval Political Thought, 300–1450* (London: Routledge, 2005), pp. 99–102.
6 Bernard of Clairvaux, *Five Books on Consideration: Advice to a Pope*, trans. J. D. Anderson and E. T. Kennan (Kalamazoo: Cistercian Publications, 1976), 2.13, p. 62.
7 Bernard of Clairvaux, *Ep.* 256, quoted in Robinson, 'Church and Papacy', p. 304.
8 Bernard of Clairvaux, *Five Books on Consideration*, 4.7, p. 118.
9 Smalley, *The Becket Conflict and the Schools*, pp. 40–5.
10 Courtney, *Cardinal Robert Pullen*, p. 260.
11 Robert Pullen, *Sententiarum libri VIII*, PL 186, VI. 56 (905 D): '*Nimirum sancta Ecclesia quae illius capitis corpus est, quae etiam contra mundum certamen suscepit, gladiis eget duobus in congressu, utroque signum crucis exprimente. Quippe nihil aliud aut defendere, aut oppugnare licet, nisi illud quo salva crucis reverentia fieri conveniat. Gladiorum alter deputatur clericis, alter laicis.*'
12 Robert Pullen, *Sententiarum libri VIII*, VII. 7 (920 C): '*Rex ergo quoniam ex ordine ministerii sui id debet Ecclesiae ut ejus alumnos, stans cum aequitate, foveat, hostes vero in justitia prorsus dejiciat; si ita se habet, utique rex; alioquin falso nomine tyrannidem exercet.*'
13 *Pol.* VI. 8; 2, p. 22: '*Duos gladios sufficere imperio Christiano Euangelii sacra testatur historia; omnes alii eorum sunt qui cum gladiis et fustibus accedunt ut captiuum capiant Christum, nomen eius delere cupientes.*'
14 *Pol.* VI. 8; 2, p. 23: '*Tueri Ecclesiam, perfidiam impugnare, sacerdotium uenerari, pauperum propulsare iniurias, pacare prouinciam, pro fratribus ... fundere sanguinem et, si opus est, animam ponere.*'
15 Letter 157, *Letters* II, p. 66; Letter 289, *Letters* II, p. 652.
16 *Pol.* VI. 8; 2, p. 23: '*in quo quisque non tam suum quam Dei angelorum et hominum sequitur ex aequitate et publica utilitate arbitrium*'.
17 *Pol.* VI. 9; 2, p. 23: '*Nec refert fideli quis militet an infideli, dum tantum militet fide incolumi.*'
18 Letter 269, *Letters* II, pp. 542–5: '*Nam sicut alii praesules in partem sollicitudinis a summo pontifice euocantur ut spiritualem exerceant gladium, sic a principe in ensis materialis communionem comites quasi quidam mundani iuris praesules asciscuntur.*'
19 Letter 269, *Letters* II, pp. 544–5: '*Vtrique uero gladium portant, non utique quo carnificinas expleant ueterum tirannorum, sed ut diuinae pareant legi et ad normam eius utilitati publicae seruiant ad uindictam malefactorum, laudem uero bonorum.*'
20 Letter 157, *Letters* II, p. 66; Letter 180, *Letters* II, p. 194; Letter 269, *Letters* II, p. 544.
21 Bernard of Clairvaux, *Sancti Bernardi Opera Omnia*, vol. 8: *Epistolae*, *Ep.* 256, pp. 163–5.
22 Allmand, *The De Re Militari of Vegetius*, p. 91.

23  *Met.* II. Prol., p. 56: '*Nam et leges ciuium ab humana constitutione plerumque uigorem sumunt, et quod publicae utilitati creditur expedire, naturali iustitiae coaequatur.*'
24  *Entheticus*, 1517-18, pp. 202-3: '*Lex divina bonis vivendi sola magistra, non veterum ritus, qui ratione carent.*'
25  *Entheticus*, 1521-2, pp. 202-3.
26  Van Laarhoven, in *Entheticus*, p. 393.
27  *Met.* II. 20, p. 96: '*ius ciuile sua figmenta nouit*'.
28  *Pol.* VIII. 17; 2, p. 345: '*Porro lex donum Dei est, aequitatis forma, norma iustitiae, diuinae uoluntatis imago, salutis custodia, unio et consolidatio populorum, regula officiorum, exclusio et exterminatio uitiorum, uiolentiae et totius iniuriae pena.*'
29  *Pol.* VIII. 5; 2, pp. 243-4.
30  *Pol.* VIII. 5; 2, p. 244: '*Recti quidem, si faciat quis alii quod sibi uult fieri et ab eo abstineat alii inferendo quod sibi nollet ab alio irrogari*'.
31  *Pol.* VIII. 5; 2, p. 244: '*Nam nimis uelle quod iustum est nemo potest, nisi forte quis queat esse iustus nimium aut beatus.*'
32  *Pol.* IV. 7; 1, p. 259 '*Sunt autem praecepta quaedam perpetuam habentia necessitatem, apud omnes gentes legitima ... Quod tibi non uis fieri, alii ne feceris; et: Quod tibi uis fieri faciendum, hoc facias alii.*' Cf. Tobit 4:16; Matthew 7:12; Luke 6:31; Augustine, *De libero arbitrio voluntatis*, ed. W. Green (CCSL 29; Turnhout: Brepols, 1970), I. 3.6, p. 214.
33  Letter 278, *Letters* II, pp. 600-1: '*cum tamen aequitatis euersionem ... nunquam ratio introducat*'.
34  Letter 172, *Letters* II, pp. 128-9: '*Hoc autem est ut in hoc conflictu potestatis et iuris ea moderatione incedat, praeuia lege, duce gratia, iuuante ratione, ut nec temeritatis reus uideri debeat aduersus potestatem quam Deus ordinauit, nec metu potestatis aut amore bonorum euanescentium iniquitati consentiat in depressionem ecclesiae*'.
35  Letter 172, *Letters* II, pp. 130-1. It is likely that Horace is the source for John's use of this term (see *Odes*, II. 10).
36  *Pol.* IV. 12; 1, p. 277: '*Est autem (ut Stoicis placet) iniustitia mentis habitus quae a regione morum exterminat aequitatem.*'
37  *Pol.* IV. 12; 1, p. 277: '*In eo autem maxime constat iustitia, si non noceas et ex officio humanitatis prohibeas nocentes. Cum uero noces, accedis ad iniuriam. Cum nocentes non impedis, iniustitiae famularis.*' Cf. Cicero, *De officiis*, I. 23, p. 24: '*Sed iniustitiae genera duo sunt, unum eorum, qui inferunt, alterum eorum, qui ab iis, quibus infertur, si possunt, non propulsant iniuriam.*'
38  Ulpian, *Digest*, i.1.10, in S. P. Scott (ed.), *The Civil Law* (1932), www.constitution.org/sps/sps.htm (accessed 10 July 2017); *Pol.* IV. 2; 1, p. 237: '*Porro aequitas, ut iuris periti asserunt, rerum conuenientia est, quae cuncta coaequiparat ratione et imparibus rebus paria iura desiderat, in omnes aequabilis, tribuens unicuique quod suum est. Lex uero eius interpres est, utpote cui aequitatis et iustitiae uoluntas innotuit.*'
39  On the significance of the early and medieval Christian tradition of Deuteronomy

as Moses's final statement of the law see MacIntyre, *Whose Justice? Which Rationality?*, p. 150.

40 Deuteronomy 17:16: 'Even so, he must not acquire many horses for himself, or return the people to Egypt in order to acquire more horses, since the Lord has said to you, "You must never return that way again."'

41 *Pol.* IV. 4; 1, pp. 245-6: '*cuius legitima quantitas est, quam ratio necessitatis aut utilitatis exposcit, ita tamen ut utile et honestum coaequentur et ciuilitas conscribatur honestis*'.

42 *Pol.* IV. 4; 1, p. 246: '*sententiam uerissimam et utilissimam esse, honestum et utile in se usquequaque conuerti*'.

43 See, for example, Cicero, *On Duties*, I. 94, p. 37: 'the essence of this [decorum] is that it cannot be separated from what is honourable: for what is seemly is honourable and what is honourable is seemly'; *De officiis*, I. 94, p. 96: '*Huius vis ea est, ut ab honesto non queat separari; nam et, quod decet, honestum est et, quod honestum est, decet.*'

44 *Pol.* IV. 5; 1, p. 250: '*ita tamen ut diuitias suas populi reputet ... cum nec ipse suus sit sed subditorum*'. See Chapter 5, p. 163.

45 Seneca, *De beneficiis*, VII. 5.1, pp. 468-9: '*Etenim sic omnia sapientis esse dico, ut nihilo minus proprium quisque in rebus suis dominium habeat, quemadmodum sub optimo rege omnia rex imperio possidet, singuli dominio.*'

46 *Pol.* IV. 12; 1, pp. 278-9: '*Princeps enim tenetur de omnibus et omnium auctor esse uidetur quia, cum omnia possit corrigere, eorum merito particeps est quae noluit emendare. Cum enim potestas publica sit, ut praediximus, omnium uires exhaurit et, ne in se deficiat, incolumitatem omnium debet procurare membrorum. Quot autem in administratione principatus extant officia, tot sunt principalis corporis quasi membra. Dum autem singulorum officia in integritate uirtutis et suauitate opinionis conseruat, quandam quasi membris sanitatem procurat et decorem.*'

47 See B. Tierney, *Religion, Law, and the Growth of Constitutional Thought 1150-1650* (Cambridge: Cambridge University Press, 1982), pp. 26-7, which discusses varieties of corporate structures. The Roman law model suggests that all power resides in the community and is delegated to an official working on its behalf; the canon law model describes power as derived from the constitution of the Church. See Canning, *A History of Medieval Political Thought*, p. 114, who points out that in John the theocratic and political dimensions of the *respublica* coexist: 'It was in this sense that the *princeps* represented his subjects: he acted in the place of the *corpus res publicae* and bore the persona of the corporation of his subjects.'

48 Kantorowicz, *The King's Two Bodies*, p. 96.

49 Kantorowicz, *The King's Two Bodies*, p. 128; Lactantius, *Divine Institutes*, IV. 25.2-5, p. 268.

50 Kantorowicz, *The King's Two Bodies*, p. 143.

51 *Pol.* IV. 1; 1, p. 235: '*in rei publicae muneribus exercendis et oneribus subeundis legis beneficio sibi primum uendicat locum, in eoque praefertur ceteris, quod, cum singuli teneantur ad singula, principi onera imminent uniuersa*'.

52 *Pol.* IV. 1; 1, p. 235: '*humanae rei publicae status optime disponatur, dum sunt alter alterius membra*'.

53 *Pol.* IV. 2; 1, p. 238: 'Sed quis in negotiis publicis loquetur de principis uoluntate, cum in eis nil sibi uelle liceat, nisi quod lex aut aequitas persuadet aut ratio communis utilitatis inducit?'
54 *Pol.* IV. 2; 1, p. 238: 'eo quod ab aequitatis mente eius sententia non discordet'.
55 *Pol.* IV. 2; 1, p. 238: 'Publicae ergo utilitatis minister et aequitatis seruus est princeps, et in eo personam publicam gerit, quod omnium iniurias et dampna sed et crimina omnia aequitate media punit.'
56 *Pol.* III. 15; 1, p. 232: 'Ei namque licet adulari, quem licet occidere.'; 'Unde et in secularibus litteris cautum est quia aliter cum amico, aliter uiuendum est cum tiranno.' See Cicero, *De amicitia*, XXIV. 89.
57 *Pol.* III. 15; 1, pp. 232-3: 'Porro tirannum occidere non modo licitum est sed aequum et iustum. Qui enim gladium accipit, gladio dignus est interire. Sed accipere intelligitur qui eum propria temeritate usurpat, non qui utendi eo accipit a Domino potestatem. Utique qui a Deo potestatem accipit, legibus seruit et iustitiae et iuris famulus est. Qui uero eam usurpat, iura deprimit et uoluntati suae leges summittit. In eum ergo merito armantur iura qui leges exarmat, et publica potestas seuit in eum qui euacuare nititur publicam manum. Et, cum multa sint crimina maiestatis, nullum grauius est eo, quod aduersus ipsum corpus iustitiae exercetur. Tirannus ergo non modo publicum crimen sed, si fieri posset, plus quam publicum est. Si enim crimen maiestatis omnes persecutores admittit, quanto magis illud quod leges premit, quae ipsis debent imperatoribus imperare? Certe hostem publicum nemo ulciscitur, et quisquis eum non persequitur, in seipsum et in totum rei publicae mundanae corpus delinquit.'
58 Van Laarhoven, '"Thou shalt NOT slay a tyrant!" The So-Called Theory of John of Salisbury', in Wilks (ed.), *World*, pp. 319-41.
59 *Pol.* IV. 1; 1, p. 235: 'Est ergo tiranni et principis haec differentia sola uel maxima, quod hic legi obtemperat et eius arbitrio populum regit cuius se credit ministrum'.
60 *Pol.* VIII. 22; 2, p. 397: 'Voluntas enim regentis de lege Dei pendet et non praeiudicat libertati. At tiranni uoluntas concupiscentiae seruit et legi reluctans, quae libertatem fouet, conseruis iugum seruitutis conatur imponere.'
61 *Pol.* VIII. 17; 2, p. 346: 'Et quidem non soli reges tirannidem exercent; priuatorum plurimi tiranni sunt'.
62 *Pol.* VIII. 17; 2, pp. 348-9: 'Habet enim et res publica impiorum caput et membra sua, et quasi ciuilibus institutis legitimae rei publicae nititur esse conformis. Caput ergo eius tirannus est imago diaboli; anima heretici scismatici sacrilegi sacerdotes et, ut uerbo Plutarchi utar, praefecti religionis, impugnantes legem Domini; cor consiliarii impii, quasi senatus iniquitatis; oculi, aures, lingua, manus inermis, iudices et leges, officiales iniusti; manus armata, milites uiolenti, quos Cicero latrones appellat; pedes qui in ipsis humilioribus negotiis praeceptis Domini et legitimis institutis aduersantur.'
63 *Pol.* VII. 17; 2, p. 161: 'sed tamen non modo in populo sed in quantauis paucitate potest quisque suam tirannidem exercere'.
64 *Pol.* VII. 17; 2, p. 161: 'a tirannide tamen omnino immunis est aut nullus aut rarus'.
65 *Pol.* VIII. 17; 2, p. 347: 'Ergo respectus honesti et iusti minimus aut nullus est in

*facie tirannorum; et siue ecclesiastici siue mundani sint, omnia posse uolunt, contempnentes quid potentiam antecedat hanc et sequatur.*'
66 *Pol.* VII. 17; 2, p. 162.
67 *Pol.* VIII. 18; 2, p. 359: '*Omnis autem potestas bona, quoniam ab eo est a quo solo omnia et sola sunt bona. Utenti tamen interdum bona non est aut patienti sed mala, licet quod ad uniuersitatem sit bona, illo faciente qui bene utitur malis nostris.*'
68 *Pol.* IV. 1; 1, p. 236: '*Neque enim potentis est, cum uult seuire in subditos, sed diuinae dispensationis pro beneplacito suo punire uel exercere subiectos.*' See also *Pol.* VIII. 19; 2, p. 371.
69 *Pol.* VIII. 18; 2, p. 359: '*Ergo et tiranni potestas bona quidem est, tirannide tamen nichil est peius. Est enim tirannis a Deo concessae homini potestatis abusus.*'
70 Berman, *Law and Revolution*, p. 281.
71 *Pol.* VIII. 17; 2, p. 348: '*Itaque et tiranni nomine rex et e conuerso interdum principis nomine tirannus appellatur iuxta illud*'.
72 *Pol.* VI. 24; 2, p. 66.
73 *Pol.* VIII. 18; 2, pp. 358–64.
74 *Pol.* VIII. 18; 2, p. 364: '*Ex quibus facile liquebit quia semper tiranno licuit adulari, licuit eum decipere et honestum fuit occidere, si tamen aliter coherceri non poterat.*'
75 *Pol.* VIII. 18; 2, p. 364: '*Non enim de priuatis tirannis agitur sed de his qui rem publicam premunt.*'
76 *Pol.* VIII. 20; 2, pp. 372–9.
77 Van Laarhoven, 'Thou shalt NOT slay a tyrant!', p. 325.
78 Van Laarhoven, 'Thou shalt NOT slay a tyrant!', p. 331.
79 *Pol.* VIII. 20; 2, pp. 377–8: '*Hoc tamen cauendum docent historiae, ne quis illius moliatur interitum cui fidei aut sacramenti religione tenetur astrictus.*'
80 *Pol.* VIII. 20; 2, p. 378: '*Non quod tirannos de medio tollendos esse non credam sed sine religionis honestatisque dispendio.*'
81 *Pol.* VIII. 20; 2, p. 378: '*utilissimus et tutissimus*'.
82 Seneca, *De beneficiis*, VII. 19.18, pp. 502–3: '*Quidquid erat, quo mihi cohaereret, intercisa iuris humani societas abscidit.*'
83 Seneca, *De beneficiis*, VII. 20.4, pp. 504–5: '*Sed haec rara nequitia est semper portenti loco habita*'.
84 Seneca, *De beneficiis*, VII. 20.1, pp. 504–5: '*Sed quamvis hoc ita sit et ex eo tempore omnia mihi in illum libera sint, ex quo corrumpendo fas omne, ut nihil in eum nefas esset, effecerit, illum mihi servandum modum credam, ut, si beneficium illi meum neque vires maiores daturum est in exitium commune nec confirmaturum, quas habet, id autem erit, quod illi reddi sine pernicie publica possit, reddam.*'
85 Seneca, *De beneficiis*, VII. 20.3, pp. 504–5: '*Et si ex toto desperata eius sanitas fuerit, eadem manu beneficium omnibus dabo, illi reddam; quoniam ingeniis talibus exitus remedium est optimumque est abire ei, qui ad se numquam rediturus est.*'
86 Rouse and Rouse, 'John of Salisbury and the Doctrine of Tyrannicide', p. 709.
87 Forhan, 'Salisburian Stakes: The Uses of "Tyranny"', pp. 401, 405.

88  *Pol.* IV. 8; 1, p. 265: '*tranquilla mentis moderatione*'.
89  Wilks, 'Tyranny of Nonsense', p. 264.
90  Wilks, 'Tyranny of Nonsense', p. 272.
91  See Chapter 1, p. 44.
92  Cicero, *De re publica*, trans. C. W. Keyes (LCL 213; Cambridge, MA: Harvard University Press, 1928), VI. 13, pp. 264–8: '*Nihil est enim illi principi deo, qui omnem mundum regit, quod quidem in terris fiat, acceptius quam concilia coetusque hominum iure sociati, quae civitates appellantur; harum rectores et conservatores hinc profecti huc revertuntur.*'
93  Macrobius, *Commentary on the Dream of Scipio*, I. 8.12, pp. 123–4.
94  Stacey, *Roman Monarchy and the Renaissance Prince*, p. 31.
95  Seneca, *De clementia*, II. 3.17, pp. 434–5: '*Clementia est temperantia animi in potestate ulciscendi vel lenitas superioris adversus inferiorem in constituendis poenis. ... itaque dici potest et inclinatio animi ad lenitatem in poena exigenda.*'
96  Seneca, *De clementia*, II. 3.1, pp. 434–5: '*reclamabitur nullum virtutem cuiquam minus debito facere*'.
97  Seneca, *De clementia*, II. 7.3, pp. 444–5: '*venia debitae poenae remissio est*'.
98  Seneca, *De clementia*, II. 7.3, pp. 444–5: '*non sub formula, sed ex aequo et bono iudicat ... Nihil ex his facit, tamquam iusto minus fecerit, sed tamquam id, quod constituit, iustissimum sit.*'
99  Seneca, *De clementia*, I. 19.
100 Seneca, *De clementia*, I. 11.4, pp. 390–1: '*Clementia ergo non tantum honestiores sed tutiores praestat ornamentumque imperiorum est simul et certissima salus. ... Quid interest inter tyrannum ac regem (species enim ipsa fortunae ac licentia par est), nisi quod tyranni in voluptatem saeviunt, reges non nisi ex causa ac necessitate?*'
101 Seneca, *De clementia*, I. 13.4, pp. 396–7: '*a tota civitate amatur, defenditur, colitur*'.
102 *Pol.* IV. 8; 2, p. 264: '*nunc rigore iustitiae, nunc remissione clementiae, ut subditos faciat quasi unanimes esse in domo*'.
103 *Pol.* IV. 8; 1, p. 264.
104 *Pol.* IV. 8; 1, pp. 264–5: '*Meditatur ergo iugiter sapientiam, et de ea sic iustitiam operatur, quod lex clementiae semper est in lingua eius; et sic clementiam temperat rigore iustitiae, quod lingua eius iudicium loquitur.*'
105 C. Straw, *Gregory the Great: Perfection and Imperfection* (Berkeley: University of California Press, 1988), pp. 28–46, p. 83. See Gregory the Great, *Pastoral Care*, II. 7.
106 R. Markus, *Gregory the Great and his World* (Cambridge: Cambridge University Press, 1997), p. 31.
107 For the chronology of the 'disgrace' see G. Constable, 'The Alleged Disgrace of John of Salisbury in 1159', *English Historical Review*, 69 (1954), 67–76; *Letters* I, Appendix II, pp. 257–8.
108 C. N. L. Brooke, 'Adrian IV and John of Salisbury', in B. Bolton and A. Duggan (eds), *Adrian IV: The English Pope (1154–59): Studies and Texts* (Aldershot: Ashgate, 2003), pp. 3–13 (pp. 9–10).

109 *Met.* IV. 42, p. 183: '*Anulum quoque per me transmisit aureum, smaragdo optimo decoratum, quo fieret inuestitura iuris in regenda Hibernia*'.
110 A. Duggan, 'Totius christianitatis caput: The Pope and the Princes', in Bolton and Duggan (eds), *Adrian IV*, pp. 105–55 (p. 141).
111 Duggan, 'Totius christianitatis caput', p. 141.
112 Letter 19 (autumn 1156), *Letters* I, p. 31: '*Serenissimi domini, potentissimi regis, inuictissimi principis nostri tota in me incanduit indignatio. Si causam quaeritis, ei forte plus iusto faui, promotioni suae ultra quam oportuerit institi, ad hoc toto desiderio cordis suspirans ut quem fortunae inuidia credebam exulantem, miseratione diuina regnantem cernerem in patrum solio, et iura dictantem in populis et nationibus.*'
113 Letter 31 (1–8 April 1157), *Letters* I, p. 50: '*Insulam egredi imaginem uidebatur habere diffugii; calumpniatorum declinare congressum esset ream conscientiam profiteri; principis non expectare conspectum caput meum laesae maiestatis obnoxium legibus faceret.*'
114 Letter 28 (c. December 1156–January 1157), *Letters* I, p. 45: '*Exinde honestius et liberius uel gratia litterarum uel occupatione alterius studii tantae sollicitudini, laboribus, suspicionibus et periculis me ipsum subtrahere potero.*'
115 *Pol.* 1. Prol.; 1, p. 17. '*Dum tamen Tolosam cingitis, ista aggressus sum et me curialibus nugis paulisper ademi, illud uoluens in animo, quia otium sine litteris mors est et uiui hominis sepultura.*' John draws on Seneca, *Ep.* 82.3.
116 McLoughlin, 'The Language of Persecution' pp. 79–82.
117 Barrau, 'La *conversio* de Jean de Salisbury', pp. 230–1, 236–40.
118 Barrau, 'La *conversio* de Jean de Salisbury', p. 240.
119 The name refers to a Maccabeean leader mentioned by Josephus in *De bello Judaico*.
120 *Entheticus*, 149–50, pp. 114–15: '*qui reges falso nulla sub lege teneri, et quicquid libuit, credidit esse pium*'. See Van Laarhoven on the signficance of pseudonyms in John's *Entheticus*, pp. 54–6, 377–8. For a survey of Stephen's reign see R. H. C. Davis, *King Stephen 1135–54* (3rd edn; London: Longman, 1990); E. King, *King Stephen* (New Haven: Yale University Press, 2012); C. Holdsworth, 'The Church', in E. King (ed.), *The Anarchy of King Stephen's Reign* (Oxford: Oxford University Press, 1994), pp. 207–29.
121 *Entheticus*, 1301–2, pp. 190–1: '*Huic, qui priscorum mores legesque revelli praecepit*'; *Entheticus*, 1335, pp. 192–3: '*Iulia lex illo dormivit rege sepulta*'. The Julian law prohibited adultery, and John draws particular attention to Stephen's lust at *Entheticus*, 148, pp. 114–15. See also *Pol.* VIII. 22.
122 *Entheticus*, 1310–14, pp. 190–1: '*qui titulo regis publicus hostis erat, ponitur exemplar regum populumque regendi, et bene vivendi formula certa datur. Iuvit eum pacis cultus, sed more tiranni, cerneret ut pedibus subdita cuncta suis.*'
123 *Entheticus*, 1341–5, pp. 192–3: '*Illa tirannorum pax est, ut nemo reclamet: quicquid agant, possint omnia, iura nihil. Iura vacant, sacras leges evertit abusus, velle suum statuunt iuris habere locum.*'
124 Liebeschütz, *Mediaeval Humanism*, p. 22. On issues of dating the text see R. Thomson, 'What is the Entheticus?', in Wilks (ed.), *World*, pp. 287–301.

125 C. J. Nederman, 'The Changing Face of Tyranny: The Reign of King Stephen in John of Salisbury', *Nottingham Medieval Studies*, 33 (1989), 1–20. See also Nederman, *John of Salisbury*, p. 49.
126 Nederman, 'Changing Face of Tyranny', p. 15.
127 Nederman, 'Changing Face of Tyranny', pp. 18–19.
128 Nederman, 'Changing Face of Tyranny', p. 17.
129 *Pol.* VI. 18; 2, p. 50: '*hominem contemptorem boni et aequi*'; '*ut eo non tam regnante quam concutiente et collidente clerum et populum*'.
130 Nederman, 'Changing Face of Tyranny', pp. 16–17, 19. See Introduction, pp. 14–15.
131 *Historia pontificalis*, II, pp. 6–7. The drama of this account conveys John's talent as a story-teller: 'For he [Theobald] knew well that obedience is better than sacrifices, and trusting in God's mercy went abroad a fishing smack which he had hired and hidden in a remote bay far from the haunts of men: a vessel that would carry no more than a dozen men and lacked even the most essential equipment; and so he crossed the channel rather as a survivor from a shipwreck than in a ship.' Such 'workaday deeds' are, according to Monagle, 'John of Salisbury and the Writing of History' (p. 232), typical of the style of the *Historia pontificalis*, which focuses on the exemplarity of the characters described.
132 *Historia pontificalis*, II, pp. 7–8: '*Licet ergo rex ille temeritate sua ecclesie Dei et nostram meruerit indignatationem, tantam tamen caritatem non possumus non approbare cuius uota cogimur exaudire.*' For Theobald's actions at the Council of Rheims see Saltman, *Theobald: Archbishop of Canterbury*, pp. 137–42.
133 *Historia pontificalis*, XLII, p. 86: '*quia res erat litigiosa cuius translatio iure reprobata est*'.
134 *Historia pontificalis*, XIX, p. 49: '*episcopo non licuerat ecclesiam scindere, ei subtrahendo fidelitatem quem ecclesia Romana recipiebat ut principem*'.
135 *Pol.* VIII. 21; 2, p. 394.
136 E. King, 'The Anarchy of King Stephen's Reign', *Transactions of the Royal Historical Society*, 5th series, 34 (1984), 133–54 (135).
137 Nederman, 'Changing Face of Tyranny', p. 18.
138 For general information on Frederick's reign see G. Barraclough, 'Frederick Barbarossa and the Twelfth Century', in G. Barraclough, *History in a Changing World* (Oxford: Blackwell, 1955), pp. 73–96; P. Munz, *Frederick Barbarossa: A Study in Medieval Politics* (London: Cornell University Press, 1969); M. Pacaut, *Frederick Barbarossa* (London: Collins, 1970); H. Fuhrmann, *Germany in the High Middle Ages c.1050–1200* (Cambridge: Cambridge University Press, 1986), pp. 135–80; K. J. Leyser, 'Frederick Barbarossa and the Hohenstaufen Polity', *Viator*, 19 (1988), 153–76; J. Freed, *Frederick Barbarossa: The Prince and the Myth* (New Haven: Yale University Press, 2016). For a survey of the papal schism in 1159 see I. S. Robinson, *The Papacy 1073–1198: Continuity and Innovation* (Cambridge: Cambridge University Press, 1990), pp. 78–84, 461–84.
139 Letter 124, *Letters* I, p. 207: '*Promittebat enim se totius orbis reformaturum inperium et urbi subiciendum orbem, euentuque facili omnia subacturum, si ei ad hoc solius Romani pontificis fauor adesset.*'; '*ut in quemcumque denuntiatis*

*inimicitiis materialem gladium inperator, in eundem Romanus pontifex spiritualem gladium exerceret*'.

140  Letter 124, *Letters* I, p. 207: '*ipsaque fortior, gratior et gloriosior Sponsi reddatur amplexibus post trihumphum*'.
141  Letter 124, *Letters* I, p. 208.
142  Letter 123 (c.May–June 1160), *Letters* I, p. 203: '*Virtus principum nullo clarius elucet indicio quam si maiestate eius pacem populus, ecclesia quietem et religio gratum Deo recipiet incrementum.*'
143  Letter 125 (June–July 1160), *Letters* I, p. 215: '*In eo maxime uiget et proficit gloria principis Christiani si pium Deo a quo omnis principatus est impendit famulatum.*'
144  Letter 145, *Letters* II, pp. 40–1: '*et ut ostendatur non esse hodie imperatorem qui ad Christum pertineat, cum scismaticus per uim et fraudem et labem haereticorum nitens insecabilem scindere unitatem, integritatem corrumpere, incestare pudicitiam, et quantum in ipso est, euertens dispositionem Dei et promissiones ueritatis euacuans, Romanum imperium Christo machinatur auferre. Instat ergo ut nomen Christi de imperio deleatur; sed ut muneris tui docet inscriptio, nomen Christi singulariter permanet in aeternum, et praesumentis imperium et de falso nomine gloriantis exinanitus est honor, et profecto humiliabit eum qui est ante saecula.*'
145  For example, Letter 239, *Letters* II, p. 454; Letter 240, *Letters* II, p. 458.
146  Letter 220 to Richard Prior of Dover (? summer–autumn 1167), *Letters* II, pp. 378–9: '*Facies caeli serenatur ab oriente, caput scismatis in aquilone conteritur, ei membra languentia contabescunt, dolent latera, squamae soluuntur, ut spiraculum per eas possit incedere, et iam in occidente suos iustitiae Sol radios uibrat.*' Cf. Revelation 12–13.
147  Letter 221 to Master Lawrence of Poitiers (summer–autumn 1167), *Letters* II, pp. 380–1: '*quia iam conteritur caput scismatis, et quae ei cohaeserunt, immo in stercore suo computruerunt membra*'.
148  Letter 219 to Alexander III, *Letters* II, pp. 376–7: '*ut et uos, qui gladium Dei uidetis eductum in capita tirannorum, in eos Petri gladium exeratis*'.
149  Letter 273 to Baldwin, archdeacon of Totnes (c.May 1168), *Letters* II, pp. 572–3: '*Quid ergo superest a Domino exspectandum, nisi ut ei compereant latera sua, et quos complices habuit in errore comites habeat in ruina?*'
150  T. Reuter, 'John of Salisbury and the Germans', in Wilks (ed.), *World*, pp. 415–25 (p. 423).
151  Reuter, 'John of Salisbury and the Germans', p. 424.
152  Letter 242, *Letters* II, pp. 472–5: '*Cum enim Romanus pontifex per patientiam Teutonicum tyrannum diutius expectasset ut uel sic prouocaretur ad poenitentiam, et scismaticus, abutens patientia eius, peccata peccatis adderet iugiter ut error in amentiam uerteretur, uicarius Petri, a Domino constitutus super gentes et regna, Italos et omnes, qui ei ex causa imperii et regni religione iurisiurandi tenebantur astricti, a fidelitate eius absoluit, et Italiam fere totam a facie furentis et praesentis tanta felicitate et celeritate excussit ut in ea nichil habere uideatur nisi tortores, quos euitat interdum, et angustiarum, quas euitare non potest, iuge supplicium.*'

153 Reuter, 'John of Salisbury and the Germans', pp. 417–19; C. N. L. Brooke, in *Letters* II, p. 474, n. 4.
154 On the casting of Becket in John's works see K. Bollermann and C. J. Nederman, 'John of Salisbury and Thomas Becket', in Grellard and Lachaud (eds), *Companion*, pp. 63–104 (pp. 64–74).
155 *Entheticus minor*, 25–6, pp. 232–3: '*lux cleri, gloria gentis Anglorum, regis dextera, forma boni*'.
156 Thomas, *The Secular Clergy in England*, p. 152.
157 *Pol*. VIII. 25; 2, p. 424: '*uide et dicta et praedica aequitatem*'.
158 *Entheticus*, 1463–4, pp. 200–1: '*Ebria fortunae donis nova curia rege sub puero credit, cuncta licere sibi*.'
159 *Entheticus*, 1437–9, pp. 198–9: '*dissimulare multa solet, simulat, quod sit et ipse furens; omnibus omnia fit*'.
160 The way in which the odds are stacked against Becket's strategy succeeding is illustrated in *Enthethicus*, 1495–1512, pp. 202–3.
161 Letter 168, *Letters* II, pp. 106–7: '*utpote qui eum scio tunc non auctoritatem praestitisse libidini sed obsecundationem necessitati, tamen quia eum ministrum iniquitatis fuisse non ambigo, iure optimo taliter arbitror puniendum, ut eo potissimum puniatur auctore quem in talibus Deo bonorum omnium auctori praeferebat, eique sit uice uersa in poenam quem habebat et laudabat suae peruersitatis auctorem*'.
162 Letter 168, *Letters* II, pp. 106–7: '*Sed esto, nunc poenitentiam agit, agnoscit et confitetur culpam et, si cum Saulo quandoque ecclesiam impugnauit, nunc pro ea cum Paulo ponere paratus est et animam suam.*'
163 Letter 168, *Letters* II, pp. 106–7: '*principes populi sunt hi duo quorum alter dispensat spiritualia, alter temporalia administrat*'.
164 Letter 168, *Letters* II, pp. 108–9: '*per poenitentiam reuertatur et magis pio utatur consilio*'.
165 The theme of Becket's change of lifestyle upon becoming archbishop is present in other biographical accounts; see, for example, the passage by William of Canterbury quoted in M. Staunton, *The Lives of Thomas Becket* (Manchester: Manchester University Press, 2001), pp. 66–7.
166 Letter 144, *Letters* II, pp. 32–3: '*Differte interim omnes alias occupationes, quantum poteritis, quia licet necessariae plerumque uideantur, quod suadeo praeeligendum est, eo quod magis est necessarium. Prosunt quidem leges et canones, sed michi credite quia nunc non erat his opus.*'
167 Letter 144, *Letters* II, pp. 34–5: '*Mallem uos Psalmos ruminare et beati Gregorii morales libros reuoluere, quam scolastico more philosophari.*' As an aside, we should note that it does seem that Becket took John's suggestions seriously; a copy of '*Warnerius Gregorianus*' was found among his books bequeathed to Canterbury library following his death, as noted in Chapter 1, p. 53.
168 Letter 187, *Letters* II, pp. 244–7: '*dum magnificus erat nugator in curia, dum legis contemptor uidebatur et cleri, dum scurriles cum potentioribus sectabatur ineptias, magnus habebatur clarus erat et acceptus omnibus ... factus est eis inimicus uera dicens et uitam corrigens*'.

169  Letter 176, *Letters* II, p. 168; Letter 179, *Letters* II, p. 190.
170  Letter 176, *Letters* II, pp. 170-1: '*exhibitione moderationis, tam in factis et dictis quam in gestu et habitu; quod tamen apud Deum non multum prodest, nisi de archano conscientiae prodeat*'.
171  On the *Vita* see Bollerman and Nederman, 'John of Salisbury and Thomas Becket', pp. 85-92. On the letter by John, *Ex insperato*, that preceded it, see M. Staunton, 'The *Lives* of Thomas Becket and the Church of Canterbury', in P. Dalton, C. Insley and L. Wilkinson (eds), *Cathedrals, Communities and Conflict in the Anglo-Norman World* (Woodbridge: Boydell Press, 2011), pp. 169-86 (pp. 170-1), and A. Duggan, 'Becket is Dead! Long Live St Thomas', in P. Webster and M-P. Gelin (eds), *The Cult of Thomas Becket in the Plantagenet World, c.1170-c.1220* (Woodbridge: Boydell Press, 2016), pp. 25-52 (p. 27).
172  *Vita S. Thomae* in *MHTB* II, p. 308: '*quidem in veste pretiosa spiritu pauper*'. Bollerman and Nederman, 'John of Salisbury and Thomas Becket' (p. 88), do not register the contrast John makes between Becket's exteriority and interiority, but simply read this passage as evidence of Becket's luxurious lifestyle as bishop.
173  Letter 305, *Letters* II, pp. 726-7: '*qui opes et omnem mundi gloriam, qui amicorum et totius cognationis affectionem pro Christi amore contempnens, exilium subiit, se et suos omnes exposuit periculis et paupertati; qui pro leges Dei sui tuenda et euacuandis abusionibus ueterum tirannorum certauit usque ad mortem*'.
174  Letter 305, *Letters* II, pp. 726-7.
175  Chapter 5, pp. 168-9.
176  Bodl. MS Canon. Pat. Lat. 131, fo. 128v (Lactantius, *Divine Institutes*, VII. 14.11), fo. 134r (Lactantius, *Divine Institutes*, VII. 26.1).
177  Bodl. MS Canon. Pat. Lat. 131, fo. 130v (Lactantius, *Divine Institutes*, VII. 17.2), fo. 133r (Lactantius, *Divine Institutes*, VII. 24.1).
178  Bodl. MS Canon. Pat. Lat. 131, fo. 134r (Lactantius, *Divine Institutes*, VII. 26.1-2).
179  MacIntyre, *After Virtue*, pp. 172-3.
180  *Pol.* IV. 11, but cf. *Pol.* VIII. 17, where John notes that ideally there would be no kingdoms at all and all would live in harmony under God's rule.
181  Nederman, 'The Physiological Significance of the Organic Metaphor', p. 212.

# Conclusion

John of Salisbury – who styled his Roman predecessors as *Cicero noster* and *Seneca noster* – was an avid consumer of classical texts, and in that respect he was a typical product of the Parisian schools of the twelfth century. However, his works are far more than a formulaic assemblage of pithy aphorisms pulled from the classical collections of the libraries to which he had access. Instead, they must be seen as genuine attempts to interrogate the classical world in order to find lessons for the medieval present. This is what differentiates him from many of his contemporaries, who used the classics only to add rhetorical flourishes to their works or as a source of illustrative anecdotes. John also employed these techniques, but went beyond them, engaging fully with the philosophical ideas the texts contained. His incorporation of key concepts from Stoicism places him at the apogee of the Roman Renaissance of the twelfth century, a revival that was, in part, crafted by his pen. John's writings, however, must be seen within the context of their production; his political thought is best understood when his works are examined within the social and cultural milieux in which he was an actor. John – as cleric, advisor, Christian, scholar and exile – used classical sources to formulate a political thought that defies unitary classification. Although the *Policraticus* has often been characterised as a 'mirror for princes' – an appellation that situates John's work in a continuum extending from Seneca's *De clementia* to Machiavelli's *Il principe* – his writings served a variety of purposes and spoke to a variety of audiences. The multivocal qualities of John's works are apparent from the variety of genres within which they can be situated: poetry, history, narrative prose and hortatory epistles.

The syncretic nature of his ideas, notably his formulation of a type of 'Christianised Stoicism', results in no small measure from the manner in which he accessed the classics. Given that many of the works to which he had recourse were available only in fragmentary form, or were accessed through a – frequently patristic – intermediary, John's understanding of the classics was qualified; it was a form of classical scholarship already filtered through a lens of Christian interpretation. This had a profound effect on his political and ethical theories. His adaptations of Stoic concepts stemmed partially from the context in which he would have encountered them (reading Ciceronian ideas in Augustine, for example), but were also the result of conscious manipulation of his sources to better suit his contemporary intellectual environment and projected readership. Take, for example, the idea of 'following nature'. John transformed this Ciceronian trope by asserting that life in accordance with nature was not simply a life lived rationally, but also a life lived in accordance with God's purpose. The virtuous man will pursue activities which conform with nature, but will do so to full effect only with the aid of grace. Here John neatly aligns the Stoic emphasis on interior orientation towards the rational good with Christian ethical ideas regarding free will and sin. We must not exaggerate the extent of John's classical knowledge, however; in the main, he drew on texts which were readily available and which were part of the literary canon of the period. The fact that Augustine engaged in literary battle with Cicero, and that Seneca was praised as a correspondent of St Paul, went no small way towards establishing these authors as integral parts of the medieval curriculum.

It is apparent, nonetheless, that Stoic writings appealed for another reason beyond their ready availability: many Stoic concepts could easily be accommodated as part of a Christian ethical system. For example, one of John's most significant borrowings from Stoicism is his adaptation of *oikeiôsis*, that is, the rational extension of care from one individual to his immediate familial and domestic circle and then, by degrees, to his broader community and to the polity at large. This concept of *oikeiôsis* underpins John's account of appropriate duties; those who are concerned for the well-being of others will carry out the role that has been assigned to them, and not impinge upon the duties or responsibilities of others. This interpretation of living appropriately reflects Christian ideas of *caritas*. Similarly, the Ciceronian *regula* necessitating a balance between the honourable and the useful was adapted by John as a guide to living virtuously in pursuit of a Christianised *summum bonum,* namely eternal salvation. While boundaries between philosophical schools are difficult to draw in this period, Stoicism arguably surpasses the role played by proto-Aristotelianism and neo-Platonism in John's works. In defence of this perspective, it is significant to note that many of the ideas promoted by Roman Stoicism – rejecting indifferent goods in pursuit of what is relevant for salvation, living in harmony with a rational nature, acting virtuously with an intention oriented towards the good – were made, with minimal adaptations by John, to work within a Christian scheme of ethics.

The effects of these adaptations are most apparent in John's recommendations for the political sphere. Roman Stoicism sees the individual as firmly embedded in a social context: it is fundamentally concerned with the promotion of the common good. Neither the ruler nor any other officials are permitted to place their own interests first. Socio-political values become, therefore, fundamental for effective public living. John's model of the body politic promoted a similar concept, with each 'limb' of the body obliged to do its own work in the service of the political whole. The body model was a uniquely effective metaphor for the division of political duties; it illustrated the interdependence between each part of the polity, while also demonstrating the necessary relationships of care that existed between those who carried out the duties they had been allocated and those who were obliged to look after their well-being. Common to both Stoicism and John's writings is a sense of social responsibility, an aspect that could be regarded as explicitly communitarian. By this reading, the preservation of the common good becomes the ultimate corporate goal and a normative ideal for the political individual. In John's account, this is married to Christian ethics; the political individual must also act in the interests of the Church. This is most clearly demonstrated in the case of the prince, who is obliged to respect the Church as well as developing his own religious character. By contrast, the tyrant, intent upon his self-promotion, fails the secular and religious social systems of which he is a part. In John's writings the pursuit of the common good becomes an ethical priority, although it remains one that sits alongside the pursuit of faith, and humanity's ultimate citizenship in the universal Church.

John was greatly influenced by the blurring inherent in Stoic ideology between public and private performance of duties: the good political leader must also be a good man. Living virtuously consisted of pursuit of the *summum bonum*, happiness attained through the perfect knowledge of God. Achievable only in eternity, it could be approximated by the performance of the virtues on earth, which was, in itself, a perfection of man's rational goal. John emphasised that the virtuous man will develop a *habitus*, a fixed ethical intentionality towards the good, that will enable him to choose virtue over vice, and to not be swayed by things which are morally indifferent. As illustrated, his account of *habitus* was intrinsically Stoic, with the mean in John's writings articulated by reference to Cicero's concept of decorum, a way of behaviour that treads a medial route between what is honourable and what is useful. In his exposition of the cardinal virtues, John described how the pursuit of the mean served as a guide for good behaviour. The frugal man, for example, knows that wealth is morally indifferent to his pursuit of the *summum bonum*, but he does not need to live a needlessly impoverished life; instead, he will cultivate a moderate balance of resources, be beneficent and give his money in appropriate circumstances.

This study has traced the ways in which John politicised abstract concepts: nature, duty, virtue, happiness. Politics, for John, is clearly something that happens outside (as well as inside) the bounds of institutions and traditional roles of power. A salient feature of his work is a concern for the personality of the political figure; an orientation towards the good expressed in intentional action and a good temperament that prioritises the pursuit of virtue are aspects which define a good political leader as well as a good person. Politics is intrinsically ethical, as demonstrated by the double meaning of his corporeal model; it was the epitome of the ideally arranged polity, but also served as a model of the ideal prince, who is obliged to live virtuously in recognition of the fact that he is guided by the rational and divine part of his body – the soul. The role played by moderation as a normative goal for all members of the polity cannot be overestimated. John required that the virtues were neither under- nor over-emphasised; a tyrant exceeds the bounds of his duties, while a selfish preoccupation with vice on the part of the prince can corrupt the polity as a whole. The political leader is obliged to improve his own character in order to live within the recommended mean; flattery is condemned as perverted self-interest, while strong parallels may be observed between John's invocations to Becket to flee the temptations of the court and Stoic recommendations of *otium*, a voluntary withdrawal from active life towards a life that focused on interior well-being.

John's adaptations of Stoic sources offer an important insight into the modalities of scholarship in the Renaissance of the twelfth century. Although the use of classical texts has long been recognised as the salient feature of this Renaissance, the focus has often been on quantitative concerns: how many texts were available, how rare were these texts, and how many people were using them? While these issues remain important, this study has attempted to shift the focus towards how John used his texts. In so doing, it has established that John engaged on a profound level with classical sources: reworking them to suit his needs, without ignoring the context from which they came. While John expressed a reluctance to accord pagan philosophers the authority of their Christian counterparts, his education was unavoidably steeped in classical learning, from the basic tenets of rhetorical argumentation to methods for dealing with more advanced dialectical matters. Such unconscious assimilation of the classical heritage has largely been underestimated in studies of the twelfth-century Renaissance. This study has illustrated that some of John's most novel adaptations of classical sources were derived from texts which would have been readily available to him. Stoicism, transmitted through the writings of Seneca and the eclectic Cicero, as well as through the works of many of John's patristic forebears, is a highly accessible ideology for scholars of this period – a potential 'third way' for medieval philosophy – and a viable alternative to Platonism and Aristotelianism on account of its adaptability for a Christian ethical system.

# SELECT BIBLIOGRAPHY

## Manuscripts consulted

Cambridge, Corpus Christi College, MS 46.
London, British Library, Royal MS 12 F VIII.
London, British Library, Royal MS 13 D IV.
Oxford, Bodleian Library, MS Canon. Pat. Lat. 131.
Oxford, Bodleian Library, MS Lat. misc. c. 16.
Paris, Bibliothèque nationale de France, MS lat. 7647.
Paris, Bibliothèque nationale de France, MS lat. 16592.
Soissons, Bibliothèque municipale, MS 24.

## Primary sources

Ambrose, *De officiis*, ed. and trans. I. J. Davidson (2 vols; Oxford: Oxford University Press, 2001).
Augustine, *Enarrationes in Psalmos*, ed. E. Dekkers and J. Fraipont (CCSL 39; Turnhout: Brepols, 1956).
—— *De civitate dei contra paganos*, trans. G. E. McCracken et al. (LCL 411–17; Cambridge, MA: Harvard University Press, 1957-72).
—— *De libero arbitrio voluntatis*, ed. W. Green (CCSL 29; Turnhout: Brepols, 1970).
—— *City of God: Concerning the City of God against the Pagans*, trans. H. Bettenson (Harmondsworth: Penguin, 1984).
—— *Expositions of the Psalms, 73-98*, ed. J. Rotelle, trans. M. Boulding (New York: City Press, 2002).
—— *Confessiones*, trans. C. J.-B. Hammond (LCL 26; Cambridge, MA: Harvard University Press, 2014).
Bernard of Chartres, *The Glosae super Platonem of Bernard of Chartres*, ed. P. E. Dutton (Toronto: PIMS, 1991).
Bernard of Clairvaux, *Sancti Bernardi Opera Omnia*, vol. 3: *Tractatus et Opuscula*, ed. J. Leclercq and H. Rochais (Rome: Editiones Cistercenses, 1963).
—— *Five Books on Consideration: Advice to a Pope*, trans. J. D. Anderson and E. T. Kennan (Kalamazoo: Cistercian Publications, 1976).
—— *Sancti Bernardi Opera Omnia*, vol. 8: *Epistolae*, ed. J. Leclercq and H. Rochais (Rome: Editiones Cistercienses, 1977).
Bernard Silvestris, *Le Mathematicus de Bernard Silvestris et la Passio Sanctae Agnetis de Pierre Riga*, ed. B. Hauréau (Paris: C. Klincksieck, 1895).
—— *The Commentary on the First Six Books of the Aeneid of Virgil*, ed. and trans.

E. G. Schrieber and T. E. Maresca (Lincoln, NE: University of Nebraska Press, 1979).
—— *Cosmographia*, trans. W. Wetherbee (New York: Columbia University Press, 1990).
Calcidius, *Timaeus a Calcidio translatus commentarioque instructus*, ed. J. H. Waszink (London: Warburg Institute, 1975).
*Cartulaire de Notre-Dame de Chartres*, ed. E. de Lépinois and L. Merlet (3 vols; Chartres: Garnier, 1862–65).
Cicero, *De officiis*, trans. W. Miller (LCL 30; Cambridge MA: Harvard University Press, 1913).
—— *De amicitia*, in *De senectute; De amicitia; De divinatione*, trans. W. A. Falconer (LCL 154; Cambridge, MA: Harvard University Press, 1923).
—— *De re publica*, trans. C. W. Keyes (LCL 213; Cambridge, MA: Harvard University Press, 1928).
—— *De finibus bonorum et malorum*, trans. H. Rackham (LCL 40; Cambridge MA: Harvard University Press, 1931).
—— *Paradoxa Stoicorum*, in *De oratore III; De fato; Paradoxa Stoicorum; De partitione oratoria*, trans. H. Rackham (LCL 349; Cambridge, MA: Harvard University Press, 1942).
—— *De inventione*, trans. H. M. Hubbell (LCL 386; Cambridge, MA: Harvard University Press, 1949).
—— *On Duties*, trans. M. T. Griffin and E. M. Atkins (Cambridge: Cambridge University Press, 1991).
Gregory the Great, *Pastoral Care*, trans. H. Davis (Westminster: Paulist Press, 1950).
—— *Moralia in Job*, ed. I. R. Gillet, A. de Gaudermaris, A. Bocognano, C. Straw and A. de Vogüé (Paris: Cerf, 1951–2003).
—— *La Règle pastorale*, ed. I. B. Judic, F. Rommel and C. Morel (2 vols; Paris: Cerf, 1992).
Gregorius, Master, *The Marvels of Rome*, trans. J. Osborne (Toronto: PIMS, 1987).
Hugh of St Victor, *The Didascalicon of Hugh of St Victor: A Medieval Guide to the Arts*, trans. J. Taylor (New York: Columbia University Press, 1991).
—— *De Institutione Novitiorum*, in *L'Oeuvre de Hugues de Saint Victor*, vol. 1: *De institutione novitiorum. De virtute orandi. De laude caritatis. De arrha animae.*, ed. H. B. Feiss and P. Sicard, trans. D. Poirel, H. Rochais and P. Sicard (Turnhout, Brepols, 1997).
John of Salisbury, *Vita S. Thomae*, in *Materials for the History of Thomas Becket: Archbishop of Canterbury*, ed. J. C. Robertson and J. B. Sheppard (7 vols; London: Rolls Series, 1875–85), vol. 2, pp. 299–352.
—— *Ioannis Saresberiensis Episcopi Carnotensis Policratici sive De Nugis Curialium et Vestigiis Philosophorum Libri VIII*, ed. C. C. J. Webb (2 vols; Oxford: Clarendon Press, 1909).
—— *The Statesman's Book of John of Salisbury: Being the Fourth, Fifth and Sixth Books and Selections from the Seventh and Eighth Books of the Policraticus*, trans. J. Dickinson (New York: Knopf, 1927).

## SELECT BIBLIOGRAPHY

——*Frivolities of Courtiers and Footprints of Philosophers: Being a Translation of the First, Second, and Third Books of the Policraticus of John of Salisbury*, trans. J. B. Pike (Minneapolis: University of Minnesota Press, 1938).
——*The Metalogicon: A Twelfth-Century Defense of the Verbal and Logical Arts of the Trivium*, trans. D. McGarry (Berkeley: University of California Press, 1955).
——*The Letters of John of Salisbury*, vol. 2: *The Later Letters (1163–80)*, ed. and trans. W. J. Millor and C. N. L. Brooke (Oxford: Oxford University Press, 1979).
——*The Letters of John of Salisbury*, vol. 1: *The Early Letters (1153–61)*, ed. and trans. W. J. Millor, H. E. Butler, and C. N. L. Brooke (rev. edn; Oxford: Oxford University Press, 1986).
——*The Historia Pontificalis of John of Salisbury*, ed. and trans. M. Chibnall (Oxford: Oxford University Press, 1986).
——*John of Salisbury's Entheticus Maior et Minor*, ed. and trans. J. van Laarhoven (3 vols; Leiden: Brill, 1987).
——*Policraticus: Of the Frivolities of Courtiers and the Footprints of Philosophers*, trans. C. J. Nederman (Cambridge: Cambridge University Press, 1990).
——*Ioannis Saresberiensis Metalogicon*, ed. J. B. Hall, aux. K. S. B. Keats-Rohan (CCCM 98; Turnhout: Brepols, 1991).
——*Ioannes Saresberiensis Policraticus I–IV*, ed. K. S. B. Keats-Rohan (CCCM 118; Turnhout: Brepols, 1993).
——'Life of Becket', in *Anselm and Becket: Two Canterbury Saints' Lives by John of Salisbury*, trans. R. E. Pepin (Toronto: Pontifical Institute of Medieval Studies, 2009), pp. 78–95.
——*Metalogicon*, trans. J. B. Hall, Introduction by J. Haseldine (Turnhout: Brepols, 2013).
Isaac of Stella, *The Selected Works of Isaac of Stella: A Cistercian Voice from the Twelfth Century*, ed. D. Deme (Aldershot: Ashgate, 2007).
Lactantius, *Divine Institutes*, trans. A. Bowen and P. Garnsey (Liverpool: Liverpool University Press, 2003).
Livy, *History of Rome*, ed. and trans. B. O. Foster (LCL 114; Cambridge, MA: Harvard University Press, 1919).
Macrobius, *Commentary on the Dream of Scipio*, trans. W. H. Stahl (New York: Columbia University Press, 1952).
Martin of Braga, *Formula vitae honestae*, in *Martini Episcopi Bracarensis Opera Omnia*, ed. C. Barlow (New Haven: Yale University Press, 1950), pp. 236–50.
Martin of Braga, *Rules for an Honest Life*, in *Iberian Fathers*, vol. 1: *Martin of Braga, Paschasius of Dumiun, Leander of Seville*, trans. C. W. Barlow (Washington, DC: Catholic University of America Press, 1969), pp. 87–97.
Peter Abelard, *Collationes*, ed. and trans. J. Marenbon and G. Orlandi (Oxford: Oxford University Press, 2003).
Peter of Celle, *The Letters of Peter of Celle*, ed. and trans. J. Haseldine (Oxford: Oxford University Press, 2001).
[Pseudo-] Plutarch, *Die Institutio Traiani: Ein pseudo-plutarchischer Text im Mittelalter*, ed. H. Kloft and M. Kerner (Stuttgart: Teubner, 1992).

Seneca, *Ad Lucilium Epistulae Morales*, trans. R. M. Gummere, vols 1 and 2 (LCL 75, 76; Cambridge, MA: Harvard University Press, 1917-20).
—— *De clementia*, in *Seneca: Moral Essays I*, trans. J. W. Basore (LCL 214; Cambridge, MA: Harvard University Press, 1928).
—— *De beneficiis*, in *Seneca: Moral Essays III*, trans. J. W. Basore (LCL 310; Cambridge, MA: Harvard University Press, 1935).
—— *Naturales quaestiones*, trans. T. H. Corcoran (2 vols; LCL 450, 457; Cambridge, MA: Harvard University Press, 1971-72).
[Pseudo-] Seneca, *Epistolae Senecae ad Paulum et Pauli ad Senecam <quae vocantur>*, ed. C. Barlow (Rome: American Academy in Rome, 1938).
Thierry of Chartres, *Commentarius super Libros De Inventione*, in *The Latin Rhetorical Commentaries of Thierry of Chartres*, ed. K. M. Fredborg (Toronto: Pontifical Institute of Medieval Studies, 1988), pp. 49-215.
Thomas Becket, *The Correspondence of Thomas Becket, Archbishop of Canterbury 1162-70*, ed. and trans. A. Duggan (2 vols; Oxford: Oxford University Press, 2000).
Victorinus, C. Marius, *Explanationes in Ciceronis Rhetoricam*, ed. A. Ippolito (CCSL 132; Turnhout: Brepols, 2006).
William of Conches, *Das Moralium Dogma Philosophorum des Guillaume de Conches*, ed. J. Holmberg (Uppsala: Almqvist and Wiksells, 1929).
—— *Philosophia mundi*, ed. G. Maurach (Pretoria: University of South Africa, 1980).
—— *Glosae super Platonem*, ed. E. Jeauneau (CCCM 203; Turnhout: Brepols, 2006).

## Secondary sources

Allmand, C., *The De Re Militari of Vegetius: The Reception, Transmission and Legacy of a Roman Text in the Middle Ages* (Cambridge: Cambridge University Press, 2011).
Annas, J., *The Morality of Happiness* (Oxford: Oxford University Press, 1993).
Atkins, E. M., 'Domina et Regina Virtutum: Justice and Societas in *De Officiis*', *Phronesis*, 35 (1990), 258-89.
Barker, L. K., 'MS Bodl. Canon. Pat. Lat. 131 and a Lost Lactantius of John of Salisbury: Evidence in Search of a French Critic of Thomas Becket', *Albion*, 22 (1990), 21-37.
Barrau, J., 'Jean de Salisbury, intermédiaire entre Thomas Becket et la cour capétienne?', in M. Aurell and N.-Y. Tonnerre (eds), *Plantagenêts et Capétiens: Confrontations et héritages* (Turnhout: Brepols, 2006), pp. 505-16.
—— 'Ceci n'est pas un miroir, ou le *Policraticus* de Jean de Salisbury', in F. Lachaud and L. Scordia (eds), *Le Prince au miroir de la littérature politique de l'Antiquité aux Lumières* (Rouen: Publications des Universités de Rouen et du Havre, 2007), pp. 87-111.
—— 'La *conversio* de Jean de Salisbury: La Bible au service de Thomas Becket?', *Cahiers de civilisation médiévale X$^e$-XII$^e$ siècles*, 50 (2007), 229-44.

—— 'John of Salisbury as Ecclesiastical Administrator', in C. Grellard and F. Lachaud (eds), *A Companion to John of Salisbury* (Leiden: Brill, 2015), pp. 105–44.
Bejczy, I. P., *The Cardinal Virtues in the Middle Ages: A Study in Moral Thought from the Fourth to the Fourteenth Century* (Leiden: Brill, 2011).
—— and R. Newhauser (eds), *Virtue and Ethics in the Twelfth Century* (Leiden: Brill, 2005).
Bloch, D., *John of Salisbury on Aristotelian Science* (Turnhout: Brepols, 2012).
Bloch, H., 'The New Fascination with Ancient Rome', in R. L. Benson, G. Constable and C. D. Lanham (eds), *Renaissance and Renewal in the Twelfth Century* (Cambridge, MA: Harvard University Press, 1982), pp. 615–36.
Bollermann, K. and C. J. Nederman, 'John of Salisbury and Thomas Becket', in C. Grellard and F. Lachaud (eds), *A Companion to John of Salisbury* (Leiden: Brill, 2015), pp. 63–104.
Brooke, C. N. L., 'John of Salisbury and his World', in M. Wilks (ed.), *The World of John of Salisbury* (Oxford: Blackwell, 1984), pp. 1–20.
—— 'Aspects of John of Salisbury's *Historia Pontificalis*', in L. Smith and B. Ward (eds), *Intellectual Life in the Middle Ages: Essays Presented to Margaret Gibson* (London: Hambledon Press, 1992), pp. 185–95.
—— 'Adrian IV and John of Salisbury', in B. Bolton and A. Duggan (eds), *Adrian IV: The English Pope (1154–59): Studies and Texts* (Aldershot: Ashgate, 2003), pp. 3–13.
Brunt, P. A., 'Stoicism and the Principate', *Papers of the British School at Rome*, 43 (1975), 7–35.
Burnett, C., 'John of Salisbury and Aristotle', *Didascalia*, 2 (1996), 19–32.
Camille, M., *The Gothic Idol: Ideology and Image-Making in Medieval Art* (Cambridge: Cambridge University Press, 1991).
Canning, J., *A History of Medieval Political Thought, 300–1450* (London: Routledge, 2005).
Chibnall, M., 'John of Salisbury as Historian', in M. Wilks (ed.), *The World of John of Salisbury* (Oxford: Blackwell, 1984), pp. 169–77.
Chroust, A. H., 'The Corporate Idea and the Body Politic in the Middle Ages', *Review of Politics*, 9 (1947), 423–52.
Clerval, J. A., *Les Écoles de Chartres au Moyen-Âge (du V<sup>e</sup> au XVI<sup>e</sup> siècle)* (Chartres: Selleret, 1895).
Coleman, J., *Ancient and Medieval Memories: Studies in the Reconstruction of the Past* (Cambridge: Cambridge University Press, 1992).
Colish, M., *The Stoic Tradition from Antiquity to the Early Middle Ages* (2 vols; Leiden: Brill 1990).
—— '"Habitus" Revisited: A Reply to Cary Nederman', *Traditio*, 48 (1993), 77–92.
Constable, G., 'The Alleged Disgrace of John of Salisbury in 1159', *English Historical Review*, 69 (1954), 67–76.
Courcelle, P., *Connais-toi toi-même de Socrate à Saint Bernard* (3 vols; Paris: Études Augustiniennes, 1974–75).
Courtney, F., *Cardinal Robert Pullen: An English Theologian of the Twelfth Century* (Rome: Universitatis Gregorianae, 1954).

Coyle, A., 'Cicero's *De officiis* and the *De officiis ministrorum* of St Ambrose', *Franciscan Studies*, 15 (1955), 224–56.

Delhaye, P., 'Le Bien suprême d'après le *Policraticus* de Jean de Salisbury', *Recherches de théologie ancienne et médiévale*, 20 (1953), 203–21.

Dronke, P., 'Thierry of Chartres', in P. Dronke (ed.), *A History of Twelfth-Century Western Philosophy* (Cambridge: Cambridge University Press, 1992), pp. 358–85.

Duby, G., *The Three Orders: Feudal Society Imagined*, trans. A. Goldhammer (Chicago: University of Chicago Press, 1980).

Dudley Sylla, E., 'Creation and Nature', in A. S. McGrade (ed.), *The Cambridge Companion to Medieval Philosophy* (Cambridge: Cambridge University Press, 2003), pp. 171–95.

Duggan, A., 'John of Salisbury and Thomas Becket', in M. Wilks (ed.), *The World of John of Salisbury* (Oxford: Blackwell, 1984), pp. 427–38.

—— 'Classical Quotations and Allusions in the Correspondence of Thomas Becket', *Viator*, 32 (2001), 1–22.

Dutton, P. E., '*Illustre ciuitatis et populi exemplum*: Plato's *Timaeus* and the Transmission from Calcidius to the End of the Twelfth Century of a Tripartite Scheme of Society', *Mediaeval Studies*, 45 (1983), 79–119.

—— 'The Uncovering of the *Glosae super Platonem* of Bernard of Chartres', *Mediaeval Studies*, 46 (1984), 192–221.

Dyck, A. R., *A Commentary on Cicero, De Officiis* (Ann Arbor: The University of Michigan Press, 1996).

Ebbesen, S., 'Where were the Stoics in the Late Middle Ages?', in S. K. Strange and J. Zupko (eds), *Stoicism: Traditions and Transformations* (Cambridge: Cambridge University Press, 2004), pp. 108–31.

Elford, D., 'William of Conches', in P. Dronke (ed.), *A History of Twelfth-Century Western Philosophy* (Cambridge: Cambridge University Press, 1992), pp. 308–27.

Engberg-Pedersen, T., 'Discovering the Good: *Oikeiosis* and *Kathekonta* in Stoic Ethics', in M. Schofield and G. Striker (eds), *The Norms of Nature: Studies in Hellenistic Ethics* (Cambridge: Cambridge University Press, 1986), pp. 145–83.

—— *The Stoic Theory of Oikeiosis: Moral Development and Social Interaction in Early Stoic Philosophy* (Aarhus: Aarhus University Press, 1990).

Epstein, S. A., *The Medieval Discovery of Nature* (Cambridge: Cambridge University Press, 2012).

Forhan, K. L., 'Salisburian Stakes: The Use of "Tyranny" in John of Salisbury's *Policraticus*', *History of Political Thought*, 11 (1990), 397–407.

—— 'The Not-So-Divided Self: Reading Augustine in the Twelfth Century', *Augustiniana*, 42 (1992), 95–110.

—— 'Polycracy, Obligation, and Revolt: The Body Politic in John of Salisbury and Christine de Pizan', in M. Brabant (ed.), *Politics, Gender, and Genre: The Political Thought of Christine de Pizan* (Boulder; Westview, 1992), pp. 33–52.

Fredborg, K. M., 'The Grammar and Rhetoric Offered to John of Salisbury', in J. Feros Ruys, J. O. Ward, and M. Heyworth (eds), *The Classics in the Medieval and Renaissance Classroom: The Role of Ancient Texts in the Arts Curriculum as*

*Revealed by Surviving Manuscripts and Early Printed Books* (Turnhout: Brepols, 2013), pp. 103-30.
Giraud, C. and C. Mews, 'John of Salisbury and the Schools of the 12th Century', in C. Grellard and F. Lachaud (eds), *A Companion to John of Salisbury* (Leiden: Brill, 2015), pp. 31-62.
Gregory, T., *Anima mundi: La filosofia de Guglielmo di Conches e la scuola di Chartres* (Florence: Sansoni, 1955).
—— 'L'idea di natura nella filosofia medievale prima dell'ingresso della fisica di Aristotele', in *La filosofia della natura nel medioevo, Atti del terzo congresso internazionale di filosofia medioevale* (Milan: Società editrice Vita e Pensiero, 1966), pp. 27-65.
—— 'The Platonic Inheritance', in P. Dronke (ed.), *A History of Twelfth-Century Western Philosophy* (Cambridge: Cambridge University Press, 1992), pp. 54-80.
Grellard, C., *Jean de Salisbury et la renaissance médiévale du scepticisme* (Paris: Les Belles Lettres, 2013).
—— 'John of Salisbury and Theology', in C. Grellard and F. Lachaud (eds), *A Companion to John of Salisbury* (Leiden: Brill, 2015), pp. 339-73.
—— and F. Lachaud, 'Introduction', in C. Grellard and F. Lachaud (eds), *A Companion to John of Salisbury* (Leiden: Brill, 2015), pp. 1-28.
—— —— (eds), *A Companion to John of Salisbury* (Leiden: Brill, 2015)
Griffin, M., *Seneca on Society: A Guide to De Beneficiis* (Oxford: Oxford University Press, 2013).
Guglielmetti, R. E., *La tradizione manoscritta del* Policraticus *di Giovanni di Salisbury: Primo secolo di diffusione* (Florence: Sismel-Edizioni del Galluzzo, 2005).
Hagendahl, H., *Augustine and the Latin Classics* (2 vols; Gotenburg: Almquist and Wiksell, 1967).
Hermand-Schebat, L., 'John of Salisbury and Classical Antiquity', in C. Grellard and F. Lachaud (eds), *A Companion to John of Salisbury* (Leiden: Brill, 2015), pp. 180-214.
Horowitz, M. C., *Seeds of Virtue and Knowledge* (Princeton: Princeton University Press, 1998).
Hosler, J., *John of Salisbury: Military Authority of the Twelfth-Century Renaissance* (Leiden: Brill, 2013).
James, M. R., *The Ancient Libraries of Canterbury and Dover* (Cambridge: Cambridge University Press, 1903).
Jeauneau, E., 'Jean de Salisbury et la lecture des philosophes', in M. Wilks (ed.), *The World of John of Salisbury* (Oxford: Blackwell, 1984), pp. 77-108.
—— *L'Âge d'or des écoles de Chartres* (Chartres: Éditions Houvet, 2000).
Kantorowicz, E., *The King's Two Bodies: A Study in Medieval Political Theology* (Princeton: Princeton University Press, 1957).
Keats-Rohan, K. S. B., 'John of Salisbury and Education in Twelfth-Century Paris from the Account of his *Metalogicon*', *History of Universities*, 6 (1987), 1-45.
—— 'The Chronology of John of Salisbury's Studies in France: A Reading of *Metalogicon* II. 10', *Studi Medievali*, 3rd series, 28 (1987), 193-203.

Kempshall, M., '*De Re Publica* 1.39 in Medieval and Renaissance Political Thought', in J. G. F. Powell and J. A. North (eds), *Cicero's Republic* (Institute of Classical Studies, 2001), pp. 99–135.

—— *Rhetoric and the Writing of History, 400–1500* (Manchester: Manchester University Press, 2011).

Kerner, M., *Johannes von Salisbury und die logische Struktur seines Policraticus* (Wiesbaden: Franz Steiner Verlag, 1977).

—— 'Römisches und kirchliches Recht im *Policraticus*', in M. Wilks (ed.), *The World of John of Salisbury* (Oxford: Blackwell, 1984), pp. 365–79.

Lachaud, F., *L'Éthique du pouvoir au Moyen-Âge: L'Office dans la culture politique (Angleterre, vers 1150–vers 1330)* (Paris: Garnier, 2010).

—— '"Corps du prince, corps de la *res publica*"': Écriture métaphorique et construction politique dans le *Policraticus* de Jean de Salisbury', *Micrologus*, 22 (2014), 171–99.

Lapidge, M., 'The Stoic Inheritance', in P. Dronke (ed.), *A History of Twelfth-Century Western Philosophy* (Cambridge: Cambridge University Press, 1992), pp. 81–112.

LeGoff, J., 'Head or Heart? The Political Use of Body Metaphors in the Middle Ages', in M. Feher, R. Naddaff and N. Tazi (eds), *Fragments for a History of the Human Body*, vol. 3 (New York: Zone Books, 1989), pp. 12–27.

Liebeschütz, H., 'John of Salisbury and Pseudo-Plutarch', *Journal of the Warburg and Courtauld Institutes*, 6 (1943), 33–9.

—— *Mediaeval Humanism in the Life and Writings of John of Salisbury* (London: Warburg Institute, 1950).

Little, L. K., 'Pride Goes before Avarice: Social Changes and the Vices in Latin Christendom', *American Historical Review*, 76 (1971), 16–49.

Long, A. A., 'Cicero's Politics in *De officiis*', in A. Laks and M. Schofield (eds), *Justice and Generosity: Studies in Hellenistic Social and Political Philosophy* (Cambridge: Cambridge University Press, 1995), pp. 213–40.

Lottin, O., *Psychologie et morale aux XII$^e$ et XIII$^e$ siècles*, vols 2–3 (Louvain: Abbaye de Mont-César; Gembloux: Duculot, 1948–49).

Luscombe, D. E., 'The Ethics of Abelard: Some Further Considerations', in E. M. Buytaert (ed.), *Peter Abelard: Proceedings of the International Conference, Louvain May 10–12, 1971* (Louvain: Leuven University Press, 1974), pp. 65–84.

—— 'Conceptions of Hierarchy before the Thirteenth Century', in A. Zimmerman (ed.), *Soziale Ordnungen im Selbstverständnis des Mittelalters* (Berlin: De Gruyter, 1979), pp. 1–19.

—— 'Peter Abelard', in P. Dronke (ed.), *A History of Twelfth-Century Western Philosophy* (Cambridge: Cambridge University Press, 1992), pp. 279–307.

MacIntyre, A., *Whose Justice? Which Rationality?* (London: Duckworth, 1988).

—— *Three Rival Versions of Moral Enquiry: Encyclopedia, Genealogy, and Tradition* (London: Duckworth, 1990).

—— *After Virtue: A Study in Moral Theory* (3rd edn; London: Duckworth, 2007).

Marenbon, J., 'Abelard's Ethical Theory: Two Definitions from the *Collationes*', in H. J. Westra (ed.), *From Athens to Chartres: Studies in Honour of Edouard Jeauneau* (Leiden: Brill, 1992), pp. 301–14.

—— *The Philosophy of Peter Abelard* (Cambridge: Cambridge University Press, 1997).
—— *Pagans and Philosophers: The Problem of Paganism from Augustine to Leibniz* (Princeton, Princeton University Press, 2015).
Markus, R., *Gregory the Great and his World* (Cambridge: Cambridge University Press, 1997).
Martin, J., 'John of Salisbury and the Classics' (PhD dissertation, Harvard University, 1968).
—— 'John of Salisbury's manuscripts of Frontinus and of Gellius', *Journal of the Warburg and Courtauld Institutes*, 40 (1977), 1–26.
—— 'Uses of Tradition: Gellius, Petronius and John of Salisbury', *Viator*, 10 (1979), 57–76.
—— 'John of Salisbury as Classical Scholar', in M. Wilks (ed.), *The World of John of Salisbury* (Oxford: Blackwell, 1984), pp. 179–201.
—— 'Cicero's Jokes at the Court of Henry II of England: Roman Humour and the Princely Ideal', *Modern Language Quarterly*, 51 (1990), 144–66.
Mazzoli, G., 'Ricerche sulla tradizione medievale del *De beneficiis* e del *De clementia* di Seneca, 3: Storia della tradizione manoscritta', *Bolletino dei classici*, series 3, 3 (1982), 165–223.
McLoughlin, J., 'The Language of Persecution: John of Salisbury and the Early Phase of the Becket Dispute (1163–66)', in W. J. Sheils (ed.), *Persecution and Toleration: Papers Read at the Twenty-Second Summer Meeting and Twenty-Third Winter Meeting of the Ecclesiastical History Society* (Oxford: Blackwell, 1984), pp. 73–87.
—— 'John of Salisbury (c. 1120–80): The Career and Attitudes of a Schoolman in Church Politics' (PhD dissertation, Trinity College, Dublin, 1988).
—— '*Amicitia* in Practice: John of Salisbury (*c*.1120–1180) and his Circle', in D. Williams (ed.), *England in the Twelfth Century: Proceedings of the 1988 Harlaxton Symposium* (Woodbridge: Boydell Press, 1990), pp. 165–81.
Miczka, G., 'Johannes von Salisbury und die *Summa Trecensis*', in M. Wilks (ed.), *The World of John of Salisbury* (Oxford: Blackwell, 1984), pp. 381–99.
Monagle, C., 'John of Salisbury and the Writing of History', in C. Grellard and F. Lachaud (eds), *A Companion to John of Salisbury* (Leiden: Brill, 2015), pp. 215–32.
Munk Olsen, B., 'L'humanisme de Jean de Salisbury, un cicéronien au 12ᵉ siècle', in M. de Gandillac and E. Jeauneau (eds), *Entretiens sur la renaissance du 12ᵉ siècle* (Paris: Mouton, 1968), pp. 53–69.
—— 'Les Classiques latins dans les florilèges médiévaux antérieurs au XIIIᵉ siècle', *Revue d'histoire des textes*, 9 (1979–80), 47–121.
—— *L'Étude des auteurs classiques latins aux XIᵉ et XIIᵉ siècles: La réception de la littérature classique. Manuscrits et textes* (4 vols; Paris: CNRS, 1982–2014).
Murray, A., *Reason and Society in the Middle Ages* (Oxford: Oxford University Press, 1978).
Nederman, C. J., 'The Physiological Significance of the Organic Metaphor in John of Salisbury's *Policraticus*', *History of Political Thought*, 8 (1987), 211–23.

—— 'The Aristotelian Doctrine of the Mean and John of Salisbury's Concept of Liberty', *Vivarium*, 24 (1986), 128–42.

—— 'Nature, Sin, and the Origins of Society: The Ciceronian Tradition in Medieval Political Thought', *Journal of the History of Ideas*, 49 (1988), 3–26.

—— 'Aristotelian Ethics before the *Nichomachean Ethics*: Alternate Sources of Aristotle's Concept of Virtue in the Twelfth Century', *Parergon*, 7 (1989), 55–75.

—— 'The Changing Face of Tyranny: The Reign of King Stephen in John of Salisbury', *Nottingham Medieval Studies*, 33 (1989), 1–20.

—— 'Nature, Ethics, and the Doctrine of "Habitus": Aristotelian Moral Psychology in the Twelfth Century', *Traditio*, 45 (1989–90), 87–110.

—— 'Aristotelianism and the Origins of "Political Science" in the Twelfth Century', *Journal of the History of Ideas*, 52 (1991), 179–94.

—— 'Freedom, Community and Function: Communitarian Lessons of Medieval Political Theory, *American Political Science Review*, 86 (1992), 977–86.

—— *Medieval Aristotelianism and its Limits: Classical Traditions in Moral and Political Philosophy in the 12th to 15th Centuries* (Aldershot: Ashgate, 1997).

—— *John of Salisbury* (Tempe: Arizona Centre for Medieval and Renaissance Studies, 2005).

—— 'Beyond Aristotelianism and Stoicism: John of Salisbury's Skepticism and Moral Reasoning in the Twelfth Century', in I. Bejczy and R. Newhauser (eds), *Virtue and Ethics in the Twelfth Century* (Leiden: Brill, 2005), pp. 175–95.

—— 'John of Salisbury's Political Theory', in C. Grellard and F. Lachaud (eds), *A Companion to John of Salisbury* (Leiden: Brill, 2015), pp. 258–88.

Nelson, N. E., 'Cicero's *De Officiis* in Christian Thought 300–1300', *Essays and Studies in English and Comparative Literature*, 10 (1933), 59–160.

Newhauser, R., 'The Love of Money as Deadly Sin and Deadly Disease', in K. H. Göller, J. O. Fichte and B. Schimmelpfennig (eds), *Zusammenhänge, Einflüsse, Wirkungen: Kongressakten zum ersten Symposium des Mediävistenverbandes in Tübingen, 1984* (Berlin: De Gruyter, 1986), pp. 315–26.

Nothdurft, K., *Studien zum Einfluss Senecas auf die Philosophie und Theologie des zwölften Jahrhunderts* (Leiden: Brill, 1962).

O'Daly, G., *Augustine's City of God: A Reader's Guide* (Oxford: Oxford University Press, 1999).

O'Daly, I., 'An Assessment of the Political Symbolism of the City of Rome in the Writings of John of Salisbury', *Medieval Encounters*, 17 (2011), 512–33.

Osborne, T. M., *Love of Self and Love of God in Thirteenth Century Ethics* (Notre Dame, IN: University of Notre Dame Press, 2005).

Pade, M., *The Reception of Plutarch's Lives in Fifteenth-Century Italy* (2 vols; Copenhagen: Museum Tusculanum Press, 2007).

Pembroke, S. G., 'Oikeiosis', in A. A. Long (ed.), *Problems in Stoicism* (London: Athlone Press, 1996), pp. 114–49.

Pepin, R., '*On the Conspiracy of the Members*: attributed to John of Salisbury', *Allegorica*, 12 (1991), 29–42.

Pocock, J. G. A., 'A History of Political Thought: A Methodological Enquiry', in P. Laslett and W. G. Runciman (eds), *Philosophy, Politics and Society*, 2nd series (Oxford: Basil Blackwell, 1962), pp. 183–202.
—— *Virtue, Commerce and History: Essays of Political Thought and History Chiefly in the Eighteenth Century* (Cambridge: Cambridge University Press, 2002).
Pouchelle, M.-C., *The Body and Surgery in the Middle Ages*, trans. R. Morris (Cambridge: Polity, 1990).
Reuter, T., 'John of Salisbury and the Germans', in M. Wilks (ed.), *The World of John of Salisbury* (Oxford: Blackwell, 1984), pp. 414–25.
Reydams-Schils, G., *The Roman Stoics: Self, Responsibility, and Affection* (Chicago: University of Chicago Press, 2005).
Reynolds, L. D., *The Medieval Tradition of Seneca's Letters* (Oxford: Oxford University Press, 1965).
—— (ed.), *Texts and Transmission: A Survey of the Latin Classics* (Oxford: Clarendon Press, 1983).
Ricklin, T., 'Le Coeur, soleil du corps: Une redécouverte symbolique du XII<sup>e</sup> siècle', *Micrologus*, 11 (2003), 123–43.
Rigby, S., *Wisdom and Chivalry: Chaucer's Knight's Tale and Medieval Political Theory* (Leiden: Brill, 2009).
—— 'Justifying Inequality: Peasants in Medieval Ideology', in M. Kowaleski, J. Langdon and P. R. Schofield (eds), *Peasants and Lords in the Medieval English Economy: Essays in Honour of Bruce M. S. Campbell* (Turnhout: Brepols, 2015), pp. 173–97.
Robertson, L., 'Exile in the Life and Correspondence of John of Salisbury', in L. Napran and E. Van Houts (eds), *Exile in the Middle Ages: Selected Proceedings from the International Medieval Congress, University of Leeds 8–11 July 2002* (Turnhout: Brepols, 2004), pp. 181–97.
Ross, W. B., 'Audi Thoma ... Henriciani nota: A French Scholar Appeals to Thomas Becket', *English Historical Review*, 89 (1974), 333–8.
Rouse, R. H. and M. A. Rouse, 'John of Salisbury and the Doctrine of Tyrannicide', *Speculum*, 42 (1967), 693–709.
—— 'The Medieval Circulation of Cicero's *Posterior Academics* and the *De finibus bonorum et malorum*', in M. B. Parkes and A. G. Watson (eds), *Medieval Scribes, Manuscripts and Libraries: Essays Presented to N. R. Ker* (London: Scolar Press, 1978), pp. 333–67.
Saltman, A., *Theobald, Archbishop of Canterbury* (London: Athlone Press, 1956).
Sassier, Y., 'John of Salisbury and Law', in C. Grellard and F. Lachaud (eds), *A Companion to John of Salisbury* (Leiden: Brill, 2015), pp. 235–57.
Scanlon, L., *Narrative, Authority and Power: The Medieval Exemplum and the Chaucerian Tradition* (Cambridge: Cambridge University Press, 2007).
Schaarschmidt, C., *Johannes Saresberiensis nach Leben und Studien, Schriften und Philosophie* (Leipzig: Teubner, 1862).
Sedley, D., 'The Stoic Theory of Universals', *Southern Journal of Philosophy*, 23 (1985), 87–92.
Shogimen, T., '"Head or Heart?" Revisited: Physiology and Political Thought in the

Thirteenth and Fourteenth Centuries', *History of Political Thought*, 28 (2007), 208–29.

——and C. J. Nederman, 'The Best Medicine? Medical Education, Practice, and Metaphor in John of Salisbury's *Policraticus* and *Metalogicon*', *Viator*, 42 (2011), 55–74.

Skinner, Q., 'Meaning and Understanding in the History of Ideas', *History and Theory: Studies in the Philosophy of History*, 8 (1969), 3–53; reprinted with some additions and changes in Q. Skinner, *Visions of Politics*, vol. 1: *Regarding Method* (Cambridge: Cambridge University Press, 2002), pp. 57–89.

Smalley, B., *The Becket Conflict and the Schools* (Oxford: Blackwell, 1973).

Sønnesyn, S., '*Qui recta quae docet sequitur, uere philosophus est:* The Ethics of John of Salisbury', in C. Grellard and F. Lachaud (eds), *A Companion to John of Salisbury* (Leiden: Brill, 2015), pp. 307–38.

Sorabji, R., *Emotion and Peace of Mind: From Stoic Agitation to Christian Temptation* (Oxford: Oxford University Press, 2000).

——'Stoic First Movements in Christianity', in K. Strange and J. Zupko (eds), *Stoicism: Traditions and Transformations* (Cambridge: Cambridge University Press, 2004), pp. 95–107.

Southern, R. W., 'Humanism and the School of Chartres', in R. W. Southern, *Medieval Humanism and Other Studies* (Oxford: Blackwell, 1970), pp. 61–85.

——'The Schools of Paris and the School of Chartres', in R. L. Benson, G. Constable and C. D. Lanham (eds), *Renaissance and Renewal in the Twelfth Century* (Cambridge, MA: Harvard University Press, 1982), pp. 113–37.

Spanneut, M., *Permanence du Stoïcisme: De Zénon à Malraux* (Gembloux: Duculot, 1973).

Stacey, P., *Roman Monarchy and the Renaissance Prince* (Cambridge: Cambridge University Press, 2007).

——'Senecan Political Thought from the Middle Ages to Early Modernity', in S. Bartsch and A. Schiesaro (eds), *The Cambridge Companion to Seneca* (Cambridge: Cambridge University Press, 2015), pp. 289–302.

Staunton, M., *Thomas Becket and his Biographers* (Woodbridge: Boydell and Brewer, 2006).

——'The *Lives* of Thomas Becket and the Church of Canterbury', in P. Dalton, C. Insley and L. Wilkinson (eds), *Cathedrals, Communities and Conflict in the Anglo-Norman World* (Woodbridge: Boydell Press, 2011), pp. 169–86.

Stirnemann, P. and D. Poirel, 'Nicolas de Montiéramey, Jean de Salisbury et deux florilèges d'auteurs antiques', *Revue d'histoire des textes*, n.s., 1 (2006), 173–88.

Straw, C., *Gregory the Great: Perfection and Imperfection* (Berkeley: University of California Press, 1988).

Striker, G., 'The Role of *Oikeiôsis* in Stoic Ethics', *Oxford Studies in Ancient Philosophy*, 1 (1983), 145–67.

——'Following Nature: A Study in Stoic Ethics', *Oxford Studies in Ancient Philosophy*, 9 (1991), 1–73.

Struve, T., *Die Entwicklung der organologischen Staatsauffassung im Mittelalter* (Stuttgart: Anton Hiersemann, 1978).

—— 'The Importance of the Organism in the Political Theory of John of Salisbury', in M. Wilks (ed.), *The World of John of Salisbury* (Oxford: Blackwell, 1984), pp. 303–18.

Summers, W., 'John of Salisbury and the Classics', *Classical Quarterly*, 4 (1910), 103–5.

Thomas, H. M., *The Secular Clergy in England, 1066–1216* (Oxford: Oxford University Press, 2014).

Thomson, R., 'John of Salisbury and William of Malmesbury: Currents in Twelfth-Century Humanism', in M. Wilks (ed.), *The World of John of Salisbury* (Oxford: Blackwell, 1984), pp. 117–25.

—— 'What is the Entheticus?', in M. Wilks (ed.), *The World of John of Salisbury* (Oxford: Blackwell, 1984), pp. 287–301.

—— *William of Malmesbury* (Woodbridge: Boydell Press, 2003).

Van Laarhoven, J., '"Thou shalt NOT slay a tyrant!" The So-Called Theory of John of Salisbury', in M. Wilks (ed.), *The World of John of Salisbury* (Oxford: Blackwell, 1984), pp. 319–41.

—— 'Titles and Subtitles of the *Policraticus*: A Proposal', *Vivarium*, 32 (1994), 131–60.

Verbeke, G., *The Presence of Stoicism in Medieval Thought* (Washington DC: Catholic University of America Press, 1983).

Ward, J. O., 'What the Middle Ages Missed of Cicero, and Why', in W. H. F. Altman (ed.), *Brill's Companion to the Reception of Cicero* (Leiden: Brill, 2015), pp. 307–26.

Webb, C. C. J., *John of Salisbury* (London: Methuen, 1932).

—— 'Notes on Books Bequeathed by John of Salisbury to the Cathedral Library of Chartres', *Medieval and Renaissance Studies*, 1 (1941–43), 128–9.

Webber, T., *Scribes and Scholars at Salisbury Cathedral, c.1075– c.1125* (Oxford: Oxford University Press, 1992).

Wilks, M., 'John of Salisbury and the Tyranny of Nonsense', in M. Wilks (ed.), *The World of John of Salisbury* (Oxford: Blackwell, 1984), pp. 263–86.

—— (ed.), *The World of John of Salisbury* (Oxford: Blackwell, 1984).

Yeager, R. F., 'The Body Politic and the Politics of Bodies in the Poetry of John Gower', in P. Boitani and A. Torti (eds), *The Body and Soul in Medieval Literature* (Cambridge: D. S. Brewer, 1999), pp. 145–65.

# INDEX

Abelard, Peter 1, 3, 72, 162, 166
Academic scepticism 8, 160
   John's interest in 6, 31–5, 41, 79
acting 98, 149–50
Adrian IV, Pope 3, 107, 125, 163, 197
Ambrose
   *De officiis ministrorum* 51–2, 65n.171, 102–4, 132, 162
Aristotle 7–8, 30–2, 72, 78, 80, 155–6
   *habitus* 153–5
   John's use of Aristotle 6, 20–1n.56, 31, 57n.69, 72, 88n.56, 100, 154–7
   mean 155–7
   reception of 7, 20n.53, 29, 153–4
   virtue 153–4
   *see also* Peripatetic
army *see* soldiers
Augustine 42, 45, 52–3, 74–5, 126
   *Confessiones* 52
   *Contra Academicos* 33
   *De civitate Dei* 36, 44, 52, 65–6n.1, 81–3, 146, 148
   *De doctrina christiana* 52, 102
   *De Genesi ad litteram* 52
   *De libero arbitrio* 52
   first movements 81–2
   nature 73–5
Aulus Gellius
   *Noctes Atticae* 34, 36, 40, 80–1, 138n.30
avarice 107, 125, 149, 163–7, 170, 198, 207

Barbarossa, Frederick 202–5, 209
Becket, Thomas 3, 8, 11–13, 15, 37–8, 45, 48, 50, 52–3, 119, 168–9, 186–7, 197–8, 205–8, 224
   *Vita Thomae* 3, 207
beneficence 167–9
Bernard of Chartres 4, 7, 77, 120

Bernard of Clairvaux 3, 17n.19, 52, 101, 183–4
Bernard Silvestris 48, 70, 120–1
Bible 30
   Acts 195
   Deuteronomy 8, 82, 187–8
   Ecclesiastes 86
   Job 124
   Luke 102, 182
   Matthew 102–3
   Pauline Epistles 101, 117–19, 131–2
   Sirach 124
   Song of Songs 102
body metaphors 107–8, 117–22
   *see also* body politic
body politic 77, 104–9, 117, 223
   corrupt 128, 131, 135, 191, 204
   feet 121, 125–8, 191, 199–200
   *see also* peasants
   hands 128–9, 191
   *see also* soldiers
   head 77, 130–4
   *see also* prince
   heart 107, 123–4, 128, 191
   *see also* senate
   John's treatment of 121–35
   reciprocity of duties 9, 92, 104–7, 116n.88, 126
   senses 124–5, 133, 135
   sides 125
   *see also* defecation
   soul 77, 130–4
   *see also* priesthood; prince
Boethius 7, 33, 37, 153

Calcidius *see* Plato, *Timaeus*
Cambridge School 10, 21–2n.63–6, n.68
charity (*caritas*) 67, 98, 101–2, 131, 153, 187, 222

239

# INDEX

Chartres
  bequest of books to 4, 12, 34–5, 42, 46
  *see also* Lactantius, *Institutiones divinae*; Lactantius, John's manuscript of
  burial place of John 1, 15n.1
  John as bishop of 1, 3, 15n.2, 17n.15, 37
  School of 2, 68, 72, 119
  *see also* Bernard of Chartres; Fulbert, bishop of Chartres; Thierry of Chartres
Christ Church, Canterbury
  John as administrator 3, 17n.20–1
  library of 34, 36–40, 44, 46, 52–4, 58n.73, 65n.164, 148, 159
Cicero 7, 30–1, 161, 191–2
  body metaphor 106, 132, 134
  decorum 106, 149–50, 165, 188, 207, 222, 224
  duty 94–9, 151
  intention 80
  John's opinion of 42, 45, 221
  justice 96
  medieval circulation 37–45
  moderation 149–50, 164
  nature 68–73, 222
  scepticism 8, 32–4
  transmitter of Stoic ideas 8, 32, 82
  virtue 152–4, 157–8, 160–2, 164, 186–7
  works 41–5
    *Academica* 41, 44
    *De amicitia* 37, 42, 44, 73, 190
    *De fato* 31, 44–5
    *De finibus* 41, 44, 94–6, 149
    *De inventione* 37, 39, 41, 44, 67–8, 154, 162
    *De natura deorum* 33, 44–5, 69
    *De officiis* 8, 33, 34, 40–3, 51–2, 82, 96–7, 102–4, 106, 150–2, 157, 160, 187–8
    *De oratore* 34, 42–4, 60n.107
    *De re publica* 44, 52
      *see also* Cicero, works, *De somnium Scipionis*; Macrobius, *Commentarii in somnium Scipionis*
    *De senectute* 37, 44
    *De somnium Scipionis* 41, 44, *see also* Cicero, works, *De re publica*; Macrobius *Commentarii in somnium Scipionis*
    *Epistulae* 45, 52
    *Paradoxa Stoicorum* 38, 44
    [Pseudo-] *Rhetorica ad Herennium* 37, 39, 41, 43, 44, 61n.116
    *Tusculanae disputationes* 38, 40, 44, 78, 80
  classical reception, modes of 11, 22n.67, 25, 35–6, 41, 224–5
communitarianism 8–9, 99–100, 223
Cornificius 67, 104

defecation 107, 163
dissimulation 167–8, 206–7
duties (*officia*)
  Christian sources for 100–4
  John on 97–107
  perfect duties 94–5, 103, 151–2
  private and public duties 100–1, 103, 157–8
  Roman sources for 93–7, 107, 157

education
  critique of 30, 67
  discernment in reading 147
  France 1–3, 16.n.8, 17n.17–18, 40
  John's teachers 1–2, 16n.9–11
  Salisbury 1
eloquence 67, 84n.4
*Entheticus de dogmate philosophorum (Entheticus maior)*
  composition of 11, 13
  forms 77
  in library of Christ Church, Canterbury 37
  Stephen, king of England 199–201
  law 185
  nature 73
  philosophers 30–2, 41–2, 45
  Thomas Becket 205, 207
*Entheticus in Policraticum (Entheticus minor)* 11, 13, 43, 205
Epicureanism 30, 51, 165–6
Epicurus 32, 51, 77, 147, 165–6

240

Exeter 40, 59n.88
exile 3, 169, 198-9, 204

fate 30-2, 56n.50, 73-4, 81
flattery 160
florilegia 34-6
  *Florilegium Gallicum* 45, 47-8
fortitude 81, 152, 159-61, 181-2, 184
fortune (*fortuna*) 68, 70-1, 75, 197, 205
free will 30-2, 56n.50, 70, 83, 222
frugality 164-7, 169-70
Fulbert, bishop of Chartres 1, 17.n.13

gambling 150
gift-giving *see* beneficence
Gilbert Foliot 201
Gilbert of Poitiers 2, 16n.9, 17n.15, 70
God 30-1, 42, 67-8, 70-80, 82-4, 101-3, 126, 183-4
  knowledge of 50, 147
  source of power 130-1, 133, 163-4, 191-2, 194, 203, 209
  *see also* 'two swords'
  *summum bonum* 146-8, 151-3
  truth in 79
  *see also* grace
grace 31, 67, 70, 78-9, 82-3, 92, 101, 147, 153-5, 165, 186-7, 222
  baptismal 155
grafting 72-3
Gregory I, Pope (Gregory the Great) 27-9, 50, 53, 206
  *Moralia in Job* 53, 160
  *Regula Pastoralis* 53, 126-7, 196
Gregory, Master *Narracio mirabilis urbis Romae* 27-8

happiness 67, 104, 146-8, 151, 158, 165-6, 169-70, 223-4
Henry II, king of England 3, 8, 12, 14, 15, 47, 50, 169, 186, 193, 196-7, 203, 205-6, 208-9
*Historia pontificalis* 3, 5, 26, 217n.131
  composition of 3
  Stephen, king of England 201-2
Holy Spirit 68, 70, 76, 184
Horace 41, 163-4
Hugh of St Victor 69, 106-7
hunting 104, 149-50

indifferents (*indifferentia*) 104, 149-50, 165, 170
*Institutio Traiani* 104-5, 121-2, 127, 135, 138-9n.30
  *see also* body politic; Plutarch
intention 80-2, 94, 98, 104, 149, 151-2, 167, 207, 223-4
Ireland 3, 197
Isaac of Stella 119

Jews 83
justice 96, 101-2, 159-61, 185-9
Juvenal 140n.53, 164

knowledge of self 101, 147-8

Lactantius
  *Institutiones divinae* 44, 49-51, 189
  John's manuscript of 50-1, 168-70, 208
law
  civil 147, 184-6
  divine 123, 126, 145, 185-7, 196, 208-9
  natural 92, 97-9, 159, 186-7
  Roman 38-40, 170, 187, 199-200
  *see also* prince, lawgiver
*Letters* 5, 26, 35, 39, 45, 48, 184, 186, 208
  chronology of 3, 11-12
  exile 169, 182, 98
  Frederick Barbarossa 202-4
  John's disgrace 196-8
  language of 198-9
  law 186-7
  Thomas Becket 186-7, 207
Livy 107-8, 115n.84
Lucan 37, 43

Macrobius
  *Saturnalia* 42
  *Commentarii in somnium Scipionis* 158
Martin of Braga
  *De ira* 48, 80
  *Formula vitae honestae* 37-9, 49, 159-60
mean 148, 150-1, 154-7, 159, 187, 224
mercy 134, 168, 195-6

241

INDEX

*Metalogicon* 5-7, 11, 29, 49, 67, 104, 154, 197
  composition of 3, 11, 36, 198
  critique of learning 29, 67, 194
  education 1-3, 41, 183
  nature 67, 71
  reason 76-7, 79
  soul 78, 132-4
  travels 3, 25-6
moderation 148-50, 155-7, 159, 170, 181, 195, 207
*Moralium dogma philosophorum see* William of Conches

nature (*natura*) 9, 67, 82, 84, 99, 157, 222
  definitions of 68-75
  following nature 42, 75, 80, 82, 92, 95, 98-9, 148, 186, 222
neo-Platonism 3, 7, 29, 53, 68-70, 72, 77, 121, 158, 222

*officia see* duties
*oikeiôsis* 93-9, 109n.2, 131, 222
  Christian sources for 101-2
  John on 97-100, 102
  Roman basis for 93-7
Old Sarum *see* Salisbury
*On the Conspiracy of the Members* 108, 115-16n.85

peasants 105, 127-8
  *see also* body politic, feet
Peripatetic 30-1, 73, 79, 132, 147
  *see also* Aristotle
Persius 148
Peter of Celle 3, 13, 26, 51, 104-5, 127, 196-8
Plato 7, 8, 32, 52, 71, 74, 80, 87n.38, 119-20, 132, 225
  *Timaeus* 7, 20n.51, 68, 70, 119-21, 136-7n.17
  *see also* soul; 'World-Soul'
Platonism 7, 32, 70-1, 77, 106, 117, 120-1, 123, 132, 225
  *see also* neo-Platonism
Plutarch 107, 126-7, 129, 138-9n.30, 191
  *see also Institutio Traiani*

*Policraticus*
  body metaphors 104-5, 107, 121-35
  composition of 3, 11
  duties 92, 97-9, 127-8
  *habitus* 155
  manuscripts of 12-15, 22n.72
  annotation in 12-15, 23n.82-24n.87
  mirror for princes 12, 15, 221
  moderation 165-7
  Rome 26-9
  Stoic first movements 81-2
  *summa bona* 146-8
  tyranny 189-93, 200-3
political language 10, 145
priesthood 130-4, 143-4n.105
prince 128-35, 170, 187-90, 192, 223-4
  body metaphor 129, 131, 134-5
  lawgiver 188-91
  prudence (*prudentia*) 42, 81, 124-5, 150-1, 159-62, 181
Pullen, Robert 2, 122, 139n.34, 183

Quintilian 35, 45

reading 29, 147
reason (*ratio*) 30-1, 67, 72-3, 75-9, 93, 96, 104, 120, 133-4, 147, 149, 151, 154, 186-7
  spark of (*scintilla rationis*) 82-3
  *see also* seminal reasons
religious orders 164-5
*res publica* 10, 98, 104-5, 107, 113-14n.66, 120, 123-4, 127-8, 130-1, 133, 157, 161, 181, 184, 189-92, 195
Rheims, Papal Council of 3
Richard, John's brother 1, 16n.4, 186
Richard l'Évêque 2, 20n.53, 57n.69
Robert, John's brother 1, 16n.4, 203
Rome
  Arch of Constantine 27-8, 54-5n.8
  John's travels to 25-6
  marvels of 27-9, 55n.14-17
  *see also* Gregory, Master
  Palatine Library 28-9

Salisbury 16n.5
  John's early years 1
  library of 40
  scepticism *see* Academic scepticism
  Scripture *see* Bible
  seminal reasons (*seminales rationes*) 73–5
  senate 77, 105, 107, 121, 123–4, 133, 191
    *see also* body politic, heart
  Seneca 29, 51, 80–1, 99, 147, 158–9, 167, 198
    body metaphor 130–1, 133–4
    duties 158
    frugality 165–6
    intention 80
    John's opinion of 45–6, 221
    medieval circulation 37–41, 45–9
    mercy 195
    nature 73
    reason 75–7
    stoicism 8
    tyranny 193
    works
      *De beneficiis* 40–1, 45–8, 73, 166–7, 188, 193
      *De clementia* 38, 45–6, 130–1, 133–4, 195–6, 221
      *De ira* 48, *see also* Martin of Braga
      *Dialogues* 48
      [pseudo-] *Epistles to Paul* 37–8, 41, 46
      *Epistulae* 38, 41, 45–6, 49, 76, 149, 151, 166
      [pseudo-] *Formula vitae honestae*, *see* Martin of Braga
      *Naturales quaestiones* 34, 45–6, 73, 81
  Seneca the Elder, *Controversiae* 37, 48
  Servius
    *Commentary on the Aeneid* 43
  soldiers 14, 105, 120–1, 123, 128, 182–5, 191
    *see also* body politic, hands
  soul 77–8, 89n.59, 130–4
    *see also* body politic, head; body politic, senses; body politic, soul
  Stephen, king of England 14, 38–9, 199–202, 209

stoicism 8, 11
  duties 93–7, 151–3
  fate 30, 81
  first movements 80–2
  indifferents 80, 84, 147, 149–51, 165, 169–70
  intention 80–2
  John's opinion of 30
  justice 187–8
  medieval reception of 29–30, 32, 50–3
  nature 69, 73–5
    *see also* reason; seminal reasons
  *otium* 198, 224
  passions 80
  political 158
  prudence 161
  reason 75–9
  virtue 80, 151–2, 154–5
    *see also oikeiôsis*
  *summa bona* 146–8, 223
  *synderesis* 83, 93

temperance 152–3, 159–62, 165, 181
  *see also* frugality
Theobald, Archbishop of Canterbury 3, 25, 39, 197, 201–3, 209
Thierry of Chartres 2, 3, 68–9, 154, 161–2
'two swords' 182–4, 202–3
tyrannicide 6, 181, 190, 192–3, 205
tyranny 135, 170, 181, 189–93, 199–205, 223–4

universals 78–9, 189

Vacarius 38–40
Vegetius 34, 182, 185
Victorinus 69, 71
Virgil 29, 37, 41, 43, 67
  *see also* Servius; Bernard Silvestris
virtue 80, 82, 145–6, 159–60, 169, 224
  craft 152–7
  mean of 148, 156–7, 159–60
    *see also* moderation
  pagans 147
  political 158–9, 194–5
  *summum bonum* 104, 146–7

243

virtue (*cont.*)
  unity of 152–3
  *see also* fortitude; justice; prudence, temperance
*Vita Thomae see* Becket, Thomas

William of Conches 2, 7, 62n.131, 70, 73, 120–1, 138n.27, 142n.78

*Moralium Dogma Philosophorum* 47, 63n.138, 162
William of Malmesbury 36, 45, 53, 173n.59
wisdom (*sapientia*) 29, 43, 78–9, 82, 94, 101, 120–1, 123, 128, 134, 147, 155, 159, 161
'World-Soul' (*anima mundi*) 68, 70, 76, 117

Lightning Source UK Ltd.
Milton Keynes UK
UKHW04n1453100718
325506UK00001B/21/P